THE NATIONAL ASSEMBLY AGENDA

A HANDBOOK FOR THE FIRST FOUR YEARS

Edited by John Osmond

Sefydliad Materion Cymreig
Institute of Welsh Affairs

ISBN 1 871726 433

Sefydliad Materion Cymreig
Institute of Welsh Affairs

The Institute of Welsh Affairs exists to promote quality research and informed debate affecting the cultural, social, political and economic well-being of Wales. The IWA is an independent organisation owing no allegiance to any political or economic interest group. Our only interest is in seeing Wales flourish as a country in which to work and live.

We are funded by a range of organisations and individuals. For more information about the Institute, its publications, and how to join, either as an individual or corporate supporter, contact:

IWA - Institute of Welsh Affairs

T ŷ Oldfield
Llantrisant Road
Llandâf
Cardiff
CF5 2YQ

Tel: 01222 575511
Fax: 01222 575701
Email: wales@iwa.org.uk
Web: www.iwa.org.uk

Designed by Payne Taylor Design Ltd. (587). Tel: 01222 255525
Front cover photograph supplied by Cardiff Bay Development Corporation

CONTENTS

PART THREE
RELATIONSHIPS

APPENDICES

ACKNOWLEDGEMENTS

Any project of this size and scope involves inputs from a large number of people. Even so *The National Assembly Agenda* is something of a departure given the wide-ranging discussion and consultation that preceded its publication. A glance at the appendices will give an indication of the extent of this process. *The National Assembly Agenda* has been the main project of the Institute of Welsh Affairs during 1998, involving six major conferences and 22 seminars in various locations throughout Wales. We estimate that more than 700 people have had an input into the content of the pages that follow, by virtue of their participation in these events. The Institute of Welsh Affairs is grateful to all those who have taken part, and in particular to the authors of the chapters. All have taken on board the many comments and suggestions that have been made, with the result that most of the Chapters have gone through at least three drafts.

Sections of this book have been written at different stages in the unfolding process of establishing the National Assembly. In particular, parallel discussions and policy formation have been underway by a variety of groups and committees co-ordinated by the Welsh Office, for example the Education and Training Action Group and the Transport Advisory Group. In some cases there has been cross-fertilisation between these processes, especially when published reports have been able to be taken into account. Of particular significance have been the publication of the Welsh Office's *Better Health, Better Wales* in May 1998, *Pathway to Prosperity: A New Economic Agenda for Wales* in July 1998, the National Assembly Advisory Group's report on the operation of the Assembly in August 1998, the draft *Education and Training Action Plan for Wales* in October 1998, and the WDA's transitional corporate plan, *Planning for Prosperity: The WDA 1999-2002*, also published in October 1998. In many instances, however, there has been no opportunity to inter-act with the official process, though Welsh Office and WDA representatives were present at most of the IWA events.

The project and the publication of this volume would not have been possible without substantial financial support from the Joseph Rowntree Charitable Trust. Many other organisations made contributions which enabled particular events to be undertaken in a way more ambitious than would have otherwise been the case. These include: Carmarthenshire County Council; Charter 88; The University of Wales Institute,Cardiff; the Friedrich Ebert Foundation; the McDougall Trust; the University of Birmingham Institute for German Studies; the Philip Morris Institute; the Europe of the Cultures 2002 Foundation; the Welsh Centre for International Affairs; the Wales Council of the European Movement; Welsh Context; and the Development Board for Rural Wales. BBC Wales, the Centre for Journalism Studies, Cardiff University, the Agency of the Bank of England and NCM allowed their premises to be used as a venue for a number of the seminars.

Much of the burden of co-ordinating the project and organising the seminars was undertaken by Ceri Black who joined the IWA as a freelance consultant during the period of the project. The IWA's Administrative Director, Clare Johnson, oversaw the whole operation. IWA Administrator Helen Sims-Coomber, and Research Officer Dr Nigel Blewitt, provided essential support. Adele Lewis, a research student, worked on the early proofs.

Finally, I am grateful to the members of the IWA's Executive Committee for their sustained support for this project and in particular the IWA's chairman, Geraint Talfan Davies.

John Osmond

Penarth

November 1998

INTRODUCTION

John Osmond

There is a view that because the National Assembly of Wales will not have tax varying and primary legislative powers, as will be the case with the Scottish Parliament, its scope for action and influence will be limited. A glance through the pages of this book should convince otherwise. When the responsibilities and budget of the Assembly are taken into account, together with the real opportunities it will have to bring about change, substantial improvements can be made to the life of Wales.

Moreover, a preoccupation of the Assembly in its early years will be to find ways to demonstrate that its existence does make a difference. Its very creation has the potential for change in at least three ways. First, it will challenge policy-makers to consistently take an 'all-Wales view'. Secondly, it will present an opportunity to transform the political culture. Thirdly, the Assembly will reinforce and give substantive civic meaning to the national dimension of the country's identity.

In this last regard, from day one the National Assembly will have a very different project to the agenda that will face the new Scottish Parliament. The Scots already have in place long-standing institutions and a strong sense of civil society that in themselves describe much of what it is to be Scottish. Until now the Welsh have been unable to depend on an equivalent civic culture. Instead, Welsh identity has relied upon a more diffuse sense of cultural belonging in which locality and language have borne much of the weight of what Welshness has meant. Moreover, this strong sense of place, and also the role of the language, have tended to be divisive rather than unifying. They have distinguished Welsh people one from another rather than promoting a unifying sense of Wales as an entity. It has been said that there are as many 'Welshnesses' as there are Welsh people.

On the other hand, over the last 30 years Welsh institutions have been growing at an increasing pace, starting with the creation of the Welsh Office in 1964, and the development of its powers and related Quangos ever since. Yet these have been largely invisible to most Welsh people, especially since the Welsh press and media do not penetrate to anything like the extent that occurs in Scotland. One role of the

Assembly will be to make them visible, and expose them to democratic debate and accountability. In this process we will begin to create for the first time a civic sense of Welshness, one in which all can share, and a new way for Wales to be understood. This is a formidable project, and one that should give a great sense of purpose to the early years of the National Assembly.

When it first meets in the summer of 1999 the Assembly's inheritance will be a Wales where change in a civic direction has been underway for some time. One example is the Welsh language whose fortunes have undergone a transformation during the past 20 years. This became clear in the way the language was largely absent from the debates that took place around the 1997 referendum. The contrast with 1979, when the Assembly of that era was defeated by a four-to-one vote, could not have been starker. The keynote of the 1970s was division and nothing underpinned it more than the Welsh language. During the 1979 campaign it was a disruptive influence. Irrational fears about the domination of the projected Assembly by Welsh speakers were effortlessly deployed by the No campaigners.

By 1997, however, the language had been swept away as an issue. Instead of a negative force in Welsh politics it had become a positive impulse. How this happened is something of a mystery. Undoubtedly a generation shift was part of the explanation: a generation that felt guilty about the loss of the language had passed on. Welsh medium schools were flourishing, and especially in the south-east were supported by mainly English-speaking parents. The role of S4C, together with many rock bands that perform through the medium of Welsh, linked the language with modernity, fashion and success, rather than an emotionally-suppressed past. When he was appointed chairman of the Welsh Language Board in 1993 former Plaid Cymru President Dafydd (Lord) Elis Thomas, pressed the case for taking the language out of the constitutional debate:

> 'Let's have more debates about the future political system of Wales and Europe through the medium of Welsh, but the future of the language itself must be above that debate. It should be the vehicle, not the cause of it. Too often in the past, political parties have played their version of the language card whenever it suited them. This reached its climax in the acrimonious devolution debate in the 1970s'. [1]

Looking back some years later Ron Davies, the former Secretary of State for Wales, noted how the transformation of attitudes to the language had changed the tone of Welsh politics:

> 'When I started out as a young councillor in the Rhymney Valley, the Welsh language was a hot potato which aroused angst and ire all over Wales. The Welsh language was something you were either 'for' or 'against': there wasn't much room for neutrality. But now that mode of thinking has been largely abandoned. Whether you happen to speak Welsh or not, there is increasingly the view that the language is part of what makes our identity as a nation

distinctive and unique. The language is no longer a political football in the way it once was.[2]

Attitudes to the language is only one indication of changing perspectives on what it means to be Welsh today. Another is a completely new outlook on Britain and, increasingly too, the European Union. Again, an explanation is the change in generations. In a little under two decades Wales underwent a generation shift which arguably was the single most important explanation for the four-to-one majority against the Assembly in 1979 being overturned into the narrow majority in 1997. Certainly this was a major finding from an in-depth survey of 700 people throughout Wales carried out within three weeks of the September 1997 referendum. Age emerged as the single most important determining factor in the way people had voted. Those under 45 were more likely to vote Yes by a margin of 3:2, while the over 45s voted No by a similar margin.[3]

This generation divide says as much about Britain as Wales. During the 1980s and 1990s Welsh attitudes to Britain have changed as markedly as attitudes to Wales itself. In 1979 the dominant generation was one that had grown up through the Second World War and, in its wake, the creation of a nationalised economy and the welfare state. For those who lived through it, the Second World War was a defining experience both in personal and collective terms. In the four decades following 1945 the nationalised industries were hugely influential in the Welsh economy. The welfare state, and particularly the creation of the health service, became embedded in the affections of the Welsh people. These were all distinctively British institutions and experiences. For a generation they described a framework of priorities and common sense within which Welsh politics and political identity were understood. In 1979 they were still determining what really mattered.

Yet in less than two decades virtually the whole of this landscape, everything that had previously described the contours of Welsh politics and economics, had changed unalterably. A generation was coming into positions of influence for whom the Second World War was history. Along with that memory the British Empire had slid from vision. Under the feet of this generation the nationalised industries had also disappeared from view. In place of British Coal and much of British Steel were now multinational firms whose main reason for being in Wales, apart from a relatively cheap and well educated labour force, was that it was a handy location within the European Union.

Of course, many of the values associated with the previous generation remained. The generosity and self-interest associated with a health service free at the point of delivery remained common sense, as did a native sense of community solidarity founded on attachment to locality, people and a shared landscape and culture. But all these things were mutating back more to what it meant to be Welsh than British, a Welshness moreover than now felt increasingly comfortable within a European embrace. In short, a new common sense about the realities of the Welsh economy, politics and identity was unfolding. These shifts were reflected in the divide between the generations in the referendum vote in September 1997.

What we are now presented with is, in a way, a normalisation of Welsh politics and identity. Britain remains important, but it is Britain that has changed and is changing. It no longer provides the primary lens through which Wales and what it means to be Welsh has to be viewed. In any event, as other parts of Britain develop their own institutions and as these evolve within Europe, the meaning of Britain will have to be re-negotiated. One forum for this will be the British-Irish Council being established as part of the Northern Ireland peace agreement, discussed in Chapter 29.

So far as Welsh identity is concerned the key reference point in future will be autonomous civic institutions, headed by the National Assembly, and embracing Wales as a whole. Welsh identity will no longer to be nationalised within Britain. Nor will it be felt in the first instance as intensely localised, with the language bearing an undue weight. The coming of the National Assembly is opening up a civic space for a truly Welsh politics to occur for the first time.

THE NATIONAL ASSEMBLY

The creation of the Assembly will challenge policy-makers to consistently take an 'all-Wales' view. In the Government of Wales Act the Assembly referred to in the White Paper *A Voice for Wales* went through a subtle metamorphosis. It was transformed from a *Welsh* into a *National* Assembly. In this area of politics presentation counts a lot. The expression National Assembly has a cosmopolitan, European ring, reflecting a belief that building an institution on a national bedrock means doing something a great deal more than changing a few local or even regional government boundaries. As Ron Davies himself put it:

> *'I have decided on the name - National Assembly for Wales - to stress that it will be for everyone in Wales - English and Welsh speakers, North, South, East and West and all political parties.'* [4]

Suggesting that the Assembly - being the National Assembly - will take an all-Wales view may sound an obvious point to make, but profound changes will flow from it. One example is the Welsh Office itself on whose customs and practices the Assembly will have to build. In its internal organisation the Welsh Office is currently modelled on the different Ministries found within Whitehall. This is partly because the Welsh Office has developed its functions piecemeal, over more than 30 years, with different powers and functions being handed down from different Whitehall departments at different times. It is also because the Welsh Office tends to take its lead from other Whitehall ministries.

A consequence of this background is a lack of coherence in policy-making. For example, many different Welsh Office divisions have an input into economic development which is also the responsibility of outside organisations such as the Welsh Development Agency, the Training and Enterprise Councils, and the local authorities. The result is that after thirty years of the existence of the Welsh Office we still do not have an economic development strategy for Wales. In October 1997 the Welsh Office at last put out a consultation document seeking views on what such a strategy might look like. However, when it published its final deliberations following the consultation, in July 1998, it retreated from the term 'economic strategy' and instead spoke of an 'economic agenda'. As the Cardiff University Devolution Group said, in their Memorandum of Evidence to the Welsh Select Committee's Inquiry into the Government's Devolution Proposals:

> '*Instead of concentrating on policy and strategy the Welsh Office has become increasingly involved in the delivery of programmes and services.*' [5]

There has always been tension within the Welsh Office between political and strategic objectives and more immediate problems of service delivery, tension exacerbated by continual scarcity of resources. This plays into the hands of civil servants who can easily present obstacles to innovative change in terms of lack of money. It is the nature of government, however, that where the political will is clear and strong resources can be found. The Assembly is about just that: institutionalising the national will that at the end of the day will be channelled through the voice of the leader of the Assembly. In this matter it is politics and leadership that will change. Effectively led, the Assembly will demand and drive forward a more integrated approach to economic policy making and management than is presently the case. This will be an enormous gain. As Brian Morgan, former Chief Economist with the Welsh Development Agency, and joint author of Chapter 13 on Economic Development, has put it:

> '*The present system is best described as a confused mixture of good intentions and conflicting objectives delivered by poorly co-ordinated agencies. This explains why a regional economic development strategy for Wales does not exist.*' [6]

A NEW POLICY-MAKING CULTURE

As presently undertaken, policy is largely the preserve of civil servants. Ministers at the Welsh Office can set a framework, dictated by manifesto commitments and by influences stemming from Whitehall. If they are determined enough they can also set a tone and atmosphere. For example, a new openness became apparent at the Welsh Office once Labour took control after May 1997. Even so, a dominant message coming from the administration is one that stresses the difficulties of effecting change, coupled with the inevitable budgetary constraints, rather than one that is inclined to explore the opportunities that exist.

Overwhelmingly the message reflects the views of civil servants who tend to be instinctively cautious and reluctant to change course. They also tend to recoil from distinctively Welsh policies since they are so heavily influenced by pressures coming from Whitehall departments. It has to be said, too, that in the past this has also been the case with Ministers at the Welsh Office who, at times, have been even more cautious than their civil servants.

This is a political culture that has the potential for change with the Assembly. And to be fair that is recognised within the Welsh Office itself. Speaking in November 1997 the Permanent Secretary, Rachel Lomax, said she had been surprised in the referendum debate that so many people seemed to think that the Assembly would make little difference to policy making in Wales:

> *'Believe me, a department that answers to sixty politicians who in turn answer to people from all over Wales is going to respond very differently from one that answers to one Cabinet Minister, whoever he or she is ... We are going to have to get used to explaining ourselves in public. Our business will be conducted more openly that in the past, and we will almost certainly find ourselves much more actively engaged with other bodies in Wales ... we will come under new and entirely different leadership. Instead of working to a Secretary of State who is a member of a Cabinet, and at best represents one Welsh constituency, most of us will transfer to the Assembly, where our political masters will be directly answerable to people from all over Wales, who will work in an entirely new and almost certainly much more open way ... We will have to listen more actively and respond more fully. We may increasingly become organisers of advice and expertise, rather than monopoly suppliers ... we will have to consciously shed the mind set - still rather engrained in civil servants everywhere - which says that the only advice worth having comes from the civil service.'* [7]

Echoing these points another senior Welsh Office civil servant described the forthcoming changes in even more graphic terms:

> *'Currently we are working for one Minister whose preoccupations are London rather than Wales centred. But once the Assembly is in being collective Cabinet responsibility will go out of the window. We are very close to being released from the strait jacket of thinking that Britain is a homogeneous community where policy diversity is a dangerous activity.'* [8]

Part of developing the new culture of policy-making described here will be the generation of policy communities across every area where the Assembly will have responsibility or an interest, from farming to health, housing and social services, to economic development, and to the arts and media. In all these policy arenas there are organisations and pressure groups which will want to ensure that the Assembly has heard what in their terms is the 'correct' message. Indeed, the legislation establishing the Assembly requires it to establish Regional Committees (at least for north Wales) to ensure that it takes on board representations from every part of Wales. In turn this will generate an interactive network of policy communication that will be a building block of a new civil society.

A NEW POLICY AGENDA

Of course, there will be a continual temptation for Assembly members to take a parochial view and concentrate on achieving advantage for their particular constituencies rather than advancing the interests of Wales as a whole. Nonetheless, the creation of the Assembly holds out the possibility of constructive change and innovative departures in policy making. At the very least, each of the parties will, for the first time, be required to develop a comprehensive manifesto for Wales. The agendas for change described in this book are an indication of the wide range of possibilities.

The first piece of paper to be handed the new Assembly members will be an account of present expenditure allocations within the £7.5 billion budget for which they will be responsible. As described in Chapter 4, this covers almost everything of domestic Welsh concern, from hospitals and roads, to farming and the environment, schools and urban and rural regeneration. The Assembly will have to establish an annual procedure for dealing with the budgetary process and decide whether it wishes to alter current priorities by directing expenditure from one part of its budget to another. Initially, the scope for change will be small. Even so, small changes from year-to-year can cumulatively produce a large effect.

In the past, whenever there has been a budget squeeze the areas of Welsh Office expenditure most vulnerable have been roads and housing. The area most protected has been health, which at £2.4bn, accounts for about a third of current Welsh Office expenditure. By comparison, the 1998-9 £114m allocation to the Welsh Development Agency is relatively small. As Nigel Blewitt points out in Chapter 4, 34.3 per cent of the block is directed at health, but only 6.9 per cent is spent directly on economic development, industry and training. Moreover, Welsh health expenditure is 13 per cent higher than in England, at £841 per head compared with £734. And it is climbing inexorably upwards in an unsustainable way, by around three per cent a year. The Assembly could decide, for example, to restrain expenditure on health and gradually direct some of the resources saved into economic development. The rationale would be that increasing spending on economic development should have the effect of reducing unemployment which in turn would be an effective, if long-term, means of improving health. Such a strategic decision would doubtless be controversial and difficult, given the public attachment to the NHS and the financial problems currently facing NHS Wales which in 1998-9 was running a deficit of between £25m and £35m. However, it is an indication of what the Assembly could do.

Such thinking would be assisted if we regarded allocations within the block fund as an essential and integral part of economic policy. For instance, we should view health expenditure as an investment in the economy rather that merely consumption. To begin with the Welsh health service employs 58,000 people. And as Chapter 20 on *Health and Social Policy* also points out, we have in Wales some of the worst morbidity statistics in Britain and, indeed, in Europe. This hardly adds to the attractiveness of our economic profile. A healthy economy needs a healthy workforce.

Additionally, we should regard key areas of expenditure within the block as the starting point for innovation in the Welsh economy. Again health spending provides a good example. Key growth industries in the coming decades will be in health-related industries, especially the production of drugs and pharmaceutical supplies and the research and development that accompanies them, together with the biotechnology and genetic engineering sectors. The huge investment in the Welsh health service, in terms of its proportion of the block, should be regarded as a platform on which to build research and development in health-related industries, especially in the less developed parts of Wales where health expenditure tends to be higher.

More generally, the Assembly should put a greater emphasis on indigenous business development in place of, or perhaps in addition to, the attention that has given to attracting inward investment in recent decades. This will require a 'business birthrate' plan for creating new firms, a plan whose main focus should be on west Wales and the Valleys, those areas where it has proved most difficult to attract inward investment in the past, but where there is a good chance of attracting European funds in the next few years.

Communications are intimately connected with economic development. Hitherto, communications within Wales have focused on east-west lines. The advent of the Assembly is likely to produce a new emphasis on north-south links - first an improved rail service, closely followed by more investment in north-south road connections. Undoubtedly the Assembly will have electronic communications as a high priority, too, not just in terms of its own communication with far-flung parts of Wales, but as a focus for business development.

Education is another area where we can expect the Assembly to make an early impact. There is a growing consensus, for example, that post-16 education needs to be broadened and that vocational studies need to be improved, given a higher status, and integrated with academic studies. This is one of the main recommendations in the Welsh Office's Education and Training Action Group's draft report, produced in October 1998 and discussed in Chapter 17. As highlighted in Chapter 18, the Institute of Welsh Affairs has developed detailed proposals for a Welsh Baccalaureate (the *WelshBac*) that would achieve these objectives. This would be a medium-term policy objective that the Assembly could adopt, and in the process effect an enormous change on Welsh life. Apart from the inherent attractiveness of the policy, it has the advantage of not requiring significant new spending, a consideration that is likely to weigh heavily with Assembly members.

The kind of initiatives that have been suggested here are largely within the conventional policy arena. In addition, the legislation establishing the Assembly has built in new policy requirements. For instance, the Assembly is required to take 'Sustainable Development' into account in its decision making. How this will work through in practice is likely to prove one of its greatest challenges and is discussed in Chapter 11.

There are other, analogous, cross-cutting policy arenas. The presence of a significant number of women within the Assembly should ensure that equal opportunities are 'mainstreamed' across its activities, issues that are explored in Chapter 8. The legislation also requires the Assembly to establish a 'Partnership Council' with local government. It is required to establish a scheme setting out how it proposes to promote the interests of voluntary organisations. And it is required to carry out appropriate consultation with CBI Wales and the Wales TUC on the impact of its activities on business and the economy. All these consultations and interactions will result in policy development running through new, broader channels, and are part of the Assembly's agenda explored in this book.

There are a number of persistent themes that recur, and between them they describe the formidable challenge that will face Assembly members. These themes can be condensed into four questions. Given that the Assembly will not be bound by collective Cabinet responsibility, how will it:

- Influence the content of primary legislation passed at Westminster and ensure it has the 'legislative space' to develop its own coherent policies?
- Have access to the same information/intelligence in Whitehall as the Welsh Office does now?
- Ensure that Wales receives its fair share of public funds?
- Ensure that its voice is heard on EU matters?

A NEW APPROACH TO POLICY

The way the responsibilities of the Assembly are co-ordinated and managed will to a large extent be determined by the committee structure that emerges. The Assembly's committees are discussed in Chapter 5. In policy terms the Subject Committees will be most important. In Part Two of this book, the main policy areas are broken down into eleven main areas, with Sustainable Development heading the list as an additional, cross-agenda context. It is possible that there will be a specific 'Programme Committee' devoted to Sustainable Development since this will affect every aspect of the Assembly's policy-making responsibilities. Surprisingly this was not recommended by the Secretary of State's National Assembly Advisory Group (NAAG) despite the fact that each year the Assembly will need to be produce an audit assessing what has been achieved in the implementation of its Sustainable Development agenda. However, NAAG did recommend that there should be Programme Committees on European Affairs and Equal Opportunities. As with Sustainable Development these will present cross-cutting demands that will impinge on most aspects of the Assembly's work.

But it is the Subject Committees that will be the engine room of the Assembly's activities, where policy options are reviewed and the Executive held to account.

This book deals with the Assembly's policy and service delivery functions under the following headings:

- Sustainable Development
- Strategic Planning
- Economic Development
- Transport
- Farming and the Rural Economy
- Tourism
- The Welsh Workforce
- Education
- Culture and the Arts
- Health and Social Policy
- Social Services
- Housing

There is a close inter-relationship between many of these policy areas, especially in the economic development and education fields, but also in social policy where there should be closer inter-action between health and social services as well as with housing provision. The fact that in the past such policy areas have been split between different agencies, and even in some cases between different layers of local government, only serves to reinforce the argument that in future we should aim for improved co-ordination. As one Welsh Office civil servant commented:

> *'There is very little communication between Whitehall departments. Its even difficult to get co-operation across divisions inside the Welsh Office. The Assembly should not be satisfied with sectoral solutions. Instead it should be pre-occupied with inter-sectoral solutions.'* [10]

The Government of Wales Act makes provision for Subject Committees but does not specify their number or subject composition. Yet how they are organised will itself determine to some extent the policy outcomes that will result. We will have to await until the Assembly is established and the first Executive or Cabinet is formed before we will know the pattern. This is because the Subject Committees will shadow the portfolios the Assembly's First Minister or Premier allots to his Executive Committee or Cabinet.

What is clear, however, is that there cannot be more than between four and six Subject Committees. The relatively small size of the Assembly, with just sixty members, dictates this. As discussed in Chapter 5, and in previous reports produced by the Institute of Welsh Affairs there are not enough members to go round to service many more Subject Committees [11]. A possible structure, indicating the new policy relationships that would emerge, might result in four Subject Committees as follows:

- Local Government, Environment, Strategic Planning, and Transport
- Industry, Economic Development, Rural Affairs and Tourism
- Education, Training, Culture and the Arts
- Health, Housing and Social Services

In each case there would need to be sub-committees specialising in different aspects of the Committees' work, but the kind of over-arching thematic approach suggested here would encourage a level of policy co-ordination and integration that just does not happen under present arrangements. Each of these Subject Committees should be regarded as inter-acting policy arenas within which a more imaginative and innovative approach to policy-making can be constructed. A key challenge in each arena will be to bring a cross-disciplinary approach to the management of scarce resources.

There could, of course be other combinations. There is a case, for example, for including Education and Training with Economic Development, since these areas are closely related. However, that might produce an over-burdened Subject Committee. And the fact is that all these policy areas inter-act with each other in one way or another. A case in point, as discussed earlier (page 7) is the relationship between health and economic development, not one that readily comes to mind within the current policy framework. Yet who would deny that a major cause of health problems is unemployment. The inexorable and increasing demands on the health budget, which will take around a third of the expenditure block, will present the Assembly with a huge challenge. One objective should be to decrease, or at least maintain at present levels, health spending, so that more resources can be directed towards addressing the underlying causes of ill health by reducing unemployment, improving housing, and dealing with under-achievement in education.

It was noteworthy, for instance, that in her last annual report on the Health of Wales 1996, the retiring Chief Medical Officer, Dame Deirdre Hine, for the first time drew attention to the close relationship between health, work and the economy. A chapter with this heading identified a close inter-relationship between excessively low economic activity rates in the Valleys and ill health. The politically charged recommendation came near the end of the chapter:

> 'General practitioners will need to understand that the key to maintaining
> people in work (with all the health-related benefits which work brings) lies in
> being appropriately cautious about certifying patients unfit for work, and
> encouraging them to return to work as soon as possible after an episode of

illness. This will not be easy, as doctors will be put under considerable pressure by patients and their families. In order to resist this pressure, general practitioners themselves will need to be reassured that suitable work is available, and that where necessary suitable training is available to qualify their patients for it.' [12]

Can spending on health provide the suitable work and training required? The answer, of course, is no. Yet while the policy direction is easy to suggest, it will be much more difficult to achieve in practice. The NHS is already among the most efficient in the world, delivering on the whole effective health provision while utilising some 5 to 6 per cent of GDP, three or four points lower than in comparable industrialised countries. If it is to control and direct health expenditure more effectively the Assembly will have to address rationalisation and, in some cases, rationing of some provision. To achieve consent for such an approach it will need to promote bottom-up democratic control of health decisions, through initiatives such as locality commissioning that have already been tentatively explored in some areas of Wales.

Health service policy is just one example where the powers enshrined in the National Assembly offer the potential for great change in strategic thinking. Education is an equally important area. The policy arenas described in the Committee Structure suggested here, and explored in depth in successive chapters in this book, offer policy approaches that together would bring a new coherence to Welsh policy-making.

A NEW BRITAIN AND A NEW EUROPE

It is not just internally that Welsh politics are changing. The very fact that we are changing our politics, just as the peoples of Scotland and Northern Ireland are changing theirs, is re-shaping British and European politics as well. The idea of a 'New Britain' has hitherto been confined to the 'New Labour' top-down, centralist project. The new politics in Wales - and in Scotland and Northern Ireland - will have the inevitable consequence of creating a new Britain in a more fundamental way, by re-defining and making more transparent what it means to be British.

It is, for example, no longer possible to talk in terms of a 'British nation' in the way that Conservative leaders attempted in the years leading to the 1997 referendums. Britain remains a state, but no longer, if ever it was, a unitary state. Instead, it has to be understood as a union state with many distinctive government arrangements amongst its component parts. These are now obvious so far as Wales, Scotland and Northern Ireland are concerned, and will progressively become transparent within England as well, as the constitutional reform agenda moves ahead. Already London has voted to have its own elected Mayor and Assembly. From April 1999 the English regions will have Development Agencies modelled on the Welsh Development Agency and Scottish Enterprise. These will be followed by Regional Chambers representing local government and other key interests, and eventually directly elected Regional Assemblies. The trajectory, if not yet the timetable, for the creation of regional governance within England has been set.

The creation of these new institutions will require new forums for communication between them. The Easter 1998 Irish Agreement which established the Northern Ireland Assembly also created the British-Irish Council which will bring together representatives from the new Assembly in Northern Ireland, the National Assembly of Wales, the Scottish Parliament, the Channel Isles, the Isle of Man, and Dublin and Westminster. And as discussed in Chapter 29, a Joint Ministerial Committee is to be established within the UK Cabinet Office to ensure liaison between the central UK government and the new governments in Wales, Scotland and Northern Ireland. This development emerged late in the day and largely unremarked, yet it is likely to have profound consequences for the devolution process.

These changes are transforming Britain as well as its constituent parts. So, too, is the emerging regionalism within the European Union which is steadily finding stronger expression in institutional terms. The outlines within the continental nation-states have long been apparent - the German Länder, the Italian regions, the emerging Belgian confederation, the evolution of the Spanish Autonomous Communities since the death of Franco, and latterly regionalism even within France. This process, which has been gathering pace in the last few decades, has now been immensely fortified by devolution within the United Kingdom. At the pan-European level the movement has found expression in the Committee of the Regions, still embryonic in terms of influence, but nonetheless highly emblematic.

In the 1990s we have been living through momentous changes in the geo-political context in which European integration is evolving. The disappearance of the Soviet bloc, the re-unification of Germany, and the Treaty of Maastricht have set in motion processes whose scale can be compared to the events following the end of World War II. We have the return of Germany to continental hegemony, monetary union and the single currency, and ex communist states to the east jockeying for entry into the EU. There is the potential for a new fluidity in the way that Europe functions and the way it relates to the people. With the emergence of regional structures, now within all the member states, we have the possibility of beginning to construct Europe from below in a more democratic fashion.

The former German Chancellor Helmut Kohl spelled out this possibility, speaking in the Bundestag in April 1998. The single currency, he said, would give a mighty push to the process of political union. The coming Austrian and German EU presidencies should agree a clear definition of subsidiarity. This would be crucial to the future acceptance of Europe by its citizens. Kohl rejected the notion of a super state. He said: 'I believe it has no chance. A centralised super state would destroy Europe's regional cultures in all their glory'. And he went on to say that the German federal system, in which much power is decentralised to the Länder and the municipalities was a model for the new Europe [13].

Such visions are not, of course, inevitable. They will not be handed down. They are there to be chosen and made. And now, in Wales, with the advent of the National Assembly we have the mechanism to enable us to take part. We need to become more aware that being part of Europe is much more than competing for Agricultural and Structural Funds. We should realise that the nature of those funds is contingent upon the kind of Europe they are being used to build. So the new Welsh politics is also about high politics. We need to decide what kind of Europe we want to see, achieve a consensus amongst ourselves on what that should be, and then seek allies across the Regions of Europe in pressing our case within the European decision-making institutions. The advent of the National Assembly will present us with an opportunity to ensure that Wales is represented more directly, and therefore effectively within Europe. The new politics in Wales has to find a new place, not just within a changing Britain, but within a changing European Union as well.

A WELSH CIVIL SOCIETY

During the 1980s and 1990s key mainstream institutions and political organisations in Scotland came together in a Scottish Convention to agree proposals for a Scottish Parliament. They included the Scottish local authorities, the Scottish TUC, the Churches, a variety of cultural organisations, and the Scottish Labour Party and Scottish Liberal Democrats - though the SNP and Scottish Conservatives refused to participate.

During this period there were calls for something similar to happen in Wales, especially in the wake of the 1992 election, Labour's fourth defeat in a row. However, the idea was rejected by the Welsh Labour Party, for a number of reasons. Labour has an even more dominant electoral position in Wales than Scotland with around 50 per cent of the Westminster vote compared with 40 per cent in Scotland. Its strongholds are not threatened significantly by any other party. This led some in the Welsh leadership to believe that by itself Labour could adequately represent the views of the people of Wales. More fundamentally, in 1992 devolution was still a divisive issue for the Welsh Labour Party. Its priority was achieving a consensus within its own ranks before taking on board views from outside.

Nonetheless, it was a missed opportunity. If Labour had led the search for a cross-party consensus in the early 1990s it would have had to face up earlier to the key issues of proportional representation and gender balance, issues that were to split the party in the run-up to the referendum and the first Assembly elections. As it was, deciding the form of the Assembly and then achieving support for it had to be done amidst the turmoil of the referendum campaign itself, an enterprise that very nearly came apart.

What this history, together with the Scottish comparison, reveals is a relatively undeveloped civil society within Wales. What we have is a *civil society in Wales* rather than a *Welsh civil society*. A developed civil society would have a mature sense of citizenship in relation to Welsh institutions. It would be composed of a wide range of social institutions and networks that thought effortlessly in Welsh terms and, through interaction with the Welsh policy-making process, shared responsibility for mobilising opinion and choosing the direction Welsh society should take. The new Welsh politics is about creating a new democracy and a new civil society to make the democracy work. When it first meets, the National Assembly will not be representative of that civil society. But it will be the essential instrument to ensure that in the coming decades a Welsh democracy and a Welsh civil society will come into being.

References

1   Western Mail, 26 October 1993.

2   Western Mail, 2 July 1998.

3   1997 Welsh Referendum Survey, University of Wales, Aberystwyth; reported in Agenda, Institute of Welsh Affairs, Summer 1998.

4   Welsh Office Press Release, Ron Davies welcomes the Government of Wales Bill, 27 November 1997.

5   Cardiff University Devolution Group, Memorandum of Evidence to the Welsh Select Committee's Inquiry into the Government's Devolution Proposals, November 1997, Para. 1.04.

6   Brian Morgan In The Economic Impact of a Welsh Assembly, Instituto of Welsh Affairs, September 1997, p. 49.

7   Rachel Lomax, Preparing for the Assembly, speech to the Institute of Welsh Affairs, 7 November 1997.

8   Interview with the author, January 1998.

9   See John David, Colin Jenkins et. al., The WelshBac: Educating Wales in the Next Century, and The Welsh Baccalaureate: Matching International Standards, Institute of Welsh Affairs, 1997.

10   Interview with the author, December 1997.

11   Institute of Welsh Affairs: Making the Assembly Work, 1007, and An Effective National Assembly, 1998

12   Deirdre Hine, Welsh Health: Annual report of the Chief Medical Officer 1996, Welsh Office November 1997, page 52.

13   Kohl pledges push for greater European integration, Financial Times, 22 April 1998.

PART ONE

OPERATING THE NATIONAL ASSEMBLY

CHAPTER 1

THE FIRST ELECTIONS

Denis Balsom

The passage of the Government of Wales Act introduces to Wales a new electoral system for the National Assembly of Wales. The adoption of a system which seeks to produce a more proportional outcome than that traditionally associated with British elections, is, in itself, a testament to the change in political culture that the Labour Government has set out to achieve. In parallel, the method of election to the European Parliament has also been reformed. More generally, the Commission of Enquiry under Lord Jenkins reported on arrangements for elections to Westminster in October 1998. Whilst the system of election adopted for the National Assembly is now in place, its operation and outcome will define the new politics in Wales. This chapter concentrates on the implications and likely consequences of the new system, rather than attempting to predict any particular political outcome from the electoral process.

THE ELECTORAL SYSTEM

The electoral system is a hybrid, combining a simple plurality election in each of the present 40 Parliamentary constituencies, with an additional member electoral system (AMS) utilising party lists in the five former European Parliamentary constituencies, now to be known as electoral regions. Each region will return four members giving the National Assembly a total membership of 60.

The combination of systems is designed to retain the traditional British link between an elected member and a specific geographic community, whilst the additional members mitigate the disproportionality inherent in simple plurality voting. An Assembly Member for a specific constituency will have a straightforward link to the electorate, but might come to be seen as a competitor to the Westminster MP who represents exactly the same community. There will inevitably be confusion as to which representative provides the appropriate channel through which an elector should raise issues. The Assembly will undoubtedly control most of the domestic concerns which affect everyday life, such as education, health, social services and housing, but it will do so within a legislative framework determined by Westminster. The recent reform of local government in Wales was justified, in part, by the need to clarify areas of responsibility between District and County Councillors. The advent of the National Assembly seems likely to raise such overlap issues again. Over time, however, the position of the Westminster MP can be expected to be eclipsed by that of the Assembly Member.

The Government of Wales Act explicitly defines the ratio of constituency members to additional members as 2 to 1. It also entrenches the co-terminousity of Parliamentary constituencies and Assembly constituencies. Wales is currently over-represented in Westminster, in comparison with England. The lower electoral quota used by the Boundary Commission to apportion seats in Wales (and Scotland) has been justified not only on grounds of rurality and sparsity of population, but also, in part, by the idea that the smaller constituent nations of the United Kingdom justify greater recognition within the Union Parliament. Thus, following the abrogation of the Stormont Assembly in Northern Ireland, Parliamentary representation from the Province was eventually increased from 12 to 17 MPs.

Current legislation requires the Parliamentary Boundary Commission to define at least thirty five seats for Wales, irrespective of the electoral quota. Should any future Commission choose to reduce the number of Westminster seats from Wales on the grounds of greater equity with England, the number of Assembly seats would also fall by the same number. Consequently, the number of additional members would also be reduced to retain the ratio of a 2 to 1, constituency to additional members. Such a step has always been thought to be unlikely in the past for sound political reasons. Prior to the 1997 general election, it was commonly believed that a Parliamentary majority for the Labour Party could only be achieved courtesy of the over-representation of Wales and Scotland in Westminster. The outcome of the 1997 election has now disproved this maxim and there can be no guarantee that a future Government might not legislate to require the Boundary Commission to apportion constituencies more equitably and thus reduce representation from Wales. Given the widely held view that the National Assembly has been constituted with too few members to undertake its many responsibilities (see, for example, the report of the IWA's Constitution Working Group *Making the Assembly Work*), any further diminution of its size would have very serious consequences.

The adoption of the former Euro-constituency boundaries to define the electoral regions for the Assembly also appears rather odd at first sight. For the European Parliament elections to be held in June 1999, Wales is to form a single electoral unit, returning five MEPs from a national party list election. The Government of Wales Act could have adopted a similar, single unit, approach to the allocation of the additional members to the National Assembly. This would have had the advantage of consistency, given that the electorate will now have to become familiar with two variants of the new electoral system. A common approach would have also allowed the d'Hondt formula, the mechanism used to calculate the highest average party vote, to achieve a far more proportional result from the Assembly elections by allocating all 20 additional members in successive rounds of the count. Retention of the former five Euro seats inhibits greater proportionality by limiting the application of the formula to four rounds of reallocation and by returning a uniform four members per electoral region irrespective of population size. Whilst the disparity between electorates in the former Euro-seats is not great, when compared to that between Parliamentary seats, neither is it trivial.

Assuming that the electoral regions will now be retained, there is also a case for these electoral boundaries to be made co-terminus with those for the Assembly's regional committees. Such a change would have the added political advantage of making the additional members specifically accountable to a territorial area.These new electoral regions would thus be meaningful units for other purposes within the Assembly and for other public bodies, such as the new Welsh Development Agency and the TECs. Without such a linkage, the additional members, the majority of whom will belong to Opposition parties, appear to be 'at large' and so subject to little national or local political accountability.

PROJECTED OUTCOMES

It is extremely difficult to anticipate the outcome of the first Assembly elections to be held in May 1999. Whilst historical electoral trends and voting patterns in Wales have been extremely well documented, the new system gives electors two votes and there exists only limited evidence so far to suggest how public opinion will divide. Reference to behaviour at past general elections is flawed because one has to assume that electors will behave consistently and vote for the same party on both ballots. Obviously ticket-splitting will occur, but it will only be on the basis of accurate opinion poll evidence, or, in time, on the historical evidence which will accumulate over the coming years of Assembly elections, that reasonable assumptions concerning ticket-splitting can be made.

In the interim, evidence of public opinion from Scotland suggests that the electorate has been quick to discriminate between elections to Westminster and elections to the forthcoming Scottish Parliament, with broadly traditional patterns being retained for the former and new allegiances being formed for the latter. To date only three opinion polls have been conducted enquiring after voting intention for the Assembly Elections. All have shown a significant shift in voter's preferences between the first and second ballots for the Assembly (see Tables 1 and 2 on the facing page).

On the first ballot, for a single constituency member to be elected first-past-the-post, Labour support predominated and, in the Beaufort polls, even exceeded Labour's share of the vote in the 1997 landslide election when Labour returned 34 out of 40 Welsh MPs to Parliament. Plaid Cymru, however, show a remarkable increase in support compared with past voting patterns. On the second ballot, for the additional members to represent the electoral regions, Labour support fell, whilst that for the Liberal Democrats increased significantly.

TABLE 1

Q: If Assembly elections were held tomorrow which party would you vote to represent you locally?

Pollster / Client	Beaufort / BBC	Beaufort / W Mail	NOP / HTV
Fieldwork	3-9/7/98	3-6/9/98	10-15/9/98
Sample size	1008	1029	1500
Labour	57%	57%	50%
Plaid Cymru	20%	19%	24%
Conservative	14%	12%	16%
Liberal Democrat	9%	8%	8%
Others	1%	3%	1%

TABLE 2

Q: And with your second vote, which party would you vote for to occupy the additional seats in the Assembly?

Pollster / Client	Beaufort / BBC	Beaufort / W Mail	NOP / HTV
Fieldwork	3-9/7/98	3-6/9/98	10-15/9/98
Sample size	1008	1029	1500
Labour	44%	52%	44%
Plaid Cymru	23%	19%	23%
Conservative	13%	13%	17%
Liberal Democrat	18%	11%	15%
Others	3%	5%	2%

As the 6 May 1999 election date comes closer, further polling evidence for Wales will be published. However, if the trends apparent from these early polls are confirmed by subsequent surveys, the Conservatives, Plaid Cymru and Liberal Democrats will pick up additional seats by virtue of the list system. Plaid Cymru's potential for success on the first ballot is more problematic, irrespective of any increase in popular support, because the number of seats where the party is able to effectively challenge Labour dominance is very limited. Only Carmarthen East and Dinefwr would appear winnable, but if Labour were to poll as well as they did in 1997, Plaid may still fail to capture the seat. Plaid Cymru's difficulties on the first ballot however, still allow the party to secure seats on the second ballot, as the d'Hondt formula favours parties with the highest number of votes per elected member.

If the outcome of the first Assembly elections were to match that of the most recent poll, that from NOP for HTV Wales, one might expect a Labour majority in the

Assembly with 35 of the 60 seats, Plaid Cymru would form the largest Opposition party with 11 seats, the Conservatives and Liberal Democrats would win 8 and 6 respectively. Such calculations however, remain highly speculative. Whilst one can expect the hybrid AMS election system to produce a more proportional election result than a first-past-the-post election, there will still be an element of bias towards the largest party. In the NOP/HTV Wales poll the combined share of the vote over both ballots gives Labour 47 percent, Plaid Cymru 23.5 percent, Conservative 16.5 percent, Liberal Democrat 11.5 percent and others 1.5 percent. If the sixty seats in the National Assembly were to broadly match this distribution, the outcome would be an Assembly made up of 28 Labour members, 14 from Plaid Cymru, ten from the Conservatives, seven Liberal Democrats and one from the other parties.

TABLE 3

Likely Political Composition of the Assembly

	Estimate based on NOP/HTV poll	%	If proportional to share of the vote in poll	%
Labour	35	58.3%	28	46.7%
Plaid Cymru	11	18.3%	14	23.3%
Conservative	8	13.3%	10	16.7%
Liberal Democrat	6	10.0%	7	11.7%
Others			1	1.7%

The electoral system adopted for the National Assembly produces a more proportional outcome than Britain's traditional method of election, but a substantial bias is still enjoyed by the largest party. In theory, the Additional Member system is capable of 'correcting' the inevitable disproportionality of the first round, first-past-the-post election, but it would require more seats to be distributed by the d'Hondt formula than the present system allows. By contrast, the system adopted for the election of the Scottish Parliament elects 73 members by a conventional ballot and 56 through the party list giving the AMS method far greater scope to influence the eventual outcome and achieve a more proportional result.

ISSUES RAISED BY AMS

The adoption of the AMS electoral system raises numerous questions for both electors and parties. Foremost amongst these is the formidable process of education that must be undertaken to inform the public, not only of the powers and structures of the Assembly, but also of the new method of election. Given the furore that followed the referendum concerning spoilt ballots, the prospect of electors being given two ballot papers must cause returning officers great concern.

It will also be the case that all political parties will now have to register. This is not a requirement for elections to the National Assembly alone, but has been adopted for Britain as a whole. In part it is to challenge the growing trend of spoilers standing for election. These are candidates who adopt titles and names designed to confuse or deceive the electorate, such as standing as a Literal Democrat. The new legislation however is also required by the adoption of party list electoral systems which can only be fought by registered political parties or individuals standing in their own name.

At the National Assembly election, the first ballot will elect a constituency member and be made up of candidate's names and party designations in the conventional way. The second ballot paper, to elect the additional members, will contain only party names. Individual, non-party candidates will also be able to stand for both ballots in their own names. As if this new system were not taxing enough, elections are also scheduled to be held to elect new County and Community Councils on the same day as those for the Assembly. It is probable that one of these elections be will postponed, but, even so, the potential for confusion and administrative problems remains high.

Following the election and the return of members to the National Assembly there remains the difficulty for electors to differentiate between their various elected representatives and their appropriate responsibilities. It is likely to be some time before the electorate is sufficiently well informed to be able to accurately assign responsibilities between local, national, United Kingdom and European representatives.

For the political parties, both the Assembly and the new electoral system raise difficult issues. The difficulties experienced by the Labour Party in fulfiling an earlier commitment to achieve gender balance illustrate the point. Parties are used to selecting candidates for simple plurality elections, though even here there have been considerable struggles in the past concerning the relative input of local and UK organisations to the selection process. Nominations to a party list however, present further problems. Firstly, candidate selection for the list is likely to be determined by the party apparatus and thus opposed by those wishing to defend local party sovereignty. Secondly, the probability of a candidate being elected from the list varies greatly and is dependent upon the fortunes of the party in the respective constituencies making up the electoral region. In some countries where AMS is used, parties use the list to elect senior spokesmen, allowing them to serve in the Assembly unencumbered by constituency duties. In Wales, where Labour might expect to return a majority of the constituency members on the first ballot, it means that Labour is correspondingly less likely to return many additional members from the list. Other parties are more likely to elect members from the list, but will not want to exclude their best candidates from individual constituency contests. These parties therefore, are likely to nominate the same individuals for both ballots. Candidates who lose a constituency contest, but who are subsequently elected from the list, will carry a considerable stigma of political defeat in the Assembly that may diminish both their status and effectiveness.

The method of election requires the number of votes collected by the respective parties in the second ballot to be divided by the number of members already elected for that party on the first ballot. The party with the resulting highest average number of votes per candidate is awarded an additional member. This process is repeated four times in each of the electoral regions to elect the four additional members. Where a party has polled very heavily in the first constituency ballot, and elected several members, the likelihood is that they will not be awarded any additional members by the application of the d'Hondt formula. For example, if Labour were to win all seven seats in the South Wales West region, it is extremely unlikely to qualify for any additional members, even if its loyal supporters had polled just as heavily for Labour in the second ballot. In effect, the second vote would be 'wasted'. The Labour Party is likely to be extremely reluctant to advocate that their supporters defect to an alternative party for the second ballot. For the other parties however, the ability to court support on the second ballot, whilst recommending that electors exercise their usual political preference on the first ballot, offers great potential for broadening their appeal. To the individual voter, a Labour-Green ballot, for example, may be more effective than a straight Labour-Labour vote. Whilst the major parties are unlikely to recommend such strategic choices various ticket-splitting options will undoubtedly emerge and be adopted. The electorate has already shown in recent elections, and at by-elections in particular, an acute awareness of tactical voting and this tendency can only be expected to increase at the Assembly elections. Yet, effective tactical voting requires foreknowledge of the likely outcome of the first ballot. In the absence of accurate opinion polling, such information is likely to be derived from an assessment of past political behaviour. In time one would expect the electorate to become quite sophisticated in its decision-making and for parties to also refine their campaigning to accommodate tactical voting.

The number of electors who will 'split their ticket' when voting for the National Assembly remains unknown. The available polling evidence suggests that political preferences for the Assembly will match evidence emerging from Scotland and show a clearly different patterns of political behaviour for elections to Cardiff from those to Westminster. Such a trend appears likely to be present at the first elections and will certainly become more pronounced in the future and as the Assembly establishes itself on the Welsh political landscape.

CAMPAIGNING FOR THE ASSEMBLY

MANIFESTO

The question of who will write each party's manifesto and what policies they will contain presents one of the more fascinating issues of the forthcoming election. The future relationship between the Cardiff offices of the political parties and their London headquarters remains intriguingly uncertain. Parties in Wales need to evolve their own agendas. These will not be unrelated to the UK policy agendas of their respective parties, but they will have to become increasingly distinct. At a practical level, parties will have to announce what secondary legislation they would seek to introduce in the Assembly and how current Westminster legislation might be tempered to suit the conditions of Wales. Parties may also wish to declare items of legislation they would wish to see Westminster introduce, so that some distinctively Welsh issues could then be addressed in the Assembly. In Wales, the party organisations and conferences will need to become more policy oriented, but in the case of the UK-wide parties, still liaise closely with their 'parent' bodies in London. This may prove a difficult and painful process. For Plaid Cymru, the sole Wales-only party, this will not present a problem. However, they will suffer from the relative impotence of their small Parliamentary group in Westminster to instigate legislation, except as private members, to address specific Welsh issues. Over time there can only be a growth of a distinct Welsh political agenda and increasingly independent political parties, perhaps linked in a loose 'federal' relationship with their equivalents in London and Scotland.

LEADERSHIP

Who will lead the Assembly election campaign in Wales? Will the parties deploy Welsh leaders or big name Westminster party dignitaries? It is important that the Welsh electorate understands who will head the Assembly as First Secretary should a particular party secure a majority. If the outcome at the Assembly election is inconclusive, it remains important that identifiable party leaders are in place to conduct any negotiations concerning coalitions or pacts. These concerns led the Labour Party to hold a leadership election in September 1998, between Ron Davies and Rhodri Morgan, followed by leadership contests within the Welsh Conservative Party and Welsh Liberal Democrats in the following months. As this book was going to press a further contest looked inevitable, between Rhodri Morgan and Alun Michael, for the Labour leadership in the wake of Ron Davies' resignation at the end of October 1998.

The political parties undoubtedly felt that such internal elections carried great risks of being both internally divisive and projecting an image of division to the electorate. The issue however, could not be avoided and, in the case of the Labour Party, the victory of Ron Davies, the former Secretary of State, was, in effect, an endorsement of the status quo. Whether that position will be confirmed following Ron Davies' resignation was a matter still to be resolved as this book went to press. More generally, as the Assembly develops there will evolve a distinct leadership cadre within all the parties, giving Wales, for the first time, a national political élite separate from Westminster.

As the work of the Assembly develops, tensions between the Welsh Cabinet and the Westminster Government will inevitably arise, even when both may be of the same party. As occurs in other political systems, such as under federalism, the parties in Wales will probably re-define themselves as the Welsh Conservatives, or the Welsh

Labour Party, with more or less independence from their central organisations. In theory this model already applies to the Liberal Democrats who espouse a federal constitution.

The authority of any party in power derives from its electoral mandate. The party of government in London governs by virtue of its majority in the House of Commons, likewise the Cabinet of the National Assembly. The Welsh Cabinet however, will have specific commitments to the people of Wales. For a London government any mandate for Wales has to be based on the level of popular support in Wales, or inferred from that claimed for the United Kingdom as a whole. Hence the argument that successive Conservative administrations in the 1980s lacked legitimacy in Wales. The greater democracy that is the essence of the devolutionary process, should establish clear lines of accountability once and for all.

BROADCASTING

During the Assembly elections it will be important for the Welsh political leadership to lead in the media coverage of politics and to present any specially produced party political and electoral broadcasts. The London party leaders may wish to endorse their candidates in Wales, but it is essential that these elections are fought within Wales, by the competing prospective members of the Assembly and on a Welsh agenda. In 1999 it may be that UK political leaders will take a fairly prominent part in the campaign. Thereafter, however, one would expect Welsh politics to become increasingly self contained.

LOCAL ELECTIONS

The Government of Wales Act establishes the National Assembly for a fixed term of four years. Future Assembly elections will continue to be concurrent with those for local government in Wales. It is important that the Assembly should establish itself 'above' local government, yet continue to be involved, so that policies endorsed by the Assembly can be implemented, where appropriate, through the provision of local government services. The creation of the Partnership Council requiring the Assembly to work very closely with local government and other public authorities should facilitate this process. Whilst it is appropriate that such mechanisms act as 'checks and balances' to any potential excess proposed by the Assembly, it remains important that the Assembly is able exercise power and leadership and not be thwarted without good reason.

Whilst levels of participation and interest in local government should increase through the greater integration of the various levels of governance within Wales, there still remains a danger of a mutual rivalry growing between the respective layers of government in the 'new' Wales. This might best be overcome by encouraging the parties to develop complementary agendas and manifestoes.

CONCLUSION

The adoption of a new electoral system to implement the most far-reaching constitutional reform ever seen in Wales places a great responsibility on those involved to promote a programme of public education and awareness-raising. The proper extension of democratic control and accountability, which is at the heart of the devolutionary process, demands public involvement and popular endorsement. For the public to exercise this responsibility requires, in the first instance, clear political leadership and commitment.

As the National Assembly establishes itself within Wales and as new political leaders emerge for all parties, the public will become, at once, both more sophisticated and more cynical. For Wales however, this development will be but one more signal of a new political maturity, entirely appropriate for a resilient, distinctive, community in an increasingly interdependent world.

CHAPTER 2

THE ASSEMBLY AT WORK

Mari James

During the referendum campaign, much was made of how innovative the Assembly would be. No plans were too visionary or too imaginative to be ruled out. Certainly the new Assembly would be different in its style to the formal and confrontational arrangements at Westminster. In the cold light of the dawn of 19 September 1997 the moment came to turn these aspirations into reality. Immediately there were a series of questions:

- How could the internal arrangements of a building be adapted so as to have both the status of a Parliament but also be more user-friendly?

- Were there any particular physical attributes that would be important to convey the new spirit of openness and transparency?

- How could the aspirations to make the Assembly family-friendly be realised in practice?

- If it was taken as given that the Assembly would operate bilingually, what would this mean in practice?

- How could the work of the Assembly be spread around Wales so that access to its work be made as easy for someone in Wrexham, in Llanfair PG or in Llandysul as someone on the doorstep of the main building in Cardiff?

- What support should be provided for Assembly members to enable them to work effectively?

- What should the full plenary sessions be like for those in the Chamber and how should they be projected to the outside world?

For the most part these questions are not the stuff of primary legislation and so were not answered by the Government of Wales Act. Some reference was made to them during debates on the Bill. Many MPs realised that decisions about such specifics would determine the real nature of the Assembly. Though many thousands of words had been written on the setting up of an Assembly, few had dealt with its actual operation. Most of the literature was, understandably, about the rationale for setting up the Assembly in the first place. There was little on what it should look like when it existed. There was no blue print that could be followed. That provides a wonderful opportunity to be creative and innovative.

The National Assembly Advisory Group was set up by the former Secretary of State Ron Davies in December 1997 to recommend ways for the Assembly to work with transparency, openness and democracy. The variety of backgrounds of the 14-member cross-party Group (including the author) meant that everyone had their own areas of expertise and interest – they were there as individuals and not as representatives of any party or interest.

The dynamic of the Group became such that it almost took on the role of the conscience of an 'Assembly in waiting'. It was determined not to accept without question the status quo of Welsh Office arrangements. It consulted widely and was determined to be innovative if existing arrangements or mechanisms did not meet their requirements. In the event the Secretary of State accepted all the Group's recommendations and passed them to the Standing Orders Commission to be written up as the first Standing Orders of the new National Assembly. This chapter is largely based on the National Assembly Advisory Group's discussions, the outcome of its extensive public consultation exercise and the final report of the Group.

THE BUILDING

The essential issues around the housing of the Assembly were:

- How could the internal arrangements of a building be adapted so as to have both the status of a Parliament but also be more user-friendly than the neo-gothic grandiosity associated with Parliament in the UK?

- Were there any particular physical attributes that would be important to convey the new spirit of openness and transparency?

Once it became clear that the main Chamber of the Assembly would be housed in a new, customised building and that supporting offices would be in the Pierhead and Crickhowell buildings in Cardiff Bay, then planning became easier. But it had always been the view of the Advisory Group that the facilities we were recommending needed to exist in the Assembly from its first day, whether this meant in temporary accommodation, a new building or an adapted City or Town Hall.

One of the key concerns of the Advisory Group was to ensure that the Assembly building should be physically welcoming. The Group's vertically challenged Chair, John Elfed Jones, often referred in public meetings to his feelings of insecurity when visiting Westminster and being greeted by seven foot high policemen peering down at him asking what he was doing there. If the House of Commons building welcomes voters going about their lawful, democratic business by giving out signs saying 'Who are you? What do you want? Let me look in your handbag? Stand at the back of that queue', then we wanted the National Assembly building to say 'Croeso. Shwmai? Dewch i mewn' ... 'Welcome. How are you then? Come on in'.

The welcome area of the Assembly main building is therefore crucial. The foyer should be a key feature. It needs to be large, open, airy and accessed straight from the main thoroughfare. Thus it will represent transparency and room for all. It should not be small, dark and accessed only after running the gauntlet of several layers of security and draughty passages. If security is necessary then it should be located after the main public access area. The staff in the foyer area should be characterised more by their expertise in customer-care than their ex-army service.

This foyer should also feature a large public-access counter facility. This would be the public access point for the Assembly's Information, Research and Education Service. The final National Assembly Advisory Group report is unequivocal in its recommendation of this facility. It says:

> 'We recommend that, from the establishment of the National Assembly in May 1999, there is a dedicated information, research and education service under the auspices of the Office of the Presiding Officer. We believe that this Information, Research and Education service should include:
>
> - an enquiry service for 'quick reference' queries from Members;
>
> - a gateway to the widest possible range of sources of information and briefing, which may include: the National Library of Wales; the House of Commons Library and the POLIS intranet database of Parliamentary materials; and other substantial library collections in Wales and beyond, including university, local authority and specialist libraries;
>
> - a research service producing specific briefings to Members on request with information from a variety of sources;
>
> - an information office which would provide the first contact point for the public on the work of the Assembly and for directing enquiries to Assembly Members, local authorities or MPs; it could also produce easily accessible information on the Assembly's activities; and
>
> - an education unit which could have a counter facility in the Assembly foyer and would deal with: school, college and youth service links and visits; curriculum materials to schools and colleges; and citizenship education for Wales' lifelong learning strategy.'

The Information, Research and Education Services recommended by NAAG should include:

- Copies of the proceedings of the Assembly plenary sessions (*Y Llyfr*) and its committees. These will be available electronically and copies will be able to be printed off for callers at the Information Counter. There is no comparative service for the public in the House of Commons.

- Information on Assembly's timetables. Anyone interested in a particular issue should be able to find out when it is next being debated in the Assembly and who will be involved in the debate or committee. There is no comparative service for the public in the House of Commons.

- A message service for Assembly Members so messages and letters can be left without the restrictions imposed on hand delivery of mail to MPs in the Palace of Westminster.

- A contact point for schools and colleges visiting the Assembly.

The proposed Education Unit of the Assembly will need to develop bilingual curriculum materials. Well thought-out proposals were put forward in the public consultation sessions for each primary and secondary school in Wales to have an organised visit to the Assembly at least once during each four year Assembly session. The Advisory Group report also stresses the importance of citizenship education for all ages within the lifelong learning strategy being developed for Wales.

The Wales Millennium Centre planned as the next-door neighbour of the Assembly will incorporate a new Urdd residential centre. Up to 1,000 young people a month are anticipated will pass through this centre, and many of these will visit the Assembly as well. Thus the Assembly foyer is likely to ring to the sound of children's voices in a way that would be very unusual at Westminster. Consequently, the foyer and welcoming area of the Assembly, both in its temporary and permanent homes will be crucial to the overall style and atmosphere of the whole Assembly operation.

One of the advantages of a new building is that accessibility for disabled people can be built in from the start. Adapting an old building will always be second best. It is also important that the new technology in the building is designed to cater for a range of needs. We heard in National Assembly Advisory Group public meetings how audio loop equipment to address hard-of-hearing problems was often incompatible with simultaneous translation earphones. Again, there is no blueprint and the National Assembly Advisory Group strongly recommended that representative groups of the disabled groups are involved in the detailed designs for the building in respect of accessibility. No-one knows how to overcome potential problems as well as those who have to tolerate them every day.

A FAMILY FRIENDLY APPROACH

The necessity for a crèche facility in the Assembly is widely accepted. Disagreement comes on the extent to which it should be subsidised. A crèche will set the example of the Assembly incorporating good employment practices for its staff as well as for Members.

Much thought has gone into how the working hours of the Assembly can be more normal than the ludicrous 2pm to 2am that is so often the norm in Westminster. Leaving the morning free of Parliamentary work so that other jobs can be undertaken is also entirely the wrong style for a full-time working Assembly. At first glance a 9am to 5pm working day for the Assembly Members would seem to ensure that they can get home to their families at the end of the working day.

However, this would not apply equally to Members based in mid, west or north Wales as it would to Cardiffians. And such hours do not appear so family-friendly to members of the public who may want to get at their Assembly Members outside of their own working hours. More effective might be an arrangement requiring Assembly Members to be in their constituencies on Mondays and Fridays and to be in Cardiff in the Assembly during the middle three days of the week. This is more likely to be as conducive to home life as any politician or person in public life can hope for.

BILINGUAL OPERATION

Members of the Assembly, and anyone dealing with it, needs to be able to operate in either English or Welsh, whichever they choose. This is the test of the Assembly's bilingualism. The Advisory Group has recommended that the Assembly develops its own Welsh language scheme. The alternative would be to adopt and then adapt the existing Welsh Office scheme. This goes to the heart of the bilingual operation of the Assembly.

The Welsh Office at present does not operate bilingually. It operates in English with some work being translated into Welsh. This is intrinsically different from operating bilingually. There is a danger that if the difference is not understood it will result in double staffing with the 'real', professional, staff being shadowed by someone whose job it is solely to translate their work into Welsh. Much translation will be necessary, but, equally, offices will often work most efficiently if one or more of the team can work in Welsh. There is no need for any panic-cries of anti-English discrimination in saying this. The Welsh language, like any other, is a skill to be learned not a racial characteristic that one either has or does not have.

It will be important that Welsh speakers as well as those who do not understand Welsh should be able to understand and read the main debates in their Assembly in their own language. This was the reasoning behind the Advisory Group majority recommendation that *Y Llyfr* (the equivalent of the Commons Hansard) should be in both Welsh and English, with the original language in which a speech was made clearly indicated.

Speakers in the main plenary sessions, as well as in committee meetings, will be able to speak in either English or Welsh, as they choose. Welsh speakers can then be listened to in either English or Welsh as the listener chooses. Some of the National

Assembly Advisory Group discussions made it clear that some non-Welsh speakers still believe that everything said in Welsh is about them. It is important to assist in allaying this anxiety by ensuring that the technology is available in all meeting places of the Assembly for Welsh to be spoken and to be translated into English. Only then will the two languages of Wales become the medium for debate in the National Assembly rather than the subject for debate.

The bilingualism will, obviously extend to evidence submitted to Assembly committees. It has been suggested that this will cause delay as papers will need to be translated from English into Welsh by the Assembly's own translation unit. It is actually likely to be a catalyst in making public bilingualism the norm in the private as well as the public sector in Wales. Most organisations, companies, individuals and others submitting evidence or proposals to a part of the Assembly will want it produced completely in a way that is under their control. The alternative may produce half the final document that the submitting body has not actually seen and approved.

THE REGIONS

One of the mantras of those working on the Internet is that there is no 'there' any more, everywhere is 'here'. Work is already underway to use this technology to ensure the Assembly is 'here' wherever someone is in Wales. A range of support mechanisms are being put in place that will provide video-conferencing in local councils and other bases around Wales. At these venues, local people will be able to watch the debates taking place in the Assembly, attend committee meetings, submit their evidence and discuss it with Assembly Members.

Perhaps the most important part of the process of 'regionalising' the Assembly will be the Regional Committees themselves. While only advisory committees, they will ensure that there is a vehicle for a regional agenda to be developed and monitored. Their meetings can be expected to be largely in the regions rather than in the main Assembly building in Cardiff. How the Regional Committees will develop will be one of the more innovative parts of the Assembly. They will be what their Assembly Members want them to be, and what the regional electorate pressurise them to be.

Each of the four Regional Committees – corresponding to the four regional economic forums of Wales – is likely to evolve differently as reflects their needs and political culture. They could be mere talking shops, with few people in the gallery for their public sessions. Or they could choose to be truly involving and interactive groups, listening to local people and inputting points to debates in the main Subject Committees, legislation debates and development of the main Assembly schemes.

The National Assembly Advisory Group consultation exercise was seen by some as a precursor of how parts of the Assembly, including the Regional Committees, could operate. An agenda was drawn up of issues to be covered, indications of the way forward on each issue or options where no view had been formed, a report put out in printed form, electronically, on audio tape, in summary, in Welsh and English and in a range of ethnic minority languages. Presentations were then held throughout Wales. Views were sought on what was put forward and, in some cases, on what was left out. The final report was then the responsibility of the Advisory Group but reflected the views of hundreds of people who had become involved. This kind of proactive, multimedia development of policy should replace the rather passive, flat exercise that so often characterises official consultation procedures and has led to much disillusion with such exercises.

Whether or not the Regional Committees take the passive or the proactive route to consultation will go a long way to determine the extent to which the Assembly, after its first few years, will be succeeding in being an Assembly of and for the whole of Wales. The sad alternative would be to replace centralisation on the south east of England with centralisation on the south east of Wales. That was not what the YES voters of Carmarthen and Gwynedd voted for. But it was what the NO voters of north Wales feared.

SUPPORT FOR MEMBERS

The Advisory Group's recommendation to establish a Speaker's Office (*Swyddfa Llywydd*) through which Assembly staff will be employed is central to achieving a clear division between the Executive and the Assembly in the devolution package. There is no other national or regional elected body that combines the executive and legislative functions that the Welsh Assembly will do. In being, essentially, the national, democratic personification of the substantial powers and functions concentrated in the single Secretary of State for Wales' post over the years of its growth, this is a clear innovation in the British constitution.

In early Advisory Group discussions the view was put forward that all the staff of the Assembly would have to be mainstream Welsh Office civil servants and therefore not able to engage in any political work. According to this line of argument, Assembly Members would not have secretaries but would have information technology equipment instead. They would not have researchers as there could be an information unit in the Welsh Office library to provide them with factual information. Moreover, there would not be a dedicated Assembly library for Members (after all, who ever heard of a library for just 60 people?). This was the logical position given the Assembly as a single corporate body staffed by 'ordinary' civil servants.

Such a position was unacceptable and would result in the Assembly being little more than an additional, and not very large, division of the existing Welsh Office.

The device of the Speaker's Office as an employment mechanism provides a means for a phalanx of expert staffers to be developed who owe their loyalty to the Assembly specifically. The division between the Parliamentary staff and staff of Whitehall departments is jealously guarded by the Parliamentary side, and rightly so. This is as important for the effective scrutiny of the work of the Welsh Cabinet as is the committee structure of the Assembly.

This is exactly the kind of issue for which there cannot be legislation. The National Assembly Advisory Group recommendations were a crucial step forward. They should be followed through in all appointments to the future Assembly staff. Decisions which will impact on the effectiveness of the Speaker's Office device are also being made outside Wales. The Neill Committee on Standards in Public Life are looking at whether to extend the so-called 'Short' money for Opposition parties in the House of Commons to the National Assembly. The Senior Salaries Review Board, where the remuneration package for Assembly Members is being considered, is also reviewing their allowances for staff and for constituency offices.

The key determinant of whether the Assembly can develop effective and independent support mechanisms for its Members will be the eternal vigilance and creativity of the Llywydd / Speaker. This is arguably the most political role in the Assembly. This position will affect the high politics of the balance of power between the Assembly, the Welsh Cabinet and the existing Welsh Office structures, as much as the every day rivalry between the political parties.

THE ASSEMBLY IN PLENARY SESSION

The main plenary sessions of the Assembly are likely to take place on Tuesdays, Wednesdays and Thursdays. This will be the theatre of the Assembly. The big issues will be played out here by the leading political figures of the nation.

Television has accustomed voters to a Westminster Chamber with only a handful of Members in it when twice and three times as many are working in committee rooms overhead with no TV lights or attention. The illustrative timetable produced by the Advisory Group recommends that the plenary sessions do not clash with meetings of Subject or Regional Committees. Membership of the National Assembly will be a full-time job. Constituents have a right to expect their representatives to take part in the major plenary debates or to know the reason why, if they cannot see them there on the video-conferencing screens in the local town hall.

The main chamber is likely to be round or horse-shoe shaped. This will reflect the spirit of inclusivity and consensus on which the politics of the new Wales is based. There may be desks rather than leather benches for Members, conveying an accurate impression of the Assembly being a place of work rather than a club lounge.

However, the new Welsh politics does not extend to the abolition of parties. It would not be Welsh politics if it did. It is likely to be in the main plenary session that the party system will be most evident. The vertically structured Subject Committees, the horizontally-structured Programme Committees and the Regional Committees – all examined more fully in Chapter 5 – are likely to have a stronger element of unity of purpose in their work.

The Advisory Group recommendations allow for a First Secretary's or Prime Minister's Question Time every week. The Leader of the Opposition will doubtless use this to try and reveal weaknesses in the majority party's work. Other Assembly Members will do likewise. Question sessions for all members of the Welsh Cabinet are allowed for as well. These sessions in the House of Commons have been perceived by some in recent years to have deteriorated into pre-scripted, advertising shows for the wares of the major party spokespeople. To overcome this the Advisory Group has recommended that provision be made for some questions to be asked without notice. The thinking was that any Welsh Cabinet member worth their salt should be able to handle such questions without detailed civil service briefings.

Although this is not allowed as such in the House of Commons, there are various devices developed over the decades which meet the same requirements, such as Private Notice Questions. There appears to be little or no public support in Wales for adopting such traditions of the House of Commons. What is more important is to look into why there was a need to develop them and if that need is also likely to exist in the National Assembly, then to allow for it in a normal way from the start.

This approach applies equally to some of the procedures to enable individual members to get their oar in to proceedings. That a debate must be held on whether or not the plenary session adjourns, in order for an Assembly Member to ask a direct question to a Welsh Minister and be able to respond to his or her formal reply, would be ludicrous. Thus the Commons style Adjournment debates would be superfluous in the Assembly. Debates of like type, however, serving the same purpose would be essential.

There will be certain annual debates that will take place in the plenary sessions. Schemes developed on equal opportunities, sustainable development, relations with Europe and other issues would be reviewed and monitored in a full debate each year. There will also be an annual debate on the reports brought forward by the Assembly Audit Committee. This will be the Welsh equivalent of the Public Accounts Committee and the status accorded to it will go to the heart of how serious the Assembly is about scrutiny of public money in Wales. There will also be likely to be between 100 and 400 items of secondary legislation that will need to be debated, maybe amended, and approved by the full Assembly in plenary session.

CONCLUSION

This chapter has only touched on some of the issues that will determine how the Assembly will work and what its style and demeanour will be. Space has precluded issues such as how the Assembly should be portrayed through broadcasting, though this together with detailed discussion of the working of the Committees is dealt with in other chapters. Much of this is the soft area of government and politics. It is not really the stuff of rules written in tablets of stone.

They will contribute the human element which will either make the National Assembly meaningful, effective and inclusive or a waste of all our time and a lost opportunity. How they are handled will determine the impressions and messages that will be given out from the beginning. If we get them wrong at the start they will be hard to change. This is no longer a rehearsal or a seminar session. When it meets in May 1999 our new Assembly will be for real. If its style is to meet the aspirations of the people of Wales then no-one can afford to sit back to wait and see what it is like and then complain they do not like it.

The character of the Assembly at work will be determined by the political style and culture of our politicians and the people who elect them. A demanding, proactive, enquiring, determined electorate will produce a demanding, proactive, enquiring, and determined Assembly. A lacklustre, whingeing, resentful and disinterested electorate are likely to find themselves reflected in the Assembly. We will no longer have 'THEM' to blame, only ourselves.

CHAPTER 3

FUNDING

R. Ross MacKay

The Barnett Formula, which is the present basis for funding the Welsh Office and will be inherited by the National Assembly, was a product of the devolution politics of the 1970s. The formula had two important objectives. First, to take division of public expenditure between England, Scotland and Wales out of public debate. The second was to give the Welsh and Scottish Offices some discretion on public expenditure and economic policy: to allow them to set their own priorities without constant reference to the Treasury. A compromise on public expenditure, a consensus which is accepted as reasonable within all three countries, becomes even more important when the National Assembly and Scottish Parliament are in place.

The Barnett Formula and, more broadly, tax and public expenditure in Wales and Scotland only became controversial when it was clear that the 1990s move to political power for Wales and Scotland was more firmly based than the devolution movement of the 1970s. Public expenditure is above tax in both Wales and Scotland. This subsidy is seen as unfair to the English taxpayer. Public expenditure is above tax in the poorer parts of a free market economy such as the United States of America and also in the poorer parts of more collective economies such as Sweden or Norway. Within the nation state people have rights and obligations of citizenship, the welfare of each citizen is weighted on a broadly equal basis. Transfer to poorer regions within the national economy (public expenditure above tax) follows naturally from the claim of every citizen within the nation state for equal treatment, irrespective of the region in which they live. Transfer is not subsidy. It follows from the attempt to ensure that payment of tax at the same rate in prosperous and less prosperous parts of the nation state will result in comparable levels of service.

Wales remains part of the British political community. There are UK standards for education, for welfare, for public services and a common base of taxation. Regional transfers develop from a deeper and more meaningful relationship than an agreement to trade without barriers. Within the nation state there is a recognition of common obligations of fair treatment and justice to one another. Redistribution to those not able to provide for their needs through market transactions depends on the UK Exchequer rather than the tax base of the region. The objective is horizontal equity, equal treatment of similar citizens no matter where located. The inevitable outcome is regional transfer, public expenditure above tax in regions with a less healthy tax base.

Without some sense of collective obligation it would be difficult to keep the Kingdom United. Transfer is consistent with federal systems which grant substantially more power than will be given to either the National Assembly or the Scottish Parliament (see MacKay, Audas, Holtham, Morgan, 1997). Transfer is political. It is important in holding the nation state together, but it also has key economic functions. Figure one shows public expenditure above tax in the poor region of a nation state and below tax in the rich region. Two functions of regional transfer are implicit in such a model. They equalise and they stabilise. Transfers contain and limit inequalities in regional income and regional spending power and they act to counter loss of economic base. Kaldor (1970) refers to regional transfer as automatic aid. The nature of market systems is constant revolution in economic structure. The old economic base withers away and new possibilities emerge, but decline and growth are not evenly spread between or within regions. Regional transfers are automatic if they adapt to change in economic circumstances without the need for detailed intervention, or political decisions. Automatic aid, like automatic stabilisers, absorb shocks and act against the cumulative impact of structural decline. Both functions, equalisation and stabilisation, develop from progressive taxation, common standards for public services (including education and health), and more substantial welfare payments in poorer regions.

Transfer is not subsidy, but there are still important questions about the scale and form of transfer. This chapter looks at transfer within other countries and also evidence of transfer within the United Kingdom prior to the introduction of the Barnett Formula. It then looks at the Barnett Formula and also explores Government spending and tax in Wales and Scotland. These countries are unusual not because public expenditure is above tax, but rather because they are the only economic regions within Great Britain for which we have data on tax and public expenditure. Later, the chapter measures transfer to Wales and Scotland. The theory of automatic aid (see Figure 1) suggests that regional transfer will be highly sensitive to differences in regional prosperity. Following the introduction of the Barnett Formula Wales became less prosperous relative to the rest of the UK, while Scotland's relative position improved notably. Scottish prosperity levels moved close to the UK average, but transfers to Scotland remained substantial. Welsh prosperity levels declined relative to the rest of the UK, but transfer has not become more generous. The last part of the chapter refers to political constraints. Scotland is generously treated in terms of both public expenditure and transfer, Wales is not. There are problems of adjustment. Without any reduction in transfer to Scotland, the Scottish National Party is already showing well in opinion polls. Even without the pressure introduced by the popularity of the Scottish National Party, there would be problems in cutting transfer to Scotland. A significant reduction in relative public expenditure in Scotland would have to be gradual in order to avoid major job losses.

FIGURE 1

Public Finance as a Regional Stabiliser

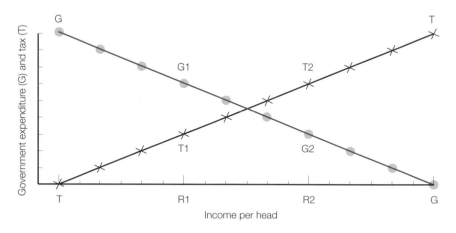

REGIONAL TRANSFERS - INTERNATIONAL AND HISTORICAL

The most comprehensive account of regional fiscal transfer in different countries is provided by the MacDougall Report (1977). The report shows a consistent pattern in five federal states (Australia, Canada, Switzerland, the USA, and West Germany) and three unitary states (France, Italy, United Kingdom): low income regions gain more from government expenditure than they pay in tax.

In both unitary and federal economies, regional transfers equalise and stabilise. They act to limit differences in living standards and spending power. They also act as automatic stabilisers. Given a shock to the regional economy, given a loss of economic base, the budget balance compensates without the need for conscious political decisions. Tax payments fall in the region that has lost economic base and local income, while social security expenditure increases. Transfers are substantial. According to the MacDougall Report, they reduced regional income differentials by an average of 46 per cent in the three unitary states and by an average of 35 per cent in the five federations. Any tendency to regional equality in mixed economies may owe much to the presence and power of regional transfers.

Figure 2 shows the relationship between regional fiscal transfer and relative prosperity in two unitary states (Italy and United Kingdom) and one federal economy (the former West Germany). In all three low income regions benefit from transfer (they pay less in tax than they receive in public services and benefits), while high income regions provide support. In all three, the scale of transfer is sensitive to relative regional income. Indeed the weight of transfer at identical levels of relative income is remarkably similar in all three countries. Italy has the highest level of transfer to weaker regions, but this is a product of greater diversity in regional income.

FIGURE 2

Fiscal Transfer

Italy, UK, W. Germany MacDougall Report

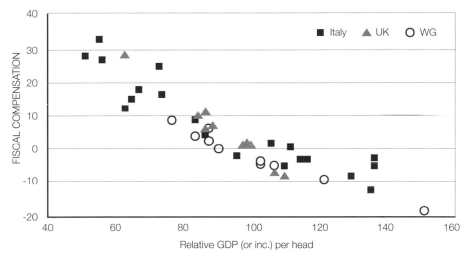

Source: MacDougall Report

Figure 3 shows regional fiscal transfers (at the time of the MacDougall Report and before the introduction of the Barnett Formula) for UK regions only. The results for Wales, Scotland and the North are highlighted. In this earlier time, Wales was a slightly more prosperous region than Scotland; and regional transfer to Wales was slightly more generous than transfer to Scotland. As we shall see, relative positions on prosperity and transfer are reversed in later years. Prosperity levels in the North of England (see Figure 3) were close to those in Scotland and the same is true for the level of transfer. The North had public expenditure above tax, not because there was any special formula designed to benefit the North, but rather because that is the common pattern for regions of below average prosperity. Figures 2 and 3 are consistent with the Kaldor idea of automatic aid and with Figure 1. The regions with prosperity levels close to the national average have transfer levels which are close to zero.

FIGURE 3

Fiscal Transfer

UK Regions MacDougall Report

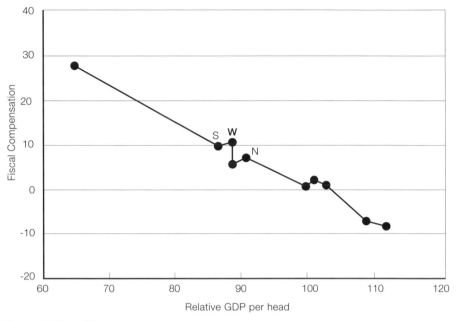

Source: MacDougall Report

TAXING AND SPENDING AND THE BARNETT FORMULA

The most reliable estimates for taxing and spending in Wales and Scotland are provided by Welsh and Scottish Office Reports on Government Expenditure and Revenue. This and the next section rely on two Reports for Wales (1993-94 and 1994-95) and three Reports for Scotland (1993-94, 1994-95 and 1995-96).

General Government Expenditure (GGE) for Scotland is estimated at an average of close to £30bn in the three financial years covered. General Government Expenditure for Wales is estimated at an average of about £15bn in the two financial years covered. Table 1 shows an approximate division of GGE between broad categories of expenditure.

Not all of GGE can be allocated according to location of expenditure. Non-Identifiable GGE (category B in Table 1) includes 'public goods' such as defence and overseas aid which are seen as bringing benefits to all UK citizens. Welsh and

Scottish Office Reports allocate Non-Identifiable GGE according to Welsh and Scottish share of UK GDP (Gross Domestic Product). As the Welsh Reports correctly indicate, the choice of GDP share provides a lower estimate of Non-Identifiable GGE in Wales than would be made if population share was used. Category C, or Other Expenditure, is mainly government debt payments (central and local) and is estimated in a similar manner to Non-Identifiable GGE (shares of debt for Wales and Scotland are close to their shares of GDP).

TABLE 1

General Government Expenditure by Broad Category

		SHARE OF EXPENDITURE	
		Wales	Scotland
A	IDENTIFIABLE:		
	1 Barnett Formula (Welsh Block, Scottish Block)	About 41%	About 46%
	2 Agriculture	1-2%	1-2%
	3 Other Identifiable (mainly Social Security)	About 36%	About 28%
B	NON-IDENTIFIABLE (mainly Defence)	About 12%	About 12%
C	OTHER (mainly Government Debt)	About 10%	About 12%

Source: Government Expenditure and Revenue in Wales 1993-94 and 1994-95; Government Expenditure and Revenue in Scotland, 1993-94, 1994-95 and 1995-96.

For both Wales and Scotland, rather more than 75 per cent of GGE is Identifiable. Other Identifiable (A3 in Table 1) is dominated by the Social Security payments that are a more important component of public expenditure in Wales than in Scotland. Rather more than two fifths of total expenditure is allocated according to the Barnett Formula (A1 in Table 1). The Welsh Block and the Scottish Block allow the respective Secretaries of State to spend according to Welsh Office and Scottish Office perceptions of needs and priorities. The main programmes within the Welsh Block and the Scottish Block are health, education, housing and other services provided by local authorities.

Figure 4 shows General Government Expenditure (GGE) per head in Wales and Scotland. For the three years shown, GGE per head in Scotland is 15 per cent above the UK average. For the two years shown, GGE per head in Wales is only 4 per cent above the UK average. Figure 4 also shows tax per head relative to the UK. Scotland is, by the mid 1990s, middle England in terms of prosperity and tax per head is slightly above the UK average. Wales is the least prosperous economic region in Britain and tax per head is only four-fifths of the UK average (see MacKay, Audas, Holtham, Morgan, 1997). In spite of distinctly lower levels of public expenditure per head in Wales than in Scotland, the gap between expenditure and tax is greater in Wales.

FIGURE 4

Spending and Taxing

Per Head – Wales, Scotland (UK = 100)

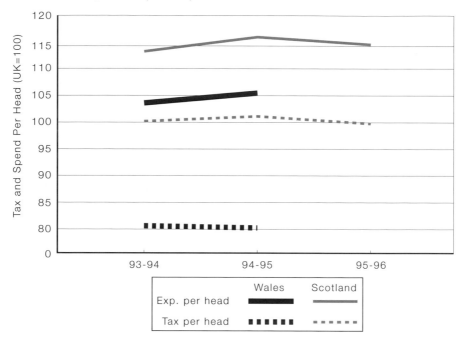

Source: Welsh and Scottish Office Reports on Government Expenditure and Revenue

Figure 5 looks at spending per head in terms of all government spending, government spending without social security (not part of the Barnett Formula and allocated according to criteria that are uniform throughout the UK) and government spending without social security and without agriculture (not part of the Barnett Formula and depends on European CAP). When we omit spending on social security and on agriculture, government spending per head in Wales is only 1 per cent above the UK average. With social security and agriculture taken out, government spending per head in Scotland is 18 per cent above the UK average.[1]

Without social security and agriculture, public spending per head in Wales is close to the UK average, but public spending per head in Scotland is substantially above the UK average. Public spending is generous to Scotland, but not to Wales although Wales is by some margin the poorer region. How does this happen? Part of the explanation rests with the Barnett Formula (see Table 2).

The Barnett Formula was designed to avoid the controversy of year by year bargaining. It provided a crude rule of thumb for allocating *increases in*

FIGURE 5

Public Spend Per Head

Wales, Scotland (UK = 100)

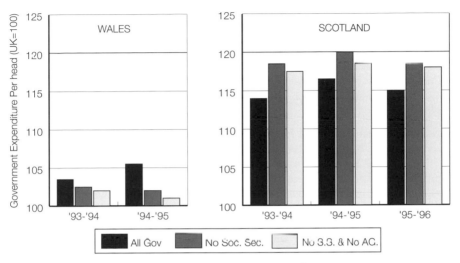

Source. Welsh and Scottish Office Reports on Government Expenditure and Revenue.

expenditure, while still preserving independence of spending. Generous treatment for Scotland has four sources. First, the Formula only allocates increases in spending. The base year (1978) is important and represented a peak in differential spending between Scotland and England. The high differential in the base year followed from a needs assessment which took note of a Scottish economy with GDP and income levels well below the levels in England. Second, no adjustment has been made to reflect improvement in Scotland's level of prosperity relative to

TABLE 2

Barnett Formula and Adjusted Barnett Formula

	England	Scotland	Wales
Barnett Formula (1978-91) Share of every £100 additional Block Expenditure	85	10	5
Share of population (1991)	85.7	9.14	5.16
Portillo Precision* Population Partition (1992 ...)	85.7	9.14	5.16

* The Treasury Committee Report on the Barnett Formula (House of Commons, I997-98) states (p.vii), 'The formula will ... be updated to take account of changes in population ... population shares will be re-calculated annually on the basis of the latest population estimates'.

Source: Scottish and Welsh Office Reports on Government Expenditure and Revenue and Treasury Committee Report.

England and Wales. Third, the population weighted formula for *increases in public expenditure* was generous to Scotland. Fourth, Scotland's share of Britain's population fell after the Barnett Formula was introduced (see Table 2). For every £100 of additional expenditure, the division to England, Scotland and Wales was 85: 10:5. That division favoured Scotland when first introduced and became more generous as Scotland's share of GB population fell (see Table 2).

From 1992 the Barnett Formula was adjusted to allocate *increase in public expenditure* according to actual rather than historic population shares. This change to the way that *increases in public expenditure* are divided will only gradually change the overall division of Block Grant expenditure between Scotland, Wales and England.

The Barnett Formula started from a needs assessment (in 1978) which set public expenditure per head in Wales and Scotland comfortably above the English level. The logic of the Formula was that increases in public expenditure are allocated according to population share and that the gaps between public expenditure in England and Wales and England and Scotland fall over time. How rapidly the gaps narrow will depend on both inflation and on real growth in public expenditure (see Heald, 1994). The implicit assumption behind the Barnett Formula was that the needs gap between England and Wales and England and Scotland were only temporary. Prosperity levels in Scotland and Wales would move towards levels in England and so would Welsh and Scottish Block Grant expenditure per head. In practice, Scottish prosperity levels moved towards those in England but public expenditure was protected by a formula that used population shares that increasingly favoured Scotland. In practice, Welsh prosperity levels declined relative to England, but public expenditure increases depended on a formula that was increasingly unfair to Wales.

The Barnett Formula was designed to take the conflict and argument out of the division of public expenditure between England, Scotland and Wales. In this, its originator, Lord Barnett, suggests, it was surprisingly successful (see evidence of Lord Barnett to Treasury Committee, 1997). The Barnett Formula (new or adjusted) is not, however, a notably sophisticated means of deciding public expenditure levels in England, Scotland and Wales. It could be turned into an automatic stabiliser by making the division of increases in public expenditure sensitive to improvement (or decline) in relative GDP per head. A different way to introduce sensitivity would be to resort to periodic revisions of public expenditure need.

In his evidence to the Treasury Committee, Lord Barnett expressed some surprise that his formula had survived so long unchanged, approved of the move to current rather than historical population shares and recommended a major review (see Treasury Committee, 1997, ps.1-7). Such a review would require a new needs assessment that reflected income per head levels. It would recognise that Scotland's relative income per head has improved, while relative income per head has fallen in Wales. Lord Barnett suggested that the Welsh 'may require an increase in their allocation' (Treasury Committee, 1997, p.2 para.3). For Scotland, he suggested a gradual rather than a sudden downward adjustment.

TRANSFER - PAST AND PRESENT

Public expenditure levels are generous in Scotland, but not in Wales. Figure 6 shows regional transfer to Wales and Scotland. The MacDougall Report estimates are compared with estimates for recent years (1993-94 and 1994-95 in Wales; 1993-94, 1994-95 and 1995-96 in Scotland). The contrast in Welsh and Scottish experience is informative. The data used in the MacDougall Report (published 1977), shows Scottish GDP per head at about 86 per cent of the UK average and fiscal transfer to Scotland was approximately 10 per cent of Scottish GDP. By the mid-90s Scottish GDP is close to the UK average, while fiscal transfer to Scotland is approximately 5 per cent of Scottish GDP. Welsh GDP per head falls from around 88 per cent of the UK average to about 83 per cent in the years 1993-94 and 1994-95. However, regional transfer to Wales does not become more generous.[2]

FIGURE 6

Fiscal Transfer – Wales, Scotland
MacDougall Report and Later

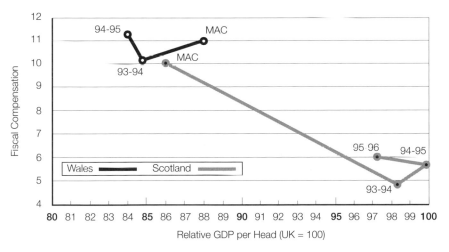

Source: MacDougall Report and Welsh and Scottish Office Reports on Government Expenditure and Revenue.

As we have seen, public expenditure per head levels in Scotland are well above the Welsh and UK levels. Scotland's generous treatment follows from an early needs assessment which reflected low prosperity in Scotland and from a population-weighted formula which did not adapt to Scotland's falling population share. The present division of public expenditure is difficult to defend, but there are obvious problems in discovering a satisfactory compromise. These are correctly identified by Midwinter in his evidence to the Treasury Committee on the Barnett Formula. Generous treatment of Scotland costs individual tax payers in the rest of the UK little because it is shared between large numbers, but is of 'considerable significance within Scotland' (Treasury Committee 1997, p.31). Moreover, to link devolution to substantial cuts in public expenditure in Scotland would not be a happy start to the re-negotiated Union between England, Scotland and Wales. It is possible to convert Midwinter's substantial significance within Scotland, but slight importance to the rest of the UK, into rough numbers. Reducing the transfer to Scotland to zero (by cutting public expenditure in Scotland) would mean a loss of £600+ per year in public expenditure per head in Scotland. Such a significant cut, introduced precipitately, would be more than unwise. Redistributing the Scottish cut in public expenditure to the rest of the UK would raise public expenditure per head by only £60+ per year.

It is doubtful if Scotland's small numbers can be a lasting defence. A new and more flexible compromise needs to emerge. It should be sensitive to the difficulties that flow from abrupt change. The argument for phased adjustment is economic as well as political. Heavy cuts in public services and major job losses would be contrary to common sense and good practice. The intention of transfer is to cushion shocks, not to create them.

CONCLUSION

'The love of our country seems ... to involve ... an earnest desire to render the condition of our fellow-citizens as safe, respectable, and happy as we can.'

Adam Smith 1759 (1984, p.231).

Transfer, including regional transfer, is not just about compassion. Automatic stabilisers are deeply embedded in advanced, mixed economies. They provide greater stability, greater security than would otherwise exist. They are a response to a weakness of capitalism. Given the loss of major industries, it takes time to prepare for useful investment. Given the loss of markets and reduced valuation of human and physical capital, built-in stabilisers provide time and opportunity to find a new sense of direction. Without transfer and guaranteed support at the earliest possible stage, cumulative forces of decline may be set in motion which prove extremely difficult to check until they have run their course. To be effective, regional transfers must be available before the full impact of decline becomes visible.

No economic system is natural, or pure. Capitalism comes in many forms, but all rely on more than market signals. Market solutions do not deliver, or develop unity and cohesion. Those who plead the cause of the market economy have been slow to recognise that the rule of solvency, if strictly applied, works strongly against certain sections of society. The groups at risk are partly formed by people and communities whose resources, including their labour, are considered surplus to requirements.

Human and physical capital take time to develop their potential, but loss of value and relevance can be rapid. Capitalism is never pure. Its imperfections may be critical to consequences, effects and results that are valued. Regional inequality cannot be analysed as if only market forces exist. When the market fails to deliver reasonable balance, as it inevitably will, society will recognise the gap (see Hirschman, 1958 and also Myrdal, 1957). Compromises and systems evolve to curb the excesses of capitalism and to protect vulnerable groups and regions. Capitalism becomes and remains acceptable when and if the economic system reflects our limited tolerance of instability and insecurity (see Hirschman, 1958 and Myrdal, 1957).

A political union, a tightly integrated economy, has other links apart from an agreement to trade without barriers. In Wales, opportunity and pay are below the UK average. In Wales, tax payments are below average and social security expenditures are above average. Without these automatic stabilisers, the painful economic and social transitions of recent decades would have been slower and harsher (see MacKay, Audas, Holtham, Morgan, 1997).

Transfer follows from the claim of every citizen for equal treatment. The objective of horizontal equity implies equal treatment of similar individuals in terms of public expenditure and tax wherever they live within the nation state. The aim is equal treatment, one consequence is regional transfer. As shown earlier, there are still questions on regional levels of public expenditure and on the extent of regional transfer. The Barnett Formula favoured Scotland and that advantage increased as Scotland's share of population fell. Public expenditure levels per head are comfortably higher in Scotland than in Wales: they are slightly higher in Wales than in England as shown above.

A measure of the balanced budget regional transfer to both Wales and Scotland has been illustrated above, as well as how fiscal transfer to both has altered over a period when relative prosperity has improved in Scotland, but declined in Wales. Relative decline in Wales has not led to more substantial regional transfer. By the standards of other countries and given the objective of horizontal equity, the level of transfer to Wales is not over generous. Scotland is different. There appears to be a recognition, even by authors who claim that the debate tends to overstate support to Scotland, that a review of need, base and formula might lead to reduction in spending levels (see McCormick and Alexander, 1996; Heald and Geaughan, 1996).

Transfer has political as well as economic objectives. Generous treatment of Scotland has been possible because Scotland's population is a small proportion of Great Britain's. For any reform to be successful, the Treasury Committee on the Barnett Formula concludes, 'there should be maximum possible agreement ... in all parts of the UK' (Treasury Committee, 1997, p. viii). The search for agreement should specifically recognise the need for gradual rather than sudden adjustment to relative public spending in Scotland.

References

Heald, D. (1994) *Formula - Controlled Public Expenditure in the United Kingdom*, University of Aberdeen, Mimeo and to be published in Public Finance.

Heald, D., Geaughan N., (1996) 'Financing a Scottish Parliament', in Tindale S., (ed), *The State and the Nation*, 167-183, IPPR, London.

Kaldor, N. (1970) 'The Case for Regional Policy', *Scottish Journal of Political Economy*, 17: 337-48.

MacDougall Report (1977), Commission of the European Communities, *Report of the Study Group on the Role of Public Finance in European Integration*, Vol. 1, General Report and Vol. II, Individual Contributions, CEC, Brussels.

MacKay, R.R., Audas, R.P., Holtham, G., Morgan, B. (1997) *The Economic Impact of a Welsh Assembly*, Institute of Welsh Affairs, Cardiff.

McCormick J., Alexander W. (1996) 'Firm Foundations - Securing the Scottish Parliament' in Tindale S., (ed), *The State and the Nation*, 96-166, IPPR, London.

Scottish Office (1995, 1996, 1997) *Government Expenditure and Revenue in Scotland 1993-94, 1994-95 and 1995-96*, Scottish Office Education and Industry Department, Edinburgh.

Smith, Adam (1959, 1984), 'The Theory of Moral Sentiments', ed by Raphael D.D. and Mackfie A.L., Liberty Fund, Indianapolis.

Treasury Committee (1997) *The Barnett Formula*, HCP 341, Session 1997-98, HMSO, London.

Welsh Office (1996, 1997) *Government Expenditure and Revenue, Wales 1993-94, and 1994-95*, Publications Unit, Statistical Directorate, Cardiff.

1   Social security spending per head of population in Scotland is much closer to the UK average than is the rest of public expenditure.

2   For both Wales and Scotland, the manner in which we have presented the results is different from the form provided by the Government Expenditure and Revenue Reports for Wales and Scotland. In these a fiscal deficit is calculated which compares General Government Expenditure in Wales (or Scotland) with General Government Revenue: General Government Expenditure is calculated after adding the Wales (or Scotland) Share of General Government Borrowing. Including General Government Borrowing ensures that regional transfers do not balance to zero. (The country as a whole and nearly all Regions are spending more than the Revenue raised). *Our calculations follow the practice of the MacDougall Report and calculate transfers between Regions as if General Government Borrowing is zero.* This balanced budget regional transfer gives a true measure of redistribution between regions.

CHAPTER 4

ALLOCATING THE BUDGET

Nigel Blewitt

In the previous chapter Ross MacKay discussed the process by which the level of the Welsh Block budget, currently around £6.7bn, is determined. This non-statutory process, based on the operation of the Barnett formula, will continue under the National Assembly. The present chapter focuses on the process by which the Block is allocated across the various spending programmes for which the Secretary of State for Wales is currently responsible, and for which the Assembly will assume control.

The Assembly will not bring with it additional public money from the UK Treasury, but it will provide the opportunity for the allocation of the limited resources to be better targeted. There is the potential for developing programmes which address the distinct social and economic problems of Wales in a more effective way. Moreover, the distribution of the budget will become the responsibility of elected politicians who will be accountable to their constituents. Assembly Members will be highly conscious of the needs and priorities of their localities. Civil servants are likely to be less directly involved in the budgetary process than is currently the case.

The Welsh Block (now also referred to as the Departmental Expenditure Limit) currently comprises 97 per cent of the expenditure within the Secretary of State's responsibility. The remainder comprises expenditure on agriculture, fisheries and food. As a consequence of the Government's Comprehensive Spending Review, figures indicating the level of the Welsh Block are available up to and including the financial year 2001-02. They are given in Table 1.

The Government of Wales Act provides little direction on the issue of setting the budget. The Assembly will have to establish its own procedures for allocating the annual budget and deciding on the priority areas of expenditure. As is evident from Part Two of this book, there will be many demands on the Assembly's financial resources. However, in the first years, although the Assembly will have complete discretion over its spending, it is unlikely that switching large sums of money between programme areas will be a feasible option, given the extent of resources currently committed to services such as health.

TABLE 1

Future Welsh Block Budget Levels

1999-2000	£7,036m
2000-2001	£7,406m
2001-2002	£7,781m

Source: HM Treasury (1998, Ch. 23)

It is informative to consider the process by which the budget is presently allocated across the various programmes under the Secretary of State's control. The procedure currently applied by the Welsh Office is outlined below. There then follows a discussion of how the procedure might operate under the Assembly.

A breakdown of planned expenditure by Welsh Office administrative group for the financial year 1998-99 is presented in Table 2. The bulk of the Welsh Office budget is directed at health (34.3 per cent of the budget), and local government support, housing and social services (43.2 per cent). By contrast, just 6.9 per cent of the budget is spent directly on economic development and industry and training.

TABLE 2

Planned Expenditure by Welsh Office Administrative Group, 1998-99

	£m	% of Budget
Agriculture	214.9	3.1
Economic Development	279.4	4.0
Industry and Training [4]	201.6	2.9
Education, Welsh Language, Arts and Recreation [4]	567.2	8.1
Transport, Planning and Environment [1]	217.0	3.1
Local Government, Housing and Social Services [2,4]	3032.2	43.2
Health [3]	2410.5	34.3
Office of HM Chief Inspector of Schools in Wales	10.2	0.1
Central Administration including Devolution (and excluding TEC management fees) [1]	86.4	1.2
TOTAL	**7019.4**	**100**

1   Excludes Consolidated Fund Extra Receipts

2   Includes some expenditure on health

3   NHS expenditure only

4   Includes Welfare to Work and Capital Receipts Initiative Expenditure

Source: Welsh Office Departmental Report 1998 - The Government's Expenditure Plans for 1998-99 (p.3)

Expenditure on agriculture in Wales is negotiated separately from the main Welsh Office Block, with about 80 per cent of the support being provided by the European Union under the Common Agricultural Policy (CAP). Following devolution, funding under the CAP will remain outside the Block, but domestic agriculture and forestry will come inside the Block.

Figure 1 also provides a breakdown of expenditure, but in terms of the combined expenditure of the Welsh Office and the Welsh Unitary Authorities (including self-financed expenditure) by main service area. The service area 'other environmental services' includes expenditure on leisure, tourism, Cardiff Bay Development Corporation and the environment.

FIGURE 1

Combined Welsh Office and Local Authority Planned Expenditure by Service Area 1998-99

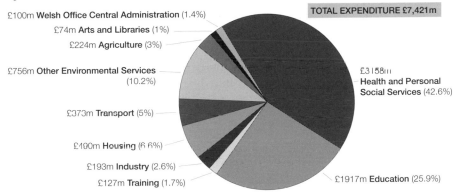

£100m **Welsh Office Central Administration** (1.4%)

£74m **Arts and Libraries** (1%)

£224m **Agriculture** (3%)

£756m **Other Environmental Services** (10.2%)

£373m **Transport** (5%)

£100m **Housing** (6.6%)

£193m **Industry** (2.6%)

£127m **Training** (1.7%)

TOTAL EXPENDITURE £7,421m

£3158m **Health and Personal Social Services** (42.6%)

£1917m **Education** (25.9%)

Source: Comprehensive Spending Review: Modern services for Wales. Spending Plans 1999-2002 Welsh Office Consultation Paper.

THE CURRENT BUDGET-SETTING PROCESS

The budget-setting process was summarised in a Welsh Office paper presented to the National Assembly Advisory Group (Welsh Office, 1998b). It begins in earnest in June when the Finance Programmes (FP) Division issues Group Directors with baseline expenditure levels for the forthcoming financial year. These take account of guidance from Welsh Office Ministers on their general priorities. Group Directors have the opportunity to bid for extra resources for their particular programme areas. At the same time, however, they must identify any possible savings which would offset these bids. Group Directors must quantify the outputs which various levels of funding will provide. Nine Groups are involved in the bidding process plus the Office of Her Majesty's Chief Inspector of Schools in Wales. At this stage of the process, total bids exceed the resources available.

TABLE 3

Main Welsh Office Expenditure Allocations, Including Expenditure on Executive Non-Departmental Public Bodies, 1998-99 (£m)

Local Authority Aggregate External Finance	2701.9
Local Government Capital Settlement	423.8
National Health Service	2480.4
Training & Enterprise	126.9
Motorways & Trunk Roads	102.4
Regional Assistance	62.6
National Assembly for Wales Capital Costs	17.0
Further Education Funding Council	175.0
Higher Education Funding Council	232.3
Qualifications, Curriculum and Assessment Authority (ACCAC)	9.6
Welsh Development Agency	113.8
Development Board for Rural Wales	9.0
Cardiff Bay Development Corporation	44.9
Wales Tourist Board	14.8
Housing for Wales (Tai Cymru)	62.9
Welsh Language Board	5.8
Arts Council of Wales	14.3
National Library for Wales	6.0
National Museums and Galleries of Wales	12.3
Cadw (inc. Royal Commission on Ancient & Historic Monuments)	10.3
Sports Council for Wales	6.6
Countryside Council for Wales	23.7
Welsh National Board of Nursing, Midwifery & Health Visiting	1.0

Source: Welsh Office Departmental Report 1998 - The Government's Expenditure Plans for 1998-99.

The Finance Programmes Division meets with each of the Group Directors in September to analyse their returns in depth. Each individual programme is scrutinised with any resources already committed for the coming year being detailed. Further off-setting savings against any bids are sought. The result is that there is some withdrawal or scaling down of bids, but bids still tend to exceed the available resources. FP Division also meet with Welsh Office Ministers to clarify their policy priorities.

During October, Ministers receive FP Division's initial set of recommendations and hold detailed discussions with Group Directors regarding the content and cost of their programmes, suggesting other possible options to be considered and requesting further details of the expected outputs from each programme. Negotiations are held until a compromise is reached. The aim is to achieve a balanced overall package for consideration by Ministers by early November.

By the middle of November, Ministers have made their decisions on the final allocations, which are passed on to Group Directors who in turn liaise with junior Ministers to decide on the details of the allocations within their programme areas. In late November, the total Block, the Local Authority revenue settlement and the agriculture figures are announced in the Chancellor's Financial Statement Budget Report. Latterly, the situation with regards to the notification of the total Block has changed as a result of the Comprehensive Spending Review, which indicates the figures for the Welsh budget for the next three years (see Table 1).

The Secretary of State announces the main features of the following year's allocations in late November or early December, usually by tabling a response to a written Parliamentary Question. Usually, there then follows a debate on the floor of the House of Commons. Local authorities and Non-Departmental Public Bodies (the Quangos) are informed of their allocations, enabling them to plan ahead. More detailed allocations are then made within each Welsh Office programme area and the final plans for the forthcoming financial year are published in the Welsh Office Departmental Report in March.

Table 3 provides a summary of the main allocation of the budget for the 1998-99 financial year, this time including expenditure by the Welsh Office on 16 of the 19 executive Non-Departmental Public Bodies for which it is responsible (as at the beginning of 1998).

THE BUDGET-SETTING PROCESS UNDER THE ASSEMBLY

The key stages of the current budget-setting process involve a relatively small group of people, namely the Secretary of State, Welsh Office Ministers, Group Directors and members of the Financial Programmes Division. With the advent of the Assembly, the process by which the the Welsh budget is distributed across the various programme areas will change dramatically. Most significantly, there will need to be discussions amongst a greater number of politicians than is the case at present. Furthermore, it is likely that the full Assembly will need to approve the final budget allocation - currently a rubber-stamping exercise performed by the Secretary of State.

The Assembly will have a clear indication as to the size of its future budget, as a result of the Comprehensive Spending Review. Nevertheless, the Secretary of State for Wales will be required, under section 81 of the Government of Wales Act, to provide the Assembly with a statement indicating the level of resources that will be available for the forthcoming financial year. This statement is to be made at least four months before the start of the financial year. Section 86 of the Government of Wales Act requires the Assembly to prepare a statement of its proposed expenditure for the forthcoming financial year. This must include:

- Total expenditure the Assembly proposes to incur that year, and what it proposes to spend it on.

- Funds the Assembly expects to receive from the Secretary of State for Wales and other Ministers and government departments.

- Funds the Assembly expects to receive from other sources.

- Information relating to local government funding under the Local Government and Housing Act 1989.

The mechanics of the budget allocation process will have to take into account a number of Standing Orders, but the Assembly itself will have to decide on the best framework to adopt. In its report to the Secretary of State, the National Assembly Advisory Group (NAAG, 1998) recommends that standing orders should provide for:

- The Finance Secretary to present the proposed budget allocation to the full Assembly on behalf of the Assembly Cabinet, and for the Assembly to debate and approve the budget.

- The Finance Secretary to ensure the Assembly Cabinet consults Subject Committees as part of the annual budget setting process.

- The Assembly Cabinet normally to set the allocation of the budget between expenditure programmes on a rolling three year basis.

- The Finance Secretary to ensure that major in-year adjustments to the budget are laid before the Assembly for approval, and for debate where the Assembly so decides.

The Assembly will need to agree on what precise roles the First Secretary, Assembly Cabinet, Subject Committees and the full Assembly will play in the process. How the Assembly spends its budget will be the subject of much public scrutiny, so the process should be as clear and open as possible. The NAAG report does not recommend the setting-up of a separate finance committee since the Assembly Cabinet should be able to oversee the budget-setting process: 'The Assembly Cabinet will provide the corporate authority to the budget proposals and any in-year adjustments; it will also be responsible for monitoring expenditure against budgets' (NAAG, 1998, p. 49).

The committee structure of the Assembly should aid the budgetary process considerably, since it will facilitate cooperation. The likely number of Subject Committees is smaller than the current number of Groups within the Welsh Office and given that each of them will be responsible for a range of different, yet related, policy areas, there will be more opportunities than at present for integrating and coordinating policies. This should in turn lead to better management of the available resources. The Assembly Cabinet should ensure that there is also cooperation between Subject Committees in order to minimise any possible conflicts in service provision.

In the first instance, there will be a need to ensure that adequate time is given to Subject Committees, the Assembly Cabinet and the full Assembly to discuss and approve programme budgets, including local government finance reports which are currently dealt with by the House of Commons. Beyond that the final decisions concerning the budget allocations should be made as soon as possible before the start of the financial year so that those involved in policy and service delivery have ample time to plan ahead.

A further factor which the Assembly may need to consider when setting its budget is making provision for emergency in-year increases in expenditure. The Government's Comprehensive Spending Review has resulted in a dramatic reduction in the size of the UK reserve, and has led to more stringent conditions under which it can be used to meet unforeseen budgetary pressures. As a consequence, the Welsh Office Comprehensive Spending Review consultation paper (Welsh Office, 1998c) suggests the possibility of establishing a Welsh 'reserve' of unallocated funds which could be drawn down when there are unexpected demands on the Assembly's resources. Of course, whilst this would allow increased in-year expenditure on some programmes without the need to divert resources already committed to other programmes, it would mean holding back resources in the first place.

CONCLUSION

With the the National Assembly, the process by which the Welsh budget is allocated between policy programmes will change considerably. From day one, the Assembly will be faced with demands for resources that will far exceed its limited budget - there will be no extra money in the pot. Increased spending on any programme will mean reduced expenditure on others. The Assembly will therefore need to devote much energy to identifying priority areas and ensuring that appropriate levels of funding are provided to support effective policy measures. Although the Assembly will also be constrained initially by inherited programme spending levels (most notably in the areas of health and education), there will be some scope for making marginal changes to spending in key areas. Over time there should be significant opportunities to alter the distribution of expenditure across programmes as long-term policy objectives and strategies are formulated.

The new budget-setting process is likely to be far more consultative and cooperative than at present, and will involve 60 elected politicians from throughout Wales, who should better understand and be more responsive to local needs and priorities than is presently the case. Furthermore, the Assembly's committee structure will enable the development of integrated policies which should in turn increase the level of coordination in the allocation of resources between different programme areas. The expectation should be that this will lead to a more effective, efficient and appropriate expenditure programme.

References

HM Treasury (1998) *Modern Public Services for Britain: Investing in Reform - Comprehensive Spending Review: New Spending Plans.*. The Stationary Office.

National Assembly Advisory Group (1998) *Recommendations*. Report to the Secretary of State for Wales.

Welsh Office (1998a) 'The Budget Setting Process'. Paper prepared for NAAG. February.

Welsh Office (1998b) *Departmental Report 1998 -The Government's Expenditure Plans for 1998 - 99*. The Stationery Office.

Welsh Office (1998c) *Comprehensive Spending Review: Modern Public Services for Wales*. Spending Plans 1999-2002 Consultation Paper.

CHAPTER 5

THE COMMITTEES

J. Barry Jones

The National Assembly will be a unique institution when it comes into being. There are similar institutions across Europe but they lack the specific characteristics that will distinguish the National Assembly. The German Lander, and their legislative powers, are defined by a federal constitution. The French Regions lack the extensive secondary legislative powers of the National Assembly as well as any sense of 'national identity' which would be anathema to the concept of a single indivisible French republic. The Spanish Autonomous Communities can be thought of as occupying a space somewhere between the German and French regional institutions.

The most distinctive feature of the Assembly will be the organisation of its executive. Initially, it was intended that the Assembly would be run along local government lines, with Subject Committees assuming responsibility for the determination of policy. During the passage of the Government of Wales Bill, the Opposition parties argued that such a diffuse power structure would reduce the status and authority of the National Assembly. It was argued that a Cabinet system of executive authority was necessary to provide effective political leadership and clear lines of accountability. However, the 'local government' committee system was not discarded but preserved to act as a counter-weight to the cabinet. Labour argued that this would ensure that the policy-making process was inclusive of all members of the Assembly, and not confined within the ranks of a small political élite. Thus, what is proposed in the Government of Wales Act (1998) is a constitutional hybrid involving a balance of power between the Executive Committee (Cabinet) and the Subject Committees of the Assembly. Whether this balance of power is inherently stable is yet unclear. Much will depend upon Standing Orders regulating committee procedures and supplemented by evolving customs and conventions.

The success of the National Assembly will depend upon the working relationship between the Cabinet and the Subject Committees and there is little doubt that ultimate political power will rest with the Cabinet. Therefore the primary concern must be to ensure that the Subject Committees in particular, possess a viable political role.

It is not the intention of this chapter to study all of the Assembly's committees. It is anticipated that certain committees can be expected to operate in the same way as their counter-parts in Westminster. The Executive Committee or Cabinet will be composed of the First Secretary (elected by the Assembly) and the Assembly Secretaries (appointed by the First Secretary). Like any Cabinet it will ensure strategic leadership of the National Assembly and public accountability. But its operation will be largely (although not exclusively) determined by the conventions of the British cabinet and the procedures of the majority party. In circumstances where there is no overall majority for one party a dé facto coalition will emerge with consequent modification for established Cabinet conventions.

The Audit Committee will be elected by the National Assembly and like its Westminster counter-part will be chaired by a member of the Assembly not drawn from the majority party. It will (and should) lean heavily on the Public Accounts Committee of the House of Commons for the determination of its procedures and will be supported by the office of the Auditor General for Wales.

The other committees, however, will be unique to the Welsh political context and can be expected to develop new procedures reflecting the needs of the National Assembly and its priorities. They are the Scrutiny Committee, Subject Committees, Programme Committees, and the Regional Committees.

SUBORDINATE LEGISLATION SCRUTINY COMMITTEE

Section 58 of the Act lays down the broad principles for the Scrutiny Committee's operation. It will scrutinise draft subordinate legislation proposed by the Assembly and report back 'drawing attention to any special features' which the Committee thinks the Assembly should take into account.

The composition of the Scrutiny Committee (detailed in Section 59) will be such as to assure the committee is independent. It will be required to reflect the party balance in the Assembly, to exclude all members of the Cabinet, and be chaired by a member of the Assembly drawn from one of the minority parties.

The Scrutiny Committee will be unique in as much as it will be considering subordinate legislation for Acts passed by the Westminster Parliament. However, it will doubtless be guided by the Joint Committee on Statutory Instruments. The Westminster Parliament has a long history of delegation by statute, a limited power to legislate, usually handed to the executive. In practise governments have exploited this facility to give themselves greater freedom of action in the application of policies. This has led to the charge that many statutory instruments no longer deal with 'means' but with 'principles' (HC 257-i, 1985-6). Accordingly more pressure has been put on the Joint Committee which reports to the Commons if there are doubts whether the instrument is intra vires the enabling statute, whether the instrument lacks clarity and requires further explanation, or, whether its drafting is defective. The extent of this supervision of statutory instruments is severely limited. Of approximately 2,000 statutory instruments made each year only about two per cent attract critical reports, a measure not so much of the high quality of statutory instruments as to the volume of work undertaken by the Committee.

One can reasonably expect the Assembly Scrutiny Committee to exercise a more comprehensive supervision of statutory instruments and secondary legislation generally. The Assembly will also devote more time to debating critical reports in greater detail than is presently the case in the House of Commons. But while positive benefits will accrue from the operation of the Scrutiny Committee, there are serious questions which need to be addressed. Given that so few members of the National Assembly will have a House of Commons background, there will be, in the short term at any rate, a deficiency in experience and expertise on the Committee. This will put more pressure on the officials servicing the Committee which could pose difficulties if they were to be appointed from the Welsh Office.

Finally, it is not clear how the Westminster Parliament would react to the new situation whereby a Scrutiny Committee acting for the National Assembly considers and approves statutory instruments derived from legislative enactments of Westminster. No doubt concordats (see Chapter 28), and evolving customs and conventions will clarify the situation in the medium to long term. In the short term, however, there is likely to be an element of uncertainty in the operation of the Scrutiny Committee.

SUBJECT COMMITTEES

Section 54 of the Act is ambiguous with regard to Subject Committees. It allows the Assembly to establish them as and when it considers them appropriate. The only guidelines relating to the Subject Committees' remit is contained in Schedule 2 of the Act which lists 18 policy fields to be transferred to the Assembly (listed at the end of this chapter). These policy fields will have to be packaged, so as to produce a viable number of Subject Committees.

The most obvious constraint on the number of Subject Committees is the availability of members. Key Assembly committees, in particular the Audit Committee and the Scrutiny Committee, will be crucial to the whole devolution exercise. One would expect senior politicians, preferably with parliamentary experience, to fill these committees. It would then be debatable whether those members serving on 'watch dog' committees should also be available to serve on Subject Committees.

It is possible that such a concession could be made in respect of the Scrutiny Committee but it would be quite unacceptable for a similar concession to be made to the members of the Audit Committee. Thus, depending on the number of members of the Audit Committee and - taking account of the First Secretary, the

Assembly Presiding Officer and Deputy Presiding Officer, neither of whom would be expected to serve on Subject Committees, and the possibility of two Assembly Secretaries without subject area responsibilities - there would be at best 50 and possibly as few as 45 members available to serve on the Subject Committees.

Significant implications derive from this mathematical exercise. Few, if any of the Subject Committees are likely to be devoted to one specialist policy area. On the contrary, the prevailing pattern will be of general multi-functional committees composed of Assembly men and women serving on two or more Subject Committees. This immediately raises questions about the degree of specialism and expertise within the Subject Committees and their ability to argue for their policy preferences. In the final analysis, could these Subject Committees take on the political executive backed by the resources of the Welsh Office with any degree of success? It will be argued that the Committee Secretariat will compensate for the initial limitations of their membership, but the personnel involved in the committee secretariats will be recruited from the Welsh Office. There will be obvious difficulties of divided responsibilities.

Another political reality will infringe on the Subject Committees. Their number and their respective policy responsibilities will be determined by the First Secretary. This is nothing new. It is the way in which the Westminster Parliament operates. The Prime Minister appoints Ministers and assigns them particular responsibilities which are faithfully reflected in departmental organisation and the House of Commons select committees' terms of reference. The same will happen in the National Assembly. The First Secretary will appoint the 'cabinet', the members of which will have policy responsibilities as Assembly Secretaries. The Subject Committees on which they will serve will thus reflect the respective duties of their Assembly Secretaries.

Consequently, the delicate balance between the political executive of the National Assembly and the Subject Committees will have to take account of the First Secretary's political power of appointment, the influence of Assembly Secretaries, and the administrative resources of the Welsh Office. Serious consideration should be given to whether the Subject Committees should be serviced by Welsh Office personnel or whether a separate category of civil servants appointed by and answerable to the National Assembly (rather like the Parliamentary clerks) should be established. This does not have to be done immediately but it might be considered desirable when the operation of the National Assembly has 'bedded down'.

The debate on devolution reiterated the point that the procedures of the National Assembly should facilitate 'inclusivity' through the mechanism of Subject Committees with their multi-party membership. It also followed that these committees should have a pro-active role in the policy making process. The attainment of these objections will depend upon the procedures which the Subject Committees evolve.

Given the considerations above, the following guidelines represent operational requirements for a successful committee system:

- Allowing for absences and illnesses, the Subject Committee membership should consist of at least seven and no more than nine members.

- The quorum for such committees should be five.

- Some committees, depending on the range of their responsibilities, should have sub-committees.

- Sub-committees should be allowed to draft in outside experts as advisors to enhance their consideration of complex and technical issues.

- Sub-committee reports would have to be considered and approved by the full committee before being presented to the Assembly.

One issue which has to be addressed is the Subject Committees' reactive and pro-active functions. Clearly the committees will be reactive in so far as they respond to the statutory instruments which will come down the line from Whitehall and Westminster. Although, as already indicated, the Scrutiny Committee will be important, one would expect the Subject Committees to develop a considerable role on this area. They will also respond to suggestions and recommendations of the Assembly. Thus having a reactive role will not in any way imply that the Subject Committees' functions have been diminished.

However, if the Assembly is to have an input into the Westminster legislative process, to ensure that Welsh interests and needs are taken into account in the drafting of legislation, then Subject Committees will need to develop appropriate procedures. It may be argued that such an input into the Westminster legislative process should be the responsibility of the Executive Committee (cabinet) and in strictly constitutional terms this is probably so. But if the Subject Committees are to develop House of Commons Select Committee characteristics (that is to say, sounding out interested parties, taking evidence, identifying problems and making recommendations) then they will, in effect, be participating in the pre-legislative consultation process.

If the Subject Committees do the things which the National Assembly Advisory Group (NAAG) expects – take evidence from interested parties, review the performance of public bodies, scrutinise secondary legislation – to whom should their views and recommendations be directed? Should it be to the Assembly for that body to consider and debate, or should it be via the Assembly Secretary to the Executive Committee? Should a Subject Committee be allowed to 'test out' its policy recommendations against those of the Executive on the floor of the Assembly?

Another issue which requires consideration is the possibility of minority reports emanating from a committee. Should such reports be tackled alongside majority reports? And should they be debated or are they doomed to 'die on the vine'? The answers to these questions will be found in the balance of power between the Executive and the Subject Committees which in turn will depend upon the party balance, good will and a willingness to aim for consensus politics and policies.

Those with experience of Welsh politics will conclude that a new political culture will be a prerequisite.

Another procedural issue, again relating to the balance of power between the Executive and the Subject Committees, concerns to the role of the Assembly Secretary (in effect the Minister) in the operation of his or her committee. There will be no clear separation of powers. The Assembly Secretary will be present when the Committee deliberates, but will be prevented from dominating its proceedings by the chair who might well be representative of an opposition party. This could have benefits leading to changes in proposed secondary legislation at an early stage and thus promote the politics of consensus. On the other hand, one can imagine that the presence (even if limited) of the Assembly Secretary during the deliberations of the Committee might inhibit its decisions and eventually undermine its autonomy. The role of the opposition parties might be seriously weakened in the long term. Plainly this would be an undesirable outcome.

PROGRAMME COMMITTEES

The National Assembly Advisory Group has suggested that the dangers of 'departmentalism' might be minimised by a 'programme' approach which is used increasingly at the local government level. Such 'horizontal' programme committees could be set up to develop specific action programmes. Doubtless real benefits can accrue from specific 'one-off' tasks. But there must be serious doubts about institutionalising such an arrangement. It would result in more committees, and more pressure on members.

However, the most serious consequence would be to erode the coordinating functions of the Assembly. The consideration of policies in terms of equal opportunities and sustainable development should be on the floor of the Assembly. If we are not careful all meaningful policy matters will be decided outside the Assembly. It cannot be the intention to marginalise the Assembly before it has even come into existence. However, a strong case can be made for one permanent 'horizontal' committee recommended by the Advisory Group, that concerned with the European Union and its developing relationship with Wales.

REGIONAL COMMITTEES

The Act requires the establishment of Regional Committees covering the whole of Wales. While there is a specific requirement that there should be a committee for north Wales, there is considerable discretion open to the Assembly in drafting its standing orders and defining the boundaries of the Welsh regions. The regions could reflect the existing administrative structures of Wales, although this has recently undergone change, and they should not transgress local authority boundaries.

However, the central argument for Regional Committees is that there are areas in Wales suffering from serious social and economic deprivation. In which case, the traditional north/south division of the country will have less significance than the east/west dichotomy which emerged so clearly in the 1997 referendum.

The Act specifies that Regional Committees do not need to replicate the party balance in the Assembly but will be composed of Assembly members representing constituencies in that region, plus the additional members allocated from the electoral regions. Recommendations made by the Regional Committees will not be binding – only advisory. Nor is there any impediment (other than representing a constituency in the region) upon whom the Regional Committees may elect as their respective chairs.

The question arises: what useful role might these 'advisory' bodies perform? Is there not a danger that the Regional Committees could degenerate into sectional lobbies, pitting region against region for financial support, and deepening the socio-geographic differences within Wales? Alternatively, might not the Committees possessing only advisory 'powers' become mere talking shops – regarded by their respective regions as futile and pointless institutions and so lead to the disaffection in one or more regions?

The Act's intention is to avoid these two extreme scenarios. A third way would doubtless be preferred by New Labour. This is one in which regional interests are articulated and taken into account by the Assembly while the process of consultation (through the Regional Committees) serves to integrate the different parts of Wales into the new devolved Welsh political system.

It is difficult to devise a formula which will guarantee to bring this about. So much depends on the membership of the committees, their personalities and the party balance. In the final analysis much will depend, too, upon the development of a new inclusive Welsh political culture. The greater the proportionality of the parties in the National Assembly the greater the likelihood of such an inclusive culture emerging.

While the ultimate success of the Regional Committees will be dependent upon the development of a dynamic nationally inclusive political culture in Wales, there are certain attitudes and perceptions which could help these Committees develop a significant role. They should concentrate on securing influence within the Assembly, building cross-party and cross-regional alliances rather than stimulating regional bureaucracies. They should meet in their respective 'regional capitals', preferably when the Assembly is not in session and at times that do not overlap with other regional committees.

The intention should be to give a focus to the region and its problems. The Regional Committees should have clearly defined and specific terms of reference. The tasks they set themselves should be attainable and each of the Regional Committees should be guaranteed access to the First Secretary to question him or her on the probable impact of national Welsh policies on their respective regions.

Finally, the Committees should be supported by an effective secretariat both at the regional level and in the Assembly where one would expect the committees to devise their strategy.

Much of the foregoing will be determined by the National Assembly and its Standing Orders. But there is much that the Regional Committees can do to enhance their role. Their procedures and objectives should be clearly stated to include the following:

- A regular calendar of meetings held when the Assembly is not in session.

- The predetermination of themes to elicit evidence and stimulate interest.

- A guarantee that Regional Committee recommendations/reports will be debated on the floor of the National Assembly.

- A promise that the recommendations will be considered by the Partnership Council for Wales which brings together representatives from the Assembly and local government.

Although the Regional Committees will only be advisory it is possible that the success of devolution to Wales will be judged on their record in spreading wealth and economic activity more evenly across Wales. The main thrust to Welsh devolution came from a perception that there were serious spatial inequalities in the United Kingdom. The National Assembly will have to address that problem from the outset, but it will have to do so in a manner which confronts and resolves the east/west dichotomy in the Welsh economy. The Regional Committees will be extremely important in this endeavour and far more so than their advisory status would suggest.

CONCLUSION

It is understandable that so many questions surround the establishment of the National Assembly. We are sailing into uncharted constitutional waters. Setting up an elected assembly with executive functions, possessing a degree of autonomy yet still subordinate to the legislation enactments of the Westminster parliament, poses difficulties and will require novel procedures. The success or otherwise of Welsh devolution will depend upon a variety of factors, including the nature of the concordats between the Welsh Office and Whitehall departments and the relationship between the First Secretary in the National Assembly and the Secretary of State in the British cabinet. It will also depend upon the balance of power between the political executive in the Assembly and the policy Subject Committees. That relationship will determine the effectiveness of devolution as a developing and inclusive process.

APPENDIX

Functions to be transferred from the Welsh Office to the National Assembly, as laid out in Schedule 2 to the Government of Wales Act.

1. Agriculture, forestry, fisheries and food.

2. Ancient monuments and historic buildings.

3. Culture (inc. museums, galleries and libraries).

4. Economic development.

5. Education and training.

6. The environment.

7. Health and health services.

8. Highways.

9. Housing.

10. Industry.

11. Local government.

12. Social services.

13. Sport and recreation.

14. Tourism.

15. Town and country planning.

16. Transport.

17. Water and flood defence.

18. The Welsh language.

CHAPTER 6

THE ASSEMBLY
AS A LEGISLATURE

Paul Silk

The obvious apparent answer to the question 'who makes the law in Britain' is Parliament. Parliament is the legislature, and legislation is therefore something emanating from Parliament. But Parliament has, at least from the nineteenth century, delegated legislative power to others, in particular to Ministers of the Crown. This delegated legislation generally nowadays takes the form of statutory instruments, normally called 'orders' or 'regulations' or 'rules', and is subject to the procedures of the Statutory Instruments Act 1946. Most of this chapter will be about this type of delegated legislation[1]. At the same time, the European Communities Act 1972 also delegated legislative power from Parliament to the European Communities, while legislation which has established devolved legislatures in the United Kingdom or in former British colonies - whether in Kenya, Ireland, Wales or Scotland - was and is itself an exercise of the power to delegate.

Delegated legislation in the conventional sense is also known as 'secondary legislation' or 'subordinate legislation' in contrast to the 'primary' legislation passed by Parliament in the form of Acts. Of these terms, 'secondary' is unofficial, but in very common use, while 'subordinate legislation' is the proper term - and is defined in that most obscure part of the statute law, section 21 (interpretation) of the Interpretation Act 1978. The terms 'secondary' and 'subordinate' imply that delegated legislation is inferior to primary legislation. In some senses, this is so: when a minister has power to make delegated legislation, he or she has that power because an Act of Parliament (the primary legislation) said so. If the Act is repealed, the power ceases. Primary, not secondary, legislation is normally necessary when policy changes of substance need to be made. Secondary legislation can also be reviewed by the courts which can find it to be invalid because of formal defects or because the minister in making the secondary legislation went beyond his or her powers. Courts have no such power with primary legislation[2]. On the other hand, delegated legislation can deal with very important areas of policy. It also has the same legal force as primary legislation, and, for example, prison sentences can follow breaches of some secondary legislation. And while the hierarchical relationship means that it is normally the case that one Act of Parliament may only be amended or repealed by another, there are now limited circumstances in which alterations of this sort may be affected by secondary legislation. As we shall see, it would be wrong to dismiss secondary legislation as 'second class' legislation.

Certainly secondary legislation is legislative big business. In recent years, there have been more than 1,500 to 2,000 general statutory instruments annually (and roughly the same number of local statutory instruments). Statutory instruments have steadily grown in number and in length over the last 40 years, and as legislative vehicles they vastly outweigh primary legislation. To give an indicative figure, there were 3,001 pages of new primary legislation passed in 1995, as opposed to 9,688 pages of secondary legislation. All of this was 'law'.

THE LEGISLATIVE POWERS OF THE ASSEMBLY

Typically, primary legislation gives power to 'the Secretary of State' to make secondary legislation. Because of the doctrine that the Secretary of State is a single office shared between a number of Secretaries of State, any Secretary of State could legally exercise a power conferred on 'the Secretary of State'. Thus, in the past, emergency secondary legislation for Northern Ireland has been made by the Secretary of State with responsibility for an English Department. But normally, where an aspect of policy has been placed within the responsibilities of a Department, it is the Secretary of State heading that Department who exercises the power to make secondary legislation by statutory instrument. In this way, the Secretary of State for Wales is a legislator, and, over the years which the Welsh Office has existed, the Secretary of State for Wales has accrued a mixed bag of powers to make secondary legislation in the fields in which the Department sets policy for Wales.

This legislative power of the Secretary of State for Wales will be exercised by the Assembly. Section 22 of the Government of Wales Act requires functions in 18 fields specified in Schedule 2 to the Act (including functions of making subordinate legislation) to be transferred to the Assembly (see the Appendix to the previous Chapter). The first draft of the transfer order listed over 300 Acts under which some or all of the functions will be transferred. Where any of these Acts confers a subordinate legislative power which is exercised in Wales by the Secretary of State for Wales, this will become a power exercisable by the Assembly. Section 22 also allows other functions exercised by ministers in relation to Wales (including functions presently exercised by other Departments, like, for example, the Home Office) to be transferred later. The Act also makes provision for powers to be exercised by the Assembly concurrently with a minister, and for ministers to continue to exercise powers in respect of transferred functions for the purpose of implementing European Community obligations. Very importantly, Section 44 of the Act removes any need for legislation made by the Assembly to be subject to any additional scrutiny by Parliament, except when the legislation is made jointly with a minister or relates to certain cross-border issues. Thus the Assembly will be a legislature, not just an executive as local authorities are[3]. That status will, for example, probably allow it to join the Commonwealth Parliamentary Association, in the same way as State Parliaments and Assemblies in Canada, Australia and India do.

There is, of course, an important distinction between the legislative powers of the Assembly in Wales and those of the Scottish Parliament and the Northern Ireland Assembly. Both of the latter will have primary and secondary legislative powers devolved to them, whereas secondary legislation made by and through the Assembly in Wales can be seen as a species of UK-level delegated legislation, - *devolved secondary legislation* - being the successor to such secondary legislation that is currently made for and applied to Wales. One possible consequence of this lesser degree of autonomy may be a greater readiness on behalf of the courts to review legislation passed at Cardiff than at Edinburgh[4]. It will also certainly be the case, as we shall see later, that the Assembly's freedom of legislative action will be more dependent upon Parliament than will be the case in Scotland or Northern Ireland.

HOW DOES SECONDARY LEGISLATION WORK AT PRESENT?

Much of the legislation which governs daily life in Wales is made by statutory instruments. Most of the 1,500 to 2,000 statutory instruments made each year (other than those affecting Scotland or Northern Ireland only) apply in Wales. However, comparatively few are made by the Secretary of State for Wales, or, at least, by the Secretary of State for Wales alone. Many statutory instruments applying in Wales are made, for example, by the Home Secretary, the Lord Chancellor, or Treasury Departments. The Welsh Office estimates that, in an average year, the Secretary of State for Wales makes approximately 50 general statutory instruments[5] on his own, and 400 with other ministers.[6]

The powers of the Welsh Secretary to make secondary legislation are normally exercised wholly independently of London when an issue:

- has application only in Wales (for example, a local pollution incident requiring restriction on food sales); or

- is in one of the comparatively rare areas of policy where the Welsh Office has a different stance from English Departments - education policy is the leading example in recent years.

But as the figures show, more typical is secondary legislation signed by English and Welsh ministers, and applying equally on both sides of the border. For example, the Local Authorities (Members' Allowances) (Amendment) (No. 2) Regulations 1998 was signed by ministers in the Department of the Environment, Transport and the Regions and the Welsh Office, and introduced identical upratings in councillors' allowances in England and Wales. Strictly, these instruments are made *concurrently* by the two ministers. However, for administrative convenience, one instrument is produced covering both countries. There are also much less frequent occasions when instruments are made *jointly*. This is because the parent Act confers power on a group of ministers to make secondary legislation. For example, the Road Traffic Regulation Act 1984 allows the Secretaries of State with transport responsibilities in England, Scotland and Wales respectively jointly to specify forms of traffic signs (for the whole of Great Britain).

Jointly made instruments will continue to be made by the Assembly in conjunction with the appropriate ministers in England (and, in some cases, members of the Scottish Executive). In the case of road signs, for example, the Assembly will not be free to determine its own signs. But there also appears to be an assumption that the Assembly will continue to follow England in that statutory instruments affecting Wales and England at present made concurrently will continue to be made in identical terms[7]. Even where separate instruments are made, Wales may follow the English template, perhaps with 'minor changes", as Peter Hain suggested in a recent Standing Committee debate on the School Standards and Framework Bill[8]. However, there appears to be no reason why this should *necessarily* happen. Indeed, there is every reason to suppose that a new Assembly will wish to be legislatively creative, not quiescent.

As we will see, the powers of the Assembly to make statutory instruments are potentially great, if the Assembly is prepared to use them. Additionally, the Assembly will not be restricted to making subordinate legislation where none has already been made. Because of section 14 of the Interpretation Act 1978, the Assembly's power to make subordinate legislation implies a power to revoke or amend existing subordinate legislation. In this way, it will have power to change existing secondary legislation in areas where power to act is transferred to it. Moreover, as already mentioned, there is nothing to prevent other powers exercisable by statutory instrument by other ministers from being transferred to it in future transfer orders, whether or not those powers are at present exercised by the Secretary of State for Wales. Nor is there anything to prevent individual future Acts of Parliament transferring powers on an *ad hoc* basis.

THE IMPORTANCE OF SECONDARY LEGISLATION

We now need to look in more depth at what precisely secondary legislation is. Almost all Acts of Parliament contain many provisions giving ministers power to make secondary legislation. These can often consist of powers to regulate very minor matters. To take one extreme, paragraph 7(2) of Schedule 4 to the Welsh Development Agency Act 1975, as inserted by Schedule 10 to the Government of Wales Act, will allow the Secretary of State, and therefore (after transfer) the

Assembly, to make regulations about the reinterment of human remains found on consecrated land compulsorily acquired by the WDA. This is an important matter, no doubt, for the relatives of those interred, but hardly the essence of exciting legislative politics. It does, however, give the feel of much secondary legislation. As de Smith and Brazier put it:

> 'Open a recent volume of **Statutory Instruments** and read the first hundred pages. The tedium of wading through a mass of abstruse technicalities, barely comprehensible to anyone lacking expert knowledge of the subject matter, is at least an instructive experience; and if one has the moral stamina, one can plough on through another five thousand pages. With such dull subject matter, delegated legislation is in fact a dull subject for many of us.' [9]

This is an accurate description of the mass of statutory instruments. Essentially, statutory instruments often amount to no more than a means of allowing civil servants to fill out the dull bits of primary legislation.

So is a power to legislate which is restricted to subordinate legislation a power worth having? Much subordinate legislation may appear to be dull and detailed, but it is essential if the purposes of the primary legislation on which it depends are to have practical life. Sometimes its contents are at the heart of the political debate. For example, the National Health Act 1977 gives the Secretary of State power to set prescription charges and to provide for exemptions. Statutory instruments, in particular the *Charges for Drugs and Appliances (Orders)* regularly alter National Health Service charges. If these instruments were not made, prescription charges would not exist. The statutory instruments are necessary for the power to impose charges to have practical effect.

Let us take another example, the *Activity Centres (Young Persons' Safety) Act* 1995. This short Act stemmed from a boating tragedy off the southern English coast, and makes provision for the regulation and safety of adventure centres used by those under eighteen. The Secretary of State is given power by order to designate a licensing authority for adventure centres, and power by regulations to set conditions such as who may hold licences, what requirements are placed on licence holders, what fees can be charged and how licences may be revoked or varied. Regulations may also create criminal offences concerned with licensed activities, though the Act itself provides for the maximum penalties. Without the order and the regulations, there would be no licensing regime for adventure centres, and the primary legislation would have been passed with no effect. It was therefore only when the 12 pages of secondary legislation were made, some nine months after the four-page was passed, that the licensing regime of activity centres was able to begin. This example is typical of the pivotal role which subordinate legislation plays. However, it is also worth pointing out that the primary legislation in this case (and, again, this is typical) severely restricted the scope for manoeuvre which the Secretary of State had in making the order and regulations. For example, the designation order could only designate a person nominated by the Health and

Safety Commission, while 12 subsections of the primary legislation provided a template of what the licensing regulations should be.

The Activity Centres (Young Persons' Safety) Act is a fairly minor example of a so-called 'skeleton' or 'framework' Act of Parliament, where the subordinate powers granted are so important that the real operation of the legislation is entirely by the orders and regulations made under it. More substantial examples of legislation which have been criticised on this basis include the *Child Support Act 1991*, the *Education (Student Loans) Act* 1990, the *Jobseekers Act 1995* and the *School Standards and Framework* Bill which was referred to earlier. The School Standards and Framework Bill is a particularly interesting case. For example, it introduces an obligation to provide school lunches. The Bill tells us that 'school lunch has such meaning as may be prescribed' and that 'prescribed' means prescribed in regulations made by the Secretary of State. In Wales, the Assembly will be able to prescribe standards for Welsh school lunches, and these could be different from the English standards. At a facetious level, this could mean brown, pink and yellow custard in Wales, and yellow only in England. At a more serious level, the *School Standards and Framework* Bill introduces numerous powers to make secondary legislation, and has therefore been drafted in such a way that its implementation in Wales could be very different from its implementation on the English side of the border.

If anything, the trend to framework legislation is increasing. This has led to a suspicion in Parliament that subordinate legislation might become more than a matter of administrative convenience, and more a means of achieving policy ends without the tedious business of requiring parliamentary approval. As the House of Commons Procedure Committee commented in 1996:

> *'there is in our view too great a readiness in Parliament to delegate wide legislative powers to Ministers, and no lack of enthusiasm on their part to take on such powers'.*[10]

Indeed, the House of Lords set up a Delegated Powers Scrutiny Committee in 1992, with a principal remit of reporting to the House on whether the provisions of any Bill 'inappropriately delegate legislative power'. There is one particular class of powers to make secondary legislation which have caused concern among some Members of Parliament. These are the so-called 'Henry VIII powers' - powers named after a King who was given sweeping power under the Statute of Proclamations 1539 to legislate without reference to Parliament. In essence, a Henry VIII clause is one which allows a minister to amend or repeal primary legislation by secondary legislation[11]. For example, there are provisions in Schedules 18, 24 and 25 of the School Standards and Framework Bill which will allow a statutory instrument to make radical changes to the major provisions in the Bill about appeals against school exclusions or admissions. Where a power to make such secondary legislation passes to the Assembly, the Assembly will have a power over primary legislation.

There is little apparent consistency in the various Henry VIII powers that the statute book contains. As the Chairman of the House of Lords Delegated Powers Scrutiny Committee has written:

> 'some deal with detail: to bring lists up to date, to uprate the amount of a fine, to vary the number of members of a Board, to adapt primary legislation to particular circumstances, to make exceptions to the operation of an Act, to make consequential and transitional provisions. Some allow a minister to change the substance of policy, but only within limits established in the Act. Others bestow on a Minister the power to change the substance of policy without limit'.[12]

All this indicates that there is no universally agreed principle on what is an appropriate power to delegate and what is not. The Renton Committee on the Preparation of Legislation[13] was hostile to anything other than 'details which may require comparatively frequent modification' being within the competence of secondary legislation. On the other hand, the Hansard Society Commission on the Legislative Process favoured a more continental model, arguing that the 'main provisions of statute law should be set out in Acts of Parliament, but that most detail should be left to delegated legislation', though they also favoured much improved parliamentary scrutiny of this delegated legislation[14]. De Smith and Brazier, while seemingly unperturbed by delegated legislation in general, thought it 'far from clear' to what extent general criteria had been formulated as to where the lines should be drawn between matters explicitly to be set out in Bills and matters to be left for amplification by the exercise of delegated powers[15].

If the line between what is appropriate for secondary legislation and what belongs in primary legislation is a fuzzy one, it would be wrong to imply that the use of subordinate legislation to fill out the details of the primary Act has normally been intended as a means of bypassing Parliament or of giving ministers wider discretionary powers. Parliament has trouble enough in dealing properly with the primary legislation it considers without quadrupling its legislative burden by scrapping secondary legislative powers and using primary legislation instead. Acts of Parliament would be impossibly long and detailed if there were no facility to make secondary legislation.

So far as it inherits the Secretary of State's existing secondary legislative functions, the Assembly will therefore have a haphazard collection of miscellaneous powers reflecting the almost arbitrary decisions taken by administrations over the last 50 years about what to include in primary legislation and what to leave for secondary legislation. In some areas powers will be minor or even trivial. In others, the Assembly may be able to use Henry VIII provisions to amend or repeal primary legislation as it affects Wales. In most cases, primary legislation will only work if secondary legislative powers are exercised in Wales in a way which is compatible with the primary legislation.

It is conceivable that the Assembly might choose not to implement secondary legislation, so frustrating the intention of primary legislation. This occurs at present with the Welsh Office deciding not to implement secondary legislation in relatively uncontroversial areas, especially in education. One example is the absence of publication of primary school league tables in Wales. However, were this to be carried through in more central policy areas, especially those affecting expenditure, then one could imagine confrontation quickly occurring.

In the future, as we shall see, primary legislation could be framed in such a way as would restrict or expand the Assembly's subordinate legislative powers. There should therefore be no necessary hang-up about the term. Secondary legislative power is real power.

THE RELATIONSHIP WITH WESTMINSTER

Unlike secondary legislation currently made by the Secretary of State, Parliament will have no role in approving or negating orders made by the Assembly alone, though Parliament will retain a role in the case of orders made jointly with English ministers and cross-border instruments. This is a real diminution of parliamentary control on Welsh affairs. Nevertheless, what happens at Westminster will continue fundamentally to affect the sort of legislative powers which the Assembly is able to exercise.

First of all, primary legislation affecting Wales is likely to continue to be made by Westminster Bills applying to both England and Wales. Unlike Scotland, there has been in the past very little specifically Welsh primary legislation. In the pre-publication stages of England and Wales primary legislation, the old Welsh Office would have been consulted. Concordats should mean that, at least when the administrations in London and Cardiff are on friendly terms, this consultation continues (see the Appendix to Chapter 28 for an account of the operation of concordats). Consultation will, however, presumably be limited to Assembly Secretaries and the staff of the Assembly: it will hardly be consultation with *all* Assembly Members if for no other reason than that MPs will not be happy for Assembly Members to be consulted when they are not. At the beginning of a parliamentary session, when legislation comes into the public domain, the Secretary of State will have a duty to consult the Assembly about the government's legislative proposals, and the Assembly will have the right to make representations about any matter affecting Wales. What will this amount to? There is a temptation to recall Hotspur's response to Shakespeare's caricature Welshman Glendower's boast that he 'can call spirits from the vasty deep'.

> 'Why, so can I, or so can any man
> But will they come when you do call for them?'

We can all read the Queen's speech and we can all make representations about a government's legislative programme. How can the Assembly be given an *effective* role? How can it ensure that it is listened to?

Plaid Cymru has proposed a fast-track Westminster procedure for Bills, or amendments to Westminster Bills, supported by the Assembly. This is possible, though not favoured by the government. Other structures are also conceivable - for example, joint committees of MPs and MWAs. The Partnership Council might be a model. But it will be important for the Assembly to establish mechanisms for effective representation of Welsh interests in the preparation and parliamentary progress of primary legislation affecting Wales in the fields transferred to the Assembly. The idea that the Secretary of State might be the Assembly's advocate in Parliament is superficially attractive, but the Secretary of State will be answerable to the Prime Minister, not the Assembly, and cannot be expected to act on instructions of an Assembly which may be at variance with the London Government.

There may be another problem in a system which allows an independent body (the Assembly) to implement the details of legislation framed elsewhere. What happens when the Assembly and Parliament (or rather, the executives in London and Cardiff) disagree? Under British constitutional theory the Queen in Parliament is the sovereign law-making body (though we have to leave aside the effect of Britain's membership of the European Union). What Parliament has given, it can take away. It did this in the case of Stormont and the English metropolitan authorities, and it could clip the wings of the Scottish Parliament or the Assembly in Wales. Parliament's powers are of course limited by what is realistically possible. For instance, the Indian Independence Act 1947 could be repealed, but India would not thereby revert to British control. The more credible the devolved legislatures prove themselves to be, the less chance there is that they will have their wings clipped. Nevertheless, there would be nothing to prevent a London government from passing primary legislation which applied only to Wales, and which was unacceptable to the majority of Welsh MPs (and to Assembly Members) but acceptable to the Westminster Parliament as a whole. In these circumstances, the Assembly would no doubt wish, through its general debates, to express its opposition to what was being done, but would have no power to resist the decisions of the Westminster Parliament. To use the school lunches example again, if London does not want choice of custard in Wales, it can simply remove the power of the Assembly to provide it.

Primary legislation passed at Westminster could also restrict the Assembly's power to manoeuvre. It need not be a straightforward pulling back to London of powers devolved to Cardiff. Primary legislation *could* be drafted to give English ministers wide powers to make secondary legislation while the Assembly is given more circumscribed powers. The secondary legislation route *could* become less favoured generally. This, incidentally, would meet quite separate concerns, widespread at Westminster, about the burgeoning of secondary legislation. Existing legislation *could* be amended so that the Assembly does not have the freedom of action of English ministers. Assembly orders *could* even be repealed by Act of the Westminster Parliament. All this might be unlikely at present, but the desire to control Wales may exert sway on Whitehall, and may in the future attract London ministers whose policies may be at variance with those of Cardiff.

There is an alternative, more positive scenario. A Whitehall which is sympathetic to the administration in Cardiff, and which wishes the Assembly to fly, is likely to frame its primary legislation in a way which gives the maximum of flexibility to the Assembly. This seems implicit in the Government's White Paper promise that:

> 'As a general principle, the Government expects Bills that confer new powers and relate to the Assembly's functions ... will provide for the powers to be exercised separately and differently in Wales; and to be exercised by the Assembly'.[16]

The Government of Wales Act itself confers on the Assembly powers to reform Welsh health authorities and other Welsh public bodies which are beyond any powers exercisable by any minister in relation to England.

Other devices could be employed in the future. These could both make it more difficult for Parliament to intervene in Welsh matters, and easier for the Assembly to legislate. For example, the Speaker of the House of Commons could be required to designate any Bill affecting only a devolved Welsh function, and a Bill so designated could be exempt from the procedures under the Parliament Acts, or subject to the consent of the Assembly or otherwise specially considered. Bills could include a 'Welsh clause' allowing the Assembly to make provision in Wales by order (subordinate legislation) so long as the order had similar effect to that brought about in England by the other clauses of the Bill.

Many possible variations of such an order are conceivable, giving greater or lesser degrees of freedom to Cardiff, and there is an interesting precedent in the case of Northern Ireland legislation. Since the Stormont Parliament was prorogued and direct rule from Westminster introduced in 1972, most legislation for Northern Ireland has been by Order in Council (a form of secondary legislation). It has become the practice in recent years for many Bills applying in Great Britain to contain a clause signalling that Northern Ireland subordinate legislation will be introduced, and will be subject to fewer parliamentary controls than would otherwise be the case, if the purpose of that legislation is to make similar provision for Northern Ireland as is made in the Great Britain Bill.

If it became the norm for England and Wales primary legislation in the fields transferred to the Assembly simply to give *carte blanche* to the Assembly to implement by secondary legislation such parts of the primary legislation as it thought fit (and with such modifications as it thought appropriate) then the Assembly would have powers which were to all intents and purposes indistinguishable from primary legislative powers. An incidental advantage would be that it is at least possible that the scope for judicial review of Welsh legislation would *dé facto* lessen if powers to legislate by secondary legislation over such wide areas were conferred upon the Assembly.

PROCEDURES IN THE ASSEMBLY

How is the legislative business of the Assembly likely to work? The Government of Wales Act is silent on many of the details of how Assembly orders will be prepared. They will have to be considered by a subordinate legislation scrutiny committee; be subject to a regulatory appraisal; and be approved by resolution of the Assembly (or subject to a negative procedure, when it is not reasonably practicable for normal procedures to be followed). But what will happen before this? The National Assembly Advisory Group (NAAG) has proposed two procedures, which it has dubbed 'fast track' and 'full scrutiny'.[17]

Fast track is intended for the less important instruments, full scrutiny for others. In both cases, initiative lies with the Assembly Secretary and Executive Committee, who are also given the role of proposing which route should be followed. Under fast track, the Assembly Secretary arranges regulatory appraisal and then submits the instrument to the scrutiny committee. Under full scrutiny, instruments are submitted to Subject Committees which arrange regulatory appraisals, consider amendments and consult with outside parties before submitting the draft instrument (amended if necessary) to the Scrutiny Committee. The Subject Committee operates within a timetable.

Fast track and full scrutiny come together at the scrutiny committee stage. This committee is likely to have a largely technical role, for example of assessing whether the instrument is *intra vires* and whether the Welsh and English versions have the same meaning. After the scrutiny committee, the instrument is submitted to the Assembly as a whole. If the Assembly wishes to amend the instrument, it may do so, but must then re-submit the instrument to the scrutiny committee. Eventually, the Assembly resolves to approve the instrument and it passes into law after being signed by the Presiding Officer.

These proposals are very different from the path followed by statutory instruments which affect Wales at present. Basically, under current arrangements, statutory instruments are formulated in government departments; officials present final drafts to ministers, and ministers present orders on a take-it-or-leave-it basis to Parliament, where it is impossible for them to be amended and where few are even debated[18]. These Westminster subordinate legislation methods were described as 'palpably unsatisfactory' by a House of Commons Procedure Committee in 1996[19], and it might therefore seem a little rich to take any lessons from what Dafydd Elis Thomas called the 'most disorganised, inefficient, unaccountable, ramshackle, theatrical so-called legislature in the Western world'. However, some very sensible desiderata for legislative procedure were drawn up by the House of Commons's Modernisation Committee in 1997[20]. These can easily be read across to the Assembly. The criteria would then be:

i   The Executive of the day must be assured of getting its legislation through in reasonable time (provided that it obtains the approval of the Assembly).

ii   Other parties and Members in general must have a full opportunity to discuss and seek to change provisions to which they attach importance.

iii   All parts of a draft order must be properly considered.

iv   The time and expertise of Members must be used to good effect.

v   The Assembly as a whole, and its legislative Committees in particular, must be given full and direct information on the meaning and effect of the proposed legislation from those most directly concerned, and full published explanations from the Executive on the detailed provisions of its draft.

vi   Throughout the legislative process there must be wide accessibility to the public, and legislation should, so far as possible, be readily understandable and in plain language.

vii   The legislative programme needs to be spread as evenly as possible through the year.

viii   There must be sufficient flexibility in any procedures to cope with, for example, emergency legislation.

ix   Monitoring and, if necessary, amending legislation which has come into force should become a vital part of the role of the Assembly.

The NAAG proposals seem to fulfil these criteria very adequately, though there is less emphasis on the bipolarity of politics so familiar at Westminster. There is probably also a greater expectation that legislation will be an open, participatory process in Wales - a route favoured by, for example, Charter 88[21]. When we recall that this better legislative process is being applied to a class of legislation which is at present being considered in Parliament perfunctorily, if at all, it is clear that there will be a great potential enhancement of democratic control.

There is one area where more might possibly be done. Charter 88 make the specific proposal that Assembly subject committees should be able to initiate Assembly legislation whereas NAAG seems to regard this as an executive act. Legislative procedures should involve active participation by all elected members, and open consultation with the electorate: it should not be a rubber-stamp legitimation process. This implies that the right to take the initiative should belong to Subject Committees, 'opposition' parties, and even to individual MWAs, as it does to Westminster backbenchers.[22]

CONCLUSION

Legislation dominates the agenda of Parliament. It is unlikely to dominate the Assembly to the same extent, if for no other reason than that the Assembly will have other roles, alien to Parliament, of, for example, setting strategic priorities in Wales and of controlling the administrative programmes at present run by the Welsh Office. The amount of time taken on legislation in Cardiff will depend on a number of factors:

- The extent to which autonomy is given by London in future primary legislation.

- What mandatory legislative requirements are placed upon the Assembly.

- The desire of Assembly members to exercise powers that they are not obliged to exercise (for example, by reviewing and amending secondary legislation already applying in Wales).

- The extent to which the Executive Committee controls the legislative process, both in terms of timetable and initiative.

Any desire to be legislatively creative will also need to be tempered by the financial reality of the block grant, and the administrative ability of the Assembly's staff to formulate and draft the legislation bilingually.

Legislation will be an important facet of the Assembly's work. In some ways, one of the key tests of the devolution settlement will be the extent to which the Assembly will be able to legislate in a way that meets the aspirations of the Welsh electorate. The Assembly will certainly need to develop legislative methods which ensure full scrutiny and democratic participation. And flaws in legislation will undoubtedly be attacked in the courts by those at both ends of the devolution spectrum. But legislative methods should not be the main criteria by which the success of the Assembly will eventually be judged. To do so would be particularly unfair when the constraints under which the Assembly is able to legislate are borne in mind. But it will be fascinating to see how the Assembly adjusts to its legislative duties, and how proactive it will be, or will be allowed to be.[23]

References

1   The Consultation Paper of the National Assembly Advisory Group (NAAG) used a wider definition of subordinate legislation, including, for example, circulars and guidance. This issue was addressed in section 19 of the IWA's Constitution Working Group response to NAAG report, *The Operation of the National Assembly*, 1998. This paper does not address the important issue of legislation implementing European Community law.

2   Though this elides the question of the courts' powers in respect of primary legislation incompatible with European Union treaty obligations, or, after the passage into law of the Human Rights Bill, the European Convention on Human Rights.

3   Local authorities exercise powers delegated to them, and may, of course, have powers to make bylaws. But they would not be regarded normally as legislative bodies.

4   It is equally possible that the courts will be more flexible in their approach to statutory instruments made by the Assembly than they are to instruments made by the Secretary of State.

5   About 100 local statutory instruments are also made annually by the Secretary of State for Wales.

6   para 7 of Appendix I to 27th Report of Joint Committee on Statutory Instruments, 1997-8 (House of Commons Paper No. 33-xxvii)

7   The resource implications of drafting instruments which are different from those applying in England, and doing so bilingually, is obvious.

8   House of Commons Standing Committee A; 10 February 1998, col. 396

9   *Constitutional and Administrative Law*, 7th edition, page 362

10 Fourth Report, Select Committee on Procedure, 1995-96, *Delegated Legislation* (House of Commons Paper 152)

11 A particularly far-reaching Henry VIII power was given under the Deregulation and Contracting Out Act 1994. This Act allows

ministers to make orders amending or repealing primary legislation which imposes a burden on any person carrying on a trade, business or profession. These orders are subject to special parliamentary procedures and are scrutinised by special committees in each House of Parliament.

12   Evidence to House of Commons Select Committee on Procedure, Fourth Report, Session 1995-96, *Delegated Legislation*, page 60

13   Cmnd. 6503

14   *Making the Law*

15   op. cit. page 371

16   *A Voice for Wales*, para 3.39

17   Consultation Paper *op. cit.* chapter 8

18   This unamendability is partly the result of the difficulty of achieving consent to amendments from both Houses of Parliament.

19   Fourth Report from Procedure Committee, Session 1995-96, *Delegated Legislation*, para 1

20   First Report, Select Committee on Modernisation of the House of Commons, Session 1997-98, *The Legislative Process*, para 14

21   *Standing Orders, A New Political Culture for the National Assembly for Wales*, Charter 88, May 1998

22   Of course, Members of Parliament have no power to initiate secondary legislation at present, and it could be argued that Members of the Assembly should therefore have no such powers but that the Executive Committee alone should inherit the powers of the Secretary of State.

23   The kernel of this paper was delivered to the *New Politics and the Operation of the National Assembly* Conference held by the Institute of Welsh Affairs in Cardiff on 20-21 March 1998. It was refined as a result of a seminar held by the Institute on 12 June. Draft versions have benefited from the comments of Philip Davies, Paul Evans, David Miers, Robert Rogers, Roger Sands, Rhodri Walters and Barry Winetrobe - to all of whom, as well as to the Institute, the author is most grateful.

CHAPTER 7

DEALING WITH PRIMARY LEGISLATION

Keith Patchett

The National Assembly will not be a full-scale legislature. Its principal concerns are with executive action, such as allocating the budget, developing and implementing policies for Wales within a framework set by Acts of Parliament, setting targets for public bodies and monitoring their performance, increasing the public accountability of those delivering public services, and the like. Its legislative competence is confined to making subordinate legislation under powers transferred to it by the Secretary of State or directly delegated to it. These powers will enable the Assembly to implement Acts of Parliament by making instruments where none exist at the moment, or to replace or amend existing instruments where a policy change or factual circumstances require. But the authority to make primary legislation on the subject areas within the Assembly's responsibility is to remain with Parliament.

It will not be surprising if, in the early stages, the demands of establishing new executive decision-making and accountability procedures, and making them work effectively, limit the amount of legislative activity within the Assembly. At first, that activity may be primarily concerned with making those instruments that are essential in order to operate legislation recently passed by Parliament, such as the Schools Standards and Framework Act 1998. But as the 2003 election comes closer, members may feel the need to show policy initiatives and achievements, perhaps involving an element of radical divergence from the past, that can only be brought about by changes in law.

However, the Assembly's capacity to legislate is affected by the limits upon its competence that are set by Acts of Parliament, both past and future. The Schools Standards and Framework Act 1998, for example, will enable the Assembly (to which the Secretary of State's powers under the Act are to be transferred) to make its own provision on a wide range of matters, and indeed expressly allows it to decide not to make any implementing legislation at all on a number of issues.

Other Acts may allow rather less room for initiatives.

The Assembly therefore will need to concern itself with primary legislation that is in preparation in Whitehall or before Parliament which has implications for Wales, particularly when it may affect the functions of the Assembly itself. The Government of Wales Act says very little specifically about this matter, but there is no doubt that the Assembly will take an interest in these matters since the Government of Wales Act expressly authorises it to 'consider, and make representations about, any matter affecting Wales' (s.33). The uncertainty lies in how it can pursue that interest most effectively.

There are in fact a number of circumstances in which the Assembly may wish to take some action concerning primary legislation. These include:

1   Securing inclusion in the Government's legislative programme of some bill dealing exclusively with a Welsh issue, for example, a Welsh language bill.

2   Becoming involved with the preparation of bills that affect some Welsh interest, especially if they are likely to extend or contract the Assembly's powers.

3   Specifically, being involved with the formulation of those provisions of bills that will confer or alter the power of the Assembly to make secondary legislation.

4   Scrutinising the text of bills affecting such a Welsh interest, and monitoring their passage through Parliament, with a view to making Assembly concerns known and, where appropriate, to press for amendment.

5   Promoting or opposing private bills (that is, bills exclusively affecting some private interest or section of the community).

INCLUSION OF WELSH BILLS IN THE LEGISLATIVE PROGRAMME

The number of statutes that are concerned principally or exclusively with Welsh matters is very small in terms of the complete statute book. It may be expected that this will continue to be the case, although a go-ahead Assembly may increasingly find circumstances in which inadequacies peculiar to, or predominating in, Wales can only be dealt with if primary legislation is first put in place. For that to happen, a bill for such a purpose must find a slot in the Government's legislative programme, for which it must compete with claims from the Whitehall departments at the Future Legislation Committee. (The alternative - that the bill be made subject to the lotteries of private members' bills and procedures - seems unacceptable).

This may be eased if the legislation can be tagged into another bill, on a related topic, that has a stronger claim to a place in the legislative programme. It is not uncommon for departments to put forward bills that deal with several rather loosely-connected topics. In such a case, much will depend upon the willingness of the lead department on the bill to cooperate. The Assembly Secretaries may have a rather more difficult task in securing agreement than might have been the case when the Welsh Office and the department were working in tandem in a particular subject area. Departments could be required by concordats to consider and consult on such requests. What the Assembly cannot do is to try to apply pressure by establishing public support for new legislation under its power to hold a national poll – section 36 of the Government of Wales Act expressly precludes the Assembly from holding polls to ascertain public opinion as to how it might exercise its function of making representations on matters affecting Wales.

If the Assembly must proceed on its own, a direct request to the Future Legislation Committee for a slot will presumably not be countenanced, since the Assembly is not part of the central Government machinery. In any case, it would stand limited chance of success since the Assembly (or an Assembly Secretary) will have no claim to participate in the horse-trading that the Committee exercise sometimes appears to involve. Will it then fall to the Secretary of State for Wales to perform the function of making the case on the Assembly's behalf? The Government of Wales Act (s.31) sees it as the responsibility of the Secretary of State to consult with the Assembly about the contents of the Government's legislative programme but only when it is about to be acted on in Parliament. But presumably it would be open for the Assembly, whether then or on another occasion, to press the Secretary of State for inclusion of the bill in the programme. The Secretary of State, as a head of a department with general responsibilities for Wales, despite the radical reduction in its subject responsibilities, presumably will remain entitled to request a place for a bill in the next programme (or even that following).

An alternative suggestion has been made for the designation of an Agent-General for the Assembly in its relations with Whitehall, who could be recognised as entitled to participate in the bidding process on its behalf. But here, as in respect of other matters, it seems improbable that such a representative from outside the Whitehall system would be readily accepted, not least as the Assembly is unlikely to be seeking a legislative slot every year.

It is more probable that the Secretary of State will retain the responsibility. But in that event concordats will need to provide for continued access to correspondence touching on departmental claims and to papers of key cabinet committees relating to bids likely to come under consideration and for liaison on these matters with Assembly officials.

Such an arrangement is not wholly satisfactory, as much would depend upon how Secretaries of State perceive their relationship with the Assembly. After all, their primary commitment will be to the Government of which they are part. Whether a particular Assembly request is taken up, and other departments consulted, and the Committee case strongly pressed by the Secretary of State (who may have little by way of bargaining power in the Committee) may depend upon how the Secretary of State views the legislation and the likely reaction of other Ministers to what it seeks to do. The Secretary of State cannot be seen as the Assembly's advocate in Parliament or Whitehall, even when the Government and the Assembly majority come from the same political party. The Assembly may find that it is faced by vague promises and little urgency in terms of a place in the legislative programme.

Even if the bill does receive a place, a number of uncertainties need to be answered. Which body is the instructing agency? If it were to be the Assembly, its officials must have access to Parliamentary Counsel, presumably because the bill is a Government bill, and thus drafting will be undertaken by them. (In any case, it is doubtful that the Assembly will have the necessary resources either in policy-making or legislative drafting). But how can the Assembly be responsible to the Legislation Committee for adherence to the preparation timetable? Who would be expected to steer the bill through the Houses of Commons and Lords?

It is more probable that the formal lead would be given to the Secretary of State if the matter concerns an exclusively Welsh issue (for example, the language) or to the relevant Whitehall department for a matter of a kind that is within their usual remit. Concordats would then need to provide for full involvement of Assembly officials in the preparation and monitoring of the bill and giving them as full access during the parliamentary proceedings to the person in charge as departmental officials now have. Might not some changes in parliamentary procedures then be called for?

Similar considerations could arise in a case where the Assembly finds, in the course of performing its functions under a particular statute, that legislative weaknesses impair its ability to produce effective administration. To what extent will the Secretary of State be able to facilitate their need for primary legislation, given that he no longer has any formal responsibility for the subject matter for Wales and the overall responsibility rests with a Whitehall department? Will the departments pay closer attention to a request if it is channelled to it by the Secretary of State, than if it is made directly by the Assembly itself? Again, concordats will need to cover the relationship between the Assembly and the departments on these matters. The Secretary of State's office could well be expected to ensure that they are fully respected.

PREPARATION OF BILLS THAT MAY AFFECT WALES

The Government of Wales Act (s.31) ostensibly entitles the Assembly to be consulted by the Secretary of State about the bills which form the government's legislative programme for the coming parliamentary session and about bills subsequently introduced. The entitlement, however, is circumscribed by qualifications. The initial consultation is to take place 'as soon as reasonably practicable after the beginning of the session'; for the subsequent bills it appears likely to take place when the Secretary of State considers it to be 'appropriate'. The consultation need not take place if the Secretary of State considers that there are 'considerations that make it inappropriate'. The nature of the consultation is such as 'appears to the Secretary of State to be appropriate'.

It is a matter of conjecture how this process will be conducted. Will the Secretary of State consult only on bills dealing with matters of a kind already within the competence of the Assembly? Or will the Secretary of State enable the Assembly to take a view on all bills other than those that must remain confidential because of tax or other financial considerations or those that have to be proceeded with as a matter of urgency? Will the consultation be a one-off occasion when the Assembly is merely able to express its views on the information derived from the Queen's speech? Or will the consultation process be a protracted one which enables the Assembly, through its committees, to examine and comment in detail on the text of the legislation to be introduced? Will the Assembly be restricted in the types of matter on which it is expected to comment, as for example those provisions that are of direct concern to it, or will it be permitted to express its views on the basic policy, including, for example, whether a known matter of concern to the Assembly has been appropriately addressed?

In principle, the Assembly could have an interest in almost all legislation that goes before Parliament. Even bills relating to matters that are outside the executive competence of the Assembly can, in theory at least, have implications for Wales, or may benefit from a Welsh perspective. In the past, such views could be expressed within the Whitehall consultation machinery through the Secretary of State, or in Parliament by Welsh MPs. Those arrangements presumably will not change, but it is difficult to see a place for any formal machinery of representation, using these channels, for matters with which the Assembly itself cannot be directly involved. The most that a concordat can do is to enable Assembly officials to forward the Assembly's views to the relevant Whitehall department for consideration, along with other representations that might be made by other organisations. Whether those views are given weight may have to depend to an extent on the willingness of the Secretary of State or some MP to espouse them.

The Assembly has a stronger case for some more formalised machinery in relation to bills touching matters on which it already has or could be given an executive role. Presumably this is the main purpose of section 31 of the Wales Act. Patently, the value of that procedure will depend on the exercise by the Secretary of State of the wide discretion in the provision. There can be no guarantee that all Secretaries of State will take this process equally seriously. Here too, it may help if officials in the Secretary of State's Office are given responsibility for vetting all proposals for legislation, with full access to Cabinet committee correspondence, with a view to ensuring that the concerned departments comply with concordats which confer a right of consultation on the Assembly.

It is in this context that an important question must be asked - what will happen to the Assembly's comments? Legally, consultation involves the right to have views expressed properly considered by the person carrying out the consultation. Here, that person is the Secretary of State, not the sponsoring department. Does that mean that the Secretary of State is entitled to evaluate the views expressed and to decide whether, or the manner and extent to which, they are to be passed forward to the departments? Presumably the Secretary of State's officials can be looked to as a guaranteed conduit to the lead department for representations, even though the Secretary of State may personally not agree with all the contents. Again, his officials could be given the responsibility for ensuring that the department follows up those representations.

It is questionable too how far the Assembly can look to the Welsh MPs to represent its views in these settings. Even if in the initial Assembly there are MPs who are also members of the Assembly, it is hardly consistent with constitutional practice for those MPs, and even less for others, to be mandated to put the Assembly's case in Parliament.

This said, there is an underlying weakness in this procedure in providing an appropriate input by the Assembly into new legislation. By the time the Assembly is consulted, the department's views on policy are settled, the policy option and the mode of legal implementation long selected and the preparation and drafting of the legislative scheme are largely complete. This greatly restricts the Assembly's ability to influence the legislative outcome. Departments will be exceedingly reluctant to re-think the basics of the legislation. Not only has the Cabinet endorsed the statutory objectives and the Legislation Committee approved the draft as government policy, but any major changes represent a threat to the government's timetable for implementing the legislative programme. The most that the Assembly can realistically hope for at this stage are modifications of the scheme to meet particular concerns.

At least on bills that would or could make substantial changes to the functions of the Assembly, the Assembly input must be at the much earlier stages when the departmental policy is being evolved, the contents of the legislative scheme worked out and the provisions drafted. The case for this needs little justification. If the Assembly is to identify with changed policies, as set by the Government and Parliament, it needs to be assured that the legislation has taken account of existing Welsh circumstances and executive arrangements, and of the capacity of the Assembly to carry it into effect. Not least of the matters to be factored in are the financial implications both for the Welsh budget (given that changes will usually be funded through the block grant), and for the competitiveness of the private sector in the Welsh economy.

The Act is silent in this respect, providing no guarantees for the Assembly. It is in this context that the concordats are likely to have special importance, particularly if major ideological or policy differences were to emerge between the parties in power in Cardiff and in Westminster. The kinds of matter that the concordats might include:

- The right to seek the support of a department for the inclusion in a departmental bill of amendments to existing legislation to rectify shortcomings that have hindered the Assembly in the performance of its functions.

- The right to be informed of any bill listed by the Future Legislation Committee which impacts on a subject area within the competence of the Assembly at much the same time as the Whitehall departments.

- The right to receive relevant documentation relating to the legislative projects for such bills.

- The right to be consulted by the lead department in Whitehall during its appraisal of policy alternatives for such a bill and, if a compliance cost assessment or other regulatory appraisal is to be carried out, whether it should include Welsh concerns by reason of circumstances special to Wales and whether it is to be carried out by the Assembly under its business consultation powers (s.115).

- The right to make representations to the Cabinet Committee, probably through the Secretary of State, if the preferred policy option appears to disregard some essential Welsh dimension.

- In cases where the bill is likely to need important provisions specifically concerned with implementation in Wales, an entitlement to have Assembly officials part of the team preparing the bill.

- In other cases, the right to be consulted fully during the preparation of the legislative scheme and the drafting of the bill.

- The right, probably through the Secretary of State, to make representations about a bill to be considered by the Legislation Committee prior to its presentation to Parliament if the Assembly considers that it fails to meet Welsh needs.

Here too it may help if officials in the Secretary of State's office are given responsibility for vetting all proposals for legislation, with full access to Cabinet committee correspondence, with a view to ensuring that the concerned departments comply with their duty to consult the Assembly.

If such arrangements are made, an issue will be the extent to which the members of the Assembly are to be involved in them. Under current arrangements, there is a degree of confidentiality about aspects of the process, which it is not too difficult to maintain as those responsible are either Ministers of the Crown or civil servants (who can determine the extent to which information is made available to others outside central government). To a point, it may be possible to maintain necessary confidentiality under the new arrangements if the only persons involved on the Assembly side are Assembly Secretaries and Assembly officials (who technically remain part of the same civil service as the departmental officials). But we should bear in mind Peter Hennessy's observation about government departments:

> 'As Shirley Williams puts it, they have banners to defend on which
> departmental traditions and orthodoxy are emblazoned like fading regimental
> colours in a cathedral - and these are defended against all-comers whether they

be pressure-groups, select committees, international organisations or other ministries'. (Whitehall, 1990, p.380)

The arrival of the Assembly could lead to new strains on what are seen as departmental prerogatives when dealing with officials owing their immediate loyalty to an entity which is outside the central government structure. The concordats will have to command considerable adherence to overcome current inhibitions on cooperation.

The issue becomes more problematical if members of the Assembly are to have a role in the preparation process. Leaving aside possible resentment by MPs that elected representatives in the Assembly might have greater access to information about the direction of government policy, the departments themselves may be reluctant to allow a wider and possibly premature disclosure of their thinking. This issue may become less pressing as the new Freedom of Information policy takes effect, though it can never disappear. No doubt the concordats will confine the involvement to Secretaries and officials (and the Cabinet structure makes this more feasible). But is it reasonable to expect, for example, the subject committees to be entirely excluded from the process, or for the officials who service them to have to decline to pass on information derived during the preparation process? If the committees are to be allowed to consider such confidential information, consideration will have to be given to the standing orders excluding the public (under s.70(1)(b)).

As the former Secretary of State acknowledged (for example, *Hansard*, vol.309, col.618), the issue of confidentiality will have to be resolved through the concordats, perhaps by allowing the departments to indicate in particular cases the matters on which information given to a Secretary or official must be treated as confidential.

DELEGATION OF POWERS TO MAKE SECONDARY LEGISLATION

Much has been made of the fact that the Assembly will have extensive powers of secondary law-making. But it needs to be stressed that at present no general power to make secondary legislation is given to the Assembly. Its law-making powers will derive from individual Acts of Parliament, including the Government of Wales Act itself (for example, ss.27 & 28 in relation to the reform of certain public bodies) to implement particular subject-matters; their delegation sections will determine the scope of the power to legislate (s.21(b)).

At the outset a large number of law-making powers in existing Acts will be transferred to the Assembly, but the issue of additional powers will arise in relation to every future bill which touches upon a subject-matter within the general competence of the Assembly. Initially, however, almost all of the Assembly's law-making powers will be acquired through the devolvement under a Transfer Order of specific delegated powers that have been conferred by existing Acts upon the Secretary of State. It is only in the few cases provided for in the Government of Wales Act that powers are delegated directly to the Assembly itself (for example, s.28, above).

It remains to be seen which of these techniques is used in future Acts. The Act (s.21) allows for both possibilities. A theoretic difference between them may have little practical importance. In principle, the removal of a delegation made by an Act requires an amendment of that Act by another, whereas a transferred power could be reclaimed for a Secretary of State by revoking the relevant transfer order provision (Interpretation Act 1978, s.14). But the latter case requires approval by resolutions of both the two Houses of Parliament and the Assembly itself (s.22(4)). Further, it was made clear in Parliament that transfer orders were intended to be irreversible; the revocation power would be used only to correct errors; primary legislation would be the appropriate method of recovering transferred powers (Lords *Hansard*, vol.590, cols.187ff).

Which method is used will be of some interest to the Assembly. If the power is initially vested by a new bill in a Secretary of State, the Assembly may need assurances about the use of transfer powers. On the other hand, if, as seems possible, it becomes future practice to confer the power directly on the Assembly, foundations will be laid for a constitutional convention that requires that device to be followed by future Governments.

Further, the Assembly has an interest in the way that provisions on functions are divided between an Act and its secondary law-making power. If the Act itself contains substantial provisions on the subject matter, the room accorded to the Assembly for secondary legislation is likely to be restricted. Whether law-making powers are conferred at all on particular matters may be an important issue. On a controversial subject on which Whitehall has different policy perceptions from Cardiff, it is not ridiculous to contemplate the lead department giving instructions for the bill to be drafted so as to resolve the issues as the Government wishes, with a delegation of powers that virtually obliges the Assembly to implement the Government's preferred approach.

In the past, delegated powers have varied considerably from statute to statute, in some cases restricted as to the objectives to be secured and circumscribed as to contents, in others conferring a wide discretion in both respects. Instruments made under delegated powers must, of course, be *intra vires* in terms of the delegated power and consistent with the objectives of the parent Act. Since the Assembly must work within the limits set by the authorising Act, it has an interest in the precise terms of the delegation in a bill, and in particular the breadth of the power that will be conferred. Its ability to institute policy changes by secondary legislation will be determined by the scope of the delegated powers.

It remains to be seen how far Parliament will be prepared to accept delegation powers drafted solely for the Assembly's use in bills that deal with England and Wales. If it insists on largely common delegation provisions for both England and

Wales, it may find it necessary, in order to give the Assembly the required room for initiative, to confer on central Government wider powers than even in the past. An unsatisfactory consequence may be that the instruments applying to England will be subject to far less scrutiny and control under current Parliamentary procedures than will be the case in Wales.

On the other hand, will Parliament be ready to give the Assembly powers to legislate on matters that for England are provided for in detail in the bill itself? In particular, will those powers be drafted to permit the Assembly to pursue somewhat different policy objectives from those conceived in the parent Act for England? Presumably, there will be reluctance to give legislative powers that allow the Assembly to implement contradictory or conflicting policy objectives. Efforts might be made to draw a line deliberately to set limits to the Assembly's scope for innovation, which will necessarily be reflected in the terms of the authorising provisions.

Conversely, Whitehall may favour the practice of conferring on the Assembly broad powers to legislate to give effect to the general policy or principles of the Act in question. For the lead departments will typically have no operative interest in the mode of implementation in Wales. The most that may be required by the department are provisions necessary to obviate major contradictions which might create implementation problems in England or political difficulties for central Government. The extent to which the Assembly is entitled not to implement the Act might be spelled out expressly, thereby removing an area of legal uncertainty. Such an approach has the added attraction of reducing the scope for judicial review of the Assembly's subordinate legislation, as it is difficult to establish that an exercise of a power cast in very broad terms is *ultra vires*.

Indications that this approach might be feasible can be found in the Schools Standards and Framework Act 1998. Indeed, the broader the Assembly's power to make subordinate legislation on a particular topic, the closer the Assembly comes to having a competence equivalent to that of making primary legislation on that matter. These issues are of such great importance that the Assembly must be involved with the preparation of the legislation at an early stage before possible solutions have hardened into legislative provisions.

MONITORING AND AMENDMENT OF BILLS

A bill passing through Parliament can be subjected to a wide range of amendment proposals, particularly where significant policy changes are required. Accordingly, the lead department and, for bills affecting the Assembly, the Assembly too, must keep a close eye to determine whether proposals raise issues that call for desirable clarification of the bill. In addition, as an unfortunate feature of the law-making procedures in the United Kingdom, bills are introduced into Parliament, typically on controversial or complex subjects, though they need further work or are likely to undergo major changes during their passage following a re-thinking of policy. New procedures (such as two-year legislative programming and pre-legislative scrutiny) may discourage the inefficiency of these arrangements which undoubtedly affects the quality of legislation. But this possibility is another strong reason why the Assembly will have to establish procedures for monitoring the progress of bills that concern it.

Presumably, such functions would be principally a responsibility of the relevant Assembly Secretaries and their officials, though again the Subject Committees may have a role to play. If the Assembly has had formal involvement in the preparation of the bill, its responses to developments would be channelled through the departmental officials in charge of the bill. The resolution of differences may have to be the subject of the concordats, though the ultimate responsibility for the final decision must lie with the department (or most exceptionally at Cabinet level).

In cases where the Assembly has not been formally involved with the bill, the most it can do is to make representations, presumably directly to the lead department. Here too it will be in the hands of the department. The Assembly will have no power, of course, to put its own amendments directly to Parliament, nor would it be appropriate for the Secretary of State to table them (Hansard, vol.309, cols.600-603). While a sympathetic (Welsh) MP might be primed to take up an issue, he or she cannot do so in the name of the Assembly, even if happening to be a member of it. The proposal would have to take its chance for selection for consideration as any other backbench amendment motion.

In more general terms, it will be of interest to see how far it is necessary for the Assembly to keep the Secretary of State informed of its activities on legislative projects, in particular potential policy disagreements, both here and in the initial preparation of a bill. It may be questioned whether the Secretary of State is entitled to make a policy input (even if the resources of his office enabled a distinct position to be developed), since his former responsibility for the subject matter has been transferred to the Assembly. But is a broader trouble-shooting or conciliation function to be accorded to him?

PRIVATE BILLS

In principle, it may be thought that the Assembly is the most appropriate forum for regulating matters of the kind conventionally dealt with by private legislation, when they affect a particular section of the Welsh community only. Such bills are usually promoted by a body outside central government and are dealt with by special parliamentary procedures. But this is still a form of primary legislation and proposals to confer such powers even of this limited nature have not been accepted, since they are outside the scheme of the Government of Wales Act (Hansard, vol.307, cols 728ff).

However, the Act does remove any doubt about the Assembly's power to promote or oppose private bills before Parliament. This was added to the Act (s.37; Hansard, vol.309, cols.594ff), though its exercise is made subject to support of a two-thirds majority of voting members.

These powers have become less important in recent times. If the primary objectives can be met by means other than a private bill, Parliament now expects those to be followed. For example, the Transport and Works Act 1992 introduced procedures under which new undertakings such as tramways, inland waterways and certain harbour developments (for which private bills have been extensively used in the past) can be authorised by orders of the Secretary of State, rather than by primary legislation. But though the power to make those orders is to be transferred to the Assembly, the power to promote or object in these cases is expressly withheld (s.37(3)). Such a power is seen as tantamount to giving the Assembly primary law-making authority in this area.

The Government of Wales Act makes no reference to hybrid bills (that is, public general legislation introduced by Government that includes provisions affecting particular private interests), in respect of which Parliament allows petitions of those specially affected to be heard and considered (as in the case of the Cardiff Bay Barrage Act 1993). In principle, there seems to be no reason why the Assembly should not be treated as able to petition Parliament, as other executive authorities established by statute can, in the (probably exceptional) case where it meets the qualifications set by Parliament for petitioners. In any case, it is unlikely that such a bill would be introduced by Government except at the request of the Assembly or at least only after consultation with it. Accordingly, its position and powers of action are likely to be no different from those it may use in respect of other public legislation that affects a Welsh interest.

CONCLUSION

The issues relating to primary legislation impact indirectly upon the Assembly's main legislative work, which will be concerned with subordinate law-making. But the discussion serves to remind us that the Assembly can only pursue policies within the terms set by Acts of Parliament. There will necessarily be circumstances in which it will be legally powerless to make the changes it would like. Great care must be taken, for example in Assembly election manifestoes, not to promise action that cannot be taken. At the same time, the Assembly and central Government must establish procedures in connection with primary law-making that ensure that Welsh requirements cannot be sidelined on the grounds that the Welsh dimension in the administration of Acts is of no concern of central government departments.

In particular, it is in the longer term interest of the Assembly to press Whitehall and Westminster in drafting future bills to confer broad legislative powers directly upon the Assembly. The form in which new Acts devolve legislative powers will determine whether the Assembly is to develop a virtual primary law-making competence. If that happens, the establishment of the Assembly will indeed be a process and not an event.

CHAPTER 8

EQUAL OPPORTUNITIES

Neil Wooding

The case for promoting equality as a tool to challenge discrimination and mistreatment has never been stronger than at the present time. The work of Assembly members both implicitly and explicitly will be judged on how effectively the needs of individuals living in Wales are met through the provision of public services. Successfully meeting this challenge will rest upon mainstreaming the principle of equality into the work of the Assembly so that all operational and strategic decisions are made with reference to sustaining fair and equal outcomes.

There are practical steps the National Assembly can take to achieve equality through its work. Firstly, it should ensure the application of British and European equality law through all of its work. Secondly, it should ensure that the principle of equality is given priority and status within its own operations. Thirdly, it should establish a framework to monitor equality of information. Finally, it should implement an equality action plan to initiate change and chart progress.

The role of individual representatives in managing this process will be considerable. The work will need to be driven by an Equality Advisory Committee supported by a specialist unit. This will enable the Assembly to meet its statutory obligations. Its establishment offers an unprecedented opportunity to achieve fair and equal treatment for all people living in Wales and for re-politicising the equality agenda to bring benefit to those who have traditionally been excluded from mainstream society and subjected to considerable mistreatment.

The principle of equality should be established as a core value in the purpose and practice of the Assembly. It should find ways to demonstrate, through the political process, fair and equal treatment for all. In doing so, it will demonstrate that equality cannot be confined to the narrative of law, but should be embodied in every action and decision that a responsible government is empowered to take on behalf of the community it represents.

A challenge lies in the capacity of the Assembly to acknowledge and value differences rather than to ignore or exclude them when they deviate from the accepted norm. It is understandably easier for us to promote equality on the grounds of sameness or similarity than it is on the grounds of difference.

Developing a shared and inclusive understanding of equality will enable the Assembly to address social and economic processes which often determine disadvantage. One example is the way paid work has been traditionally organised without reference to family responsibilities. This has had a disproportionate effect upon women, who continue to carry the major responsibility for child and adult care. Another is the way public services are delivered which, often unintentionally, have fallen short of responding effectively to those with greatest need. Differing patterns of illness and disease which are determined by cultural and gender considerations have regularly resulted in elderly people, or those of a different racial background, being marginalised or excluded from effective healthcare, often at the time when they need it most. Mistreatment of this kind is often a process rooted in institutional behaviour.

Within the wider community, it is readily apparent that those who become dependent forfeit the right to question or challenge the public services which they receive. Relationships between the providers and users of such services are often based upon consumer or patient philosophies which deny such rights. In these circumstances, dependence can become in practice a disqualification for citizenship. People who, through no fault of their own, are dependent on public service provision, can for that reason be denied being treated in a fair and equal way.

PRESENT PATTERNS OF DISCRIMINATION

The under-representation of women in key areas of Welsh employment and public life reflect a pattern of historical inequality. Women on average earn 20 per cent less than men and have the second lowest earnings of any economic region across the United Kingdom. Only 22 per cent of public appointments go to women even though they involve the provision of services which are often predominantly used by women. Despite increasing skills and experience, women are still excluded from many senior management decision-making positions in the public and private sector revealing a pattern of systematic discrimination.

The treatment of black and ethnic minority groups inside and outside of the workplace indicates significant levels of racism ranging from physical violence to illegal job discrimination. Across south Wales incidents of racial harassment have been increasing faster than in any other part of the United Kingdom. This is generally unseen and unheard of by the majority white population who are inexperienced in recognising this form of treatment, but nonetheless are the perpetrators of it. Across Wales this has contributed to a culture of disbelief which often refuses to acknowledge the experiences of black people in relation to racial mistreatment.

The experiences of disabled people, although different, also testify to a pattern of mistreatment, denying access to education and employment. The exclusion of disabled individuals from the planning and delivery of services because of their disability, has often resulted in marginalising associated needs. These are, in turn, seen as problematic and of less importance.

To add further weight to this profile, the experiences of less 'socially acceptable' groups, such as lesbian women and gay men, people with mental health problems, ex-offenders and travelling communities, provide evidence of a catalogue of mistreatment which is often directed towards the most powerless and excluded in society. For these groups and many others, the process of exclusion has been driven by widespread cultural contempt and social hostility. This has often been expressed in subjecting such groups to public humiliation, physical violence and exploitation. In these circumstances, public disapprobation has been used to justify mistreatment often by those holding power and authority.

There is however, a paradox in the mistreatment of such groups and individuals. On the one hand they are exposed and made vulnerable to public discrimination and ritual abuse. On the other hand, however, they are rendered invisible as citizens and service users in the policy planning and public service process.

To effectively alleviate disadvantage and bring an end to mistreatment, the Assembly will need to address the processes that lead to inequality. Often the reasons for institutional and individual discrimination are unseen, resulting in action which addresses individual incidents rather than root causes. This rarely provides an opportunity to reflect upon the way we act and think as individuals and organisations.

As a consequence, we often think of discriminatory behaviour as exceptional rather than part of normal experience. To bring positive and lasting change, the Assembly will need to develop a programme of action to remove unfair discrimination and mistreatment from the management and delivery of public services in Wales. It should also support other organisations with whom it works to do the same. Simultaneously, it must seek to promote through policy and best practice, more equitable and humanitarian ways of treating groups traditionally excluded from mainstream Welsh society.

THE LEGAL IMPERATIVES

Members of the Assembly will be subject to British, European and International law. In addition the Assembly will be bound by its own statute. Clauses 47 and 113 of the Government of Wales Act declare:

Clause 47

The Assembly shall make appropriate arrangements with a view to securing that its business is conducted with due regard to the principle that there should be equality of opportunity for all people.

Clause 113

1   The Assembly shall make appropriate arrangements with a view to securing that its functions are exercised with due regard to the principle that there should be equality of opportunity for all people.

2   After each financial year of the Assembly, the Assembly should publish a report containing:

a   A statement of arrangements made in pursuance of Subsection (1) which had effect during the financial year; and

b   An assessment of how effective those arrangements were in promoting equality of opportunity.

To give effect to these statutory requirements, members of the National Assembly will need to engage in the following activities:

- Ensure the application of British and European Equality Law both in relation to its own work and the business of organisations working to its direction.

- Develop an organisational framework to ensure the principle of equality is given priority and status within the National Assembly.

- Establish a framework for monitoring and evaluating activity including the development of an ongoing database of relevant equality information.

- Implement an action plan to address inequalities through the provision of public service.

Members of the Assembly will also be subject to the following pieces of equality legislation:

- The Equal Pay Act of 1970 as amended in 1983

- The Sex Discrimination Act of 1975 as amended in 1986

- The Race Relations Act of 1976

- The Welsh Language Act of 1995

- The Disability Discrimination Act of 1996

In addition to this and as an emanation of the British State, the Assembly will be directly bound by Article 119 of the Treaty of Rome. This involves a responsibility to implement Directives, Recommendations and Codes of Practice in the spirit of promoting equality for specific disadvantaged groups across Wales.

POLICY OPTIONS FOR THE ASSEMBLY

Assembly representatives need to clearly understand the requirements of the law in order to identify and avoid discriminatory practice. They will also need to understand the differences between direct and indirect discrimination and acknowledge the importance of identifying unintentional mistreatment. There is a wealth of evidence that suggests that the majority of legal breaches occur as a result of ignorance rather than through deliberate action. The policy implications for the Assembly should be to:

- Ensure that all members are briefed on their individual responsibility to promote the law.

- Encourage members to use the law as a development framework for all groups and individuals rather than be a minimum standard of operation for some groups and not for others.

- Establish a strategic framework for achieving equality change across the work of the Assembly within specific time periods.

Developing an organisational framework to support the promotion of equality will be intrinsic to ensuring it becomes central to the work of the Assembly. Evidence suggests that success in challenging discrimination and reducing disadvantage is contingent upon establishing an open and ongoing discussion about inequality and ways to overcome it. This could be achieved by establishing an advisory committee linked to all the Subject Committees of the Assembly. This would ensure consistency in the promotion of equality across all areas of the Assembly's work. In turn this would encourage the exchange of best practice and establish a visible standard of operation.

To assist the committee, an Equality Unit responsible for coordinating action and supporting development would need to be established. Acting in an advisory capacity, the Unit would support the Assembly in meeting its equality objectives. It would offer a framework for promoting best practice across all public services and establish itself as an information resource to public service agencies working within the remit of the Assembly. Taking forward these initiatives would enable the Assembly to discharge its statutory responsibilities, ensuring that everyday business was carried out with due regard to promoting equality and avoiding discrimination. The policy implications of these proposals are as follows:

- Within the context of the Assembly's Standing Orders, an advisory group on equality issues should be convened.

- A framework for promoting a comprehensive and inclusive understanding of equality to inform the policies of the Subject Committees should be established.

- An Equality Unit should be established, clarifying its role in relation to the work of the Assembly.

- The assurance that the conduct of Assembly Members reflected a commitment to promoting equality.

Developing an equality monitoring strategy will require consideration to be given to the way in which services are carried out and organised. Strategies designed to tackle social and economic exclusion will need to be regularly monitored in order to measure success. This will need to occur in relation to all public services falling within the scope of the Assembly's work.

Developing a comprehensive monitoring system will enable each Subject Committee to reflect upon current practice by asking a number of questions relating to the way in which different groups access or benefit from its services. For example, in the field of economic development, these might include how many new businesses have been started by men, women, people belonging to a minority ethnic group or disabled persons, and which groups have been more successful in obtaining employment and why. Once gathered, this information will need to be critically analysed against current patterns of under-representation and exclusion.

To use monitoring data as the basis for developing action plans and remedial strategies, information will need to be dis-aggregated by gender, race and disability. Over time, this should become more sophisticated to include other groups that may be currently marginalised or excluded from any such analyses. This will enable a comparison of experience between different groups and individuals, highlighting any trends or patterns of activity which may be considered discriminatory. The policy implications of these recommendations are that:

- A monitoring framework to record all information appropriate to carrying out an equality audit should be developed.

- The internal operations of the Assembly as well as the delivery of public services should be monitored.

- A monitoring schedule is established to provide a framework for collecting, analysing, interpreting and publishing information each year.

- An equality audit, in effect a 'Social Trends and Practices Survey' should be published annually. This would bring attention to the treatment of specific groups and the role of the National Assembly in alleviating disadvantage.

The Assembly should develop a programme of action to introduce change to those public service areas failing to promote equality in their current arrangements. This may involve the need for positive action to counter the effects of long-term disadvantage and discrimination.

Such action programmes might be modelled on those developed by the European Commission. They are a tried and tested formula for achieving change and have been used extensively by public and private sector organisations throughout the United Kingdom. Taking action to remove discrimination and improve practices offers the only effective solution to removing discrimination and alleviating disadvantage for all people. The policy implications are as follows:

- A detailed social survey should be carried out to establish an accurate picture of disadvantage caused through mistreatment across Wales. This should be used to establish a base line against which the work of the Assembly can be measured over time. This could be supported by the experience of agencies working with disadvantaged groups across Wales.

- A framework for agreeing and initiating action within Subject Committees should be developed.

- Although action plans will be weighted according to the subject area and the degree of change required, it will be useful to focus upon key themes which offer ways of making equality happen in a mainstream way. These will include developing equal status partnerships, democratising decision-making, and inclusive approaches to consultation.

CONCLUSION

This chapter has provided a case for developing a new and inclusive definition of equality, one which comprehensively reflects the experiences of those who have been mistreated and discriminated against in Welsh society. The purpose of this has been to raise the level of individual commitment through knowledge and understanding in order to generate and sustain a programme of effective equality action within the National Assembly for Wales.

For the principle of equality to thrive within the working life of the Assembly, it must rest on the commitment of individual representatives to ensure equal treatment for all people living in Wales.

To learn the process of equal treatment, all Assembly representatives should be aware of the reasons for inequality, the different forms it takes, and how such acts are perpetrated. It is often the case that we believe in equality for some and not for others, and that we promote it as an act of generosity rather than an intrinsic right ascribed to all individuals.

CHAPTER 9

OPERATING THROUGH TWO LANGUAGES

Colin H. Williams

Bilingual or multilingual decision-making assemblies are the norm in contemporary world politics, whether within European Regional Legislatures, such as in Catalunya and Euskadi, within the organs of the European Union or within other supra-national organisations, such as the Council of Europe, NATO and the United Nations. In conforming with this international practice the National Assembly will be signalling its intention of being a modern, representative political institution and committing itself to serving its constituents in both the languages of Wales.

Nevertheless, to what extent has the role of the language changed now that we have achieved a National Assembly? The late J.R. Jones (Professor of Philosophy at the University of Wales, Swansea)used to say that, in the absence of other markers, we needed the language to act as the badge of the distinctive Welsh identity (J.R. Jones, 1967). Is that the case still? Is the purpose of the language to establish ourselves as a bilingual nation and thereby register our difference from our neighbours? Or, as some have argued recently, does having the Assembly in some way obviate that need, for other symbols have come to play the defining role in terms of our citizenship and participation in the national democratic process?

Social scientists have argued that the Welsh language is no longer the central symbol defining our separate identity within the UK. Major institutions established in the post-war era have taken its place as the key marker of national separateness. None is more significant than the proposed National Assembly, which together with similar developments in Scotland and Northern Ireland will recognise in formal terms the internal cultural political distinctiveness of the United Kingdom. Consequently Welsh socio-political life will be characterised increasingly by a robust civil society, which promises to be inclusive, community oriented and consensual. The language will remain an important but relatively minor component of national identity. The operation of the Assembly might itself become the defining characteristic of national identity. Politically this is a crunch issue, and within it lies a major danger to the Welsh language. There is a clear element within Wales which is non-Welsh speaking and deeply resents any implication that it is not truly Welsh. The argument is well known. Identity does not depend upon specific cultural markers but can be established, or even manufactured, around institutions. Hence 'nations' are not necessarily linguistically based. The Scottish and Irish experience is cited, where the Celtic languages are not greatly relevant to the maintenance of national identity for the vast majority of citizens. Countries like the USA and Australia have no distinctive linguistic basis (Ricento and Burnaby, 1998).

Others argue that the Welsh language has become de-politicised as a result of a number of reform measures culminating in the passing of the Welsh Language Act in 1993 and the establishment of the statutory Welsh Language Board. The Welsh language has been normalised and serves mainly as a medium of communication rather than as a symbol of a minority culture. It will have an important role within the Assembly as a functional means of expression, and consequently the old politics of confrontation will give way to a more accommodating approach to language choice. Following endorsement of Labour's devolution proposals in the Autumn of 1997 a new, more inclusive politics is said to characterise Wales. The cornerstone of this new political culture is participatory democracy which promises a new era of inclusive and consensual civic affairs. The previously fragmented nature of Welsh public life, divided by region, geography, history and, above all, language, may now be ameliorated by the establishment of a truly representative bilingual National Assembly.

A third viewpoint is that the 1979 devolution referendum reinforced deep linguistic and cultural divisions which have not disappeared over the last decade and a half. Severe doubts remain as to whether the Assembly, despite the rhetoric of the 'new politics', with its focus on 'open', 'inclusive' government, will initiate a new era of normalised use of Welsh. The Assembly may promise more than it will be able and/or willing to deliver in terms of promoting Welsh as a co-equal language of the nation. This viewpoint maintains that the Welsh language will continue to be a more potent symbol of national identity than the Assembly, especially as the latter is not a fully fledged Parliament. Doubtless the Assembly will be able to build on the reforms undertaken by the Conservatives, such as the support for S4C, the promotion of Welsh in the National Curriculum and the creation of a statutory Welsh Language Board. Nevertheless, it is difficult to be optimistic about surrendering the fortunes of the language to majoritarian British political parties whose language policies have been characterised more by short-term expedience than by absolute conviction.

However, to counterpose the Assembly and the Welsh language as alternative bases of national identity is to offer a mischievous view of the current reality. Surely they are more profitably seen as complementary and mutually reinforcing features of an evolving society? This was certainly the view of the overwhelming majority of Welsh speakers who voted Yes by a factor of seven-to-one in the 1997 referendum favour of the Assembly, according to one survey (Richard Wyn Jones and Dafydd

Trystan). Rather than view Welsh as a symbol of our separateness it is more constructive and realistic to view it as a social fact and as a natural medium of communication of a significant proportion of the population.

A cardinal rule is not to allow the Assembly's language policy to be embroiled in a long running political squabble, but to establish clear, firm guidelines for the promotion of both languages. These can be considered under three headings: the guiding principles by which guidelines will be adopted, the policies that will be necessary, followed by an analysis of the process through which the policies should be put into effect.

PRINCIPLES

While it is fair to assume that the Assembly, in legal and functional terms, will seek to operate in a comprehensive bilingual manner, legislation alone cannot create a supportive environment within which bilingual working practices will flourish. Rather it is the attitude of Assembly Members towards Welsh and promoting bilingualism which will be the determining factor. A range of opinion will be represented by the Assembly Members with most favouring institutionalised bilingualism, some content with symbolic bilingualism, and others displaying a hostile regard for Welsh, or presuming that it is irrelevant to our future, not realising perhaps that the increased numbers of young Welsh speakers, especially in south east Wales, has already changed the geo-linguistic landscape. Thus, the Assembly will be as Welsh in atmosphere as the majority of Members so desire, or ultimately as determined by the First Secretary.

Critics have cautioned that any attempt to rush the implementation of bilingual proceedings prior to the establishment of a proficient bilingual secretariat will alienate participants and damage the Assembly's credibility and commitment to the equal use of Welsh and English. Thus one of the first items for deliberation will be how to prioritise which elements of work, and determine which type of public documents, will be published in a bilingual format. There is a wide range of experience of these matters, especially at local government level where, among others, Gwynedd County Council may be cited as a model of how to operate a bilingual administrative system. Its commitment to clear guidelines, comprehensive oral and written translation facilities, and a supportive attitude on behalf of its members and officers, has minimised potential conflict between Welsh and non-Welsh speakers.

Establishing a strong bilingual infrastructure for the Assembly is an essential pre-requisite for being able to operate effectively. The guidelines need to be agreed well in advance of the election so that prospective members understand the rules of engagement. Leaders of the political parties recognise this necessity but need to convince some of their members that the Assembly could be the biggest boost yet to the promotion of Wales as a bilingual society and not as a society comprised of a majority and a minority linguistic community.

POLICIES

It is recognised that a fine balance needs to be maintained between priority, precedence and pragmatism in the execution of policy. There has been speculation whether use of Welsh within the Assembly will be seen mainly as a *symbol,* as a marker of Welsh differences, or whether it will seek to develop policies aimed at promotion, access and strategy? The example of Ireland contains important lessons. The Irish language in the Republic is highly visible at a superficial, symbolic level but rarely used on an everyday basis. The current consensus in Wales is that the Assembly will be committed to developing a substantive bilingual policy within a multicultural context. In time, of course, it could also seek to adopt a stronger multilingual line, in keeping with the demands of a rapidly evolving European Union.

The Assembly should prepare its own internal language plan and, given its pre-eminent position, the quality of the plan's implementation will be of vital concern to all other public bodies, as the Assembly should be seen to lead by example.

National language policy will likely focus on three important aspects. First, language policy needs to be developed in relation to citizenship, rights and the socialisation of Welsh youth. This would involve issues such as interaction with the British state and its unwritten constitution, the European Convention on human rights, European Community language policies, the development of bilingual education, bilingual service provision in local government, health and social services. Secondly, there is a need for economic policies and regional development initiatives which seek to stabilise predominantly Welsh speaking communities, to create employment, and to promote bilingual working opportunities. Thirdly, there should be consideration of the interests of Welsh language and culture as they are impacted upon by town and country/structure planning and improvement's to the transport system (James and Williams, 1997). In addition the pressing housing, property control and rural service issues highlighted by various bodies including Jigso and Cymdeithas yr Iaith (1998) should be addressed directly.

A fundamental precept of the Assembly's mission should be that its policies on bilingualism should be complemented by the promotion of positive attitudes to Welsh culture and heritage.

PROCESS

The central issue is how the Assembly operates as a bilingual institution. Basic guidelines for the use of Welsh and English in the National Assembly have been specified in clause 46 of the Government of Wales Act:

1   The Assembly shall in the conduct of its business give effect, so far as is both appropriate in the circumstances and reasonably practicable, to the principle that English and Welsh languages should be treated on a basis of equality.

2   In determining how to comply with subsection (1), the Assembly shall have regard to the spirit of any guidance under section 9 of the Welsh Language Act 1993.

3   The standing orders of the Assembly shall be made in both English and Welsh.

While the Welsh Language Act (1993) speaks of treating Welsh and English on a basis of equality in the conduct of public business, the Act, in Clause 46, is less limited in its scope. The Assembly must treat both languages equally (as far as is both appropriate in the circumstances and reasonably practicable) in the conduct of its business; that is, *all* of its business, whether public or not. This is a more far reaching norm than that previously encouraged under the Welsh Language Act. The Labour Government's unambiguous commitment in the White Paper *A Voice for Wales* to give equal status to both languages has therefore been transferred to the Government of Wales Act and has been warmly welcomed by many agencies and political parties.

Thus the Assembly's standing orders will need to translate the principle of equal treatment into practice. Initial deliberations on these matters have been entrusted to the National Assembly Advisory Group whose consultative document outlined three principles regarding bilingual practice:

- The Assembly should adopt and extend the Welsh Office's existing Welsh language scheme;

- Members should be able to use English and Welsh in Assembly debates and Committee Meetings;

- Members of the public should be able to use English and Welsh when communicating with the Assembly.

On the basis of submitted evidence NAAG anticipate that there will be practical barriers to full implementation of these principles and suggest that a target date be set by which comprehensive bilingual provision will be in place(1998: 27). Until then they suggest the following key priorities:

- Simultaneous translation (Welsh into English) for Assembly debates and committee meetings;

- Simultaneous translation (Welsh into English) available for meetings with the public;

- Publications, and documents available to the public being in both English and Welsh;

- Papers submitted for consideration by Assembly Members in plenary sessions and committee meetings to be available in both English and Welsh;

To this we may add:

- Preparation of the equivalent of *Hansard* for the Assembly should reflect the principle of equal validity. That is to say, it should record the contributions verbatim in whichever language they are spoken. Contributions spoken in Welsh should be translated into English, following the simultaneous oral translation, but the first and primary version recorded will be in the language of the speaker.

- The Assembly's physical infra-structure, its chamber and offices, together with its administrative routines and electronic networks, should be constructed so as to enable bilingual and multilingual technical facilities to be employed in the most user-friendly and unobtrusive manner.

- The visual identity of the Assembly and its capital buildings should reflect its bilingual character.

- Members of the public who wish to interact with the Assembly in an electronic format should be able do so in either Welsh or English.

All the above are essential if Welsh and English are to be considered co-equal languages of Assembly life from the outset. Indeed, if this were not achieved there would be a permanent campaign to rectify the situation. Such an arrangement would reflect both the principle of equal validity of Welsh and English and the principle of equal opportunity. This would empower citizens and members by enabling them to exercise their language choice as a matter of right rather than as a reflection of administrative convenience.

NAAG (1998) anticipate practical barriers to realising the above priorities 'in the early days' and suggest a timetable for full implementation. However, it would be unsatisfactory to try to 'tack' a comprehensive bilingual practice on at a later date as this would undermine the principles of equal validity and opportunity. One barrier, currently an unknown quantity, will be the resources in terms of staff able to provide bilingual service. This is an issue of the utmost delicacy. Current plans to train in-house Welsh Office staff and to recruit new bilingual employees are well advanced, but there is no clear indication so far as to whether they will be employed in general across a range of Assembly functions, or whether their work will be concentrated in specific departments. This will be discussed below. Pragmatic considerations will determine the timetable for achieving a comprehensive service, but it is imperative that an unswerving commitment to this goal be given from the outset. A parallel and precedent exists in the application of the Education Act of 1988, under which several Local Education Authorities were given time (in accordance with a strict deadline), to engage qualified Welsh-medium staff before implementing the National Curriculum in its entirety.

It may be that the question of drafting statutory instruments in Welsh will also take a little longer as suitably qualified translators are trained to the highest possible standard. However, the aims should be clearly specified before the first Assembly term so that it does not become embroiled in a long drawn out debate on first principles.

The Standing Orders will have to incorporate a general ruling whereby the issue of a disparity between two language versions can be resolved without necessarily giving automatic preference to one version over the other. It is also probable that a Language Standardisation Centre will need to be established at the earliest possible date, in line with the 1995 recommendations of the Official Welsh Panel of the Welsh Language Board.

RELATIONSHIP OF THE ASSEMBLY WITH THE WELSH LANGUAGE BOARD

To what extent, and in what ways will/should the Assembly take over the role of the Welsh Language Board? How can its functions be better realised in a possibly different, more democratic, organisational format? Will we need a dedicated, specialist body to continue to achieve this, or could it be done by a committee of the Assembly working directly with the civil service? Should the Assembly include a Language Planning Centre in addition to a Language Standardisation Centre? Should the Assembly consider the need to establish the office of a Language Ombudsman to oversee/audit the operation of the Welsh Language Act, as in Canada? How is it possible to change the current procedures so that a correct usage of Welsh in all signs and public documentation is realised?

Welsh has achieved a renaissance not through the operation of an overt democratic process but rather via the exertions of pressure groups, the activities of influential networks, strategic enabling legislation and the operation of a Quango. For some, the notion that somehow 'democracy', as expressed in the Assembly, will advance the language is unrealistic when the overwhelming majority of the constituency does not speak Welsh. There may now be a sentimental regard but there is no guarantee that it will carry the day when hard financial decisions have to be made. There is a crucial need, therefore, for a dedicated specialist body responsible for language matters. Clearly it would have to be accountable to the Assembly, but it should not be a committee of the Assembly. Bluntly, however it is dressed up for public appearance, it should remain in essence a quasi-autonomous but democratically accountable body. Again, from the operation of such a body a Language Planning Centre should emerge so that the impact of socio-economic decisions, as well as physical planning, can be evaluated in relation to language well-being.

There are limited grounds for arguing that the responsibilities of the Welsh Language Board could be transferred to the Assembly, with the shouldering of such responsibilities shared by the majority of Assembly Members. One direct implication would be that the Assembly had a mandatory duty to promote Welsh. However, should this transfer of responsibilities happen it is possible that the Assembly *en masse* would be less committed to the language than is the Welsh

Language Board. If this is likely, then there is little merit in initiating a transfer of responsibilities. Far better to strengthen the co-ordinating function of the Language Board which would militate against the severe fragmentation which has bedevilled previous efforts at language promotion.

In addition to these organisational considerations, two other technical problems remain. First, which organisation within the Assembly will be responsible for the development of language policy? Secondly, which internal body will consider appeals in relation to the content of language schemes and to make a decision to request judicial advice to take action against a public body? The latter question is far from straightforward in legal and procedural terms.

The Language Board should be retained in its current form with the Assembly taking over the role of the Secretary of State with regard to it. The strengths of the Language Board lie in its ability to plan strategically, its partnership links with statutory and voluntary grassroots bodies, and its ability to call on expert knowledge from among its ranks. Too great a proximity to the day-to-day business of the Assembly might detract from these strengths. As long as clear lines of accountability exist between the Welsh Language Board and the Assembly it should remain 'at arm's length'. The Board should be answerable directly to the appropriate First Secretary and would work in close liaison with the Chair of the Welsh Language and Culture Committee should one be established.

It is too early to gauge the full impact of the success of the Welsh Language Board, especially in relation to its Language Schemes, but there can be no doubt that it has achieved a great deal in a short space of time. It is a matter of considerable debate as to whether the Language Board should accrue more powers to itself and be responsible for the disbursement of most, if not all, grants which are targeted toward the promotion of either the Welsh language or Welsh medium organisations. Such a move may have a logical premise but could be politically damaging as it would make the language over-dependent upon the nuanced values and policy directions of just one organisation. However, should the Language Board yield to the Assembly its influence in directing change through grant disbursement, it is difficult to envisage it retaining any real power and control over the fortunes of Welsh.

With regard to the approval of language schemes, in as much as these are agreed between the Language Board and individual bodies it is difficult to see where the Assembly would usefully play a role. The Assembly's political role is to identify the broad principles of Welsh language policy, to decide how far to move along the spectrum from voluntarism to compulsory bilingualism, to identify priorities such as promotion, access or consolidation, and to integrate the interests of Welsh into all spheres of life in line with current holistic views on language planning.

A key question is whether or not the Assembly would have the authority to grant to the Welsh Language Board the right and the duty to monitor Assembly deliberations and actions with regard to the Welsh language. Conversely, should the

Assembly operate a co-equal bilingual policy it could be argued that there is little need for a separate Welsh language and culture subject committee. However, operating a bilingual policy is one thing; having a watching brief for the fortunes of Welsh culture is quite another and the two should not be conflated. There is a *prima facie* justification for a Welsh Language and Cultural Committee separate from, but directing the activities of the Language Board, as well as determining national language and cultural policy.

There is considerable merit in the idea of a Language Planning Centre which would have a holistic brief to monitor material issues which influence the development of both English and Welsh. This could either be a unit within the Language Board or, more likely, a joint venture with a specialist academic centre. Additionally, the Assembly could lead the way in establishing a body devoted to language standardisation and to devising and diffusing technologically innovative and proficient ways of working in a bilingual environment. Many caution that such an institution should not be the preserve of language purists and should not take on a language policing function. That is to say, those varieties of contemporary Welsh which are heavily influenced by English should not be condemned nor praised, simply recognised as a fact of social life.

It is doubtful whether the Assembly has the authority under clauses 28, 29 and 33 of the Act to establish the Office of a Language Ombudsman who could intervene in disputes over the language schemes of public authorities. This was clearly a significant omission from the 1993 Bill as the very fact of agreed language schemes begs the question of assuring compliance.

Current wisdom suggests that, notwithstanding the success of the Language Ombudsman in Canada, Wales is unprepared for yet another agent of language implementation and is only slowly accommodating to the reality of the Welsh Language Board exercising real statutory power. There may be scope for including elements of language-related grievance and compliance within the remit of the current Ombudsman, or there may be scope for devolving some of these functions to a strengthened Language Board. The idea of a Language Ombudsman should not be rejected, however, as our neighbours in Ireland, in considering a new Irish Language Act, have already decided to establish a Language Ombudsman as an integral part of implementing the new Act.

All these matters will ultimately be down to political will which will remain an unknown variable until the Assembly is in place and matures as an effective instrument of change. It could be argued that the *ad hoc* nature of Welsh language policy making in the 1980s and 1990s lacked transparency. The inclusion of the Welsh language as a foundation subject within the National Curriculum in English-medium schools across Wales in 1988 exemplified this. The issue of transparency does not just relate to policies regarding the Welsh language. The referendum campaign itself demonstrated a broad lack of awareness about how decisions governing services were made in Cardiff rather than London, which reinforces the perception of Wales lacking a civic identity and a sense of ownership about some of its institutions and administrative practices. The Assembly will bring much more transparency to decision making and, in turn, this will impact on the development of Welsh language policy.

PRACTICAL PROBLEMS

An important, hitherto unresolved issue is the division of responsibilities between the Assembly and other arms of the UK government in relation to the Welsh language. For example, how may responsibilities for the Welsh language and culture be divided between the Assembly and the Department of Heritage in Whitehall? The White Paper did not raise this issue, but the Assembly may well be interested in the question.

The Welsh Office is currently recruiting and training translators and proficient bilingual administrators. There is a real worry as to the bilingual capacities of senior administrators, and a presumption that there will be an unevenness in the quality of the bilingual service provided within different sections of the Assembly's work. It is feared that this unevenness will derive both from the relative commitment of the Committee Members to operating in a bilingual fashion, and also from the standard of fluency displayed by key officers in different departments.

A central issue will be the extent to which Welsh can become a cross-cutting medium of governance and administration and not limited to its own Committee for the Welsh language and culture - that is, not become commodified and separated out as a 'problem area'. This should not happen if the principles enunciated at the beginning of this chapter are put into effect.

A second issue is the degree to which establishing a bilingual Assembly will influence the language-choice behaviour of the public. Critics sympathetic to the promotion of Welsh have observed that local authorities have invested heavily in Statutory Language Schemes which in reality are of little interest to all but a handful of Welsh speakers. It would be regrettable if the Assembly's commitment were not matched by the public's adoption of Welsh as a language of interaction with national government. In this context the Assembly should use its position as an exemplar, a testing ground, an educator and a significant actor to influence behaviour in this regard.

A third issue is the supply of specialists to operate the Assembly. Critics have warned that just as the development of a bilingual media (between 1982-1997) drew mainly on the talented professionals of Welsh-medium schools and chapels, so the fresh opportunities afforded by the Assembly and its associated domains will pose a second threat to the staffing levels of the education system. This is a major challenge to the University sector which as a matter of urgency should provide training courses and bilingual specialist diplomas in matters related to a range of functions which fall under the remit of the Assembly.

The Assembly has the potential to be a major fillip to the fortunes of Welsh but it should not be viewed either as the 'saviour of the language' or the sole agency for language promotion. Other voices should be encouraged as I have detailed elsewhere (Williams, 1995).

The Assembly's language policy will certainly impact upon the private sector, both directly and indirectly. A precedent for this may be found in the banking sector whose official standpoint in the mid-1980s was 'English is the official language of business in Wales'. Now, following the Welsh Language Act, they are competing with one another to provide bilingual services as they have realised that such moves are popular with a proportion of their customers. We do not necessarily have to wait for additional legislation for the private sector. Making current public policy more effective and thereby inducing behaviour modification should suffice for the private sector in the short term.

TRANSLATION PROCEDURES AND FACILITIES

The Welsh Office is aware of the translation requirements of Assembly provision under the Government of Wales Act. What is not known is the extent of the additional work likely to be produced as a result of the decisions of the Assembly. The Welsh Office's Translation Unit together with the Welsh Language Board have explored the implications of two key areas, namely those determined by the Assembly's Standing Orders, which establish its procedures and also the Executive Department's dealings with Assembly members. In its official advice on these matters the Language Board's Translation Committee (WLB, 1998) gave particular consideration to the following issues:

- The *Report of the Proceedings* of the Assembly itself or any of its committees or sub-committees to include a translation of the exact words spoken in Welsh into English (the Committee assumed that the reports would be in *Hansard* format, rather than traditional minutes).

- Equal status for both languages at every meeting.

- The right of every member to speak in both languages.

- The right of every member (and of course the public, which is not a matter for Standing Orders) to have a simultaneous translation into English.

- Every document produced by the Executive Department for members for any meeting to be bilingual (or to be available in both languages at the same time).

- The Act states (in clauses 65(4) and 114) what standing orders will have to ensure as far as the language of subordinate legislation is concerned.

The Translation Committee summarise that there are three main aspects of this work:

- Word for word translation of minutes.

- Translation of documents for members from Welsh into English and English into Welsh (it is assumed that officials will be able to provide documents in either language).

- Provision of simultaneous translations from Welsh into English for all meetings governed by standing orders.

In determining the Executive Department's dealings with members simultaneous translation requirements are likely to go further and include:

- Meetings between members and officials.

- Less formal meetings between members/party members and so on.

- Non-public meetings between members, officials and others (for example, briefing sessions).

Documents likely to be translated include the following:

- Directions, signs and advice for members together with all general information about the Assembly.

- Members forms (for example, costs, declaration of interest).

- Messages, including bulletin boards, oral and electronic messages, and external correspondence.

An important consideration is whether the Assembly will provide a translation service for members, so that constituency correspondence, for example, could be conducted in Welsh. A related need would be Welsh language tuition for those members wishing to improve their linguistic skills. These exemplars raise an important issue, namely that it is of little value declaring that both English and Welsh are co-equal languages of the Assembly if the supporting infra-structure is not available to realise a free language choice. Thus it is crucial that investment be made both in the human resources of the Translation Unit and in the technical field of information technology. The current potential of the latter is not fully developed. It might consist of constructing databases of standard and specialist terms so that one Welsh term would correspond to one English term and vice versa; the upgrading of *CySill* and *CysGair*; the licensing of Welsh versions of standard computer packages and office systems; the development of speech to text procedures; the production of the *Welsh Academy Dictionary* and the *Legal Dictionary* on CD-ROM; and the incorporation into the Assembly's computer network of all previously released specialist publications such as *Termau Adeiladu*

(Terms for the Building Industry) or *Geirfa Amgylchedd y Dŵr* (Terms for the Water Environment).

The Translation Committee have also considered the possibility of information technology enabling most documents to be issued electronically. However, for both paper and electronic versions to be available at the same time, they will not have to be distributed bilingually. Members can choose either version, or both (in the case of learners, for example). They recommend that paper documents should always be prepared bilingually, and in the case of word-to-word minutes, both versions should appear side by side, with the original words on one side and the translation on the other.

Sensitivity to the whole question of translation is vital, but the Assembly has an excellent opportunity to display positive discrimination in favour of bilingualism and in promoting the exciting idea that both languages are the natural heritage of all residents of Wales with a view to establishing not greater bilingualism in Wales but a bilingual Welsh society (Williams, 1988).

LINGUISTIC POLICIES AND THEIR INFLUENCE ON NATIONAL DEVELOPMENT

How far will the Assembly be part of the process of creating (or re-making) Wales as a bilingual country, as opposed to one comprised of two relatively discrete linguistic communities? At present there is a fairly thin patina of bilingualism in place. What trigger factors can the Assembly influence which will deepen the whole process of operating effectively within a bilingual context? Alternatively, is there a danger that the Assembly might encourage or even promote the slide backwards to separation of the languages? Is there a role for the development of a policy of bilingualism within a multicultural framework as opposed to bilingualism within a bicultural framework to take account of Wales's culturally plural population?

If the Assembly can be widely seen as operating an effective bilingual policy it could bring a great deal of benefit in normalising the language. Success will rest with the way in which the operation of the Assembly is conducted and conflicts between Welsh-speakers and non-Welsh-speakers, if not avoided, are at least mediated. The Assembly *can* remake a bilingual Wales but it will rest largely on the expertise and sensitivity of those in government. It can also directly influence related organisations by the manner in which it exercises its fundamental commitment to operating as a bilingual institution. Achieving this would include the comprehensive televising of key debates and selected committee meetings and the adoption of sophisticated tele-communication systems to disseminate information.

If the Assembly adopts a robust attitude towards functional bilingualism it will serve as a tremendous fillip to other organisations. However, should it adopt a lukewarm or patronising attitude this will serve to undermine many of the real gains made subsequent to the Language Act.

The Assembly's recruiting policy and training programme could also impact on the public sector and especially local government. Currently there is an acknowledged shortage of competent accredited translators, experienced language tutors, and skilled bilingual administrators and technical specialists. The training infra-structure for a bilingual workforce is woefully inadequate. Consequently, special attention should be paid to how the Government's training agencies, such as the TECs, are resourcing or failing to resource the required training programmes for an increasingly sophisticated, bilingual economy. There is a skills gap in the workplace which needs to be addressed urgently if the relationship between the Assembly and the rest of the public sector is to operate harmoniously. The Local Government Management Board suggests that the Welsh Office and the TECs should acknowledge this skills shortage and establish industry-recognised accredited courses for training tutors. This would necessitate a partnership between the Further Education Colleges, the Universities and the WJEC together with the TECs to develop accredited intense and part-time courses. Government agencies should recognise Welsh language courses as a necessary skills-based training qualification for those searching for employment. In recognising the necessity for such skills, agencies should pay both course and examination fees and lobby to receive government assistance for upgrading the skills level of its employment force as a consequence of the changes set in train by the Welsh Language Act, 1993.

In addition, strong positive messages on the societal value of bilingualism will not go unheeded within the private sector, and surely this is how cultural development takes place. If the National Assembly is to succeed as a political institution people from all over Wales must be able to engage with it and feel a sense of shared **ownership**. This would contribute to the emergence of a common Welsh **civic identity** based upon a mutual respect for both languages.

References

Anderson, B, (1991) *Imagined Communities*, London: Verso.

Cymdeithas yr Iaith (1998) *The Welsh Language in the Next Millennium*, Aberystwyth:Cymdeithas yr Iaith Gymraeg.

Hobsbawn, E. and Ranger, T. (ed.), (1983) *The Invention of Tradition*, Cambridge: Cambridge University Press.

James, C. and Williams, C.H. (1997) *Language and Planning in Scotland and Wales*; in MacDonald, R. and Thomas, H. (eds.), *Nationality and Planning in Scotland and Wales*, Cardiff: The University of Wales Press, pp. 264-302.

Professor J.R. Jones (in translation, originally published in Welsh in 1967) *Need the Language Divide Us*, Planet No. 49/50, January 1980.

Jones R. W. and Trystan D. *How We Voted on Wales' Future, Agenda*, Institute of Welsh Affairs, Summer 1998.

Lewis, S. (1926) *Egwyddorion Cenedlaetholdeb*, Caernarfon:Plaid Cymru.

NAAG (1998) *National Assembly for Wales*, Cardiff: National Assembly Advisory Group Consultation Paper, Welsh Office.

Ricento, T. and Burnaby, B. (eds.), (1998) *Language and Politics in the United States and Canada*, Matawah, N.J.: Lawrence Erlbaum Assocs.

Welsh Language Board (1998a) *1997-98 Annual Report and Accounts*. Cardiff: Welsh Language Board.

Welsh Language Board (1998b) *Meeting the Translation Requirements of the National Assembly for Wales*, Cardiff: Welsh Language Board.

Williams, C.H. (1988) *Addysg Ddwyieithog yng Nghymru Ynteu Addysg Ar Gyfer Cymru Ddwyieithog?* Bangor: Canolfan Astudiaethau Iaith, 1. 1-28.

Williams, C.H. (1995) *Questions Concerning the Development of Bilingual Wales* in R.M.Jones and P.A.Singh Ghuman(eds.), *Bilingualism, Education and Identity*, Cardiff: University of Wales Press, pp. 47-78.

Williams, G.A. (1982) *The Welsh in their History*, London: Croom Helm.

Acknowledgements

This chapter is a synthesis of ideas received in response to a briefing paper distributed by the author between March and June 1998 to a cross-section of public bodies, representatives of political organisations, academic specialists and private citizens.

Written responses were received from and /or interviews were conducted with the following: Professor Harold Carter; Cymdeithas yr Iaith Gymraeg; Cynog Dafis, MP; Eifion Davies, Gwyn Jones and John Walter Jones of The Welsh Language Board; Lord Gwilym Prys Davies; The European Bureau for Lesser Used Languages, Dublin; Gwynfor Evans; John Albert Evans; Ifor Gruffydd, Isle of Anglesey County Council; Gwilym Humphreys; Clive James, Chief Executive's Department, Gwynedd County Council; Mari James, National Assembly Advisory Group; Huw Lewis; Iorweth Morgan; Euros Owen and Rhian Huws Williams, Central Council for Education and Training in Social Work; John Phillips; W.H. Raybould; John Rowlands, Environment Agency Wales; Gill Stephen, Local Government Management Board; Dr Alys Thomas, The University of Glamorgan; Gareth Thomas, MP; and Sharon Williams, Torfaen County Borough.

John Shortridge (The Welsh Office) gave an excellent account of current strategic planning for the Assembly at a seminar in my department on 28 April 1990 which proved very helpful. I am grateful to my colleagues Professor Glyn E. Jones and Jeromy Evas for their constructive criticism of this chapter.

CHAPTER 10

THE PRESS AND MEDIA

Geoff Mungham and Kevin Williams

The success of the Assembly depends on broad-based support from the people of Wales and the mass media will play a vital role in building that support. The process of political change will, of course, turn upon the impact the Assembly has on Welsh life, in all its aspects. Yet the Assembly has still to excite the popular imagination in Wales. The referendum campaign failed to stir half the nation into even bothering to vote. Events since September 1997 (for instance, the damaging wrangle over the siting of the Assembly) have hardly served to raise the level of public enthusiasm for the 'project'. How the media choose to cover the work of the Assembly will, to a large extent determine the profile of the new body and popular perceptions of it. In turn, the Assembly's own effectiveness will depend in part on how well it manages to communicate with the electorate.

Ours is a culture of change. The Assembly is part of a wider process of 'redefining' our political culture. At the same time there are other forces at work (commercial and technological) which will not only act to reshape the media in Wales, but also affect the Assembly. Take, for example, the speed and impact of technological innovations. These include the start-up of digital broadcasting, the spread of cable and satellite systems and the opportunities presented by the Internet and other forms of interactive media. Properly used, the new technologies could determine not only ways in which the Assembly is covered, operates and delivers its services, but affect those services themselves. The potential for job creation, inward investment and innovation in service provision - which can ride on the back of these new technologies - are highly relevant to the work of the Assembly, especially in the areas of economic development, education and skills training. The same technology also offers the prospect of linking the Assembly to its various constituencies in new and imaginative ways. For the media in Wales, the new technologies provide both opportunities and problems, some of which (as we suggest below) the Assembly should become involved with.

THE STATE WE'RE IN

Before we consider the relationship between the media and the Assembly, it might be helpful to provide a brief guide to the media 'map' of Wales. A few words about the history of the Welsh media should preface these points. Perhaps the most significant feature of the history of the Welsh media has been their failure to establish themselves as national entities. This failure has led the sociologist Jeremy Tunstall to state that the 'Welsh media are much less Welsh than the Scottish media are Scottish' (Tunstall, 1983, p 228). The lack of a national media in Wales can be seen as a factor in the outcome of the 1997 referendum. Much of the information people gained about the Assembly came from media sources based outside of Wales, and the vote against the Assembly was strongest in those areas where the presence of Welsh newspapers and television was weakest, mainly along the borders with England: the north east and south east of Wales and especially in Cardiff and the surrounding area. The contrast in media consumption patterns between Wales and Scotland has been highlighted to account for the difference in the outcome of the vote in the two countries. Only 10 per cent of Scots buy daily morning newspapers produced outside of their country, while nearly 87 per cent of people in Wales buy daily morning papers not produced in Wales. For broadcasting (radio and television) it is estimated that 40 per cent of the population live in areas which overlap with English transmitters, whereas only 2.5 per cent of Scots live in such areas (IWA,1996). The lack of a highly developed Welsh media system has political consequences for Wales.

Nonetheless, since the early 1980s there has been a rapid growth in the media industries in Wales led by the broadcasting institutions. The first development was the decision, in 1977, to split BBC radio into two channels, broadcasting in Welsh and in English. This division set the pattern for broadcasting in the 1980s. The most significant step forward was the setting up of *Sianel Pedwar Cymru* (S4C) in 1982. Both Radio Cymru and S4C treat Wales as a distinct political constituency. This is done by providing Welsh speakers with a Welsh perspective on national and international affairs through current affairs programmes such as *Y Byd ar Bedwar* and *Taro Naw*, as well as feature programmes and dramas representing popular culture and life in Wales. The success of Welsh language broadcasting has led to calls for the development of a similar service for English language speakers in Wales. Overall, Welsh television broadcasts around 88 hours a week of programmes specifically made for Wales, but only just over 25 per cent are in the English language. There is only around 24 hours of television every week for English speakers in Wales, who make up four-fifths of the population. The creation of an English language service for Wales could consolidate the efforts to provide an all-Welsh perspective for English speakers and would confirm the developments which have taken place since the early 1980s. These are leading to the emergence, for the first time, of a distinct national media system.

What follows is a sketch of some of the salient features of the media in Wales, such as ownership, markets, audiences and regulatory mechanisms. There is no space to set out a comprehensive review and we also need to remember the media form a dynamic sector where today's arrangements are liable to sudden change, especially in the fields of ownership, technical innovation and regulation.

MEDIA REGULATION

The issue of regulation is not confined to Wales. One of the issues facing the Assembly is where it might have regulatory powers, where it might have influence and how sensible it would be to try and exercise either.

The principal regulatory body for the press in Wales (as elsewhere in the UK) is the Press Complaints Commission (PCC). Established in 1991, the PCC is a self-regulatory body, which has drafted its own 'Code of Conduct' governing the conduct and content of newspapers and magazines. Concern about the effectiveness of the PCC as an 'enforcer' led to the PCC announcing a series of reforms to strengthen press self-regulation in 1993. These included making non-press members a majority on the Commission, tightening up the Code and setting up a hot-line to aid the public in making a complaint. Despite these changes the PCC has come in for criticism as being an ineffective regulator. Nevertheless, there is little appetite among politicians (and probably none among editors and journalists) for any statutory regulation of the press. In addition to the PCC, a handful of newspapers have appointed Ombudsmen to deal with readers' grievances, while the Advertising Standards Authority – another self-regulatory body – deals with complaints about newspaper and magazine advertisements.

Unlike the press, broadcasting in Britain is heavily regulated by a myriad of statutory bodies. These include the Broadcasting Standards Commission (BSC), the only organisation within the regulatory framework to cover *all* radio and television. The BSC's three main tasks, as laid down in the 1996 Broadcasting Act, are to produce codes of practice on 'standards' and 'fairness', adjudicate on complaints, and monitor and report on standards and fairness in broadcasting.

The Radio Authority (RA) oversees all non-BBC radio services and licences and regulates all independent radio services, national, cable, satellite and restricted services (the latter includes short-term, special event radio and highly localised permanent services, like hospital radio). The RA is responsible for monitoring the performances of licencees and to regulate programming and advertising, with the power to apply sanctions to rule-breakers. RA Board members are appointed by the Department of Culture, Media and Sport and its operating costs are met by annual fees paid by licence holders.

Commercial television services in and from the UK are licensed and funded by the Independent Television Commission (ITC). Its 'Programme Code' aims to ensure 'quality and diversity' in programme content and the ITC publishes an annual review commenting on the performance of its licencees. The terms of HTV's licence includes a commitment to producing a minimum number of hours of programming specifically for Wales. The ITC has a Cardiff office and an advisory

Viewers' Consultative Council for Wales. The ITC works with other regulatory bodies when considering licence applications. For example, bids are assessed for 'technical acceptability' in conjunction with the Office of Telecommunications (OFTEL) and the Department of Trade and Industry (DTI). Part of the ITC's remit is to identify areas for new local delivery services and to advertise and assess franchise bids. Its income derives mainly from fees paid by licencees, while Commission members are government appointees. Recently the ITC was given responsibility to establish Digital Terrestrial Television, which will carry services provided by the BBC, HTV and S4C.

The BBC - as a public service broadcaster - operates under a Royal Charter. The current Charter, awarded in 1996, runs for ten years. Broad policy guidelines are laid down by the Board of Governors (appointed by government), with day-to-day decisions taken by the Board of Management. The Governors' responsibility for programmes is shared with the Broadcasting Council for Wales which advises on programmes and services.

S4C is accountable to the seven member S4C Authority who monitor management and programme policy. Authority members are central government appointees and funding comes from a government block grant. Viewer feedback on S4C's output includes audience research, running a 'Viewers' Hotline' and holding public meetings at various locations around Wales.

This regulatory framework applies within an important European dimension. The issue of broadcast regulation has exercised the European Commission (EC) and its thinking has implications for all aspects of UK broadcasting. The EC's 1984 Green Paper (which become a Directive in 1989), *Television Without Frontiers*, examined the idea of creating a single market for broadcasting by trying to 'sweep away the national regulatory obstacles' to a free market for the circulation of television services within the EU. This idea brought into conflict two sets of interests. The lobby in favour of deregulation was backed by key figures in the European advertising industry and the Association for Commercial Broadcasters. The other included the established broadcasters (joined in the European Broadcasting Union) who, while favouring an 'integrated European broadcasting zone', argued for regulation to protect public service broadcasting. The Directive represented a victory for the deregulators and set a course which seems unlikely to change. As the 1997 EU Green Paper on *Media Convergence* put it: 'The global nature of communications and the difficulty of exercising control within a given Member State are leading to solutions which draw on self-regulatory practices by industry, rather than by formal regulation'.

There is relatively little the Assembly can do (even if it were so minded) to alter these regulatory structures. Instead, the structures themselves may well crack under the weight of increasingly powerful national and trans-national commercial forces in the broadcast market, towards more 'deregulation' and away from forms of public accountability. Options open to the Assembly in this field might be:

- Breaking up those quangos responsible for broadcasting in Wales (like the Broadcasting Council and the ITC in Wales) and replacing them with more genuinely accountable and regulatory bodies.

- Pushing for a say in the appointments of key figures in the public service media.

- Working with the Media Division of the Government Relations Unit (a specialist source of advice and assistance to media industries about how best to lobby decision-makers in Westminster, Whitehall and Brussels).

Other ways in which the Assembly could possibly support the broadcasting culture in Wales are discussed in the final section of this paper.

OWNERSHIP, MARKETS AND AUDIENCES

The press in Wales has three distinct features. Not much of it is locally owned. Recent years have seen what has been described as 'fairly dramatic concentration of ownership' (as elsewhere in the UK). Much of the press read in Wales is London produced and written. Local ownership is mainly confined to North Wales Newspapers (whose holdings include the *Wrexham Evening Leader* and a clutch of paid and free weeklies), The County Press, and some small circulation Welsh language papers. In October 1998 two of the largest remaining independent weekly newspapers in Wales, the Aberystwyth-based *Cambrian News* and *The Brecon and Radnor Express*, were taken over by the Tindale Newspaper Group.

The concentration of ownership has been marked by the 1995 take-over of the *Western Mail and Echo* by Cheshire-based Trinity International (now Trinity plc.). Trinity, the largest owner of regional newspapers in the UK, also owns the *Daily Post, Wales on Sunday* and 26 other titles in Wales (which include paid and free weeklies covering various localities mainly in south Wales and along the north Wales coast). Another major owner is Southern Newspapers, whose ownership includes the *South Wales Argus* and around a dozen weeklies operating largely in south and west Wales. Smaller 'stables' of titles are run by Tindle Newspapers (mainly in south and west Wales), the Bailey Newspaper Group (based in south-east Wales) and the Northcliffe Newspaper Group, mainly covering Swansea and west Wales. Southern are based in Hampshire (and expanded their holdings in Wales when it bought the Welsh interests of United Provincial Newspapers in 1996), Tindle in Surrey, Bailey in Gloucestershire, while Northcliffe is a provincial newspaper group of the Daily Mail & General Trust, one of the top UK media owners.

Outside of these groupings are a number of Welsh language publications. These include the weeklies *Y Cymro* and *Golwg* (the latter depending on public subsidy) and the *Papurau Bro*. There are around 50 of these monthly, community newspapers, with a combined circulation of about 50,000. Part-subsidised by the Welsh Language Board, they exchange information and news and play an important role in helping maintain the Welsh language.

The London-based press has a significant presence in Wales and enjoys sales figures not matched by any of the newspapers produced in Wales. For example, of the morning dailies, *The Sun* has the highest household penetration in Wales (22.5 per cent), *The Mirror* (12.5 per cent) and *The Daily Mail* (10 per cent). By comparison, *The Western Mail* and the *Daily Post* - which claim, respectively, to be 'the National Newspaper of Wales' and 'the Paper for Wales' - have only 12 per cent between them, 6 per cent each. London press 'penetration' is even more marked on Sundays, when their only competitor is *Wales on Sunday* with a circulation of about 65,000 (Mackay and Powell 1996, p.15).

The coming of the Assembly presents a challenge to the Welsh-based press and we discuss later ways they might respond, and the - admittedly limited - ways in which the Assembly might help sustain a diverse print media in Wales. Arguably a much bigger issue is how to attract interest in the Assembly from the London press and it is by means no certain they will be prepared to offer regular and systematic coverage.

Welsh television and radio - but especially television - face a number of challenges. The three national broadcasters (BBC, HTV, S4C) operate in an increasingly competitive market place. Competition from cable and satellite systems will intensify as broadcasting moves into a new digital age. Before looking at these developments and their implications, it is worth outlining the present state of Welsh broadcasting.

BBC Wales, HTV and S4C have often been seen as having a 'cultural mission'. That is to say, they are seen as not only providing information and entertainment, but also as helping develop a Welsh 'identity' (cf Talfan Davies, 1996: Williams, 1997). The BBC Wales Controller has declared that 'BBC Wales programmes should be dominated by that which is significant to the lives of the people of Wales'. HTV, in its fight to retain its franchise in 1991 claimed, in the words of its then Director of Television, that the purpose of the company was 'the reinforcement of our identity', while the 'missionary' role of S4C in promoting Welsh language broadcasting is well known.

HTV is required to provide a distinct programming service for Wales. The 1996 ITC Annual Report showed HTV broadcasting an average of nearly 12 hours of Welsh programmes each week, an hour above the licence requirement. S4C broadcasts around 33 hours a week of Welsh language broadcasting. Ten hours a week are provided free of charge by BBC Wales (an obligation set down in the 1990 Broadcasting Act), with the rest coming from independent producers, including HTV. This entails a rescheduling of Channel 4's programmes, generally at non-peak hours, underlining S4C's role as a commissioning broadcaster, not a programme producer. BBC Wales produces around 630 hours a year of English language programmes made specifically for Wales (mostly news, current affairs and sport). Radio Cymru and Radio Wales each broadcast about 120 hours a week. The former is listened to at some time during the week by about half of the adult Welsh speaking population, while the latter has a regular audience of 400,000, around 17 per cent of those in the transmission area (Mackay and Powell, p.17).

BBC radio and Welsh television face a common problem: the knowledge that many potential viewers/listeners are tuned into English transmitters. Around 40 per cent of the population can access television programmes coming from England. It has been estimated that 55 per cent of households in the Vale of Glamorgan tune their aerials to HTV West rather than HTV Wales. In Cardiff the figure is 57 per cent and Newport 46 per cent. These are estimated figures and can be disputed. For instance, many aerials directed towards England along the south Wales coast can also receive Welsh signals off the back of the aerial. There is no way of knowing the extent to which choice is exercised in these cases but there can be no doubt that there is an important 'leakage' of potential Welsh television viewers to English signals. In north Wales HTV is challenged by Granada. The problem is just not one of 'refuseniks' (who make a conscious decision to reject Welsh TV), but also those who may not be aware they can pick up Welsh services and those who cannot do so (cf Williams, 1997, pp 29-30). This will be a problem for the Assembly, as well as the broadcasters. In its 1997-98 Annual Report, the Broadcasting Council for Wales commented: 'With the coming of the Assembly, no part of the Welsh population should be deterred from getting news and information services tailored to Wales' own situation'.

If the audience is a problem, so too are the finances of Welsh television. The BBC is dependent on the licence fee as its main revenue source, but is under pressure to increase its funding from commercial ventures. The more the BBC is pushed down this path, the more opposition is likely to grow against the retention of the licence system. When the BBC Wales Controller wrote recently about 'the financial walls ... closing in' he was simply acknowledging the pressures on BBC finance (Talfan Davies, 1996). S4C, until 1998 funded by a percentage of net advertising revenue from ITV, which generally provided an expanding income base, has now moved to a static one under the terms of the 1996 Broadcasting Act. HTV's problems stem from the burden of having to pay the Treasury £23.5m every year to operate its franchise, a figure it is trying to have reduced.

New media technology will alter the contours of Welsh broadcasting, though in ways as yet far from clear. Probably the biggest challenge is posed by the new digital technology. What, then, does the digital age promise? Digital television services can be sent from terrestrial transmitters and by cable and satellite. To receive services, viewers need either a new digital set, or a decoder for their existing sets. The digital system, through 'compression', allows many more channels to be squeezed into the same frequency space as one channel on today's analogue signal and will give better reception. Since digital technology economises on the use of frequencies, services can be 'bundled' and transmitted together on one frequency, leaving the digital receiver to 'unbundle' them into the different services. These bundles are called 'multiplexes'. Radio will have seven of these; one allocated to the BBC, the rest to commercial broadcasters. Television will have six multiplexes. The BBC has been given one. S4C as S4C Digital Networks Ltd (SDN) – has been licensed to operate another, in partnership with United News and Media (owners of HTV) and the cable company NTL (which operates in south Wales as NTL Cable-Tel). SDN is obliged to broadcast S4C and Channel 5 in digital format, but is free to use its remaining capacity for new programming. SDN is currently in talks with satellite providers, as well as planning to market its programming in conjunction with Ondigital, a terrestrial pay-TV group owned by Carlton Communications and Granada. Another multiplex will be shared by ITV - which includes HTV - and Channel 4.

There is certainly no shortage of hyperbole surrounding the impending 'digital revolution'. Typical is S4C's prospectus on the digital age: '... hundreds of new channels will be available. Large, wide screens will deliver a cinematic experience in the home ... increasingly television will be used in conjunction with the telephone and the PC to enable the viewer to interact with the programme provider ...' (S4C, 1997, p.3). But as history shows, new media technologies do not always bring the kind of change the pundits have envisaged.

For example, S4C's plans to fill the space on its multiplex by forging links with commercial operators could compromise its cultural mission. As the BBC has discovered, partnerships between a public service broadcaster and a commercial enterprise, raises the controversial issue of how to avoid cross-subsidy from public funds. Digital technology may also split the broadcast audience in Wales, between those who can access the digital world and those who cannot. It is likely that only some transmitters in Wales will be able to carry the digital system, at least in the beginning. Because of the 'brute facts' of geography, Wales has more transmitters than any other part of the UK, meaning greater costs in putting a digital transmitter on every mast. Even if some of the gaps can be filled by satellite digital service delivery, there will be still be a large minority - as much as 35 per cent by some calculations (cf. Mackay and Powell: and Williams) stuck as analogue-only users, either through no links being available, or because they cannot afford the cost of the new technology.

There is also the important point about the future of English language programming made specifically for a Welsh audience. How the resources are to be found to expand English language provision to something like that in Welsh through S4C, will require closer collaboration between Welsh broadcasters. On the face of it, it does not seem particularly cost-effective or sensible for S4C to be planning to increase its English language broadcasting, while the BBC and HTV struggle to find the funding to expand their own English language output. However, S4C will be using its 'spare' public service digital channel to broadcast proceedings of the National Assembly. In the longer run it has declared a willingness to collaborate with BBC Wales, HTV and others to develop this channel into one providing a comprehensive English language service for Wales (IWA,1998).

Finally, we need to recognise that in a digitally-driven, multiple channel universe, 'finding' Wales will be that much more difficult. This is in a world where the consumer has (nominally) much more choice. More channels, targeted towards specific interests will inevitably fragment the audience. All the more reason, then, for broadcasters to cooperate to help give programmes made in Wales a clear place on a vastly expanded broadcast schedule.

POLICY RECOMMENDATIONS

Our recommendations range from the short to the long-term. Some, if adopted, could be acted upon immediately. Others require the longer view to be taken and substantial pre-planning and discussion involving Assembly members, the media industry and other relevant bodies. The recommendations are grouped under three main headings: communicating the message, covering the message, and media policy and governance.

COMMUNICATING THE MESSAGE

A central part of the 'brief' of the Assembly is the pledge to make it a political forum which will be 'democratic, effective, efficient and inclusive'. The effectiveness of the Assembly will, to a large extent, depend on the ways it manages to communicate with the electorate. In turn this will mean devising structures enabling people to communicate with the Assembly.

There is no shortage of ideas on how this might be done, based on the application of the technologies currently available. Ideas already put forward, include:

- Adopting 'best practice' models being deployed elsewhere (for example, in Norway and Singapore) to ensure that all government departments, committees and agencies become Internet-led and then build network links with outside bodies. Closer to home, is the 'Central Computer and Telecommunications Agency (CCTA) Government Information Service', designed to help improve public service to the citizen. Its website offers information on Government On-Line, among other services.

- Developing 'electronic democracy' by establishing tele-conferencing facilities to link the Assembly with different interest groups and constituencies. Placed in various locations across Wales, a network of this kind could provide inter-active 'highways' between the Assembly and those it seeks to serve.

- 'Gavel-to-gavel' television coverage of the Assembly's plenary and committee sessions. One model to follow could be C-Span's coverage of Congressional politics in the USA, which mixes 'straight' televising of political business, expert commentary and opportunities for viewer participation in matters under debate. Another model will be the new BBC Parliamentary Channel replacing the cable Parliamentary Channel service. The latter had a number of shortcomings: the rules governing coverage were too restrictive and there was little provision for interpretation or comment.

- Other useful ideas can be found in the last Government's Green Paper, *Government Direct*, the present Government's White Paper, *Better Government* and the 1997 Fabian Society pamphlet, *Information Age Government*. Between them they suggest, among other things, ways of merging central and local government offices into a network of 'one-stop' information and service shops, making government more accessible, efficient and 'citizen-friendly' and – more grandly – proposals to 're-engineer' the machinery of the central and local state.

To order this plethora of ideas we suggest the Assembly should set up a Communications Committee responsible for shaping and directing the Assembly's own communications. In addition to reviewing those proposals already listed, the Committee would also need to address: the rules of broadcast coverage; how to compile a bilingual, online equivalent of *Hansard*; the most effective ways of covering the Regional Committees to convey the Assembly's work in different parts of Wales and meet the needs of the local press; and to consider the problems some have identified around the issue of providing simultaneous translations of the business of the Assembly. The Committee will also have to consider, at some point, the implications of the promised Freedom of Information Act. More immediately, the Committee will need to address the relationship between the Assembly and the growing number of public relation firms and lobbyists in Wales who will, no doubt, surround Assembly members after May 1999.

COVERING THE MESSAGE

How effective the Assembly is in communicating its message will depend partly on how the media in Wales cover its work and proceedings, a point which also extends to how the media will cover the campaigns for the first Assembly elections.

The broadcasters in Wales are already discussing how best to cover the Assembly. The BBC has announced its 'post-devolution dividend' with news of a 'substantial fund' having been set aside by the BBC in London for Assembly coverage, along with 'ambitious plans' to cover the first elections. This promised investment means the BBC, unlike most of the smaller media in Wales, will have the staff and resources to cover most aspects of the Assembly's work. It will probably be in a position to field subject and regional as well as political correspondents, which could significantly help to show the Assembly's relevance to people's lives in the different parts of Wales. HTV has also publicly stated that it will invest in staff and resources to provide comprehensive coverage of the Assembly.

As part of their preparations for the Assembly, BBC Wales, HTV and S4C have joined together to launch a determined bid to win back those viewers who have turned their backs on Welsh television by watching programmes coming from Bristol, Birmingham and Manchester (most of the 'boycotters' live in south-east and north-east Wales). To this end, HTV built, in 1997, its own broadcast aerial to serve Wrexham – one of the biggest 'blackspots' for television from Wales – and is planning a major publicity campaign to persuade the 'boycotters' to turn back to Wales, citing the Assembly as a good reason for doing so. BBC Wales also installed a new transmitter in Wrexham for BBC 2 in the suummer of 1998. In the case of HTV, just how much it can invest may depend on its bid to get a reduction in its annual £23.5m licence fee it has to pay to the Treasury, a bid which should be supported by the Assembly.

The matter of how to provide running broadcast coverage of the Assembly will be decided by the Welsh Office. It has shortlisted applicants interested in either supplying and installing the necessary technical facilities, or providing the operational service (or both). The prospect of gavel-to-gavel coverage of the Assembly raises some complex issues. At present this could only be done on cable (but large parts of Wales will never be cabled). On the other hand, digital broadcasting, which has already begun on satellite and will begin shortly on terrestrial television, with its promise of a multi-channel universe, offers new opportunities. While S4C will have the capacity to deliver 'total' Assembly coverage via S4C Digital, it may not have the resources to do so, raising the difficult question of how to fund a dedicated channel.

Broadcasters and the Assembly need to think about how to deal with the problem of the large proportion of people in Wales who do not watch Welsh television at all. This issue will certainly engage the attention of those Assembly members with constituencies in areas that overlap with English transmitters. But quite apart from their interest in seeing their voters as Assembly viewers, it will be damaging if the National Assembly cannot access, through television, the new national political community it is there to represent.

There are two rather more specific points to make about broadcast coverage, which the broadcasters and the Assembly could endorse in the spirit of encouraging more open and transparent government. The first is the restrictions placed on broadcasters by the Representation of the People Act. The Act was a major frustration in their attempts to cover key constituency campaigns in the 1997 General Election and in reporting the subsequent referendum on devolution. As framed, the law should more properly be called the Representation of the *Politicians* Act. The Assembly should support broadcasters in calling for either the repeal or amendment of that part of the Act which seriously constrains broadcast election coverage. The case for change is made the more urgent because of the (partially) new method of voting for the Assembly, with the introduction of multi-member constituencies under a system of proportional representation.

Second, a commitment to open government means the Assembly must oppose any attempt by press or broadcasters to replicate the Parliamentary Lobby as a mechanism for reporting on the Assembly. The Assembly's First Secretary and other major office-holders should, instead, be expected to hold regular, televised press conferences. Further, through tele-conferencing and/or Internet links Assembly leaders should be encouraged to answer questions put directly by members of the public, which would give some substance to the concept of an 'electronic democracy' at work.

The Assembly also presents new opportunities for the press in Wales. There is every sign that Wales' biggest morning and evening daily papers are preparing to take them. One way they could do so would be by providing extensive online coverage of all aspects of the Assembly's work - using technology they are already applying with some skill and imagination.

A bigger challenge is around the issue of the local press. They are important to the communities they serve and often have a high level of household penetration in their circulation areas. Few, though, will have the resources to give the Assembly any thorough coverage. Some local papers may be reluctant even to send a reporter to cover the nearest Assembly Regional Committee, if only a small part of committee business is directly relevant to the paper's locality. There are ways in which these problems might be overcome. For instance, the Press Association (the UK News Agency) is working on how to provide a news service for the local press. Again, if committee proceedings are put online (either by broadcasters or via the net) then local papers could pick up items of local interest without having someone physically attend meetings.

MEDIA POLICY AND GOVERNANCE:

Although we believe the Assembly needs a media policy it is clear – as we said before – there are major constraints on what it can or should do. However, there are several areas where the Assembly could give a lead, with the aim of helping shape policy and directing resources into Wales' media and cultural industries. This much was recognised in the Welsh Office's July 1998 report, *Pathway to Prosperity: A New Economic Agenda for Wales,* which drew attention to the potential of these sectors to create jobs, add to the 'business birth-rate' and attract investment. Elements of a media policy could include:

- Strengthening the independent film and television sector. Wales is fortunate in having a large, diverse and well established independent sector for TV, film video and animation production, with potential for further growth and development. Consideration should be given to ways of supporting the work of independent producers, especially in raising finance, and there may be a case for some mergers in this sector to strengthen performance by combining resources. There is also certainly a case for direct public investment, using the 'investment and payback' formula applied elsewhere. For instance, there is a line in the Scottish Office budget for film-making, something the Assembly might want to consider as one way of supporting the Welsh film industry. The Assembly could also act as a 'facilitator', by helping independent producers identify other sources of public and private sector funding, possibly through joint venture capital deals.

- The Assembly should be alert to the different challenges facing film-makers in Wales. The recent announcement by Channel 4 that it will be increasing its regional commissioning by 30per cent, offers opportunities for local film-makers, 100 of whom met in early 1998 with the Head of Factual Programmes and Features at Channel 4 to discuss the network's requirements. The recently formed 'Wales Film Action Group' – comprising all segments of the film industry in Wales, brought together by Sgrin – was a response to Government proposals for British film-making in its document, *The Bigger Picture*. Concerns about these proposals, and the Group's call for a more equitable share of film finance for Wales, are ones in which the Assembly should take a close interest.

- Having the Assembly act as a support for Welsh media and cultural industries by, for example, sponsoring exhibitions and trade fairs and by Assembly leaders playing an 'ambassadorial' role in promoting the work and achievements of our media and cultural workers.

- Encouraging cooperation between broadcasters. As BBC Wales' Controller put it: 'We will not solve the three great challenges of sustaining Welsh language broadcasting, addressing the imbalance of Welsh and English language provision, and finding our place in a much, much wider market-place, unless we consider our problems in the round and seek collaborative solutions'. There is scope for the Assembly to play a role here by: considering how broadcasters might pool and share resources to produce the software for the new multi-channel digital environment; and helping identify issues and concerns common to the broadcasting community in Wales.

- Consider an extension of public investment and other means of assistance to the publishers of minor papers and magazines in Wales, to help sustain and promote a more diverse print media.

- Providing a forum for representatives from the Assembly and the press in Wales to exchange views and discuss issues of mutual interest.

- Promoting education and training programmes to equip young people in particular with the skills and knowledge necessary to service the media and cultural industries. Some good work is already being done in this area and should be built upon and where possible coordinated in ways outlined in *Pathway to Prosperity* and other recent reports on how best to invest in 'human capital' in Wales.

- Effective policy-making needs an accessible, comprehensive and reliable data base. The Assembly requires a regularly updated 'media register' for Wales, logging details of ownership, finance, employment patterns, labour force skills, output and other relevant information. Some information of this kind exists, but not as a single, definitive 'audit'. Such a reference source would be a useful tool for Assembly policy-makers, for the industry itself and for the wider public. It is an essential starting point for any informed discussion about the future of the media and cultural industries in Wales.

- Developing Internet uses in ways that go beyond the applications already mentioned. For example, the Internet, linked with desktop publishing technology, could help secure the future of those community papers (*papurau bro*) which have taken root in Welsh speaking areas, Or again, the Internet offers immense possibilities for tapping into the Welsh 'diaspora', especially the five to ten million North Americans of Welsh descent. The resources of this diaspora, if harnessed, could raise the global profile of Wales, encourage more educational and cultural exchanges, and be a possible source of inward investment and job creation.

CONCLUSION

The Assembly came about as the result of a hard-fought and close-run referendum. It faces a daunting task: to live up to the expectations of those who campaigned and voted for it, and to win over those who could not be persuaded to give the Assembly their support, or even the benefit of the doubt. In this regard those who failed to vote in the referendum are as important as those who voted No.

The Assembly, as our new national forum, needs to present a distinct image and a clear voice - both within Wales and beyond. It is largely through the mass media that this can be most effectively achieved. Assembly members have to grasp this point, and in doing so, come to appreciate the vital role the different media can play in helping shape the political, cultural and economic life of the 'new Wales'.

References

Drummond, P et. al. (eds) (1993): *National Identify and Europe: the Television Revolution*, British Film Instituto.

Humphreys, P. (1997): *Mass Media and Media Policy in Western Europe*, Manchester University Press.

IWA (1996): *The Road to the Referendum*.

IWA (1998): *Submission to the Welsh Select Committee's Inquiry into Broadcasting and the National Assembly*.

Mackay, H. and Powell, T. (1996). 'Wales and Its Media: Production, Consumption and Regulation', *Contemporary Wales*, 9, pp 8-39.

S4C (1997): *S4C Digital...The Plans*, S4C, Cardiff.

Talfan Davies, G. (1992): 'Broadcasting and the Nation', *Planet*, April-May, pp 16-22.

Talfan Davies, G. (1996): *Broadcasting in Wales in the Digital Age*. Address to the Celtic Film and Television Festival, Bangor, 28 March.

Tunstall, J. (1983): *The Media in Britain*, Constable.

Williams, K. (1997): *Shadows and Substance: the Development of a Media Policy for Wales*, Gomer Press.

PART TWO

POLICY PROCESSES AND OPTIONS

CHAPTER 11

SUSTAINABLE DEVELOPMENT

Gareth Wyn Jones

Sustainable Development requires the 'progressive integration of the economic, social and environmental issues in the pursuit of development that is economically efficient, socially equitable and responsible and environmentally sound' (*Agenda 21*). It recognises our responsibilities to generations yet unborn and to other peoples and nations.

The goal of Sustainable Development is not to turn the clock back to some imagined 'nirvana'. It seeks to minimise our 'ecological footprint', so ensuring the continuing health of the Earth's life-sustaining biological and physical processes. It involves the positive management of our natural heritage, as well as respect for our cultural inheritance, for the benefit of this and future generations. It requires appropriate social and economic initiatives to maximise human welfare without damaging the environment. Sustainable Development is not a synonym for environmental conservation although a realistic appraisal of environmental constraints and a concern for environmental quality is central to it.

While depending on participation and public consent, progress requires the use of a range of public policy tools, including taxation, the planning system, grants and financial incentives, regulations, laws and legal redress. These will not all be directly at the disposal of the National Assembly.

Although the broad objective of Sustainable Development has been ratified at the UK, European and international levels and is incorporated into the Government of Wales Act, the economic, social and environmental parameters for measuring progress to increased 'sustainability' are not well developed or agreed internationally. While the weaknesses of GDP or GNP *per capita* as realistic measures of the quality of life or human welfare are widely recognised, alternatives such as Index of Sustainable Economic Welfare or Genuine Progress Index do not enjoy a wide currency. Equally a number of important social and environmental issues are unresolved and relevant economic theories unconvincing.

While Sustainable Development has engendered a comprehensive political philosophy and agenda (see, for example, M. Jacobs, *The Politics of the Real World*, Earthscan, 1996), it embraces three broad themes:

- Measures to improve the quality of life, such as warmer homes, clean air, safer streets and healthier, more socially coherent and culturally dynamic communities (see, for example, the Welsh Office's *Sustainable Communities in Wales for the 21st century: Agenda 21 Strategy*).

- Measures to ensure the health of the processes that maintain the long term stability of the biosphere. Issues involved include global climate change, ozone depletion and other global pollutants, biodiversity decline, changes in oceanic currents, desertification.

- The management of our heritage of natural beauty and wildlife and of human artefacts and cultures to enrich our own and future generations.

Initiatives espoused to promote each of these themes are not axiomatically mutually consistent and conflicts are likely to arise between environmental objectives as well as with commercial and consumer aspirations.

Conventional civil service processes, including budget line allocations and policy development are strongly sectorial and usually orientated toward specific, well defined but limited goals. Integrative policies and holistic initiatives are difficult to accommodate.

Notwithstanding these problems, the Sustainable Development agenda has implications for all elements of the work of the National Assembly and hence all the chapters in this book. It should influence the structures and working practices of the Assembly as well its policies and initiatives and relationships with outside bodies and other levels of government.

The emergence of the Sustainable Development agenda is due to the paradoxical nature of the triumph of the global market economy. Whilst bestowing unparalleled wealth and opportunity on a significant minority of humanity in global terms (a majority in Western society), it has created economic precariousness and social dislocation for a majority of individuals and communities. This is reflected by crime, drug abuse, communal fear, economic migration, increased investment in personal security and prisons, in a disillusioned, disenfranchised underclass and in a loss of cultural heritage, including many of the world's languages. Both the free market and the central command systems (especially the latter) have extracted a heavy price in local and global pollution, land degradation, loss of wildlife (biodiversity), loss of habitats and landscape heritage.

There are unresolved issues between the continuing internationalisation of the markets in goods and services and the free flow of capital, and the emphasis given by Sustainable Development on community values and the local sourcing of goods to minimise the ecological impacts of production and distribution.

Sustainable Development nevertheless aims to harness the dynamic of the market to the service of humankind and of the environment while seeking to prevent them from being pawns subject to unregulated global market forces. This position harmonises strongly with traditional Welsh values and is reinforced by the recent experiences of our urban and rural communities. It recognises the validity of enterprise and a role for 'goods' and 'services' produced both by private and the public sector, as well as contributions from the civic and co-operative sectors.

It must also be emphasised that, while 'development' implies future change, the reconciliation of our social and economic aspirations with environmental priorities will require urgent changes to current lifestyles and political priorities.

The scale of the Sustainable Development agenda is formidable, and given the difficulties alluded to so far, it is dangerous to be too prescriptive. To produce an integrative, holistic approach, a matrix is proposed here which allows the implications of putative actions arising from the Sustainable Development agenda to be taken into account. These will be discussed in relation to the interaction of three broadly distinct but overlapping 'environmental themes' with eleven policy areas. The three environmental themes are:

1 Personal Space/Environment

Since the quality of personal space in many Welsh communities is poor, it is a major concern. Problems range from the need for fresh air; clean water; for sufficient, affordable, untainted, safe food; for safety from natural and man-induced threats (especially to children and the elderly); and for a comfortable home in a congenial community. These must be combined with opportunities for meaningful work, education, relaxation and entertainment, cultural expression, and some physical and social mobility. The precise ways in which these aspirations are expressed may vary widely from society to society but their fundamental importance is universally accepted (see for example, the United Nations Charter).

2 Global processes

The products of a global population of six billion and growing, and our technical capacity and prolificacy means that human activity is impacting at a planetary level, even given the massive scale of the global biogeochemical and biophysical fluxes that support life on Earth. While this planet is undoubtedly resilient, there is substantial concern about:

- Global climate change and consequential increases in the frequency of extreme events, changes in sea level and oceanic current flows.
- Atmospheric O_3 depletion.
- Radioactive pollution on a continental scale.
- Forest destruction and soil loss.

- Depletion of water resources.

- Major oceanic and terrestrial pollution, for example NO_x, SO_x, pseudo hormones.

- The loss of biological genetic diversity – through terrestrial habitat loss, species extinction, and marine over-exploitation and pollution.

An international consensus of scientists, politicians and many business leaders, for example Cor Herkstroter, President of Royal Dutch Shell, supports the application of a prudent precautionary approach to such issues.

3 Natural heritage

In addition to the macro, global or continental environmental issues, whose solution is of obvious self-interest to humankind, there is a concern to conserve the fabric of the countryside and cherish the natural beauty of landscape and wildlife. This heritage is a reflection of human management and regional and national cultural history interacting over the last several thousand years with biology and geomorphology. It is as important an element of our collective history in Wales as our literary, musical and built heritage and is, indeed, woven into them. It is also a major asset in promoting commercial activity, for instance tourism, and makes a significant contribution to our aesthetic experiences and to the quality of life.

As already noted, conflicts may well arise in policies designed to promote specific objectives within each of these environmental themes as well as with more conventional commercial or personal objectives.

The eleven policy areas referred to above are:

1 Energy Generation and Use

2 Rural Land Use

3 Water Resources

4 Resource Use Minimisation and Pollution Control

5 Transport and Communication

6 Marine Resources

7 Urban Land Use and the Built Environment

8 Industrial Production

9 Recreation, Sport and Entertainment

10 Tourism

11 Culture and Community

These policy areas and possible actions in relation to the three themes are discussed in detail below. First, however, a number of important procedural and structural reforms need to be considered since they will influence all other matters. These are addressed in the following Section on such reforms. Wales may be the first country in history to have Sustainable Development formally written into its founding constitution. However, our economy is small and highly integrated into that of England and the international economy. Lacking a solid historical base, we have a major challenge in formulating and implementing practical policies that will put Wales at the forefront of international sustainable development. The example of Tir Cymen, transmuted into Tir Gofal – the scheme that integrates farming practices with environmental conservation – illustrates some of the possibilities and the frustrations.

STRUCTURAL AND PROCEDURAL REFORMS

THE MECHANISM OF GOVERNMENT

The application of the concept of Sustainable Development is a statutory obligation placed upon the National Assembly by the 1998 Wales Act. This will require it to adopt an integrated approach to decision making and the development of methods to evaluate the long-term environmental and social implications of decisions as well as conventional fiscal and political considerations. The Assembly will need to work inclusively with all public and private bodies and individuals in Wales to encourage the adoption of 'sustainable practices'. The Assembly will need to establish mechanisms to inform itself about 'best practice', technical innovations, and relevant social and economic initiatives elsewhere.

Actions:

- The National Assembly should make a firm commitment to the principles of Sustainable Development as set out at the Rio Earth Summit in 1992 and subsequently agreed by the UK government.

- Each of the Assembly's committees should be required to assess their actions in the light of these principles, with environmental as well as other objectives and targets being set for each government department and agency. The implementation of the objectives should include partnership actions with locally elected and voluntary bodies and subsidiarity within broad strategic objectives.

- A small Welsh Environmental Audit Office should be set up to establish Sustainable Development criteria (including Strategic Environmental Assessments and Environmental Accounts) and to review the funding decisions of the Assembly against these criteria. The main Assembly audit committee should be required to take advice from this body and to review progress towards Sustainable Development.

- Decision-making should be open, democratically accountable and taken at the lowest appropriate level. Strenuous efforts should be made to inform the Welsh public about the scientific reasons informing environmental concerns and supporting such decisions as well as socio-economic issues.

- The Assembly should produce a quinquennial national 'State of the Environment' Review assessing our use of resources and 'environment capital', and local authorities should be encouraged to do likewise. Progress should be reported annually to the Assembly and the Welsh people.

- The Assembly should establish a Joint Advisory Committee on Sustainable Development to play a major role in setting targets, defining issues, and reporting on the Assembly's own environmental and Sustainable Development performance. This Committee should include external specialists charged with bringing to the Assembly's deliberations relevant information from around the world.

- The Assembly should address the relationships between its various agencies in promoting the Sustainable Development agenda, in particular the Welsh Development Agency, Countryside Council for Wales, the Environment Agency, the Farm and Countryside Advisory Service, the Wales Tourist Board, and the Sports Council for Wales.

LOCAL AUTHORITIES

The National Assembly should respect the concept of subsidiarity, devolving decisions and policy implementation to the county/borough and community council level as appropriate. Nevertheless, the Assembly, making use of both the Environmental Audit Office and the joint Sustainable Development Committee, should provide clear guidance to local authorities on how the principles of Sustainable Development should be applied more locally.

Actions:

- Local authorities will be required to produce, co-ordinate and regularly update their Agenda 21 implementation plans.

- Local authorities will be required to address the issues raised by the various policy reform areas discussed below.

- Local authorities will be encouraged to co-operate actively with community and voluntary groups to promote local initiatives furthering Sustainable Development, especially through the use of local products in line with the proximity principle.

- While National Guidance will be required to co-ordinate the planning functions of local authorities, community involvement and rights in the planning process will need to be strengthened. Two main initiatives can be envisaged:

    i   More emphasis should be placed on effective participation of local communities, individuals and groups in developing local strategic plans through techniques such as Planning for Real, and a greater role for community councils.

    ii   People should be given the right of appeal against planning decisions where there is a *prima facie* case that the permission is contrary to the Local Plan.

- Local Authorities will be required to cooperate to produce local integrated transport plans across their boundaries reflecting regional 'travel to work' and shopping/recreational patterns.

- Consideration should be given to allow local authorities to raise local sales taxes to generate extra funding from tourism for reinvestment in local environmental and social projects such as footpath maintenance, recreational facilities, and cultural events.

EUROPE AND THE WIDER WORLD

The National Assembly should enforce European and international environmental and social standards rigorously. The Assembly should do all it can to encourage the EU and others to adopt progressive environmental standards.

Actions:

- The Assembly should seek to implement European Directives and Regulations relevant to Sustainable Development through its secondary powers in the most positive ways possible.

- The Assembly should ensure that representation for Wales is secured within the Council of Ministers when relevant issues are discussed.

- The Assembly should ensure the effective and imaginative implementation of European and international environmental obligations to support 'green job' creation and secure the retention of EC funds to carry out these requirements.

- The Assembly should establish close co-operative relations with other European Regions to exchange information on best practice as well as to influence EU policy debate.

- The Assembly should use its representation on the British-Irish Council and the EU Committee of the Regions to address Sustainable Development issues.

RESEARCH AND TECHNICAL INNOVATIONS

The National Assembly should establish mechanisms to promote research and development into environmentally-sound, socially-enlightened and economically advantageous technologies in collaboration with national and international business and industry; and into the development of criteria for the improved definition of environmental, social and economic policies that underpin sustainable development.

Actions:

- The Assembly should address the role of the Universities and other Research Institutes in Wales in making available to them the best international knowledge and practices and in devising new environmentally benign technologies and novel approaches to social issues, using its financial power to promote this approach.

- The Assembly should promote studies into the issues involved in the implementation of integrated 'sustainable' policy-making.

- The Assembly should ensure that training is available both to elected members and to its civil servants in the management of Sustainable Development and undertaking the necessary economic, social and environmental analyses.

EDUCATION AND TRAINING

The National Assembly should ensure that the concepts and principles that underpin Sustainable Development are fully integrated into the educational curriculum at all levels and in both languages. The Assembly should also ensure that practical training opportunities are widely available at many levels.

Actions:

- The role of the Welsh Environmental Education Council should be reviewed and strengthened.

- Training in environmental management skills should be promoted at all levels.

PARTICIPATION AND EMPOWERMENT

The National Assembly should adopt transparent practices to encourage public participation in its proceedings and should de-mystify the process of Sustainable Development. The Assembly should ensure that the best possible scientific and technological information is available to the public and their representatives to encourage rational, informed debate and realistic assessment of hazards and risks.

Actions:

- The Assembly should ensure that its agencies, for example the Countryside Council for Wales, will carry out their obligations to inform and empower the public and work in tandem with elected bodies.

- The Assembly should ensure the integration and effective use of organisations such as Jigso, Bro, Groundwork, Gwaith Maes, and the British Trust for Conservation Volunteers, to facilitate voluntary action by all age groups and allow communities and interest groups to make direct contributions to solving local environmental and social issues and to promote Sustainable Development initiatives.

- The Assembly should ensure that all sections of society irrespective of gender, age, cultural or ethnic background are fully engaged in the effort to identify and secure a 'sustainable future' for themselves.

- The Assembly should have a permanent exhibition in the main foyer of the Assembly building describing how it is promoting Sustainable Development in its work.

OBLIGATIONS TO OTHERS

The concept of Sustainable Development emphasises our obligations to future generations and to less fortunate peoples, countries and individuals all over the world. Our small nation has a proud record of international service and this spirit of altruism should be encouraged. The National Assembly, despite its limited powers, should seek mechanisms to allow Welsh people, especially our youth, to participate in projects that promote international Sustainable Development and overseas co-operation.

Actions:

- The Assembly should co-operate with the Welsh Centre for International Affairs, the Urdd and other organisations, to promote strong interaction between Welsh youth and those abroad to promote a wider appreciation of Sustainable Development.

- The Assembly should seek in all possible ways to make its views and its commitments known internationally.

- The Assembly should enable a specifically Welsh contribution to be addressed to international problems and proceed by effective collaboration with others.

POLICY REFORM AREAS

This section considers the main policy areas that must be addressed as part of the evolution of a more sustainable society in a healthy environment. In each case the interplay of the suggested actions with the three 'environmental themes' outlined above is considered. Informed policy decision-making must initially recognise and then seek practical methods of reconciling, as far as is possible, the conflicts between different 'environmental objectives' as well as social and economic pressures.

1. ENERGY GENERATION AND USE

General Policy: To respond to the international consensus on climate change (see Intergovernmental Panel on Global Climate Change). The Assembly should seek:

- To break the historic link between wealth (measured by GDP per capita) and energy use.

- To achieve a significant decrease in anthropogenic emission of CO_2 and other greenhouse gases over the next 20 years.

The objective should be a decrease of 50 per cent in CO_2 emissions by 2020 by

- a 25 per cent increase of efficiency in energy use in all sectors; and

- a 25 per cent increase in electrical energy production from renewable sources, including bio-mass, wind, small-scale hydro, tidal and photo-voltaic solar.

Actions

- Decrease heat loss and increase passive heat gain in domestic, business and commercial premises by improved insulation, and higher building standards (see also the Urban Land Use and the Built Environment sections).

- Promote fuel-efficient transport by improving public transport, and discouraging developments that increase car use (see also the Transport and Communication and Urban Land Use sections). Information technology should be used to decrease certain transport components.

- Require investment in energy efficiency by all government agencies and government funded institutions, for example hospitals and local authorities. They could be required to invest 5-10 per cent of annual fuel bills on increased fuel efficiency with penalties in the event on non-compliance.

- Collaborate with industry and commerce to encourage the adoption of best energy efficiency practices in both space heating and production technology (see also the Industrial Production section).

- Undertake a comprehensive review of the renewable energy resources and options, both terrestrial and offshore, and bring forward fully costed, environmentally audited proposals.

- Support a programme of combined public/private investment in renewable electrical energy generation - including reappraisal of the Severn Barrage and newer technologies to harness tidal flows, Bio-mass, Hydro, Solar and possibly including a levy on energy utilities.

- Promote policies to encourage a variety of local energy supplies while retaining links to the National Grid as a secure backup.

- Commit to phasing out nuclear power because of the unresolved environmental problems of radioactive waste disposal and storage.

Thematic Interactions: This policy is driven primarily by the 'Global Processes' theme but will, in general, contribute to several aspects of the 'Personal Space' theme by improving air quality and housing standards. However, major conflicts can be anticipated in relation to the curbing of transport-generated CO_2 and other emissions with potentially reduced access to out-of-town shopping, and various recreational facilities (all heavily dependent on personal car transport). A significant conflict exists between maximising renewable energy production and aspects of the 'Natural Heritage' theme. Potential clashes include wind turbine farms and landscape values and new small scale hydro or tidal power schemes and 'nature conservation'. The Assembly will need to make a detailed analysis of the renewable energy resources of Wales including 'environmental impact assessments' on the various options. However, the clear priority must be the reduction of CO_2 emissions to near Wales' global share.

2. RURAL LAND USE

General Policy: To integrate high quality food, fibre, timber (primarily hardwood) and other novel crop production with the positive management of the semi-natural wildlife/habitat and landscape heritage. To make maximum sustainable use of renewable natural resources. To add value locally to maximise job opportunities and to maintain viable and vital communities and the rural population. To reinforce and market a positive brand image of Welsh rural products by enforcing high standards of animal welfare, and product traceability. To promote high standards of environmental management coupled with the development of rural tourism and recreational opportunities. To fulfil all-Wales' obligations to wildlife and habitat conservation under European and international agreements.

Any approach must be compatible with evolving European policy (especially the Common Agriculture Policy) and international treaties. A comprehensive all Wales agri-environmental scheme linked to a comprehensive food and timber production and promotion policy would provide the basic strategy for combining the environmental, social and economic objectives noted. Major initiatives must be developed using both public and private finance, especially from the farming and land-owning sectors, to brand, promote and market Wales' rural products (see Chapter 15). This should be reinforced by initiatives in the urban and peri-urban areas of Wales and through the tourist industry to extend the markets for quality Welsh products.

Actions

- To promote and fund a comprehensive all-Wales agri-environmental scheme, also enabling the sustainable management and use of existing broad-leaved woodlands. This would allow the positive management at least 80 per cent of our remaining semi-natural habitats including all biological Sites of Special Scientific Interest, Special Conservation (general ecology) and Special Protection (birds) Areas.

- To make sustainable use of 20-30 per cent of the annual increment of hardwoods for added value products.

- To promote an increase of 50 per cent in the hardwood cover in Wales in 20 years.

- To promote organic farming, assist farmers to convert to this system, and to use established mechanisms to market Welsh organic products.

- To establish throughout the livestock industry, high animal welfare standards, high food quality, and create a strong Welsh Food Promotion and Marketing Agency so that Welsh rural products are synonymous with 'quality'.

- To establish a research and development programme into novel crops including energy crops, herbs and medicinal plants, and chemical stock for synthesis to support commercial diversification and landscape diversity.

- To develop more comprehensive methods for landscape appraisal and management throughout the country to make these part of the local planning process. To reappraise the roles of National Parks and other Designated Areas, with the aim of producing a more holistic rural planning and sustainable development framework relevant to the whole of rural Wales.

- To develop plans to promote rural, cultural and green tourism associated with landscape and wildlife assets and linked to local sustainable products. To ensure a comprehensive network of paths and bridle-ways for walkers and riders (see also the Recreation, Sport and Entertainment, and Tourism sections).

- To arrange for appropriate recreational facilities in the countryside. This should involve accommodating motor and other noisy sports in agreed zones mainly in the urban periphery (see also the Recreation, Sport and Entertainment section).

- To increase public involvement in and acceptance of planning and development control systems (see also the Urban Land Use and the Built Environment sections).

Thematic Interactions: This policy area is mainly driven by the need to secure our 'natural heritage'. At the same time good land management practices also contribute to elements of the 'global processes theme' such as soil and water conservation and maintenance of biological genetic diversity. However, in Wales the former is not a major issue and our contribution to the latter is rather restricted. The policies suggested would also have a significant positive impact on the 'personal space' of local people and visitors. Potential negative interactions include possible higher food prices. Environmentally sound land management and high animal welfare standards can impose extra costs, part of which must be met by the consumer. The management of our natural heritage is a public good with costs accruing to the public purse. However, this should be partly off-set by improved food quality and hygiene standards, by improved market penetration and a decrease in incidence of food poisoning, as well as enhanced urban enjoyment of the countryside's natural beauty and wildlife.

3. WATER RESOURCES

General Policy: To recognise that 'water use efficiency' is as important as energy use efficiency so as to secure supplies of high quality water to all domestic users, while protecting the quality and flow rates of rivers, and lake levels. To assess the possible contribution of existing and new small-scale hydro to the economic generation of renewal energy. To create incentives to minimise water wastage, and to avoid harmful discharges into water courses.

Actions

- To set strict limits on water leakage from the distribution grid.

- To encourage water metering to reward commercial and household water conservation.

- To achieve high standards of chemical and biological water quality.

- To encourage the distribution and use of water-use-efficient appliances.

- To encourage water sports, including angling, sailing and windsurfing, in appropriate locations.

Thematic Interactions: In a Welsh context the policy is mainly driven by the conservation of 'natural heritage' but will have some modest implication for 'global processes'. Water quality is also important to the quality of personal space.

4. RESOURCES USE MINIMISATION AND POLLUTION CONTROL

General Policy: For the National Assembly to work in close collaboration with the WDA and industry to ensure that non-renewable resource use is minimised. Resources should be recycled or re-used wherever environmentally and economically feasible. The emissions of pollutants must be tightly regulated to ensure high standards of air, water and soil quality/purity. The need is to promote a culture in which everyone, including business, government and its agencies, local authorities, community groups and individuals think and act upon the real resource and environmental implications of their businesses and way of life. Part of the role of the Assembly will be to interpret for Wales the policy framework derived from the EC and International Treaties as well as UK legislation. The Assembly must work with industry to find outlets for 'waste products' and to provide the practical infrastructure to make this feasible. The objective must be to decrease substantially (to less than 50 per cent) landfill disposal and to generate new job opportunities (following the Washington State model) as well as controlling other emissions.

Actions

- To establish targets for resource use and waste minimisation for all policy areas under the authority of the Assembly.

- To establish emission standards into air and water from point sources and from dispersed activities.

- To establish comprehensive investment criteria that enable the real impacts, including external impacts, of decisions to be evaluated. These criteria should recognise both fiscal and non-fiscal values.

- To provide a framework for the co-ordination of local authority strategies for waste minimisation, recycling, promoting local product and service use in line with the 'proximity principle', and to decrease transport-based emissions.

- To work with industry to encourage new waste-using commercial processes.

Thematic Interactions: This action area is relevant to the three environmental themes but perhaps especially to the retention of our 'Natural Heritage' and improving our 'Personal Space'. It implies changes in life-style, for instance placing requirements on households to pre-sort rubbish, some curbs on consumerism, a requirement for companies to move quickly to adopt integrated low emission production systems and positive steps to encourage new innovative uses of waste materials.

5. TRANSPORT AND COMMUNICATIONS

General Policy: The National Assembly should work to ensure that effective Information Technology facilities and management are accessible throughout the country. Regional and local development plans must be elaborated so as to minimise the need to travel, and to decrease car dependency. Quality public transport must be developed to match local and regional demands. Further integrated transport policies should be devised at the national and regional levels which address the various sectors of the transport market to minimise the impact of unnecessary and leisure travel on our Natural Heritage, and drastically decrease transport-generated pollution.

An overall decrease in car-derived congestion and pollution can best be achieved by the careful analysis of journey types and a concentration of investment in predictable urban 'travel to work' journeys and inter-conurbation travel and goods distribution, for which trains are well suited.

Actions

- To instruct local authorities to co-operate to produce integrated transport plans with improved public transport in the main conurbations in Wales – Cardiff/Newport and the eastern valleys, Swansea/ Neath and adjacent valleys, Llanelli/Gwendraeth, Glannau Menai, Llandudno/Colwyn, and Wrexham and its hinterland.

- To bring pressure to bear to improve rail links within Wales, especially north-south, and to England and mainland Europe.

- To identify and develop a minimum, essential 'strategic road' network in Wales for social and commercial reasons while vigorously promoting traffic calming elsewhere. To identify and carry our road improvement schemes within the strategic network which decrease the negative impact of traffic on the 'personal space' of communities and allow access to the facilities in Wales' capital.

- To collaborate with industry to develop the use of low emission vehicles, for example fuel cell and combined power technologies. To ensure the vehicle manufacturing sector in Wales is well placed to benefit from the new technologies as they come on stream.

- To develop an information technology (ISDN/fibre-optic) network and promote its use throughout Wales. The Assembly should take a direct lead in using IT to communicate with the people. This would assist in distributing its administrative functions throughout Wales, thereby decreasing environmental and economic overheating pressures in Cardiff and distributing job opportunities.

- To consider road pricing in urban areas and the management of parking more widely as methods of regulating traffic flow and promoting economic development (one example is the Northern Snowdonia Traffic Management Scheme).

Thematic Interactions: In this area there is the potential for major conflict between various components of the Sustainable Development agenda as well as commercial interests. In the eyes of many, cars contribute to their 'personal space'. However, vehicle emissions are increasing contributors to global pollution as well as to local air contamination and health problems. International comparisons show clearly that in urban/suburban regions of high population density cars and road building cannot solve mobility and congestion issues. Motor manufacture is also a major employer in Wales and its decline would have serious social consequences. The country's political and economic history has resulted in primitive transport in many areas and the specific problems of rural, low population density areas, where car dependence is likely to continue, need to be addressed.

6. MARINE RESOURCES

General Policy: The National Assembly should work to conserve and enhance the biological diversity of Wales' inshore coastal waters. This would promote sustainable local fisheries and also, where appropriate, aquaculture while adopting and pressing others to adopt, high chemical and biological sea water quality standards. The Assembly should also maintain and, where possible, improve the amenity and scenic quality of the coast and beaches, by preventing unsightly developments and removing eye sores. The Assembly should strictly enforce EU standards for sea water and beach quality, both to protect wildlife and promote the tourist industry. Serious consideration should be given to protecting the coast from unsightly developments and to the removal of, for example, caravan parks from scenic areas to promote a quality tourist product. Regulations should prevent over-fishing by sports and semi-commercial divers, while protecting the interest of established local fishermen.

Actions

- To move rapidly to curb marine discharges.

- To regulate tanker traffic and oil discharges in Milford Haven and Liverpool Bay to minimise pollution risk.

- To monitor and regulate catches of fish and crustacea to conserve stocks, specifically protecting the interests of local fishermen against semi-commercial and sports divers.

- To promote non-invasive, remote techniques to view marine and coastal life.

- To encourage integrated coastal management schemes.

7. URBAN LAND USE AND THE BUILT ENVIRONMENT

General Policy: The National Assembly should issue strategic planning guidance to the planning authorities to ensure the highest standards of human environment in urban areas.This would involve discouraging 'greenfield' housing development, and out-of-town shopping malls and precincts. It would encourage town centre regeneration, ensure the retention of open, recreational spaces in or near population centres, and provide clear zones for commercial, industrial, and housing land use. There should be a strong integration of planning with the regional and local integrated transport strategy. In addition, the Assembly should promote, in collaboration with local authorities, the use (and re-use) of local materials and a local vernacular style in contrast to the uniform 'mid-American/Essex' style of most retail outlets and housing developments.

Actions

- In addition to establishing local, and regional development plans, to take positive steps to involve people in their development by consultation, for example *Planning for Real* exercises. Respect should be given to the principle of internal subsidiarity by making full use of community councils.

- To seek private-public partnerships to upgrade housing stock, ensuring a high level of insulation and where possible positive heat gain.

- To encourage retail outlets to sell local products and to develop local and regional distribution networks.

- To ensure the integration of transport and planning control.

- To consider new methods for regenerating town and city centres.

- To conserve urban parks and open spaces and wildlife havens.

- To redistribute development pressure from hot-spots, including the dispersal of public service jobs from Cardiff to avoid environmental and social pressures in the area.

- To regulate unsightly development on the coast and in the countryside.

- To retain older, retired people in their communities, thereby increasing a sense of community and family and discouraging retirement communities/villages'.

- To utilise the Regional Committee structure of the Assembly to promote strategic planning.

Thematic Interactions: This area is mainly concerned with the quality of 'Personal Space' and the protection of the 'Natural Heritage' from insensitive exploitation. In certain instances Wales' contribution to global wildlife diversity is threatened. It is a policy area where public involvement and ownership of the plans is particularly important. Conversely there is also a critical need for national and regional structural planning.

8. INDUSTRIAL PRODUCTION

General Policy: The National Assembly should work closely with industry and the trade unions to promote high environmental and social welfare standards. This would give Welsh industry a competitive advantage in anticipation of continuing international pressures for improved pollution standards, protecting biodiversity, and conserving the natural heritage. The Assembly through the Welsh Development Agency should work to position Wales at the vanguard of new applied technologies which contribute to providing solutions to environmental problems. for example fuel cell technology, photovoltaics, and waste re-use. Such activity should contribute to prosperity and social welfare.

As industrial processes are changing rapidly, the Assembly, operating mainly through the Welsh Development Agency, should encourage industry to adopt the latest, low emission technologies. This would position Wales to benefit from the economic opportunities that will arise from stricter environmental standards. Lifecycle analysis of the impact of products and production should be encouraged.

Actions

For detailed recommendations see Chapter 13 on *Economic Development*, by Brian Morgan and Kevin Morgan.

9. RECREATION, SPORT AND ENTERTAINMENT

General Policy: The National Assembly should encourage sports and recreation, especially those which have the least environmental footprint and which contribute to community spirit. It should ensure that facilities are adjacent to population centres and can be readily accessed by public transport. Links between planning, public transport and tourism need to be addressed to promote greater integration in both urban and rural Wales.

Actions

- To ensure that a comprehensive and appropriate network of local, regional and national footpaths are provided.
- To ensure that a network of safe bridle paths are available for horse riders.
- To provide a network of safe cycle paths near the conurbations as well as long distance routes together with appropriate paths for mountain bikes.
- To encourage the provision of facilities such as mountain bunk houses, and appropriate farm house accommodation.

10. TOURISM

General Policy: The National Assembly should view tourism as a major industry, one largely dependent on the sensitive, sustainable development of our natural, built and cultural heritage. Recognising that the family beach (caravan and guest house) holiday is in decline, the future shape of Welsh tourism has become a serious issue. It is likely that the future lies in generating a quality product emphasising Wales' environmental and cultural heritage.

Actions

- To increase the daily visitor spend and to promote weekend breaks through the year.

- To develop an improved image of Wales to counter the caravan/'kiss me quick' image.

- To develop much stronger links with the Welsh food and catering industry.

- To address the issues of transport and parking related to tourism.

- To ensure a range of novel as well as traditional recreational and cultural activities and events for visitors.

- To consider making much more imaginative use of buildings such as Caernarfon and Caerffili castles for public events and concerts (involving the provision of wet weather cover).

11. CULTURE AND COMMUNITY

General Policy: As the Sustainable Development agenda implies a commitment to socially inclusive values as well as the environmental principles noted earlier, the National Assembly should seek to promote a strong sense of cultural cohesion in Wales. This should operate across both languages and reinforce community purpose to achieve the Assembly's social, economic and environmental aspirations.

A wide variety of voluntary and community initiatives and mechanisms exist throughout Wales. These are heavily dependent on EU funding, for instance the Leader projects in rural Wales. These should be encouraged and their funding protected. Methods should be explored to encourage business and industry and civic organisations to undertake a greater role in cultural events. The Welsh language and culture should be encouraged and made more accessible.

CONCLUSION

The analysis offered here can, at best, only sketch out a strategy relevant to the National Assembly's obligation to pursue Sustainable Development. The strategy has the capacity to generate thousands of new jobs. Through well-directed public investment it has t'_____ _____ _____ _____ ivate and civic investment in area:_____ __ _____ ____ _____ __ ___ssing, catering, recreation, renewa___ energy production, certain types of ___facturing, the provision of servic__ such as IT, public transport and _____ parking. The strategy also suggests investment in _____ research and _____ent on the basis of public-private partnership.

The World Business Council for Sustainable Development has described two scenarios that might be pursued to promote greater international sustainability. One, the so-called *Geopolity scenario*, emphasises rigorous environmental regulations and enforcement, though working with the grain of the markets. The second, the *Jazz Scenario*, envisages greater public choice and commercial pressure to adopt best environmental practice, leading to a world of greater transparency and dynamic reciprocity. These two scenarios are not incompatible. It is likely that with its limited legislative powers, at least initially, the National Assembly will rely heavily on indirect and co-operative methods, and subtle incentives to achieve its objectives.

CHAPTER 12

STRATEGIC PLANNING

Mark Tewdwr-Jones

Residents oppose landfill tip. Threat to greenfields from houses. Old mineral site to be worked again. Major investment announced for town centre ...

These are familiar headlines that regularly appear in the newspapers around Wales. All raise issues that affect our everyday lives in one way or another. They are either a cause of celebration (more jobs), or they are a matter for concern (environmental impact). Occasionally, they are both. Witness the LG company's semiconductor and electronic development in Newport. This investment will create over 6,000 jobs to give the Welsh economy a boost, but at the expense of building over part of a Site of Special Scientific Interest. Such decisions entail difficult choices.

What ties together all these issues is the town and country planning process. Planning sits in the middle of social, economic and environmental change in our communities. Planners are charged with ensuring local economic development and protection of the best of our landscapes. They attempt to provide the right development in the right locations, as well as stopping development going to the wrong places. For the most part, planners do provide better environments for people. Imagine what life would be like without planning. People could build where they wanted to, without regard to other people, or the environment. Some sort of framework and strategic coordination must be necessary.

Town and country planning is a very different activity today from that which emerged in the early years of the twentieth century, and it is no longer solely the preserve of local government. Planning is shared between central government, local government, public organisations, and the private sector. It is a process that facilitates development on the one hand, and regulates protection of the environment on the other. It is a partnership which can assist numerous levels of government achieve their strategic and local objectives. The number of organisations existing in Wales that possess planning duties in one form or another means that it is important for the National Assembly to generate effective Welsh strategic planning coordination.

Contrary to popular opinion, town and country planning is not simply a process that stops people building their household extension, or building a house on a plot of land. Planning is a much broader all-encompassing activity, since it exists to coordinate policy, cement partnerships, and facilitate much-needed change. Strategic coordinative planning should identify national policy objectives for Wales as a whole, promote cooperation between different levels of government, assist Wales' position in Europe, and encourage the public to take some stake in the policy and decision-making processes.

Planning is therefore a major governmental activity and will be a core policy area for the National Assembly of Wales. The Government of Wales Act transfers town and country planning policy-making from the Welsh Office to the Assembly. Implementation of economic, environment, transport and housing policies will have to occur within a strategic planning framework that also takes into account Sustainable Development. The Assembly will be required to set planning policy for the whole of Wales and to provide planning policy guidance to the unitary local authorities to enable them to make the right local decisions.

The town and country planning process will be at the heart of the Assembly's ability to set future policy for Wales. This will be new territory for the planners and the politicians. It will not only be a case of trying to get some coordination and consistency. A specifically Welsh agenda has to be created.

Planning could be viewed as an umbrella term for government agencies' intervention in a wide range of policy areas related to the built and natural environment. In this context, it is not just a matter for the National Assembly and unitary local government. Other public organisations in Wales take decisions which either impact on or are affected by the planning system. Examples include the Welsh Development Agency and its quest for major inward investment sites, the Countryside Council for Wales' commitment to rural areas and the environment, the Environment Agency's role in preventing environmental pollution, the Wales Tourist Board's attempts at enhancing tourism, and the Sports Council of Wales' policy towards furthering sport and recreational opportunities in our communities.

The objectives of these organisations are potentially in conflict with one another. For example, the WDA might identify several large inward investment sites in north and south Wales. At the same time, however, they might also be areas the Countryside Council for Wales wishes to see protected in the interests of the environment and landscape. Diverse but inter-related policy objectives need formal coordination which will be a core function of the National Assembly. It will need to use the planning system to ensure that no one interest dominates the agenda at the expense of others. This is the main purpose of our planning system: balancing the different pressures and expectations in the natural and built environment.

A DISTINCTIVE WELSH PLANNING SYSTEM

The similar legal and administrative planning arrangements in England and Wales support the assumption that, from purely a land use perspective, Wales is merely a western extension of England. Welsh planning has an identical legal dimension but a subtly different policy approach. The land use planning system in Wales comprises Planning Policy Guidance and circulars at the all-Wales level with unitary development plans at the local level. In addition, development control processes and applications for planning permission are determined at the level of the 22 unitary local authorities and the three national parks.

The Welsh Office has not attempted to implement a radically different policy approach to the planning system in Wales from that operated by the Department of the Environment in England. Both central government departments have released circulars and Planning Policy Guidance Notes (PPGs) that set out the objectives of planning under joint-authorship over a long period of time, thus reflecting the government's view of the planning system being essentially identical in both countries. Occasionally, however, some circulars and PPGs have been issued in Wales separately from the policy documents in England, either on topics that have a distinct Welsh flavour, or because legal and administrative systems in the two countries are, in these instances, separate. Examples are Circular 61/81 *Historic Buildings and Conservation Areas*; Circular 30/86 *Housing for Senior Management*, and Circular 53/88 *The Welsh Language - Development Plans and Planning Control*. The latter two circulars reflect what is probably the most distinctive policy difference between land use planning in Wales compared to that for England, and although welcomed by relevant Welsh organisations are limited compared to the plethora of other guidance that has been jointly released.

The implementation of joint English and Welsh guidance has led to critics of the planning system, in particular political representatives from rural Wales, to highlight the inadequacy of strong planning guidance for local authorities at the Welsh level. This, they argue, reiterates an alien set of planning policies that are inappropriate for Wales since they fail to take into account geographical, cultural and social considerations distinctive to Wales. This was debated at length in the Parliamentary Welsh Affairs Select Committee's sessions in 1993 for their report on *Rural Housing*.

What is clear from almost all of the central government circulars and Planning Policy Guidance Notes is the lack of a distinctly Welsh policy dimension. It is questionable why so many other policy topics were not considered appropriate to warrant the issuing of separate policy guidance appropriate for a Welsh audience. In addition to the policy guidance on the countryside and the rural economy, other substantive planning issues covered by these common policies included economic development, retailing, telecommunications, recreation, coastal planning, tourism, renewable energy, and mineral extraction. These covered some of the more politically sensitive issues within the planning system operated in Wales. For far too long, planning at an all-Wales level has been formulated in England and given a 'rubber stamp' by the Welsh Office. Until now, there has been nothing Welsh about Welsh planning policy. The Welsh Office, partly as a result of insufficient resources and staff but also because of a lack of initiative, have failed to provide Wales with a distinctive planning agenda. Policy towards retailing and shopping developments, new housing, minerals extraction, coastal planning and conservation, energy developments, and the provision of sport and recreational facilities have all been identical to the position in England.

In the 1980s and early 1990s, the political role of the Welsh Office in relation to planning was one of centrality with the Department of the Environment. On occasions, separate planning agendas emerged, causing political embroilments throughout political circles on such issues as rural housing, wind farms, opencast mining, urban renewal, and out-of-town retailing. Yet these were debates sparked by essentially reactionary politics. Although Peter Walker, the Secretary of State for Wales between 1987 and 1990, was widely applauded for his interventionist role in facilitating an urban programme for the Valleys, the methods employed by the Welsh Office to progress and encourage economic change and urban renewal were outside the land use planning system. They relied on a combination of central government grants, government agencies (in particular the Welsh Development Agency and the Land Authority for Wales), private sector investment, and political cooperation across government agencies. A Welsh Office role in providing a national planning policy framework was not apparent.

Uncertainty over Wales' planning policy agenda was exacerbated further in 1993 by the appointment of John Redwood as Secretary of State. A change in Welsh Office policy caused principally by personal political ideology on the part of the Minister resulted in no further Planning Policy Guidance Notes being released in Wales. The withdrawal of the Welsh Office from the planning policy guidance resulted in Wales (and Welsh local authority planners) undergoing a period of disillusionment and the creation of a policy vacuum that was more devastating for planning's role in Wales than at any time in the 1970s or 1980s. Indeed, the Welsh Office, that had never particularly believed in promoting an independent planning policy approach, now found itself slipping behind on planning policy issues initiated across the border. Between 1993 and 1995, five PPGs were released by the Department of the Environment that normally would have applied equally to Wales. The Welsh Office refusal to release a PPG on transport, for example, resulted in a separate policy approach between the Welsh Secretary and the Environment Secretary in England on controlling transport in urban areas, protecting the environment, and encouraging more investment in public transport, some of the more rational areas for the planning system's intervention in the 1990s.

Following the appointment of William Hague as Secretary of State for Wales in July 1995 and in one of the last acts sanctioned by John Redwood as Welsh Secretary, two new draft Planning Policy Guidance Notes were released. The two documents, *Unitary Development Plans in Wales* and *Planning Guidance Wales: Planning Policy* incorporate the 'missing PPGs'. However, the contents and format of the two drafts was radically different from the joint English/Welsh planning guidance previously released. The principal change in the two draft documents compared to their former and English counterparts centres on the number of PPGs that will in future provide the Welsh national planning policy agenda. The Welsh Office replaced all the existing PPGs, some seventeen documents together with a number of circulars and other government statements, with just the two revised PPGs.

The establishment of the National Assembly provides an opportunity to consider whether the time is ripe to create a separate Welsh planning process, a process that meets the needs of the different stakeholders in Wales – at European, UK, Welsh and local levels. Wales will still possess a common legal system for planning with England, but the interpretation of that law through policy mechanisms can be different. This does not mean to say that Wales should produce a completely new blueprint. It would merely be a reflection of how all the different Welsh needs – geographic, social and economic – can start to make sense together. There should be an effort to coordinate all the competing claims on what the planning system is expected to deliver: jobs, environmental protection, improved public transport, better housing, greater choice in recreational facilities, and the promotion of culture.

THE NEED FOR AN ALL-WALES PLANNING POLICY

The Welsh Office's *Planning Guidance Wales* covers such topics as green belts, economic development, housing, coastal planning, the countryside, retailing and town centres, nature conservation, historic buildings and conservation areas, transport, sport and recreation, tourism, renewable energy, and pollution control. This 221 paragraph document was first published in May 1996, and was updated in late 1998. It outlines how the Welsh Office expects planning decisions to be made by the unitary authorities, and provides a broad framework within which the private sector and other public sector organisations in Wales should make decisions about where (and where not) to site new developments.

We might possess a separate planning policy guidance document compared to the English policy guidance, but it has only been the format that has changed. The policy document contains just eight statements that are distinctly Welsh. If one scrutinised the contents of English planning policy, the two sets of planning guidelines would be practically identical. The content of Wales' present national planning policy merely discusses how local government should operate planning, and does not cover national planning objectives.

DISAPPOINTMENT AND FRUSTRATION

There is a current debate in Welsh planning policy about the need to use the planning system to attract inward investment, to site new employment development along the major transport routes in Wales, and to protect the best landscapes. But the document is virtually devoid of a spatial dimension. It does not contain any guidance on where major new development should be located. Nor does it adequately provide national targets for, say, sustainability, biodiversity, or even economic development. Current Welsh policy is restricted to simply broad vacuous declarations that contain very little direction. It is true to say that most of the planning system operates - quite rightly - at the local level of government, and this permits local people to decide matters locally. However, the ability of local people tp decide matters locally has often been thwarted in Wales through the intervention of the Welsh Office.

During the last few years there has been concern that land use planning is becoming increasingly politicised. Some local politicians, particularly in rural areas, are frustrated with their inability to apply local interpretation of national guidance to local circumstances. The principal substantive policy areas affected by these decisions relate to affordable housing in rural areas and the preservation of the Welsh language. Planning policy is being used in these areas for social advantage in a way that was never intended. Rural authorities are increasingly promoting housing policies to develop affordable housing for local people and to secure distinctive cultural differences. These two areas of social concern sit uneasily within the planning policy process although there is evidence to suggest that their prominence may increase in the near future as more authorities attempt to integrate the issues into the planning system.

Almost all 221 paragraphs of *Planning Guidance Wales* repeat the English position, almost word for word. This tendency to apply English-formulated planning policies in Wales hasn't gone unnoticed, of course. Rural planners and politicians have on times become frustrated with what they see as inappropriate planning policies to deal with the social, economic and environmental problems of their communities. After all, how could a housing development policy drafted to apply across England and Wales be just as suitable for the landscape of mid Wales as the Home Counties? Local authorities have tried to deviate from the norm. But this has only landed them in trouble with the Welsh Office which has accused them of 'malpractice', simply because they have not strictly followed the national approach. Local authorities do have some discretion to set their own agendas, but these are within a strong framework provided by central government.

The professional officers, aware of the limitations to the statutory planning process, are conforming to the policy planning constraints. However, elected members tend to be more reluctant to follow imposed central government guidance. This leads to occasions when local members reject professional advice, down play central government planning policies, and thereby contribute to reports of mis-representing the purpose of the land use planning system. Because this is in part a political reaction it is especially difficult for a planning officer to deal with. The professional has to recognise and manage politicians' requests to implement an anti-institutional decision -making process against the imposition of central government policies for everyone in the authority's area. It is one thing for local politicians to deliberately ignore established government planning policies for the benefit of everyone in the authority's area. On the other hand, it is another matter when the opposition is enacted only when it benefits people born in the locality. Research should be undertaken to consider the extent to which the Welsh language is being used as a material consideration in the planning policy process by local authorities, and to assess ways in which both affordable rural housing needs and the Welsh language have the potential to be incorporated into the Welsh planning system. Guidance is required for professional planners and elected members on how cultural issues and social considerations should be treated in the development plan process.

A position where the Assembly does not release any planning guidance to the unitary authorities on these issues is not an option. A change can be made to ensure that the guidance provided is both suitable for the unique problems Welsh authorities face and responsive to local people. The Assembly should therefore have two objectives in relation to planning policy:

- To provide planning policy guidance that is relevant to the unitary authorities to enable them to implement planning locally (ensuring best practice in the activities of local government).

- To provide planning policy direction on certain issues of national importance to Wales. The Assembly has to possess some strategic policy-making function in relation to planning, especially those planning issues which can only be addressed at an all-Wales level through planning policy promotion and strategic coordination.

It is to this second dimension that we now turn.

MAJOR DEVELOPMENTS OF NATIONAL SIGNIFICANCE

The sort of development issues which should be addressed at the all-Wales level include the siting of new airports, prisons, hospitals, major manufacturing sites, barrage developments, major cultural and recreational facilities, and the routing of new roads and new railways. Currently, these major decisions lack a framework. The location of such high profile schemes are left either to the Secretary of State (for instance, location of the Assembly itself) or to government agencies (for example, major inward investment by the WDA, hospitals by the health trusts, and prisons by the Prison Service).

Perhaps this is not an essential task of the Assembly, but in its monitoring of other agencies the Assembly will need to adopt strategic and sustainable objectives in overseeing locational and investment decisions. The situation east of Offa's Dyke is also changing. The development of major infrastructure projects will occur within a stronger planning policy provided by the Department of the Environment, Transport and the Regions at an all-England level. This is to ensure that the enhanced power awarded to the English regions does not result in their competing with one another to attract particular major developments. Scotland, too, is working towards the preparation of a National Physical Plan. If the Assembly does not perform a similar role in Wales - either by releasing an all-Wales national planning policy covering these developments or through enhanced scrutiny and monitoring of public sector organisations - greater inter-authority competition will occur that would undoubtedly lead to public accusations of wasteful bidding, secrecy and lack of accountability.

WALES IN A EUROPEAN SPATIAL PLANNING CONTEXT

An all-Wales planning policy document would also be helpful in placing Wales on a European agenda. *Planning Guidance Wales* contains no reference to the European Union or to structural funds, even though their importance in Wales has been extremely significant. Scotland and the English regions are about to change the content of their planning policies to highlight more explicitly the European dimension. In future they will highlight the areas of the country designated to receive Objective 1, 2 and 5b funding from Europe, to ensure that planning policies are then developed that coordinate physical land use and the resources and finances available for investment. Such a change is bound to benefit the Regional Development Agencies and Scottish Enterprise, in providing a competitive edge over Wales through a coordinative policy mechanism. The Welsh Development Agency should be viewing this with some concern.

The merging of strategic planning policy with wider financing issues is a major change in policy in England. However, the Welsh Office does not seem inclined to follow suit. Consider how effective an all-Wales planning policy would be if it not only highlighted overarching policies related to the natural and built environment, but additionally the spatial locations of major infrastructure projects and the areas of eligibility for financing. The planning ministers of the European Union have already produced a *European Spatial Development Perspective* (ESDP) that attempts to move further down the road of integrating land use planning policies with resourcing issues. The UK government has signed up to the ESDP. England and Scotland are already working on enhanced Euro-friendly national policy statements. Can Wales afford to do nothing?

RECOGNISING THE PLANNING NEEDS OF WALES

The creation of the National Assembly provides an opportunity to formulate a planning policy that meets the needs of the Welsh economy, the environment and our communities. In the process the Assembly will have to balance competing claims for its attention. Strategic planning should ensure that environmental protection *and* economic development are catered for in an integrated and sustainable whole. One way to proceed would be for the Assembly to produce a 'State of the Nation Planning Framework', that reflects the particular needs of Wales, rather than England, identifies broad strategic policy direction, and encourages public and private sector agencies to implement the strategy at a more detailed local level.

The town and country planning process has to recognise the following aims, that were developed as part of an all-Wales strategic planning guidance exercise in the early 1990s. They are still relevant today and can be used as a foundation for the Assembly's development of a strategic planning framework:

- To ensure that Wales can enjoy a quality of life at levels comparable with the best in the European Union.

- To develop land use planning policies that reflect the principle of Sustainable Development.

- To protect and enhance the natural and built environment.

- To recognise the distinctive language and culture in Wales.

- To improve the economic health of the principality.

- To improve access to housing.

- To secure public and private investment in transportation and infrastructure.

The Assembly's duty in relation to planning is strategic. It should not intervene excessively in the activities of local government or frustrate the options available to the private sector. It should merely set the broad framework. On housing, we must ensure that the best of our landscapes are conserved and future housing development is targeted on derelict or brownfield sites. On the economy, we must also build on the success of the Welsh Development Agency and other organisations in providing suitable strategic sites for inward investment, to plan for future job creation. This does not mean that the new Welsh Development Agency determines the whole strategic policy for Wales. We cannot afford to put employment creation above all other policy sectors. It requires the Assembly asserting its Sustainable Development remit over the WDA and, as a democratic forum, insisting that economic development decisions are transparent and coordinated.

The Assembly must oversee an efficient, effective and integrated transport network for Wales. This has to be sustainable and meet the needs of businesses and communities. Strategic planning should also take more account of the different social and cultural dimensions of Welsh life: protection of the Welsh language, providing the means for affordable housing to meet needs, and regulating second homes if they seriously affect local housing supply.

More importantly, the Assembly has to be sensitive to the landscape and settlement patterns of Wales. This is an area where planners, landscapers and architects should work together in controlling development and providing quality buildings in sensitive locations.

IMPLEMENTING PLANNING POLICY AND STRATEGIC COORDINATION

The first year of the Assembly will witness extreme pressure on its members to deliver on a wide range of issues apart from planning. The priority areas for Assembly members are likely to be health, education, and the economy. We should not expect a 'big bang' to occur in Welsh planning, but the Assembly can make a start in transforming the system. In particular, the Assembly should work to the following programme:

- Adopt a strategic planning framework to harness the diverse and competing policy areas of Wales into a sustainable 'State of the Nation Planning Framework', that identifies the issues that local government, the quangos and private sector can work together to deliver.

- Establish mechanisms that pull together the aims and objectives of the various governmental agencies in Wales (in particular the WDA, CCW, and the TECs) into a coordinative sustainable policy agenda, and to review those policies regularly.

- Delegate the monitoring of the implementation of this policy framework to the four economic regions of Wales.

- Issue national infrastructure planning policy statements on those matters that require addressing at the all-Wales level, to ensure Wales possesses a strong spatial planning voice in Europe and to avoid costly public inquiries and delays.

- Review the various sectoral policy needs of Wales to assess how policies could change to make them more responsive to people of Wales.

- Work in partnership with the quangos and unitary local government and the private sector in providing an effective framework to ensure that planning delivers.

CONCLUSION

By creating a strong policy on all these interconnected matters a sound strategic planning platform will be provided. The Assembly, local authorities, the quangos, the private sector and voluntary organisations will be better able to act in partnership to deliver a sustainable all-Wales policy. Strategic planning policy cannot be prescriptive over the detailed work of local authorities. Local communities must keep some discretion to decide what is best for their local areas. Different parts of Wales will have to adopt their own interpretations and approaches to an all-Wales policy.

Yet we can devise a strategic planning system that is both responsive to local needs and robust as a national agenda. That policy will be essential in overseeing local authorities' approaches to planning and the environment. But it also has to act as a shop-window for Wales in forging links with Europe, in attracting EU structural funds, and enhancing Wales' position in the global economy.

The draft replacement to *Planning Guidance Wales* released in 1997 is a long way from setting the required Welsh planning agenda. We need to start thinking about planning *for* Wales, not planning in Wales. With the National Assembly we have an opportunity to create a strategic planning vision for Wales that is integrated, sustainable, and above all, Welsh.

CHAPTER 13

ECONOMIC DEVELOPMENT

Brian Morgan and Kevin Morgan

Of all the measures by which the National Assembly will be judged none will be as important as the challenge of raising the level of economic well-being, north and south, east and west. Although economic well-being is influenced by macro-economic factors outside the Assembly's control, much can be achieved through more concerted and dynamic action at the Welsh level. Regional aid still plays an important role in promoting economic well-being in Wales, but this can never be an adequate surrogate for a skilled and versatile workforce, a stock of innovative firms, and a robust networking culture in which the public, private and third sectors collaborate for mutually beneficial ends.

Given that Wales is one of the poorer parts of the UK, with a wide array of deeply-entrenched problems, the design of a new economic development agenda could easily degenerate into a wish-list. This would be a recipe for disaster since the Assembly would inevitably dissipate its energies in an orgy of self-indulgent activity.

To avoid this scenario the Assembly will have to establish clear priorities at the outset. In deciding where to focus its energies, it will have to strike a judicious balance between two essential, but competing, principles:

- On the one hand it cannot avoid addressing fundamental weaknesses in the Welsh economy, such as the weak skills base, the poor research and development record, the low rate of new firm formation, all of which require long-term attention before they begin to pay dividends.

- On the other hand it is politically important that the Assembly demonstrates it can make a difference on the economic front and this requires 'little victories' sooner rather than later.

To succeed the Assembly will need to promote new forms of economic development in Wales. This chapter sets out some ideas for maximising the opportunities for indigenous growth based on the creation of a skilled workforce, the growth of competitive firms and the reform of the institutional infrastructure.

The chapter begins with a frank picture of the economic and institutional problems which the Assembly will inherit. There follows some development priorities which the Assembly should address as a matter of urgency. Finally, we emphasise that 'process' is as important as 'content' when it comes to making public policy more effective.

THE ASSEMBLY'S ECONOMIC INHERITANCE

I. MANUFACTURING SUCCESS

In many respects the performance of Welsh manufacturing, in both the UK and European contexts, continues to be above average, with manufacturing output in the last decade out-performing the UK average by a considerable margin. Also Wales is likely to have been one of the few UK (or European) regions to increase manufacturing employment over the same period. See figure 1:

FIGURE 1

Employment Change 1986-1996

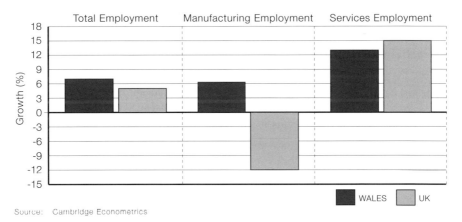

Source: Cambridge Econometrics

The reasons for this Welsh manufacturing success are (at least) threefold:

- High levels of inward investment, with substantial re-investments emphasising the competitive advantage acquired by relocating firms.

- Considerable capital investment and productivity growth in metal manufacturing and related sectors.

- Integration of new SMEs into the manufacturing sector - a sector that is now highly price competitive with a large and growing export content.

These developments have combined to produce enormous improvements in manufacturing productivity since the mid 1980s and Wales is now one of the most productive regions in the UK (see figure 2). However, prosperity in Wales (as measured by GDP per head or personal incomes), has failed to match the growth in manufacturing output. This is largely because the expansion in manufacturing has not generated sufficient spin-offs in other sectors to raise total factor productivity.

FIGURE 2

Manufacturing Labour Productivity (value added per head) 1995

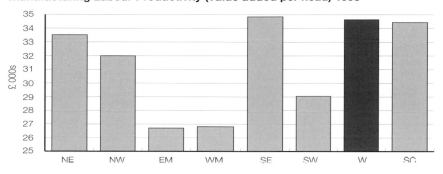

Source: dti 'Regional Competitiveness Indicators Feb 1998'

II. RELATIVE PROSPERITY

Consequently, it is doubtful whether the policies that have generated economic growth have been equally successful in boosting regional economic development. Indeed, the latest GDP per capita figures remain stubbornly low at 83 per cent of the UK average and the trend remains significantly downwards. See figures 3 and 4:

FIGURE 3

GDP Per Head (UK = 100)

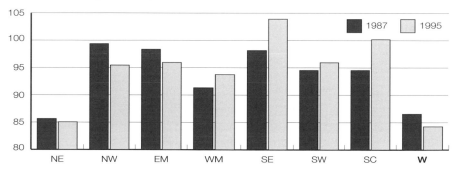

Source: dti 'Regional Competitiveness Indicators Feb 1998'

FIGURE 4

Welsh GDP per Head (UK=100)

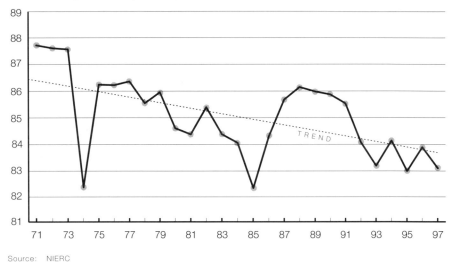

Source: NIERC

Other areas of concern are low levels of firm formation, a poor transport infrastructure, low R&D activity and poor vocational qualifications. See figures 5-7:

FIGURE 5

Manufacturing and Services Gross Average Hourly Earnings for Full-Time Employees (£s per hour)

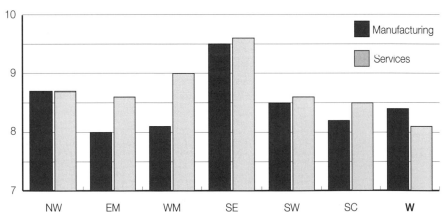

Source: dti 'Regional Competitiveness Indicators Feb 1998'

FIGURE 6

Welsh Share of New UK VAT Registrations

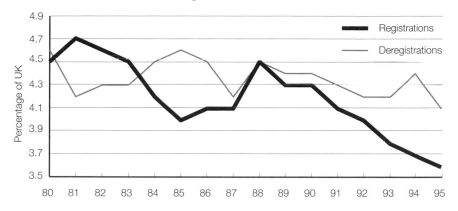

Source: ONS

FIGURE 7

VAT Registrations as a % of Firms, 1996

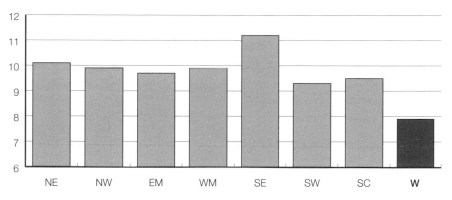

Source: dti 'Regional Competitiveness Indicators Feb 1998'

Many reasons have been put forward to explain the continuing dichotomy between manufacturing success and personal prosperity in Wales (see figures 8 - 12):

- The growth prospects for the Welsh **service sector** in terms of output, employment and productivity are way below the UK average and this is reflected in low wages in the service sector compared with manufacturing ~ not helped by the fact that 40 per cent of Welsh service sector employment is in public administration.

- Economic activity rates are, in general, below the UK average and in certain areas of rural Wales, where employment opportunities are poor, participation rates are considerably lower.

- The number and growth of indigenous firms is below the UK average but in some key sectors - especially the high value added service sectors - the trends are even worse (despite the expensive Financial Services Initiative and the attractions of Cardiff Bay).

- Significant inward migration has taken place in recent years, often of retired people, which has lowered GDP per head figures by adding directly to expenditure but only indirectly to output.

- There is low integration of foreign-owned manufacturing companies into the regional economy. Despite some notable successes with local sourcing such as those undertaken by Sony and Ford, the typical inward investor has low levels of local sourcing and undertakes little or no high value-added R&D. Hence, inward investment may be creating 'islands of excellence' within a sea of mediocrity.

FIGURE 8

Sectoral Employment Growth: 1980 - 96

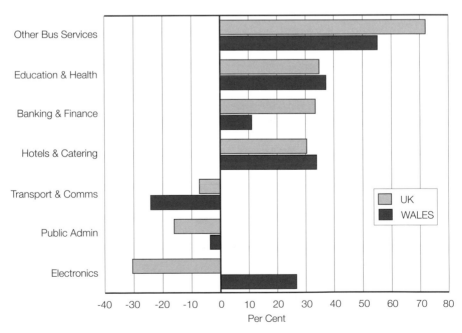

Source: dti 'Regional Competitiveness Indicators Feb 1998'

FIGURE 9

Welsh Service Sector Employment: 1996

Total Service Sector Employment = 786,000

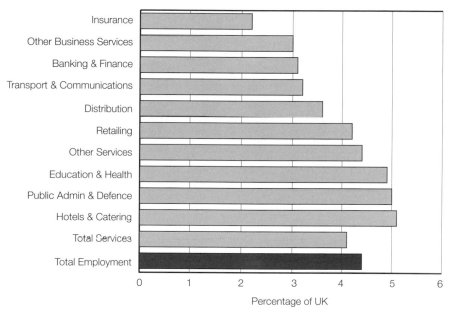

Insurance
Other Business Services
Banking & Finance
Transport & Communications
Distribution
Retailing
Other Services
Education & Health
Public Admin & Defence
Hotels & Catering
Total Services
Total Employment

Percentage of UK

Source: Cambridge Econometrics (February 1997)

FIGURE 10

Inward Investment Jobs by WDA Division

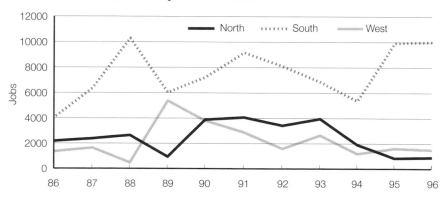

North ▪▪▪▪▪▪▪ South West

Jobs

Source: WDA

FIGURE 11

Business R&D and Hightech Specialisation, 1995

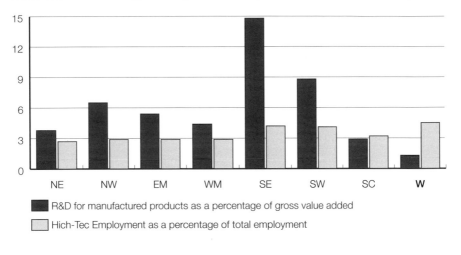

R&D for manufactured products as a percentage of gross value added

Hich-Tec Employment as a percentage of total employment

Source: dti 'Regional Competitiveness Indicators Feb 1998'

FIGURE 12

Forecasts for UK Growth Sectors: 1997-2010

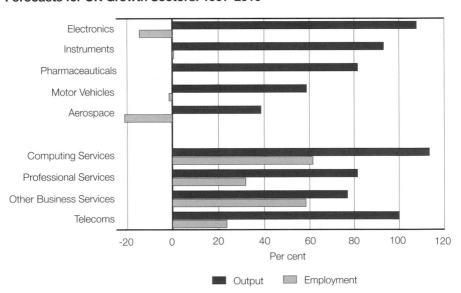

Source: Cambridge Econometrics

The conclusion seems to be that although the positive impact of inward investment on the manufacturing sector is indisputable, there is still much that needs to be done to improve the contribution that inward investors make to the economy of Wales. There is also a need to develop policies that achieve more for indigenous companies.

III. KNOWLEDGE AND INSTITUTIONS

Policies to reduce the prosperity gap with the rest of the UK are discussed below but to be effective they will need to address two further inherited weaknesses:

- the knowledge gap
- the institutional deficit

The **knowledge gap** refers to the dearth of information on the sectoral performance of SMEs and of SME needs. Consequently, there is currently little in the way of proactive business support services being provided to indigenous firms. To become more proactive, Business Connect will need to improve not only the information flow to SMEs but also improve the information flow about SME needs to partner organisations in economic development. Hence there is a need to create a stratified, representative database of manufacturing and service sector firms that is targeted at relevant sectors, such as 'producer services' – that is, those services that add value to the manufacturing sector.

Some information already exists on small firms but the aim should be to develop a data base that can be used to target firms who are growing and also firms with the potential to grow. This information is a vital pre-requisite for the development of innovative programmes that can effectively assist these firms to achieve their growth prospects.

The **institutional deficit** is characterised by the numerous institutions currently involved in delivering business development programmes to indigenous firms in Wales. Indeed, the one thing that would probably do more to generate long term growth than anything else would be the rationalisation of these diverse organisations. An effective strategy for indigenous growth will require the integration of these economic development organisations into an **effective partnership**.

In this respect, the institutional deficit also refers to the lack of a partnership approach in Wales to developing mechanisms that can focus regional development policies on SME 'needs'. For example, the next section highlights the opportunity for the Assembly to develop institutions similar to Scottish Trade International in order to promote a radical rationalisation of business support services to Welsh SMEs.

DEVELOPMENT PRIORITIES FOR THE NATIONAL ASSEMBLY

All economic development programmes are destined to disappoint some constituency because they are obliged to be selective and this one is no exception. We have identified three development priorities for the first term of the National Assembly – skills, business development and infrastructure – each of which has a major bearing on the health of the Welsh economy in both the short and the long term. This means that the Assembly ought to be able to devise staggered targets which enable it to strike a judicious balance between the two competing principles outlined in the introduction. This is to secure 'little victories' in the short-term without losing sight of long-term goals. In discussing the following development priorities we are more concerned to establish the case for action than to elaborate the policy details.

I. SKILLS

With notable exceptions, Wales is a low-skills economy in which most companies do not make adequate provision for the training of their employees. We believe there are at least three dimensions to the skills challenge:

- Vocational
- Graduate
- ICT-related skills

As regards **vocational skills** this demand-side problem is compounded on the supply-side by the fact that FE colleges, the main delivery mechanism for vocational skills, are heavily constrained by a funding mechanism which allots pride of place to student preferences rather than to the needs of the Welsh economy. What makes matters even worse is that the post-16 Vocational Education and Training (VET) system is plagued by competition, pitting schools against colleges, with the result that young people may not be getting the best careers guidance to suit their needs, be they vocational or academic.

Critics claim that the current VET system satisfies neither students nor employers. The most graphic illustration of the vocational skills deficit is that blue chip inward investors cannot secure an adequate supply of young people for their apprenticeship programmes. If large firms cannot get what they want from the VET system, what hope is there for SMEs in Wales?

If the Assembly wants to make an early impact in redressing the vocational skills deficit in Wales it would do well to build on existing good practice. The *Action Plan for Manufacturing Training in Wales*, produced by the Council of Welsh TECs, identified a series of targets to upgrade the skill base in Wales. It has the additional merit of having been produced through a process of consultation, thereby commanding respect and legitimacy from the public and private sectors throughout Wales.

Wales needs to be much more creative about the use of **graduate skills** because we are the Cinderella of higher education in the UK: in 1998/99, for example, the funding per student is £5,645 in Scotland, £4,760 in England but only £4,611 in Wales. With some exceptions the HE sector in Wales does not engage with the Welsh economy on anything like the scale that is necessary. Recent events suggest that this may be changing:

- LG Semicon, the new Korean firm in Newport, has set a precedent for interacting with HE because of its graduate skill requirements.

- The Heads of Higher Education in Wales commissioned a study of the impact of higher education on the Welsh economy which sought to identify good practice.

- Progress is being made with the supply of 'High Level Graduates' who combine academic and industrial expertise.

- The Teaching Company Scheme has been well-received by the corporate sector.

Overall, however, Welsh firms, especially SMEs, make little or no use of graduate-level skills. This must be a priority if we are to retain these high level skills in Wales. In conjunction with the Higher Education Funding Council for Wales, the Assembly should build on current initiatives to promote the use of graduate skills in the Welsh economy, particularly within the SME sector.

Finally, the Assembly would do well to pay particular attention to **Information and Communication Technology (ICT)** skills because these are routinely required in the 'learning society'. The Wales Information Society (WIS) Project, which can be accessed at its website (http://www.wis.org.uk), has signalled the danger of a new polarisation in Wales between the 'information haves' and 'information have-nots'. A WIS survey (contained in the report *Wales Information Society*, IWA, 1997) revealed some alarming results: general awareness about ICT skills in Wales was low and there were marked differences by age, class and gender.

If the Assembly took it upon itself to pioneer a 'digital democracy' in Wales, in which new forms of interaction became possible between people and politicians, this would really put the spotlight on ICT skills.

II. BUSINESS DEVELOPMENT

No country can aspire to a viable future without a robust business sector, the key element of economic well-being. Business development policy in Wales should have at least four important dimensions:

- Raising the business birth rate.

- Improving support for indigenous businesses.

- Making the most of the foreign-owned sector.

- Raising the status of community enterprise, which affords important opportunities to socially excluded parts of Wales.

The **business birth rate** in Wales is lamentably low compared to other regions of the UK, as we can see from the VAT data. Although there are deep social and cultural reasons for this poor record, not least poverty, the Assembly would do well to emulate the Business Birthrate Initiative in Scotland, which has begun to address these deeper barriers to new firm formation. As things stand, there is nothing remotely like this exercise in Wales and the WDA should be encouraged to conduct a similar initiative here. To inform this strategy, urgent action is needed to address the knowledge gap identified above because an understanding of the characteristics of growth firms will be an important pre-requisite for starting and growing **new** firms.

In this respect, support for new firms must go hand in hand with better support for existing **indigenous businesses,** the long-neglected sector of the Welsh economy. The debate about how best to support this sector (that is, what services to offer, who should offer them and how support should be organised), is inextricably tied up with the debate about the future configuration of Business Connect, which urgently needs to be reformed.

Business Connect is essentially a loose consortium of public agencies that is not funded properly to carry out its task. This is in sharp contrast to the significant new funding made available to Business Links in England and the Business Shop structures in Scotland. Moreover, Business Links is being set ambitious new targets to drive up quality and as part of this reform the providers of business support services are to be regularly monitored.

The main problem in Wales is that the real delivery of business advice, together with more than 50 per cent of the 'access points' for Business Connect, is provided by the local enterprise agencies and voluntary sector organisations which are part of the consortia. However, these are the only Business Connect members which are not fully and directly Welsh Office funded.

Ideally the 'new' Business Connect Wales should be allocated funding centrally in partnership with the Welsh Development Agency and these funds should be targeted on encouraging indigenous companies to grow. The funding and the associated employment targets would have parity with those set for inward investment. The importance of this recommendation can be gauged from the figures. In 1996-97 the WDA achieved an employment target of 18,000 jobs. Of this total, about 15,000 jobs came from inward investment. In fact on average over the last five years the target for indigenous job creation has been less than 20 per cent of that for inward investment. Hence, this new organisation would be set the objective of achieving a better balance between indigenous business growth and inward investment in terms of parity of esteem, parity of objectives and parity of resource.

However, this option could require the creation of a new Quango and this might prove to be politically unacceptable. In this case some intermediate solution might prove necessary. Initially for example, it could mean the creation of a 'company limited by guarantee' which would rationalise the structure and co-ordinate all expenditures on business development. This organisation might be formed by a partnership between the Welsh Office and the new WDA along the lines of Scottish Trade International.

A re-launched Business Connect should be granted powers to audit and agree the business plans and corporate strategies of existing organisations to ensure some consistency in objectives across the target markets. Formal agreements and a simplified structure (based on the WDA regions) would be required, but funding would then be dependent on business plans conforming to a co-ordinated strategy.

In the context of an effective Business Connect, the development of networks of SMEs will be crucial because it is now well understood that firms learn best from other firms in a network environment, and not from business advisers. Hence a prime objective for each partner would be to encourage firms to participate in networks and to highlight the cost advantages of such activity. Linkages should be further developed and strengthened - not just along the supply chain but in terms of broader customer networks for diverse products and services. These networks would then be used as a mechanism for bolstering SME growth and stimulating economic development across Wales.

Although Wales has done well in attracting **foreign direct investment (FDI)**, we need to appreciate that the foreign sector accounts for less than 8 per cent of total employment in Wales and much of this is heavily biased towards the south-east and north-east parts of the country. The Assembly could usefully address two major FDI issues: first, how to promote a more balanced spatial spread of new FDI projects and, second, how to encourage the 'embedding' of existing FDI facilities.

As regards new FDI projects the Assembly should work with the WDA to explore the possibilities of a more tiered system of incentives where they become progressively weaker the closer they get to south-east and north-east Wales. One of the key factors here is availability of good sites and premises, and the west and the north should be given top priority in this respect.

The embedding of existing foreign plants can be encouraged in two ways: by improving the quality of the WDA's aftercare service on the one hand and by improving the quality of technical skills on the other. At the same time the competence of indigenous suppliers should be improved together with the R&D capability of the Universities. The WDA has earned a sound reputation for its *Source Wales* programme, and this needs to be extended to new sectors of the economy. One example is agri-business where there are new opportunities for indigenous firms to supply UK retailers with high quality, especially organic, food products.

Finally, business development initiatives should no longer ignore the **community enterprise** sector and the **cultural industries**, both of which afford important training and employment opportunities for socially excluded sectors of society. The community enterprise sector is not a marginal part of the economy. According to the Welsh Local Government Association, there are now some 500 community enterprises in Wales, with a combined annual turnover of £30m, and these have created a total of 5,000 jobs.

Similarly, the development of arts, culture and media activity is already generating a significant number of jobs in all parts of Wales. These sectors provide enormous returns for very little (financial) investment. For the sake of social justice and economic development the Assembly should support cultural innovation and community entrepreneurs.

Some of the policy options that would help address these issues include:

- Improving the productivity and growth of small firms by identifying potential growth SMEs; embedding multinationals into the local economy and developing supplier networks for these firms; using these large firm / small firm links to encourage innovation in product and process development; and focusing business support services on networked SMEs with the aim of extending these links to high value added services and R&D facilities.

- Raising economic activity rates in Wales to the UK average by revitalising business start-ups and developing retraining schemes and incentives that encourage people, particularly women, to re-enter the labour market.

- Identifying opportunities for indigenous businesses to become more focused on international markets and developing international / SME linkages that encourage SMEs to access the global economy and benefit from inward investment successes.

- Using the cultural and artistic strengths of Wales, such as the Welsh National Opera, and bands like the Manic Street Preachers to enhance the image of Wales as an arts community having European significance; and creating scope for community enterprise and cultural activities to generate new jobs in the provision of local retailing services, social care, education and entertainment.

III. INFRASTRUCTURE

When discussing infrastructure we make a distinction between traditional infrastructure (like land, roads, rail and air) and technology-related infrastructure (like information and communication technologies), both of which are equally important to economic well-being.

As regards traditional infrastructure, the Assembly will want to satisfy itself that Wales is not becoming more disadvantaged as a business location on account of its road, rail and air transport systems. Legitimate concern has arisen about Wales being left behind at a time when many premier business locations in the EU already have access to high-speed rail systems, regional airports, and intra-regional motorway networks. These problems are compounded in Wales by the high tolls on the Severn bridges.

With the growth of a new, digitally-based ICT infrastructure, the Assembly will want to assure itself that Wales is not being marginalised in the Information Society. As we have argued, the best way to ensure that we stay abreast of this challenge is to ensure that Wales is equipped with the skills to participate in the emerging Information Society. To make early progress with this priority - and indeed with all the other priorities discussed here - the Assembly should build on good practice, in this case the WIS Project, which has identified the problems and possibilities for Wales in the Information Society.

THE NEW POLICY-MAKING PROCESS

The birth of a new institution tends to induce atavistic human desires such as reinventing wheels, empire building, and power struggles. In this final section we simply want to highlight two policy-making challenges which could make or break the Assembly:

- Externally, there is a need for the Assembly to work with its partners through a process of ongoing consultation.

- Internally, there is a need for the Assembly to build robust horizontal working methods to enable Subject Committees to interact in a creative and effective manner.

As regards the external challenge, if the Assembly wanted a practical illustration of an inclusive policy-making approach in Wales it could not do better than to look at the experience of the Regional Technology Plan (RTP), which is managed by the WDA and governed by a Steering Committee chaired by a well-respected industrialist. The RTP has been an exemplary policy initiative: over 600 organisations were consulted before the Action Plan was drawn up and key projects have been devolved to those organisations best equipped to carry them forward. If the Assembly can extend the partnership model of the RTP – by focusing on excellence and by harnessing the energies of a wide spectrum of expertise – it will have paid its way.

On the internal challenge it is clear that the Subject Committees will need to develop innovative cross-functional working methods if the Assembly is to be more than the sum of its parts. For example, the Economic Development Committee will have a direct interest in Transport, Education & Training and European Affairs, and these cross-functional working methods need to be embedded in the routines of the Assembly from day one.

If the Assembly can address these priorities in a collaborative and inclusive way, it will begin to make a difference. What the Assembly does is important but, even more important, is what the Assembly enables others to do for themselves.

CHAPTER 14

TRANSPORT

Bob Daimond

This chapter sets out the current level of provision for all forms of transport within Wales and summarises the main channels of responsibility for them including those which will pass to the Assembly when it is established. There is a wide level of agreement concerning the major problems and deficiencies in transport infrastructure and these are identified. Targets and longer-term objectives that the Assembly might adopt are suggested. The chapter then looks at options for developing the Assembly's relationship with the Westminster Government and with Welsh local government.

The Government has already carried out a major review of transport and associated policies, and published during 1998 the following documents:

- *A New Deal for Transport: Better for Everyone* - the White Paper on Integrated Transport Policies

- *Transporting Wales into the Future* - the Welsh supplement to the White Paper

- *Driving Wales Forward* - the Welsh Office Policy Statement on Trunk Roads in Wales

It should also be noted that the deliberations of Welsh Office Transport Advisory Group, chaired by Welsh Office Minister Peter Hain, may well influence the Assembly's agenda. The Welsh Local Government Association also has a Transport and Communications Advisory Group which it will also seek to influence the Welsh Office and the Assembly. Early in 1998 the Government published *Opportunities for Change* a consultation paper on the revised UK strategy for Sustainable Development which includes transport among its subject areas. There is to be a further White Paper and no doubt the policies to be set out in that will have to be taken on board by the Assembly.

The Government is also in the process of a major consultation exercise on the future of local democracy. Although not directly relevant to transport, this process could result in a wider competence for Local Government, could strengthen the potential partnership between the Assembly and Local Government, and hence improve the climate for addressing some of the deficiencies in co-ordination of transport highlighted in this paper.

THE CURRENT DEBATE

The concepts of sustainable transport and Sustainable Development are not new and have been addressed by transportation professionals as well as the environmental lobby for some time. The debate has however intensified in Britain since the 1997 General Election. The Government's commitment to addressing the widely acknowledged problems of congestion, pollution and sustainability has moved the debate onto a more realistic level and is to be welcomed.

Transport is not, however, a matter for discussion in isolation from other policies and subjects. It is not an entity capable of management by government or any other agency by decree. Transport is a complex interaction of all elements in a modern society and consists of millions of individual and separate decisions. While government and other organisations can promote measures and practices to assist the solution of some problems and reduce the worst effects of transport on society, the overall situation remains dependent on the exercise of choice and the availability of viable options.

There is a real danger when considering transport on a UK basis of generating solutions which address problems in certain areas but which are wholly inappropriate for other situations. The prime risk is that legislation designed to solve the obvious problems in London, Manchester or Birmingham may prejudice the rest of the country. In Wales there is a wide variation between the situation in the urban areas of south Wales or north-east Wales and the rural heartland of, say, Powys, Ceredigion, or Gwynedd. The Assembly must therefore take care in addressing this subject to give full weight to all parts of Wales and their particular circumstances.

Any meaningful changes to transport operations in Wales must entail significant improvement in the infrastructure. This requires financial investment whatever mode of transport is under consideration. The Assembly should therefore be aware that policies will have economic implications and these need to be addressed before implementation is attempted. Partial or piecemeal implementation of measures which would otherwise have a beneficial effect could result in negative results if they are perceived as failing due to lack of financial support.

RESPONSIBILITIES FOR TRANSPORT

Responsibility for transport is not vested in a single authority and there are elements for which no one could be said to be 'responsible'. Various parts of central and local government and, indeed, other agencies have responsibility related to transport and most have powers in respect of other functions which may be exercised on a discretionary basis. Currently responsibility is distributed four ways, as follows:

1   The Secretary of State for the Environment, Transport and the Regions is the Highway Authority for trunk roads in England. He is also responsible on an England and Wales or UK basis for the following:

   *   Highways and Traffic Legislation

   *   Setting the policy framework for public transport generally

   *   Regulating the railways and the provision of financial support for passenger rail services

   *   Regulating the bus industry and the promotion of safety, competition and reliability

   *   Setting the regulatory framework for taxis and private hire vehicles

   *   Promoting and regulating air services and setting the policy framework for airports

   *   Promoting and regulating shipping and setting the policy framework for ports

2   The Secretary of State for Wales is the Highway Authority for trunk roads in Wales. This entails responsibility for maintaining and managing the trunk road network and reviewing the adequacy of the network. He also has powers to carry out improvements to safeguard the safety of road users or to meet public need. While not directly responsible for the matters listed above, the Secretary of State is involved in, and has influence over, the formulation and implementation of these policies. The Secretary of State is responsible for allocating Transport Grant to Unitary Authorities (total budget approximately £40m) for:

   *   Road improvement schemes valued more than £5m.

   *   Integrated transport package schemes valued at more than £1m (1998-99 onwards).

   The Secretary of State for Wales is also responsible for allocating both revenue and capital funds to Unitary Authorities for transport purposes. However, these allocations are unhypothecated and it is each authority's responsibility to allocate its budget between various services according to its own priorities, aims and objectives. He also awards Capital Challenge funding for which Unitary Authorities make bids for specific schemes. The Secretary of State's other specific powers include:-

- The power to pay grants towards the cost of facilities to transfer freight movements from road to rail or inland waterway (Freight Facilities Grant).

- The power to pay grants towards the cost of setting up innovative public transport services in rural Wales (Rural Transport Innovation Grant).

- Limited regulatory powers in relation to the subsidised public transport services which local authorities are required to operate, for example on tendering.

- Limited regulatory powers in relation to the concessionary fares schemes operated on a discretionary basis by local authorities, for example an order making power to extend the classes of people eligible for travel concessions.

- A requirement to consider proposals for the sale or financial restructuring of local authority owned bus companies.

- Rural public transport support - £2.5m allocated in the March 1998 budget and a promise of more to come in the White Paper.

- Limited direct funding of the cycle network SUSTRANS in Wales.

3   Unitary Authorities are the Highway Authority for all highways maintainable at the public expense except trunk roads. Under the Transport Act 1985 they have powers to support public transport as follows:

- Provision of infrastructure, for instance bus stations and stops

- Concessionary fare schemes

- Non commercial services - bus or rail, either by tender or by agreement with operators

- Publication of timetables

Unitary Authorities also have powers to make Traffic Regulation Orders but enforcement is the responsibility of the Police except where decriminalisation schemes have been implemented and the Local Authority undertakes the enforcement. Unitary Authorities are responsible for Road Safety education, training and publicity, and for Education Transport.

4   The Traffic Commissioners are responsible for licensing heavy goods vehicles and public service vehicle operating companies. They have responsibilities, together with the Police, for enforcing elements of the Construction and Use Regulations in respect of commercial and public service vehicle condition.

COMMENTARY

It can be seen that in Wales there is no overall responsibility for co-ordinating public transport and that rail, air and sea transport operators are not responsible to the Welsh Office or local authorities. It should be noted that in the current proposals for a Strategic Rail Authority, the new body will be responsible to the Secretary of State for Environment, Transport and the Regions, but it is likely that it will be required to consult with the Secretary of State for Wales or the Assembly. This situation relies very heavily on voluntary co-operation to achieve what level of transport co-ordination there is. It includes co-operation between:

- Individual public transport operators - train-train, train-bus, bus-bus
- Public transport operators and individual Unitary Authorities
- Neighbouring Unitary Authorities through joint arrangements
- Public transport operators and joint Authority Groups
- A number of public transport operators and joint Authority Groups

While this primarily affects the actual provision of the services it also affects the more peripheral aspects of the public transport service, such as:

- Comprehensive time tabling - some unitary authorities do publish comprehensive train and bus time tables
- Through ticketing, which can have significant financial implications for some operators
- Concessionary fares - compatibility and acceptability
- Accessibility for disabled travellers at change of mode or service
- Provision of infrastructure

Various alternative arrangements for better co-ordination or joint working, either on a regional or sub-regional basis, have been discussed. However for any of these to be effective would require the overall direction of a third party, such as the Welsh Office, the Assembly or a specialist body.

CURRENT TRANSPORT PROVISION IN WALES

It is widely accepted that east-west channels of communication or transport within Wales are of a much higher standard than those for north-south. In particular, the relatively high standard of roads along the south and north coasts (M4 and A55), together with the good rail links in the same corridors, mean that there is much better communication with the neighbouring regions of England than with each other. Indeed in most cases for rail, and many cases for road it is necessary or preferable to travel via England to go from north to south Wales. As far as the rural heartland of Wales is concerned, 30 per cent of the population have no access to a car and hence have very limited access to transport of any kind.

It should be remembered that on a map Bangor and London are roughly the same distance from Cardiff, but the journey from Bangor to Cardiff by train takes twice as long as Cardiff to London Most journeys within Wales are longer and less commodious that similar journeys in England. It is also important to note that whatever mode is used (car/bus/train), the journey times are not reliable or consistent due to a number of different factors.

While the service within the two main coastal corridors may be considered reasonable, the provision of rail services for the bulk of Wales is minimal. Services on the Cambrian Coast and Heart of Wales rail lines are slow and infrequent. While they arc used for school and other commuting journeys they need much more frequent and speedy services to compete as viable transport options. While the service eastwards from Cardiff, and to a lesser extent Swansea, is considered acceptable, there is concern that west Wales is poorly served by the current rail operations. Similarly many of the Valleys are not served as they should be.

Along the north Wales coast while journey times have improved between Bangor and Chester/Crewe, there is still great concern about the reliability of the service, condition of the rolling stock, and the lack of commitment by Railtrack to upgrade the speed of the line. The service to Holyhead is also inadequate, although recent announcements give more hope for the next millennium. In addition the network in north-east Wales (which could give much shorter times from north to south Wales) is completely underused and has a poor quality of service.

In the major urban areas of Wales buses have recovered considerably over recent years, and, for example, service a significant proportion of school and shopping trips. As the *Wales Bus, Rail and Tourist Map & Guide 1988/99* shows, the bus service within rural Wales is fragmented and somewhat sparse. Whilst some progress has been made in improving the quality and accessibility of local bus services in certain areas, much of Wales is not reached by a regular and frequent bus service. With a high proportion of buses run by relatively small local firms, and with an unhelpful tax and duty regime, there is still a problem of age and quality of the bus stock. In rural areas, buses are dependent on the roads which often has a negative effect on bus travel. In the more urban areas of Wales less progress has been made in bus priority measures as compared with some other parts of the UK. This situation is improving and should develop further with the opening of Transport Grant to 'package schemes' in 1998/99, but funds are severely restricted.

As noted, the north and south coasts of Wales have reasonable east-west road provision. From the M4 north there are good road links for short distances (for example, to Merthyr Tydfil, Abergavenny, and Monmouth) but the overall network is not of a high standard, and has substantial lengths which are sub-standard for the level of traffic which they carry.

FIGURE 1

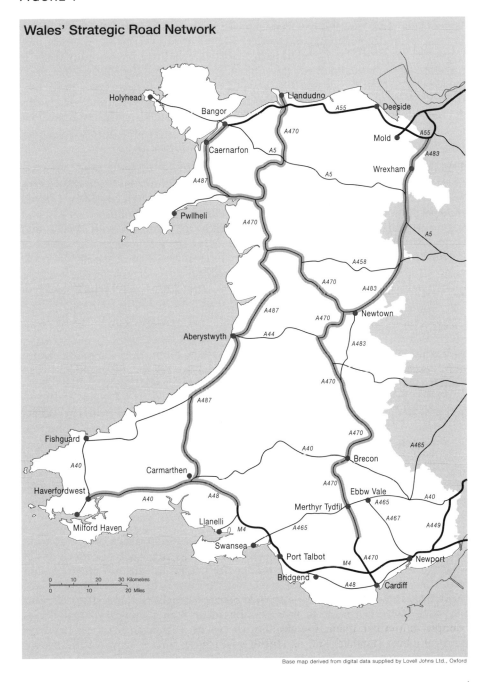

Wales' Strategic Road Network

Base map derived from digital data supplied by Lovell Johns Ltd., Oxford

In particular the A470 – the main north-south Wales trunk road – is of variable and generally low quality. The A487 and A483 (the other two main north-south Wales trunk roads) are also of variable quality with significant lengths substandard in terms of width, horizontal and vertical alignment and overtaking provision. An important point to be considered in any discussion of road provision in Wales is the effect of the virtual non-existence of alternative modes of transport. The road network therefore carries the full range of traffic from pedestrians and cyclists through to 38 ton (soon to be 40 ton) lorries. Such a mix of traffic is dangerous enough on roads built to modern standards of width and visibility. On roads that are substandard in every respect, there is both an increased level of risk and a very much increased perception of danger for the non-motorist.

There is virtually no internal air transport service within Wales, although a number of attempts have been made to establish a service from north to south over recent years. Of course, in terms of sustainability and environmental considerations air transport is not desirable. However, it can be effective in terms of time and cost and has a good safety record. The only major airport in Wales is Cardiff -Wales, and this has potential for further development as an international centre. The same can be said of Manchester which is the 'local' major airport for north Wales. Given the almost universal criticism of the continued development of Heathrow, it is unfortunate that more use of regional airports in the UK has not been encouraged. Not only would this mitigate some of the problems at Heathrow and Gatwick themselves, but could make a significant contribution to removing traffic from the motorway system.

As has already been pointed out, cycling and walking on much of the road network of Wales is dangerous. This arises not only from the dangers of traffic and road conditions but also from the general perception of vulnerability of individuals in unprotected situations. This tends to be seen as more of a threat to children, women and the elderly who are also the sections of the population least likely to have access to the car and for whom cycling and walking would otherwise be a viable option. In addition, other changes over the last 30 to 40 years have led to a decline in cycling or walking to school, work, and the shops. These changes include the closure of local schools, shops, post offices, and so on and a trend away from local employment of the resident population. Although some considerable investment has been made in certain areas in cycle routes and footpaths, these have generally more relevance to recreational use rather than everyday travel or movement needs.

The situation concerning freight transport is varied within Wales. Considerable use of rail is made for freight movement into and out of south Wales but much less in other areas. There is also a certain amount of coastal freight movement around Wales but shipping is again more relevant to import or export. Most freight movement within Wales is by road and there is virtually no alternative. Various proposals have been made to increase rail freight traffic along the north Wales coastline but to date the economic case has not been sufficiently robust. To make effective use of rail freight on either the north Wales line or to west Wales would involve changes to ferry operations at Holyhead and Fishguard and in the Irish

Ports. There have been encouraging signs of late in that Railtrack are upgrading the Cambrian Coast line for freight use and EWS are looking to develop the rail freight business in Wales in similar ways to their achievements in Scotland.

When considering the overall subject of transport in Wales attention should be given also to reducing the need for travel. Recent developments in Information Technology have created massive possibilities in this area. Video conferencing, E-mail, the Internet all offer scope for communication without the need to travel. The weakness in this area, however, is the ad-hoc nature of the development of the infrastructure for such methods of communication. There does not appear to be an overall co-ordination of provision of infrastructure and perhaps this should be reviewed.

As is the case for many areas of public sector responsibility current budgets are inadequate to maintain the existing transport infrastructure. They are certainly insufficient to finance any significant improvements in any of the modes discussed. The Welsh Office Trunk Road budget and Transport Grant have been reduced by 50 per cent over three years, Unitary Authorities have all had to reduce their Transport and Roads budgets. In Gwynedd this has been the case for eight years in succession. Generally, the smaller public transport undertakers cannot on their own generate a commercially viable case for new investment. The Government has made certain additional moneys available of late, and more is indicated in the future, although this may be relatively small compared with the assessed need for more resources.

THE AGENDA FOR TRANSPORT

The National Assembly will assume all the responsibilities and powers for transport which are currently held by the Secretary of State for Wales. For any significant additional responsibilities or powers to be given to the Assembly primary legislation would be required, and hence Whitehall Departments' approval. Some secondary powers will devolve to the Assembly which will allow flexibility to the Assembly to take initiatives. The extent of the discretion open to it will still reflect political considerations, however, and foremost amongst these will be budgetary constraints.

As we have seen, there are a number of Government reviews in progress and a series of White Papers have been produced. New legislation in the transport field is imminent and it would be appropriate to seek to influence that legislation to vest responsibility for as much as possible in Wales with the Assembly rather than on an 'England and Wales' basis. The former Secretary of State for Wales, Ron Davies, continually stressed the need for the Assembly to take an 'all Wales' view on all matters. For this to be more than a vain hope, surely it must first apply to transport and communication.

As Highway Authority for trunk roads in Wales, the Assembly could immediately make a commitment to achieving a strategic network of roads of an acceptable standard of comfort and safety within reasonable reach of all parts and people of Wales. The map on the following page shows such a possible network. Part of this network should be achieved as a result of the three schemes currently planned by the Welsh Office – the extension of the A55 across Anglesey, the M4 Relief road at Newport, and dualling the A465 from Abergavenny to Hirwaun. It is also not greatly different from the core network identified in the Welsh Office White Paper *Driving Wales Forward.*

Equally the Assembly should address the problem of rail transport within Wales and use its limited powers and considerable influence to achieve an improved and more direct service between north, mid and south Wales. It should be the Assembly's goal to become the Strategic Rail Authority's agent in Wales, subject in the first instance at least, to the overall responsibility of the Secretary of State for Environment, Transport and the Regions.

The Assembly would also wish to work with the Unitary Authorities and Welsh Local Government Association in addressing the major public transport problem of buses. It may be that with some secondary legislation powers it could amend the regulations affecting local authorities' support of bus services and the 'de minimis' financial limits to encourage much wider and innovative co-operation with bus operators. The current proposed increase, on which views have been sought, is far too modest and would not achieve significant advances.

To extend the argument further and to address the deficiencies highlighted above the Assembly could undertake a driving, or empowering, role in the co-ordination of all public transport in Wales. This could be exercised in such a way as to build upon the 'partnership' concept which has already been identified as key to the Assembly's remit. Acting either centrally, or perhaps through its Regional Committees, the Assembly could bring together the relevant private and public organisations to work within an overall Public Transport Strategy to enable significant advances to be made in all of the areas of concern identified above. It might be that some powers of compulsion or arbitration would be required to resolve difficulties but these should not be too draconian.

In the field of Information Technology, the Assembly should take a lead in achieving a greater measure of co-ordination of interests to ensure that cable or radio networks are compatible throughout Wales and as extensive as is commercially possible to encourage greater use of the communications network. If this could be achieved then the communications network could provide a vehicle for an integrated and real time information system for public transport.

When the civil service now working with the Secretary of State become responsible to the Assembly, there could be a change in the emphasis and direction of their activities. In turn this might have significant staffing implications. While not exactly replicating the role of local government officers in relation to Unitary Authorities, they will become subject to the aims and objectives of the Assembly. With the vast knowledge, experience and ability that they have at their disposal steered in a new direction, and building upon the existing good working relationship between Welsh Office and Unitary Authorities, it is possible that a much more integrated and positive momentum could be generated. This could be developed into an overall 'Best Value' philosophy for transport in Wales.

RESOURCES

Reference has already been made to the severe restrictions on traditional transport related budgets. Reference has also been made to the variety of specific funds available for particular types of scheme or expenditure. It could be argued that public sector funding has become a mess, with so many different 'pots' available, subject to a plethora of different regulations, and often allocated on the basis of 'beauty parade' competitions and bids. These funds are variously controlled by Department of the Environment, Transport and the Regions, the Welsh Office, Unitary Authorities, Welsh Development Agency (now embracing the Development Board for Rural Wales and the Land Authority for Wales), the Countryside Council for Wales and other bodies. They also include European funding under the INTERREG, ERDF, and EAGGF programmes, Capital Challenge, and so on. There has been a growth industry for some entrepreneurs in holding seminars explaining what the various funds and grants are for. It is also widely accepted that competing for so many special funds has distorted public sector strategies, priorities and programmes.

Given the Assembly's wide range of responsibilities which will include some direct transport functions together with Planning and Sustainable Development, Health, European matters and so on, it will be well placed to examine transport in its wider context. It will be in a position to reconsider all the various funding mechanisms related to transport and to generate new policies and strategies for their application. It should also be in a better position than ever before to consider these matters on an all-Wales basis and determine meaningful assessments of need and priorities.

A further consideration is that the Welsh Office Transport and Highways Division was basically a roads department a few years ago, and is now undertaking a much wider role in transport. For the Assembly to receive the support it will need to establish a new direction in transport for Wales, will undoubtedly require increased resources.

CHAPTER 15

FARMING AND THE RURAL ECONOMY

Terry Marsden

The Assembly is being established at a critical time for the rural economy. It faces an immediate economic crisis and a longer-term process of marginalisation. Both need to be addressed by a new strategic vision, supported by practical policies. There also need to be new mechanisms for the articulation of Welsh rural and agricultural issues at the different levels of policy making.

Before considering the policy response, the nature of the problems need to be understood. Members of the Assembly, its secretariat, and its various committees, will need to understand what is possible and what can be achieved through short and long-term means. In particular, it is imperative to reconsider the specific public contribution that agriculture and the food sector can play in the economy of Wales, as well as the rural economy more specifically.

The key question is this: *how can a more integrated and strategic policy for the rural economy be evolved which is sensitive to the differing conditions that exist across rural Wales?*

GLOBAL TRENDS AND RURAL DISTINCTIVENESS

A starting point has to be the recognition of new patterns of diversity and differentiation which are emerging in the rural areas of Wales and the UK more broadly. Common trends affecting rural areas can be divided into those affecting the whole of society and those which are specific to rural localities. Amongst the former are:

- Globalisation of many areas of the economy, increased competition, and restructuring of enterprises.

- Maintenance of a 'free market' ideology which is continuing to strengthen macro-economic management and control in the direction of finance capital and exchange.

- A consequential search and contestation for new forms of governance – locally and regionally based rather than relying on heavy state intervention, with an emphasis on private and public 'entrepreneurship' and innovation.

- Privatisation of formerly State owned or regulated activities.

- Increasing efforts to internationalise the *terms under which trade takes place*, and removal of economic and other barriers to trade, including most notably production subsidies, for example through the General Agreement on Tariffs and Trade and the World Trade Organisation.

- The uneven spread of new technologies, especially information and communications technologies.

- Demographic changes, leading to the ageing of the rural European population and increasing dependency ratios.

- Increasing personal mobility, including commuting, migration, tourism and recreation.

- Changing *cultural values* in relation to individualism and community, responsibility for future generations and the development of democratic practice and citizen involvement.

- The emergence of new winners and losers from these processes of change, and especially the appearance and recognition of 'excluded groups' suffering from poverty and various types of deprivation.

These trends are affecting all advanced countries differentially, and they set the context for assessing the policy options available for rural areas. While there is much talk about viewing rural areas as 'holistic entities', it needs to be recognised that many of these processes of change are shaping rural areas and life chances in uneven and contradictory ways. They are anything but integrative or compatible. It will be a test of the success of the National Assembly as to how well it can manage the change. It will need to look outwards as well as inwards and translate international processes in ways which are compatible with the interests of rural Wales.

A problem is that rural Wales is becoming progressively less self-sufficient and ever more open to the wider forces shaping European and global development. Apparently similar areas can demonstrate quite different characteristics in terms of key indicators like net migration, commuting, deprivation, new enterprise formation, the degree of social cohesion or fragmentation and so on. It is becoming apparent that different rural areas display distinct capacities in the face of global markets and social change. The Assembly will need to find ways to foster these distinct capacities. This will require an Integrated rural development policy. The positive contributions of agriculture and food to the rural economy will be a significant element in increasing Welsh rural capacities and resources. A *strategy of innovation* is central.

WELSH FARMING AND THE RURAL ECONOMY

Wales is a predominantly livestock farming region with milk, finished cattle and finished sheep and lambs representing 84 per cent of the total value of agricultural products, followed by poultry (8 per cent) pigs and potatoes (2 per cent each). Agriculture still accounts for one in four jobs in rural Wales. For the UK as a whole, Wales provides two-thirds of the specialist beef sector, most of it coming from the Less Favoured Area designated areas which account for 80 per cent of the total agricultural area of Wales (Bristow, 1997).

However, such statistics do not elucidate the profound role that agriculture and, more broadly, the food supply industry play in Wales as a crucial element in delivering social and environmental sustainability objectives as well as promoting wider patterns of local economic development. These issues are generally well documented. Yet, they have even more profound significance in the present context of uncertainty and crisis facing the sector. To persuade people of the depth and seriousness of the rural crisis (farmers are perceived as 'crying wolf' far too often), we have to view agriculture as part of a complex and changing food supply system (Williams et. al., 1998). Moreover, to distinguish agriculture as a separate and distinctive sector for specific treatment is increasingly likely to obscure and prolong the problems being experienced.

To answer the questions facing the livestock industry in Wales it is necessary to begin to ask some specific questions about the contribution and constraints operating in food supply chains in Wales; what the potential is for harnessing social, economic and environmental benefits, and how the assumed 'marginal' characterisation of much of Welsh agriculture can be redefined and linked to new innovative strategies for rural development.

One of the tendencies in the recent past has been to try to deal with problems in the short term, as they arise, without tackling the longer-term issues. We should remember that the BSE crisis is now ten years old and the problems of regulating agriculture through modifying the CAP dates back at least to 1984 when milk quotas were first introduced. In addition, despite some fluctuations, gross capital formation in the agricultural sector began to decline from the mid-1980s, representing the end of the post-war rise in capital intensity on farms in the UK. The agricultural sector, most notably in upland Britain, continues to suffer what can only be regarded as a form of 'arrested decline'; whereby the state apparatus continues to project a dependency culture, but one which it finds increasingly difficult to uphold for financial and political reasons.

The key issues will be dealt with under the following headings:

- The immediate crisis

- Basic causes and trends

- The pivotal role and position of corporate retailers and their supply chain influences

THE IMMEDIATE CONDITIONS

If 1996 reaffirmed the significance of the BSE problem and its deepening effects upon beef markets both at home and abroad, 1997 was the year when a series of other shocks combined to reinforce the uncertainty and economic insecurity of livestock agriculture and its markets. They included:

i Growing financial uncertainty and insecurity with net farm incomes down on average by 23 per cent, more farmers slipping into the red, and prices for finished cattle down by 25 per cent. Increases in the supply of lamb and pig meat only added to the problem, with lamb prices down about 28 per cent and pig meat 15 per cent.

ii These conditions, initially stimulated by the BSE crisis, were compounded by the high level of the Green Pound and the reductions in compensation payments associated with Hill Compensation and Livestock Allowances (HCLA payments in Less favoured areas) of the order of 27 per cent since 1992.

iii There have been particular uncertainties experienced by specific sectors. Deregulation is increasing the costs – the rise in collection charges and fall in prices of standard quality milk – of the smaller end of the dairy farming sector and making continued investment more uncertain.

iv An issue which has quite recently come to the fore has been the growing realisation on the part of the farming community and beyond that imports of beef products have been increasing (not least because of the strength of the Green pound). Prices have fallen by 12 per cent for French beef and 14 per cent for Irish and Dutch beef products. This has led, further, to accusations that downstream retailers and processors are able to 'make a profit out of a crisis'. Evidence is provided by the 'price spread', that is, retail price minus producer price as percentage of retail price. The price spread for beef in Britain increased from 48.6 per cent in 1996 to 54.4 per cent in November 1997; and for lamb from 36.6 per cent to 51.9 per cent over the same period (Welsh Office, 1998). Imports of beef increased by 10 per cent during 1998, which added to the negative balances in food trade which have been a feature of the 1990s.

These latter realities have fuelled questions about the 'mark-ups' inherent in the post-farm parts of the food chain, particularly given the lack of evidence of equivalent falls in retail prices, growth in imports, and a perceived lack of 'trust' in food supply chains more generally. Producers are realising that they need to consider direct action towards both the traditional state authorities and, increasingly, the supermarkets and caterers, and their internationally-based distribution systems.

It is important to appreciate that these combined outcomes are also associated with deeper structural problems which have been set in train over a longer period. Successive attempts to deal with these have largely failed. Added to this should be the recognition that overall subsidies to Welsh agriculture reached £135m a year (by 1995), representing more than 50 per cent of total income for an LFA farm. Recent attempts to reduce this vulnerable dependence upon the public purse only heightens the degree of acute uncertainty in the farming sector.

UNDERLYING TRENDS

Foremost among these is the continuing and profound demise in the effectiveness and legitimacy of the EU's Common Agriculture Policy (CAP), and its associated supply and production regulation to solve the problems farmers face. Impending World Trade Organisation (WTO) pressures to reduce farmer support, in addition to the reluctance of some European countries to be seen as upholding the existing CAP arrangements, will result in farmers increasingly having to fend for themselves. Options include developing diversification enterprises and joining environmental schemes. Faced with the WTO and the annexation of new eastern countries to the European project, we are entering a *'race to the bottom'* scenario which most Welsh farmers will find difficulty in winning. There is a growing disparity between east and west Britain, and between lowland and upland farmers. The technically advanced are the only ones capable of competing in world markets. The rest sit waiting for reconstituted rural welfare payments.

In short, the current trajectory of global competitive agriculture will reward those producers who can reduce their costs still further. For the majority of Welsh farmers the cupboard from which resources can be taken to achieve this are already bare. Moreover, in an era of public spending restraint, it is difficult to envisage much positive discrimination towards the smaller end of the farming industry.

If these conditions are left unheeded we will witness the further marginalisation of small family farms, not least from the progressive out-migration of the young to other occupations and lifestyles. There is evidence that fewer farmers sons and daughters are planning to succeed the farm. External circumstances only accentuate this tendency.

Perhaps less dramatically but just as pertinent has been the increasing salience in food supply chains of the construction and use of food quality criteria as a convention of market entry. Combining together are the food scares of the late

1980s, the passage of the Food Safety Act in 1990, the rise to power of the corporate retailers, and now the possibility of a Food Standards Agency. They all point towards a complexity of criteria being placed upon producers not just in terms of the physical quality of their products, but the assurance of their delivery to the intensely competitive retail sector. This has been matched with a shift in added value within food supply chains towards the 'end-user.' This means that most of the value can be both added and then redistributed *after* the farm gate. The gradual superimposition of quality standards only tends to reinforce this trend.

The problems of the CAP and the emergence of *privately-regulated quality control in supply chains*, governed particularly by the large retailers, mean that farmers now have even less to gain from 'going it alone'. In many of the intensive farming areas of East Anglia and Humberside for instance, buying and marketing alliances between potato and other horticultural producers have been formed to co-ordinate and maintain market entry to the retailer-led supply chains. On their part, the retailers are designing environmentally friendly food supply relationships as a marketing tool, enrolling those farmers who have the capacity and the know-how to deliver consistent products under formal contracts. Of course, not all producers can be involved, but the general trend in the innovation of food supply is for production to be increasingly harnessed to a range of quality standards. This also means that there is unlikely to be any such thing as a complete 'free-market' or level playing field in food goods which farmers can simply exploit. Rather, we see the emergence of a rather slow but decisive shift from a universalistic CAP *regulated supply system* based upon quantitative production targets, to a more *privately regulated supply chain* approach which gives precedence to quality control. This is placing new organisational and management demands upon farmers, and tends to empower the consumer end of the supply chain.

The main point to consider concerning these basic shifts in the regulation of food and agriculture can be summarised by the following questions: How can Wales, as an agricultural and rural nation, develop a strategy for leading and innovating in terms of these trends? How can we turn it into a *race to the top* rather than the bottom? These questions must face two realities:

- Problems with the social, economic and environmental sustainability of much of Welsh agriculture.

- The lack of effective processing and retailing infrastructure in Wales which could begin to create triple dividends between maintaining a family farming structure, enhancing the local value-added economic development and leading to the production of quality-assured foods for an international market.

We need to move away from a dependency culture on decreasing amounts of CAP support for agricultural production. And we need to move towards a strategy for indigenous rural and agricultural development.

THE PIVOTAL ROLE OF THE CORPORATE RETAILERS

There have been unprecedented levels of growth and rates of return in the corporate retail sector during the 1980s and 1990s. This far outstripped that for manufacturing in general terms and food manufacturing in the 1980s. It was assisted by the abolition of retail price maintenance and a decline in regulatory restriction. Other countries, for instance, have put limits on store size and protected their independent grocery sectors.

In the 1990s, faced with food scares, 'careful consumption' and increased competition from the discount sector, *competition* and *innovation* have been by-words for the corporate retailers' pre-eminence. As the 'quality revolution' has gained pace, they have been particularly adept in projecting themselves as the new custodians of both the consumer and the food-supply chain. It is estimated that they receive 70 per cent of Welsh livestock products, and through their 'due-diligence' obligations, they are able to insist upon arms-length control over the quality of their supply as well as indirectly affecting the destiny of the rest of the products.

While it is now being recognised that this market and regulatory power may not always be in the interests of Welsh agriculture, and especially the smaller upland farmers, it is important to point out that the innovation and competitive strategies adopted by the retailers in the 1990s have tended to encourage them to place more emphasis upon competition with:

- Their supermarket rivals through product innovation, own-branding and customer loyalty labelling.
- Their rivals at the local level, in the market towns as well as in the conurbations.

One result is that in Wales we now have the presence of the corporate retailers in most of the market towns. They are leading the restructuring of food consumption and retailing at the local level. These two dimensions of retail competition and innovation have meant that the process of securing quality food supply has at best been only one of their key concerns. Their competitive and innovative energies have been placed where the intense competition has been greatest - that is, between themselves.

Corporate retailers, by dint of the relatively low levels of concentration particularly in the small farm sector and the universalistic approach of CAP support, have not had to seriously compete with each other about which farmers from which to source. Neither have they been required to be seen to be acting positively towards particular groups of farmers. Moreover, by putting in place more effective packaging and processing of foods they have indirectly added value down the supply chain, away from the farm gate and the smaller abattoir. In short, they have established an increasingly international *food 'grid'* which extends far beyond their local stores or head offices and incorporates, through selective contracting, local abattoir, wholesalers and processors. They have, until quite recently been intent upon establishing a distribution system which increases the costs of transport relative to the costs of farm-gate products. When the costs of adding packaging and processing to meat products is also included, one can begin to see how the relative value-added has shifted down the supply chain.

By the mid-1990s the contrast in the general economic health of the corporate retailers sector vis à vis the beleaguered farm sector could not be more stark. The onset of a UK-wide food distribution system may have helped those farmers who gain lucrative access to quality supply chains, but for many more it tends to constrain local and regional added- value strategies. A recent report on supply chain links in Wales for instance, points to these growing constraints (DBRW, 1997). There are a combination of problems:

- An inability of Welsh food processors to access sufficient resources to progress market development.

- A lack of vertical linkages in the supply chain which leads to the widespread view among producers that processors are 'conspiring' to withhold a share of profits derived from processing the output from their farms.

- A lack of co-ordinated product branding strategies.

Moreover, the development of more centralised distribution has reinforced reductions in the throughputs of local abattoir and processing facilities. In the dairy sector there is a shortage of primary processing capacity in Carmarthenshire and Pembrokeshire. Smaller companies have limited resources for market development and establishing cost effective distribution systems for engaging with the wider retail markets. In the beef and lamb sectors there is a recognised lack of confidence among primary processors, compounded by slaughtering 'over-capacity' affecting margins and investment capital. Despite the efforts of Welsh Lamb and Beef Promotions, there is a lack of incentive for improvements to meet the quality requirements of processors and retailers.

These observations, based upon only a small amount of detailed research suggest that the evolution of the retailer -led 'food-grid' has tended to reinforce the constraints for the development of a regionally-based food supply chain infrastructure. This has made the possibilities for value-added 'leakage' from the farm gate and potentially out of Wales even greater.

In many policy circles the conditions and prospects of the retailing and agricultural sectors have been seen as far removed from each other. The former is associated with a dynamic and innovative service sector, and the latter with primary production hooked into a highly regulated and state supported system. Yet even as the disparities grow between them it is becoming clear that they are critically related through the operation of food supply chain links. Moreover, it is these supply chain links that hold the key implications for rural development.

Recently, as a part of their innovation strategies, corporate retailers have begun to consider local sourcing as a serious possibility in providing consumers with more trust and assurance about their food purchases. In addition, the retailers have begun to source more selectively on the basis of local identity and environmental value. These may be trends that will continue and ones which Welsh agriculture can more fully exploit. So far its significance has not been quantified.

Nonetheless, it is clear that Welsh agriculture, and more generally the food supply chains that incorporate Welsh locations and foods, are at a cross-roads in terms of future development.

RETAILERS AND THE WELSH FARM CRISIS

There is considerable confusion about the degree of price mark-up between farm gate prices and retail prices. However, the evidence suggests that the retail margins have been getting larger during the recent period of 1996-8. It is not clear what effects other links in food supply chain make to these price changes – for example processing, distribution, packaging plants – or the degree to which exclusive contracting between the various firms affects prices and quality of goods.

Producers are likely to face increasing quality criteria, both from government and from the private sector. How can they cope with this and what effect will it have in marketing Welsh products? How significant will regional sourcing become in the marketing and innovation strategies of the food retailers? How can a higher level be achieved? A strategy for Welsh agriculture and food needs to be developed which will:

- Promote the capacity of the farmers to engage in contracting directly and indirectly with retailers.

- Provide the stimulus for indigenous growth in value-added capacity within Wales.

- Develop more sustainable and organic food supply chains for a variety of local and international markets.

- Shape the current levels of CAP support in ways which stimulate indigenous development, rather than maintaining a 'dependency and a marginal culture'.

It is clear that Welsh agriculture and food cannot wait for the protracted process of CAP reform. Agenda 2000 does not so far provide a real stimulus for Integrated Rural Development. Action is needed now to promote an innovative Welsh agriculture capable of leading rather than following changes in European policy. We need to develop a rural strategy for Wales which places agriculture and food at its centre.

A REALISTIC AGENDA FOR THE ASSEMBLY

Rather than agriculture being viewed as a distinct and separately regulated sector, it needs to be *re-integrated* into the rural economy and assessed as such. More specifically, it needs not only to be seen to be the producer of quality foods that can increasingly attract a price premium, but also as the sustainer of a wider range of local rural employment and environmental opportunities. This requires a focus upon stimulating economic development along *food supply chains* as opposed to considering agriculture as a land-based occupation in isolation.

This is by no means easy. For instance, there are dangers with the development of the *All Wales Agri-environment scheme*, which has been built upon the success of *Tir Cymen*, that it will be blind in its operation to the demands of quality food production, the stimulation of organic agriculture, and the types of marketing relationships farmers are participating in. In short, the Agri-environment scheme will need to have wider objectives and contributions than just protecting the local farm environment.

In unravelling the inconsistencies and distortions of current rural-based policies the Assembly should take a medium and long-term view. It should not be 'hemmed in' by the more immediate pressures of allocating payments to farmers or dealing with this or that food scare or environmental conflict. This is an opportunity for Wales to take the creative lead rather than become victim to the marginalised 'gridlock' of agricultural politics and policy implementation. It is particularly a time when, through the effective development of an *innovative rural and farm policy*, Wales can develop comparative advantage in social, economic, cultural and environmental terms in a European context. It could, within a decade, turn what has for too long been regarded as a 'marginal agricultural region' into a leading European Region for agricultural innovation and food quality. How can the Assembly assist with this important medium term goal?

A NEW FOOD STRATEGY

The Assembly needs to develop a four-fold approach to rural and environmental policy within which agriculture and food innovation should be central. It needs:

- An integrated rural policy
- A strategy for food
- Strategic environmental planning
- A system of environmental duty

The second of these focuses most directly upon farming and the rural economy and should be urgently prepared. The following considerations should be taken into account:

i   The new food strategy should be organised to foster the overall objective of integrated rural development. It should aim to bring the countryside and the town closer together, for instance by fostering new organic supply chains, urban farms, and farmers markets.

ii   Following some of the principles of the Regional Technology Plan, the strategy needs to develop an innovation plan for the Welsh food industry, which both considers how new indigenous businesses can be supported and created and how Welsh producers and food businesses can participate in wider national and international markets.

iii   The food strategy will need to address the diversification of the Welsh agricultural base. It should incorporate incentives for developing premium products for the main food supply chains.

iv   There is increasing demand in the manufactured meats sector (for example, ready meals and catering). Improved partnerships need to be given a priority with the UK and EU wide food manufacturing and catering sectors. The new WDA will be central here, and needs to be charged with more responsibility for the food sector.

v   Attention needs to be focused upon the small-scale abattoirs. These are suffering from under-capacity due to the increasing centralisation of the main food supply chains. Opportunities should be sought for groups of farmers to cooperate with processors?

vi   Quality food standards need to be set for Welsh foods which give clarity to their provenance and 'green worth'. An overall 'green grade' for the main Welsh products needs to be given urgent consideration (that is, for lamb, beef and milk). This could be linked directly to the development of the all - Wales Agri-Environmental scheme. Here it will be imperative that the Countryside Council for Wales collaborates with the new WDA. A plan of action to increase the number of organic conversions needs to be made over a ten year period.

vii   The corporate food retail and manufacturing sectors need to be made much more aware of the quality and consistency of Welsh food produce. This will require improved quality regulation by all those in the supply chain.

viii   The Assembly, through the operation of the Welsh Food Strategy will need to develop more effective communications with policy making both in Brussels and Whitehall. In particular it is necessary to articulate Welsh agricultural and food interests from a distinctive and innovative base. Here the green and quality credentials of Welsh agriculture need to be given more prominence. Wales needs a distinctive voice built upon the principle of sustainable agriculture and sustainable family run enterprises. It will need to articulate the importance of the continuity of family farming as a key element in environmental protection and quality food goods.

ix The food strategy will need to consider, over a generational time-scale, the future structure of Welsh agriculture, how it intends to protect family succession, encourage new entrants and promote innovation on relatively small holdings.

x The food strategy should consider the differential contribution of agriculture and the food economy in the four economic regions of Wales. It will need to develop partnerships in the regions between the regional economic forums, the local authorities and community and farmer groups. These partnerships could be given the responsibility to produce regional innovation and co-operative plans for the farming and food economy.

xi The food strategy needs to consider what the possibilities are for the Assembly to modify the conditions upon which agricultural support funding is allocated to align it more specifically with the goals of the food strategy and integrated rural development more generally. In principle, production support will have to be more geared to premium production and green worth criteria. This is an urgent concern which cannot be allowed to drift or lie dormant on the basis of the slow reform process of the CAP.

CONCLUSION

The establishment of the Assembly comes at a time when tensions between the *realities* of globalisation and *visions* of Sustainable Development are becoming increasingly acute (see Chapter 11). The Assembly will sit at the centre of this contradiction. It will be necessary for it to act as a robust and strategic intermediary between the increasing internal pressures for change, and the turbulent external context of the policy debate.

Given the continued significance of the EU and Whitehall in policy development, it will be crucial that the Assembly articulates positive and alternative models of development which can inform policy change. Alliances will need building with other rural areas in Europe which may be further advanced in developing integrated rural development strategies which are more sustainable. In addition, it will be necessary to compare, within the UK, the differential process of rural adaptation associated with 'upland' agricultural conditions. It is interesting to note in this regard that the Scottish Office is currently running a focussed programme of policy research which is identifying such areas for action once the Scottish Parliament is established.

While there is a growing consensus concerning the need to shift rural Wales in the direction of more integrated rural development and sustainability goals, there are now two interrelated problems that policy- makers, not least Assembly-members, need to address quite urgently:

i   How to decide priorities for action.

ii How to turn policy rhetoric into deliverable policy instruments.

In the run-up to the creation of the Assembly, we already have policy commitments to a new agri-environmental scheme, to a new food strategy, and to a new national rural partnership. These innovative developments need to be linked together and given an overall strategic approach which progresses both integrated rural development and Sustainable Development objectives. They need to become practical policies over the Assembly's first term.

It will be important to avoid duplication between organisations across the different sectors. We will need a hierarchy of objectives and strategies, from the specific (such as food) to the general (such as sustainability), with integrated rural development acting as both an organisational and policy-based bridge. Wales holds the capacity to be a creative leader in European terms concerning progressing and delivering integrated and Sustainable Development policies. There are plenty of good local examples. The advent of the Assembly can give new impetus in turning these local exemplars into common practices. While much of the policy rhetoric surrounding rural areas has perceived them as inherently 'holistic' and integrated entities, the reality is, as the recent farming crisis exhibits, that they are subject to volatile and contradictory forces, mostly not of their own making. In short, rural integration and sustainability needs to be *constructed* by the building and operation of new policies which identify rural opportunities. This demands strategic policy change rather than simply a reliance upon the competitive and quite random stimulation of 'bottom up' development and partnership schemes. The latter should not be denied, but they need to be made part of an overall strategic policy frameworks.

References

Bristow, G. (1997) *Making the CAP fit: an integrated development strategy for rural Wales*. Institute of Welsh Affairs, 1997.

Welsh Office (1998) Evidence to the Welsh Affairs Committee Inquiry into the problems facing the livestock industry. *House of Commons Welsh Affairs Committee Second Report*. HMSO.

Development Board for Rural Wales (1997) *An assessment of the existing and potential utilisation of Welsh agricultural products in the Welsh food processing industry*. Nowtown, 1997.

Williams,S, Bristow,G, Price-Jones,C, Marsden, T.K (1998) *A Review of Food Supply and Marketing Chains in Wales*. Cardiff Food Group Working Paper, Department of City and Regional Planning, Cardiff University.

CHAPTER 16

TOURISM

Terry Stevens

Tourism is second only to agriculture as Wales' most important economic activity contributing some seven per cent of gross domestic product. The industry is subject to significant vagaries in demand resulting from factors in the wider political and economic environment. As a result, it is an industry that constantly has to respond to rapid changes in the market place and to the emergence of competition from new products and destinations. With agriculture in decline, tourism offers scope for further growth and the potential to become Wales' most important industry.

The tourism industry in Wales needs to be able to respond effectively to these challenges. This requires an efficient and appropriately resourced organisational structure with political support and recognition. For the past thirty years the industry has struggled to achieve the recognition its contribution to the economic and social life of Wales has deserved. The National Assembly provides a unique opportunity for the industry to be fully acknowledged and for rationalisation of the structure of tourism to meet the challenges of the new Millennium.

Changes have already been announced in the organisation of tourism elsewhere in Britain as well as in Ireland. It seems particularly relevant, therefore, that the structure of tourism in Wales should also be reviewed. The Department of Culture, Media and Sport has recently announced the possible restructuring of tourism in England with increased devolved responsibilities to the Regional Tourist Boards, hitherto carried out by the English Tourist Board, and a strengthening of overseas marketing activities for the British Tourist Authority (BTA) who, under this arrangement, will continue to promote Wales in the international market place[1].

A month earlier the Secretary of State for Scotland announced the results of his review of the Scottish Tourist Board[2]. His decision was to retain the Scottish Tourist Board but to make significant changes to its operation to focus more on supporting the industry. Finally, in Ireland the Minister responsible for Tourism has announced that, in the wake of the Good Friday peace agreement, Bord Failté (the

Irish Tourist Board) will be replaced by a new cross-border tourism body[3].

These changes are designed to achieve an improvement in the strategic leadership of the tourism industry in the respective countries. Such a strategic re-orientation now needs to be considered for Wales. Simply because change is taking place elsewhere is not a reason for changing the approach in Wales. However, at a time when the Wales Tourist Board is reviewing its strategy and relationships with the Regional Tourism Companies it would seem appropriate to look at roles and responsibilities This is not an argument for the dissolution of the Wales Tourist Board. Far from it. Tourism in Wales needs a strong lead body. The industry cannot afford to be wholly subsumed into the single economic body that is the new Welsh Development Agency. Tourism requires that the Tourist Board grows in strength and influence gaining additional resources to reflect the importance of the industry.

The organisational structure of the tourism industry in Wales has evolved gradually over the past 30 years since the Development of Tourism Act 1969. This established the Wales Tourist Board (WTB) along with the other national tourist boards in England and Scotland (the Northern Ireland Tourist Board was established in 1948) together with an overseas marketing body, the BTA. The major changes to the structure of tourism since the 1969 Act has been the establishment of three private companies in 1991, these Regional Tourism Companies, took over some of the responsibilities of the Wales Tourist Board's Regional Councils in North, Mid and South Wales established earlier by the Wales Tourist Board.

Other changes have included the establishment of Tourism Quality Services to undertake the operational work of the grading schemes and the powers granted to the Wales Tourist Board in 1992 to market Wales overseas. Over the years the Wales Tourist Board has attempted to become more strategic in its activities, delegating many of the operational activities which it used to undertake itself to other organisations such as the Regional Tourism Companies and Local Authorities. The Wales Tourist Board is, however, the only one of the organisations set up by the 1969 Act to retain all the powers which it inherited under the Act. Some suggest that this indicates that the Wales Tourist Board has done a good job. Others say it indicates that tourism in Wales has been given a lower priority than elsewhere.

Local authorities across Wales have also become more active in the development and promotion of the tourism industry over the past 30 years. During the 1970s and 1980s they took a leading role in developing tourist attractions (for example, country parks, historic houses, museums). They also became active in the funding of marketing and the management of tourist information centres. Since reorganisation of local government in 1996 this involvement has been more difficult to achieve as local authorities struggle to prioritise and contain spending within government guidelines.

The first part of this chapter will discuss the current performance of tourism in Wales in the context of Britain and Europe. This is followed by an analysis of some of the key issues currently affecting the industry in Wales. In particular there is an examination of those factors which are affecting the growth of the industry and looks at the need for strategies that allow businesses to flourish within a framework of sustainable development. The main conclusions are that tourism should be:

- taken seriously as a strategic economic development priority;
- embraced within the organisational structure of the new National Assembly and its various committees; and
- appropriately resourced.

THE ASSEMBLY'S LEADERSHIP ROLE

A key factor that permeates this whole discussion is the industry's need for strong leadership and strategic direction. It is time to change the perceptions of the industry and establish tourism as a fundamental part of the future of a vibrant new Wales and a priority item in terms of the Assembly's economic agenda.

Tourism is the world's largest economic activity with a projected 48 per cent growth potential over the next decade. Tourism is already a well-developed part of the Welsh economy contributing over £2bn and represents some seven per cent of GDP. Recent research by the Wales Tourist Board suggests that annual growth rates have been maintained over the past five years but that the rate of growth, and Wales' market share, has not kept pace with other European destinations – and Europe generally is loosing market share to new destinations. Europe and Wales, therefore, have to become more competitive.

During the Summer of 1998 there was a sustained and, often vitriolic, criticism of the Wales Tourist Board's marketing and development policies by a small number of tourism operators. This was provoked by the onset of a downturn in trade in some traditional sectors resulting primarily from factors outside of control of the WTB. These included the poor weather and the strength of the pound. At the same time the discontent was fuelled by strategic weaknesses and general disenchantment with the WTB's marketing campaigns.

Much of the criticism was ill-founded and the Board's attempt to target new domestic markets is a sound strategic initiative.The problem is that it has been at the expense of other more pressing tactical campaigns. More importantly and, irrespective of the reality of the actual level of tourism activity, the perception in many sectors of the industry was that the WTB was not being sufficiently positive about countering the problems or proactive enough in responding to the challenges. The trade must also recognise that it needs to put its house in order. More investment has to be made improving the tourism product, its quality and reliability. If standards are to rise more resources will have to be committed to marketing and training.

In addition, operators in Wales have turned jealous eyes to the perceived success of tourism in Ireland. Irish tourism has witnessed a doubling of overseas arrivals to

5.2 m over the past 10 years and a similar increase in tourism-related employment from 60,000 to 120,000 over the same period. Ironically tourism in Ireland is not without its critics and dissenters. For example, tourism operators in western Ireland complain about their loss of market share to Dublin and the East Region and the Irish Times has been denouncing tourism as the primary cause of environmental degradation. The success of Irish tourism is, however, a direct result of the high priority given to tourism by successive Irish Governments[4].

The Assembly, therefore, presents a fresh opportunity to afford tourism full recognition in terms of its integration within the economic and land use planning systems, and with other aspects of social and cultural policy. This is a defining moment and a chance to give new momentum to the strategic leadership and direction of tourism in Wales. It is appropriate to establish a long-term vision for the industry and to collectively work to achieve this vision. The place of tourism within the Assembly's Committee structure is, therefore, a fundamental concern.

One proposal is for tourism to be dealt with by an 'Industry and Innovation, Economic Development and Tourism' Committee[5]. In such an environment tourism must not become the 'Cinderella' industry. It offers real potential to grow indigenous Welsh enterprise, especially SMEs. Tourism has the potential to develop local supply chains and, in so doing, contribute to spreading prosperity to communities throughout Wales. It can assist in the development of a positive image of Wales as a distinctive destination. In addition, the primary infrastructure requirements for tourism are facilities and services of use to the residents of Wales. The growth of tourism is particularly important to rural Wales and areas which have experienced difficulties in other industrial sectors and have failed to attract other forms of investment.

A key function of the Assembly will be to ensure policy integration across committees. Consequently, tourism's contribution to the policy interests of the other Subject Committees must be assured from its position within the 'Economic' Committee. There is an opportunity here for the Assembly to give this important dimension of the Welsh economy some much needed leadership.

TOURISM'S POTENTIAL

Tourism's contribution to the Welsh economy and its potential for future growth needs to be assessed in a global context. The World Travel and Tourism Council (WTTC) estimates that the industry currently generates 255m jobs world-wide (one in every nine) and produces 10.7 per cent of global GDP[6]. By 2006 both the WTTC and the World Tourism Organisation (WTO) agree that travel and tourism is projected to grow by four per cent per year to $7.1 trillion adding 130 million more jobs and producing 11.5 per cent of global GDP[7].

This growth phenomenon creates opportunities and challenges, together with winners and losers in the global industry. The WTTC, as the industry's lead organisation, has published its *Millennium Vision* which is a strategic platform for private and public sector policy initiatives to capitalise upon the enormous potential of this growth in a manner which is sustainable in line with Agenda 21 principles[8]. This strategy is predicated upon the following strategic goals:

- Making travel and tourism a strategic economic development and employment priority by factoring it into mainstream policy decisions.

- Moving towards open and competitive markets through continued liberalisation of international trading systems and enhancing marketing.

- Eliminating barriers to growth with an investment in human resource development, stimulating an expansion and modernisation of infrastructure and intelligent taxation policies on tourism;

- Pursuing sustainable development with advancing Agenda 21 using new public/private sector delivery mechanisms and translating global principles into local action.

WTTC, the WTO, and more recently, the Commission of the European Communities have fully recognised the economic importance of tourism and its complex interrelationships with a wide range of economic, social, and cultural activities[10]. The European Commission refers to the fact that 'tourism is a phenomenon which involves the majority of European citizens, as users and as providers of tourism-related services'[11]. This sentiment is echoed in the Wales Tourist Board's strategy for tourism in Wales and in the subsequent progress report, in which the WTB state that 'tourism is a major contributor to the economy of Wales, but it also touches peoples' lives throughout the Principality in a whole variety of other ways'[12].

This theme that tourism is everybody's business and an integral and essential part of community development as a whole was noted in the Proceedings of the Welsh Select Committee on Tourism in Wales in 1987[13]. It was subsequently advanced as a central thesis in the Minority Report of that same Committee. Herein lies the basis of the challenge facing the future of tourism in Wales. How can Wales most effectively harness and grow the economic potential of tourism whilst at the same time achieving its appropriate integration into many other aspects of life in Wales in a manner which is sustainable?

The European Union still maintains its leading position in world tourism with a growth rate in 1996 of 4.2 per cent in terms of international arrivals and of 4.5 per cent in terms of tourism receipts[14]. Europe's share of the global tourism market has, however, been in decline since 1990 as a result of increasing competition from new destinations and products. In the period 1990-1996 Europe's share of the world market decreased by seven per cent in receipts and four per cent of arrivals.

In the U.K. tourism generated £102bn in 1996 and this is expected to grow by 2.9 per cent per annum to £178bn by 2006. In the process it is expected to add 310,000 more jobs to the 3 million currently employed. Tourism produces 5 per cent of

GDP at present and represents 13.8 per cent of U.K. exports. Growth is projected by the WTTC and the BTA over the next decade 14. However, the significant shifts in demand in Europe generally are prevalent in the U.K. This includes the shift to shorter-stay leisure trips, the long-term decline of the traditional family holiday, the growth of business tourism, and the increase of outbound holiday tourism. Wales is heavily dependent upon the U.K. domestic and on Northern European markets.

THE CURRENT STATE OF THE MARKET

The former Secretary of State for Wales, Ron Davies, acknowledged the 'substantial contribution' that tourism makes to the economy of Wales in his new economic agenda, *Pathway to Prosperity*[15]. This document refers to the Wales Tourist Board's estimates for 1996 that tourism was responsible for employing nine per cent of the workforce – the equivalent of 90,000 jobs – and contributing, as we have seen, some seven per cent of G.D.P. The WTB also indicates that there are over 6,000 private sector businesses directly involved in tourism.

Using these measures of performance, tourism is seen to have a bigger impact on the economy of Wales than other parts of Britain receiving almost 12 million tourist trips with a total spend of almost £2bn each year. The majority of these tourism trips are made by staying visitors from elsewhere in Britain with some 910,000 overseas tourists. In addition there are some 50 million leisure day visits to destinations and attractions in Wales.

Recent survey results have shown that there has been overall growth in domestic tourist numbers over the past five years. This growth has been in-line with the performance of U.K. tourism in general reflecting the increase in short breaks. Consequently Wales appears to have retained its share of the domestic markets. This has not been the case however in terms of spending by domestic tourists, which has shown a decrease in Wales' market share.

The Wales Tourist Board's 1994 *Tourism 2000* forecasts for overseas tourism were set higher than the forecasts for the rest of the U.K. This required Wales to increase its market share from the extremely low base of 3.6 per cent of all overseas trips to the U.K. There has been some growth in the number of trips allowing Wales to retain market share and there has been some growth in overseas visitor spending. Overall, however, Wales continues to under-perform in this aspect of tourism activity.

These figures mask the reality of an industry which exhibits a considerable range and differentiation in its tourism performance. Whilst, for example, business and short-stay leisure markets are in growth in South East Wales, there is a general downturn in trade in many of the traditional holiday resorts and in much of rural Wales. Operators in parts of rural Wales are reporting major and sustained decreases in visitor number over the past 10-15 years. This reflects the fact that Wales is strong in tourism products which are in structural decline. The problem has been that, up until recently, the growth sectors have not provided the volume needed to make up for the loss of hitherto core business. This is a key dilemma for Wales; solving it will not be easy. There is no simple or quick solution. The tourism industry is far more complex than the data produced by the WTB would imply. Our detailed knowledge of the sophisticated workings of the industry in Wales must continue to develop.

A PROGRAMME FOR CHANGE

What is clear, however, is that the success of tourism in general is directly related to the image of Wales in the market place, the ease of purchasing a tourist trip, and the ability to access and move around Wales. The Assembly must be concerned with the kind of image that will be used to promote Wales in the U.K. and international markets. The importance of Wales' image in the world is recognised in *Pathway to Prosperity*. It needs to be positive and distinctive, reflecting a modern, vibrant country that is respectful and proud of its culture, heritage and environment.

At present there is little knowledge or awareness of Wales as a tourism destination in the international tourism market place. This has been consistently demonstrated in research over the past twenty years most recently in the *Tourism Scoping Study for Industrial South Wales*[16]. The problem has been analysed in an Institute of Welsh Affairs report by John Smith MP, and is being addressed by the *Branding Wales Group*[17]. The WTB is represented on this group. However, there is no other direct tourism input to this process. The absence of a strong image of Wales is widely regarded as the major weakness. The existing profusion of destination marketing initiatives does not help the situation. The marketing effort is diluted as a result of too many organisations being involved. Resources should be better co-ordinated and an overall strategy agreed.

If tourism is to be encouraged there has to be a close interrelationship between the image used in marketing and the development and accessibility of product on-the-ground for our visitors. All too often this is where major weaknesses in the industry are exposed. The tourist requires a seamless supply of information services (information centres, reservation systems, directional signage), an integrated approach to national and local transport systems and a quality customer service at their destination. There are difficulties in meeting these basic conditions due to the fragmented and under resourced nature of provision in Wales.

The past ten years have witnessed the further fragmentation of tourist information and transport services in Wales. As a result, the basic infrastructure to facilitate tourism growth has been severely diluted. A good example of this is the lack of a connecting train service to meet the ferries from Ireland to Fishguard and the closure of the tourist information centres at key international gateway locations.

Significantly, however, the range and quality of the tourism product in Wales stands comparison with some of our direct competitors. Inevitably there are certain products which are outdated and in need of upgrading and investment. There are often products which are incapable of change and, that will suffer the consequence of a loss of business. Such a process of renewal and business casualties is inevitable. Product evolution takes place in response to market demand. Many operators in Wales need guidance to understand and respond to these changes in demand. They also need access to finance to assist their upgrading of their products.

As part of this process, Wales has introduced a number of innovative quality assurance schemes for different sectors of the industry. These have been successful in raising awareness and standards and, as a result, have been replicated elsewhere. These schemes are, however, all voluntary other than those that fall within scope of the Adventure Activities Licensing Authority. There is a consensus view in the tourism industry that the statutory regulation and registration of tourist accommodation is urgently required. At present the existing range of accreditation and inspection schemes is confusing for the tourist and the trade. A simpler, statutory, scheme needs to be introduced that reflects the special characteristics of tourism in Wales, whilst giving complete assurance to the consumer. It must be noted that the 1969 Act contained proposals for the statutory registration and classification of accommodation. They have simply not been implemented by successive governments.

The enhancement of quality standards will be further assisted by the arrival in Wales of more international brand operators. Although there is a tendency for these investments to centre upon Cardiff and Swansea their impact will be rapidly experienced throughout Wales especially in terms of developing our human resources and stimulating interest in working in tourism. The recent establishment of Springboard Wales / Sbardun Cymru – a UK-wide initiative to promote employment opportunities in the hospitality sector – will help raise the profile and image of the industry as will other U.K. and sectoral schemes.

This is an important issue. It would appear that the tourism industry is still dogged by the images of antisocial hours, poor working conditions, low pay and the absence of a career structure. As a result, operators are reporting labour shortages, recruitment difficulties, and high rates of staff turnover. Recent research has also revealed that there are significant gender issues within the industry. Tourism has a high proportion of women operating in reception, waiting, and kitchen jobs but relatively few appear to have attained management positions.

Some of these issues are part and parcel of working in the industry. It is a fact, for example, that tourism jobs involve anti-social hours. There has been significant progress on other fronts. The industry now has good quality training programmes, there are a wide range of vocational qualifications and career development opportunities are available. In addition, Wales is well resourced with FE and HE colleges offering training and education in tourism. A number of private sector, specialist, training agencies complement the public sector provision. There is also evidence that the various Government 'into work' initiatives are being used by the tourism industry[18]. There is a need to promote training and career opportunities in the industry. The importance of colleges providing relevant training which meets the needs of the industry still needs to be addressed. Further work remains to be done on the whole issue of training.

We need to create an industry that people of all ages want to be part of and which engenders pride and self-esteem. The appearance of larger companies and brand names in the industry is beginning to have this effect. Indeed one of the benefits of these larger scale operations is their more structured approach to employment and human resource development.

THE MILLENNIUM IMPACT

The industry in Wales is, and is likely to remain, heavily dependant upon a high incidence of small scale family-run enterprises and correspondingly fewer numbers of larger operators. The situation is changing. The 1990s has heralded the arrival of a long-awaited appearance of large scale tourism developments by indigenous investors. These include, for example, the T.B.I. Group (Cardiff International Airport and the Hilton International Hotel in Cardiff), the MacNamara Family (Oakwood Park and Canaston Bowl) and Terry Matthews with the Celtic Manor complex at Newport.

The past three years has dramatically witnessed a fundamental change in the nature of tourism-related investment in Wales. During this period Wales has experienced an unprecedented level of investment in tourist attractions as a result of Millennium Commission funding. The total funding involved in the National Botanic Garden of Wales, the Millennium Centre, the Millennium Stadium, the National Cycle Route (SUSTRANS), the Welsh Highland Railway Project and the Millennium Coastal Park exceeds £300m. A further tranch of European Regional Development funding for projects in the Industrial South Wales Region is also about to be announced. There appears to be a strong emphasis on investment in south east Wales leaving the industry in north west and mid Wales feeling somewhat isolated and neglected. There is a strong perception in north Wales of a North/South divide and in south west Wales of a East/West divide. These regional challenges must be addressed.

These flagship projects present Wales with exciting opportunities to attract and retain new visitor markets. Inevitably, however, there are many existing operators concerned about a potential displacement of visitors from their businesses. The dynamic impacts created by these new projects are difficult to predict. However, on the basis that they will generate a net increase of tourists there is scope for many operators to secure an increase in their market.

The conditions of much of these grant sources requires that those successful projects are sponsored by public sector organisations. These organisations generally have no commitment to commercial viability. As a result, many of these grant aided projects will always need to be subsidised, In addition, indigenous private sector operators are unable to secure support of any scale from these sources. An imbalance in funding tourism exists. The process is exacerbating a real and widely accepted issue; namely, that Wales already has an oversupply of visitor attractions. Many of these are under performing and of marginal viability. Whilst the flagship attractions are intended to generate new visitors to Wales, many remain sceptical about this actually happening. For many private sector operators any further decline will mean closure. The impact of these grant-aided projects needs to be carefully assessed.

Significantly, the cumulative effect of this investment together with the burgeoning of publicity associated with Rugby World Cup (1999) and the European Summit (1998) has stimulated wider interest in the potential large-scale development in Wales. Proposals for a £500m themed resort near Newport and for a £230m International Sports Village have been met with a guarded response from some key organisations concerned with economic and tourism development in Wales. There is a considerable amount of scepticism about the viability of such mega-scale projects and concern as to their relevance to tourism in Wales which is predicted on the principles of sustainability.

As a result, the response to large-scale tourism investments differs considerably from the warm welcome shown to inward investors in other sectors, such as manufacturing or call-centres. This is a result of scepticism that investors of this scale are seriously interested in locating in Wales combined with an uncertainty as to whether such large-scale developments are appropriate for Wales and our tourism industry. We should not be surprised, however, that there is an increasing level of international interest in Wales as a focus for their tourism investments:

- Public sector policies and strategies encourage private sector initiatives.

- Wales has a well publicised and successful track record in attracting inward investment for other industrial sectors.

- International developers and investors seek locations that offer easy access to markets and land acquisition at a reasonable price.

- Investors recognise the relative strength of the Welsh economy and the inherent qualities of the landscape, culture, and heritage.

These investors have reported a degree of concern that Wales has had difficulty in responding to their tourism proposals. This is a key issue. It has long been recognised that tourism in Wales needs to be internationalised, that there needs to be some well-known international operators associated with tourism in Wales as a balance to, what must be, a strong and distinctive indigenous tourism industry.

For 15 years at least, the Wales Tourist Board and others have desired inward investment for tourism and have courted the interest of some leading developers but with only limited effect. The emergence of the recent spate of projects has exposed our collective unpreparedness as to how to respond to such proposals.

The experiences of other countries indicate that such large scale projects bring mixed fortunes. On one hand they create jobs, raise profiles and boost the economy. On the other hand there is a potentially high level of leakage from the economy and the projects could do more to reflect and respect local heritage and culture. There urgently needs to be a strategy to guide our response to these projects and mechanisms that ensure that Wales derives real benefits from these developments.

These large-scale developments not only present challenges from a strategic tourism perspective but also highlight the current inadequacies of our land use planning system. Present statutory plans rarely make policy provision to cope with the issues raised by tourism in general and large projects in particular. This frailty of the planning system has been recognised by the Association of District Councils, which calls for a more positive approach to tourism by local authorities. The Assembly provides the unitary authorities in Wales with the opportunities to re-examine their plans and policies for tourism development over the next ten years. Under the previous Governments the Policy Planning Guidance system was diluted and replaced by more bland Technical Advisory Notes. The Assembly needs to put in place more detailed planning advice for large-scale projects.

The role of the National Museum and Galleries of Wales and of Cadw: Welsh Historic Monuments in managing and marketing key heritage attractions should be more fully exploited. Between them these two organisations are responsible for hosting over four million visitors, many of whom are overseas tourists. Their policies and plans to attract visitors need to be more effectively integrated into the work of local authorities, the Regional Economic Forums and others. They also play a key role in helping to create a distinct and recognisable Welsh tourism product. This has to be prioritised by all concerned with tourism in Wales.

MEASURES FOR REFORM

The disparate and small-scale nature of the industry in Wales and the absence of large operators means that the industry as a whole has a weaker marketing profile and a reduced lobbying power. The small-scale nature of tourism results in the under capitalisation of the business, lower levels of employment, and marginal viability. In addition, resources for training and for development are limited. There tends to be a high proportion of business failures and regular changes of ownership in many of these businesses. This in its own right is not necessarily counter productive. However, it is not conducive to a sustainable tourism industry.

One of the main advantages of an industry composed of small operators is that it should be possible to bring local character to product development. There are numerous examples in Wales where this has been successfully achieved, for example in the south west Wales area as a result of the work of SPARC, Antur Cwm Taf and Antur Teifi. This good practice should be widely promoted.

There are, therefore, advantages which arise from small-scale tourism in Wales.

These also include the potential to offer guests a friendly service, the potential to integrate tourists into the local host community and to encourage visitor spending in the local economy. Sourcing of goods and services from local suppliers tends to be more prevalent at this level. Overall, however, a more balanced composition to the industry in Wales is needed if overall growth is to be achieved and sustained. SMEs already in tourism and those considering entry to the industry need careful counselling and support.

Crucially this requires a clear vision and strategy for the tourism industry. This, in turn, demands leadership and a structure that allows all sectors of the industry and the community voice to be heard. The Assembly is not likely to influence change in the primary legislation affecting tourism in Wales. It is, however, able to put in place a structure to support its work and that of the Wales Tourist Board, thus fostering effective interrelationships between all parts of the industry. This is necessary for tourism in Wales to flourish. The Wales Tourist Board is currently reviewing its tourism strategy in advance of the establishment of the Assembly. This must be a strategy that creates the way forward for tourism in Wales.

The Wales Tourist Board is often regarded as being too distant from the trade and elusive. Its status as a 'quango' is being eroded due to recent policy changes introduced by the Government. The industry would welcome more Board members drawn from the industry and the potential for a chairperson elected by the industry. There is a need for a strong, focused, Wales Tourist Board.

The emergence of the Assembly creates an opportunity to make significant changes to improve the potential for tourism in Wales to grow in a strategic fashion. This requires that there is:

- Confirmation of the Wales Tourist Board as the lead organisation in Wales, following a review of its activities.
- Clear planning policy guidance and guidelines at the local Government level.
- A co-ordinated and strategic approach to marketing.
- The full integration of tourism into the work of the Regional Economic Forums.
- Strong industry representation and involvement at all levels throughout Wales.
- An ability to instigate rapid changes in response to changes in the market place.

Consideration should be given, therefore, to the radical reform of current structures in a way that creates this effective dialogue between the industry, local government, the Wales Tourist Board and the Assembly. This requires the establishment of:

- A Local Government Tourism Planning Forum to ensure an adequate and appropriate planning framework.

- Four Regional Tourism Councils, corresponding with the Regional Economic Forums.

- The establishment of a new visitor and tourism marketing bureau for Wales.

Finally, there is scope for a National Tourism Task Force to provide strategic leadership and guidance for the industry as a whole. This Task Force should bring together the private and public sector to create a strong platform for policy advice to the Assembly.

CONCLUSION

Significantly, tourism is the one area of economic activity that involves the majority of the citizens of Wales either as consumers, providers or as hosts in communities which receive tourists. Several authors have referred to the fact that tourism in Wales is 'everybody's business'. In addition to the direct contribution made to the economy, tourism also brings wider benefits through a multiplier, or ripple effect, through the economy.

In short the tourist pound is re-spent several times through the economy as a result of payments for wages, services and other supplies. The aim must be to achieve levels of high local spending and the prevention of 'leakage' of both primary and secondary spending to maximise the value of every pound spent. This is relevant to the concept of sustainable development.

Tourism creates opportunities for sustainable development throughout Wales, from urban centres to remote countryside and coastal locations. This allows Wales to respond positively to a wide range of markets by establishing and marketing products of international standards that reflect local conditions. As a result, tourism needs to be increasingly recognised as a positive force when managed carefully. Throughout the industry there must be a collective strategy to create a sustainable and distinctive Welsh tourism product irrespective of the scale and location of the investment. There are numerous examples of good practice in sustainable tourism development in Wales, especially amongst the National Park Authorities. These experiences need to be made available to others.

Tourism needs to be accepted by the community as a potent and valuable source of economic activity and a contributor to other social and cultural activities. From this base it will be possible to develop a constituency for tourism with politicians acknowledging that there are votes in tourism. The industry needs a major public relations campaign to achieve this recognition.

The starting point for this process must be the production of credible and reliable statistics. For too long the industry has paraded data that does not appear to have altered significantly over 20 years and, as a result, has failed to capture media attention. As a priority, therefore, the Assembly members must be given robust data about the current and future contribution of tourism to the Welsh economy. More resources have to be available for tourism research, to improve the situation.

The industry in Wales needs to prepare for an increasingly competitive and demanding tourism environment. This requires an organisational structure that is relevant to the needs of the industry, responsive to the markets and respectful of communities. It needs unambiguous political support and recognition, and a strategy which reflects the full potential for tourism in Wales. Strategic targets need to be established which are aggressive and competitive. This demands direction and leadership. The Assembly has the potential to create the right framework conditions to ensure that the tourism industry is able to achieve continued growth over the next ten years. The time is right for change and for a fresh initiative within the industry – an initiative that creates leadership and direction establishes cohesion, and stimulates effective partnerships in this key economic sector.

References

1   *New Approach to Investment in Culture*, Department of Culture, Media and Sport, 24 July 1998.

2   Written response to a question by D. Browne MP, Hansard, 15 June 1998.

3   Irish Times, 6 July 1998

4   *Ibid.*, 19 August 1998

5   John Osmond, *Addressing the Welsh Policy Vacuum: The National Assembly's Agenda for Change*, Welsh Economic Review, Cardiff Business School, Winter 1997/8

6   *Travel and Tourism's Economic Impact*. WTTC, 1996

7   Travel and Tourism Growth Forecasts WTTC, October 1996; *Tourist Arrivals -Annual Growth Projections*, WTO, Madrid

8   *Millennium Vision*, WTTC, 1996

9   *Towards Sustainable Development*, WTTC & Earth Council, 1995

10   *Final Community Measures Affecting Tourism,* European Commission, Brussels, July 1997

11   Ibid.

12   Wales Tourist Board, *Tourism 2000*, 1994; *Tourism 2000: A Progress Report* 1994-1996,

13   Welsh Affairs Committee, *Minutes of the Proceedings on the First Report from Proceedings of the Committee*, HMSO. February 1987.

14   WTTC, *UK – Millennium Vision* 1996;

15   Welsh Office, July 1998

16   Welsh European Programme Executive, *Tourism Scoping Study ISW Objectives 2 Region*, 1998

17   John Smith MP, *The Welsh Image*, Gregynog Papers Vol 1 No 4, Institute of Welsh Affairs, 1998

18   Stevens & Associates, *Tourism Employment Action for the Millennium*, South Glamorgan TEC, 1988

CHAPTER 17

THE WELSH WORKFORCE

Stephen Hill, Annette Roberts and Nick Miller

Current and future skills and training provision provides an opportunity and a major challenge to the National Assembly. Improving the skills level and capacity of the Welsh workforce would be a substantial achievement and a major boost to prosperity, immediately giving the Assembly stature, influence and relevance to the people of Wales.

Resources devoted to people development need to be recognised as investment rather than consumption, investment that creates and nurtures Wales' greatest asset - the productive and creative potential of its people. Unlocking this potential is a complex and vital task, with decision-making at personal, corporate and national levels needing to be informed by first-class research and data. There is a daunting list of real issues to be addressed, including:

- The quality and quantity of work.
- Lifelong learning and skills acquisition, including for the existing workforce.
- Nurturing an enterprise culture within Wales.
- Finding the right balance of initiatives to maximise personal, corporate and economy-wide growth.
- Potential conflicts between wealth creation and social exclusion.
- The quality of information available to decision-makers.

An Assembly cannot be expected to resolve all of these issues in its first few months, particularly given that many of them have been around for some time. However, the Assembly will need to quickly develop a long-term strategy that recognises the different needs and aspirations of the different regions of Wales. The Education and Training Action Group - established within the Welsh Office in November 1997 has identified many of Wales' skills and training problems in Wales, highlighting key issues such as:

- The high rate of economic inactivity in Wales compared with the UK (see Table 1).

- One in nine pupils leaves school without any GCSEs.

- Around 370,000 adults of working age have no qualifications.

- Less than half of the working age population has an NVQ level 3, or equivalent qualification (that is, two A levels or an advanced GNVQ).

- Over two-fifths of the working age population have low numeracy skills.

- One in six has low reading skills.

TABLE 1

Employment position of those of working age in the UK and Wales, Spring 1998 (thousands)

(Note: figures in brackets are the percentage of the working age population)

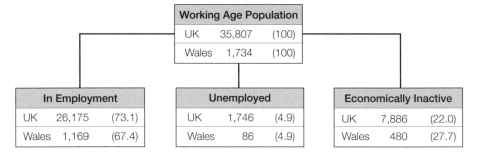

Working Age Population		
UK	35,807	(100)
Wales	1,734	(100)

In Employment		
UK	26,175	(73.1)
Wales	1,169	(67.4)

Unemployed		
UK	1,746	(4.9)
Wales	86	(4.9)

Economically Inactive		
UK	7,886	(22.0)
Wales	480	(27.7)

Source: *Education and Training Action Plan for Wales* – draft consultation document produced by the Welsh Office Education and Training Action Group, October 1998.

The Group's draft *Education and Training Action Plan for Wales,* published in October 1998, made a number of proposals to tackle these problems. Some of them are outlined later in this chapter and others are reported in the Appendix at the end.

'PEOPLE DEVELOPMENT'

Being competitive in a global information society and receiving an appropriate return on investment increasingly relies on finding the right balance between corporate, public and private infrastructure, including intellectual capital. Hence investment in human capital is a necessary complement to investment in public infrastructure (ranging from roads to universities) and investment in corporate capital. At the same time the 'people resource' is increasingly becoming identified as the primary determinant of company development. It is this 'people resource' in all its dimensions ranging from schools to continuing professional development, that will determine the future prosperity of Wales.

the lifelong learning and skills development that will be necessary in 21st Century Wales will require a combination of individual initiatives and public sector support, with the public sector role increasingly helping individuals to take responsibility for their own personal development.

Similarly, the provision of appropriate skills and training is no longer simply the operational matter of being able to meet current production requirements. People development is becoming a strategic issue for companies seeking a competitive edge in tomorrow's markets, as well as a fundamental requirement for economic growth. Escalating change is the dominant characteristic of modern markets, making the management of change the primary corporate, social and individual development issue.

Overlaying the task of managing people development is the crucial matter of educating management itself. Management competence requires a mix of education, training and experience.

People development policies cannot be provided exclusively by the State. Individual companies and persons should take responsibility for corporate and personal development, within an enabling context. Common ownership of policies and responsibilities is essential to potential growth maximisation, in individual development, corporate performance and the Welsh economy as a whole.

IDENTIFYING SKILLS NEEDS

The industrial structure of Wales has changed beyond all recognition over the last two decades. The virtual demise of the coal industry, the drastic reshaping of steel-making, the decline of heavy engineering and the substantial restructuring of Welsh agriculture have opened the door to a new employment base in electronics, automotive components and a significant market services sector, including the growth of personal, hospitality and tourism services. These changes, combined with wider developments in manufacturing and communications technology, have radically redefined the skills requirements of both the current and future workforces, with a new emphasis on customer satisfaction alongside more traditional attributes such as productivity gains and the assimilation of technological change.

Structural changes are super-imposed on to a backdrop of new employment practices such as increased flexible working, the rise of multi-skilling, portfolio employment and serial career changes. The number of full-time equivalent male jobs in Wales has been falling gradually over time, from 87 per 100 men of working age in 1971, to 79 in 1980 and just 64 in 1996. Corresponding figures for the UK are 90, 84 and 71 respectively, demonstrating the widening jobs gap between Wales and the UK. These full-time male jobs are being, to some extent, replaced by predominantly part-time, female employment which has been steadily increasing. The pursuit of efficiency has led many employers to downsize to a core workforce, with temporary or contract workers being engaged as required to meet fluctuations in demand. There is a new concentration on the workforce development as a cost centre rather than a corporate investment.

All these changes have impacted upon the skills needs and occupational profiles of industries in Wales. A polarisation is taking place in Welsh industry, with growing and sometimes urgent demands for highly skilled individuals in key sectors, such as electronics and higher level financial services, accompanied by a falling requirement for low-skilled, and even middle-skilled workers.

In occupational terms, steadily expanding demand for managers, professionals and associate professionals/technicians (the so-called knowledge workers), has been accompanied by a sharp decline in numbers of traditional craft and trades level employees. At the lower end of the skills ladder, future demand for plant and machinery operators may be strong in the short term, especially in the context of some expanding sectors within Welsh manufacturing. However, operatives can no longer be confident of such continuing employment without the skills necessary to thrive in a flexible and fast-moving work environment.

Since the wide definition of skills complicates any analysis of the skills market it is necessary to separate skills into skill types that are much easier to analyse. The table below gives one possible categorisation:

TABLE 2

Skill Types

Workplace Specific Skills	Formal Skills
Working Practices, Organisational Policy, Unique Processes	Engineering, Accountancy, History, Geography, etc.

Generic / Key Skills
Communication, Problem Solving, Ability to Learn, Numeracy, Literacy

Personal Attributes	Transferable Skills
Assertiveness, Leadership, Decisiveness, Motivation, Initiative	IT Skills, Driving, Management, Sales etc.

Different situations require different skills. For example, a highly technical engineering position will require formal skills and qualifications, whilst a sales assistant might be recruited on the basis of a positive attitude and some communications ability. As the labour market tightens, employers are recognising the need for key competencies and transferable skills in new recruits, with in-house training increasingly being used to provide the formal and workplace-specific skills required by particular situations, but albeit within the context of the drive for higher productivity in the immediate term.

Employers complain of a lack of basic skills of many new entrants to the labour market, suggesting either some shortcomings in school education or a perceived lack of relevance amongst some school-leavers. Employer research suggests that some prospective recruits need to improve their literacy, numeracy and communication skills, in addition to adaptability, motivation and team-working abilities, in order to match business requirements.

At the same time, there is increasing concern within Wales about the labour market exclusion of a significant proportion of school-leavers. The artificial distinction between education and training may be doing a disservice to young people in Wales. There is a need for curriculum development in post 11 education that will enable schools to place appropriate emphasis on general vocational competencies such as confidence in interpersonal relationships, awareness of customer needs, enterpreneurship and basic presentational skills.

The Education and Training Action Group report points out that the move towards telephone service operations, and the growth of jobs in the service sector, especially leisure and tourism, have the potential to attract the economically inactive back into the workforce. It says there is a need for people to have a core repertoire of transferable skills. These were defined in the *Future Skills Wales* project, undertaken by a consortium of Welsh organisations that surveyed more than 5,500 employers in the Summer of 1998. The project provides information on the skills available within the workforce and how they relate to those skills demanded by employers now and over the next five years. Provisional results from the project view the following skills as most important:

TABLE 3

Skills Demanded by Employers

	Percentage of Employers
Communications skills	88
Understanding customer needs	88
Ability to learn	81
Team working	81
Showing initiative	80
Ability to follow instructions	79

Source: The *Future Skills Wales* project

The project also identified the following additional skills which, along with those above, would become more important in the future:

TABLE 4

Additional Skills Demanded by Employers

	Percentage of Employers
Basic IT	47
Product Knowledge	41
Organising own learning	38
Problem solving	38
Literacy	34
Management skills	34
Numeracy	32
Job specific skills	31
Advanced IT	29
Leadership skills	27
Formal qualifications	27
Welsh language	19

Source: The *Future Skills Wales* project

SKILLS SUPPLY

There are several distinct groups within the population who could potentially provide (or be equipped with) the necessary skills to fulfil Wales' future needs. However, skills provision in Wales has to be viewed against a background of turbulence and organisational change in the structure and supply of vocational training over the past 50 years.

SCHOOL LEAVERS

School leavers are a key source of new skills, and one that can be quite accurately predicted in terms of numbers. However, there are serious issues surrounding the drive to encourage students into sixth form and higher education. Many employers perceive that the quality of school-leavers is inadequate, although the introduction of the high profile Modern Apprenticeship Training Scheme is making some inroads into industry's perceptions of school leavers. Important areas that should be addressed in this context are:

- Improve students' own perceptions of careers in manufacturing (and especially engineering).

- Create a parity of esteem between vocational training and more traditional academic routes.

- Attract more young people in schools to take up science and technology options and to consider careers in manufacturing industry.

One particular difficulty from a planning perspective is that information on leavers' qualifications by subject area is not collected centrally - with a significant shortage of data on vocational course outcomes in schools.

FE AND HE COLLEGE AND UNIVERSITY LEAVERS

Further Education colleges are the main providers of intermediate level vocational skills. At present, however, course provision is largely determined by student demand rather than employer needs. This has led to an over-supply of some skills in certain sectors, notably tourism, leisure, and media studies. Higher Education equips students with high-level skills in both vocational and academic disciplines, although employers still complain about a lack of transferable skills, including inter-personal ones, and about the absence of what may be called 'enterprise initiative' amongst new graduates. There is at least a case for the inclusion of enterprise training in further and higher education curricula across the subject range.

THE EXISTING WORKFORCE

Upskilling within the workforce is a key area of new skills provision in Wales and one that is easily overlooked in the concentration of State assistance on new entrants and the unemployed. Employee training, both outside the workplace and increasingly within, (since the introduction of NVQs), allows for the continuous development of human resources in industry. Quantifying the contribution of workplace training to skills development is an extremely complex task, especially in relation to gathering data on NVQ training.

THE UNEMPLOYED

The measured number of unemployed people in Wales has declined steadily for several years. They remain, however, a potentially rich source of new employees to meet rising demand. Initiatives such as the New Deal have refocused Employment Service activities towards greater marketing of client potential. However serious problems remain, particularly in the acquisition of skills and in the re-motivating of some who may have become accustomed to life without significant employment or income opportunities.

THE ECONOMICALLY INACTIVE

High levels of economic inactivity provide a serious challenge to economic success and prosperity in Wales. Existing programmes of Foundation Training need to be supplemented with new initiatives to bring the inactive into the labour market. Some categories of the inactive population, such as women returners can be assisted more easily by reducing the barriers to work and training. The introduction of better childcare facilities is one basic example of this. Other, often older, groups of economically inactive may need more motivation and information about new opportunities to participate.

THE ECONOMIC IMPACT OF EDUCATION AND TRAINING

There is a growing body of evidence that Education and Training is an expanding industry in its own right in Wales. For example, the Higher Education sector alone contributes an estimated £1bn to the Welsh economy (either directly or indirectly), supporting over 23,000 full-time equivalent jobs. These financial advantages are however a only by-product of education and training's principal activity. The main role is to provide individuals with skills and to advance the knowledge base of the wider economy – spending on education is an investment, rather than consumption activity.

The economic implications of education and training range from the directly measurable financial activities of institutions, to the less quantifiable impacts of education and training on the economy, through upskilling, productivity gains and technological advancements - all essential ingredients of modern competitiveness. The magnitude of these impacts will however depend on other factors. For example, one of the main disincentives against training from an employer perspective is the risk that employees, once they have acquired transferable or industry-specific skills, will then seek employment elsewhere.

In an economy where labour is increasingly mobile, the benefits of education and training may be felt more at an economy-wide level, as employees move between firms. If the objective is to educate and train the workforce, and to keep those skills within the Welsh economy, then skill enhancement incentives need to be in place for both individuals and firms. Education and training activities need to happen at the same time as new and existing firms grow and develop.

POLICY OPTIONS

There is a wide range of relevant policy issues in skills development in the contemporary and future Welsh economy - only some of which are amenable to public policy. Issues include:

- Employment versus employability - the quality and quantity of work and transferable skills.

- Responsibility for training the employed.

- Small firm development in the enterprise culture in Wales.

- The balance of initiatives to promote economic development in Wales.

- The possibility of employer levies to finance continuing training.

- Rural needs and priorities.

- The potential conflict between wealth creation and social exclusion.

- The growth of national institutions and identity.

- Local versus regional strategies, and the need for appropriate incentives to overcome any perceived 'motivation gap'.

The Education and Training Action Group recommends that the National Assembly develops a strategy to:

- Promote intensive training courses, designed in conjunction with employers, to upskill people to fill vacancies, especially where skill shortages are particularly acute.

- Encourage more of our young people to pursue vocational qualifications and acquire a bilingual capacity.

- Promote modern apprenticeships as quality programmes providing progressive routes to higher education qualifications and further develop them to meet the needs of Welsh industry and commerce.

- Encourage employers to give equal status to all qualifications and progressively to use vocational qualifications as entry criteria for work in all occupations.

- Promote collaboration between schools, colleges and industry to effectively deliver more hard-edged technology-based GNVQs and NVQs together with science and technology to school pupils.

- Increase the number of graduates in engineering and technology, particularly with design skills.

Small and medium-sized enterprises (SMEs) are a significant part of the Welsh economy - creating around 63,000 jobs in the years between 1967 and 1985 (Census for Employment). However, they tend to invest very little in training and development. Moreover, they are unlikely to have links with schools and colleges and employ comparatively few graduates. The *Future Skills Wales* Project found that in 1998 around half of employers in SMEs did not arrange off-the-job training for any of their workforce. The Education and Training Action Group report contains a number of specific recommendations about skills development in relation to small firms. In particular it suggests that:

- Fiscal incentives should be examined to see if more employers can be persuaded to undertake training initiatives.

- Skill sector groups should be established across all the major areas of industry and commerce to encourage them to work in partnership with schools, and further and higher education institutions.

CONCLUSION

Responsibility for skills and training development is currently shared by a range of institutions across Wales. The recommendations of the Education and Training Action Group, discussed above and in more detail in the Appendix, provide one prescription for bringing a much-needed coherence to the system. It offers the prospect of significantly improving Wales' skills profile, integrating the provision of vocational and academic education, and saving money in the process. It is an example of the kind of initiative that will be available to the National Assembly to put into practice.

APPENDIX

The Education and Training Action Group was convened under the chairmanship of Welsh Office Minister Peter Hain in November 1997. In October 1998 it produced a draft *Education and Training Action Plan for Wales*. The following statement reports on some of the main issues raised by the Group.

Welsh industry is having problems in recruiting skilled people, especially in the electronics, automotive and aeronautics sectors, all of which have been successful in attracting inward investment in recent years. However, the Education and Training Action Group's report warns that the skills shortage is putting future expansion at risk:

> 'Highly skilled engineers and technicians will continue to be needed in many of the growth sectors in manufacturing and in supporting service sectors. Their availability will influence the location of design and research teams which are of growing importance in relation to higher value manufacture. However, there are already shortages of engineers, technicians and IT specialists in Wales and the statistical evidence supports concerns that Wales is not equipping existing and new members of the workforce for the technological challenges of the next century.' (page 12).

The Group's report underlines the wide range of organisations currently responsible for delivering post-16 education and training, as the following table shows:

Post-16 Student Numbers* and Distribution Across the Sector

Funded By		%	Delivered By		%
FEFCW	196,000	(69)	Colleges	214,000	(75)
LEAs	24,000	(8)	Schools	24,000	(8)
TECs	34,000	(12)	PPs	28,000	(10)
Adult Ed.	32,000	(11)	Adult Ed.	20,000	(7)

* Numbers exclude Higher Education Provision

Key

FEFCW:	Further Education Funding Council for Wales - 29 Further Education Colleges
LEA:	Local Education Authorities (22) - 188 11-18 schools
TECs:	Training and Enterprise Councils (6, being reduced to 4)
PPs:	Private Providers - about 200, via the TECs
Adult Ed. :	Adult Education Centres/Providers - 200 via the 22 LEAs

The report argues that there is an urgent need to achieve better links and use of resources across this complex post-16 education and training provision. It says we need a more 'joined-up' arrangement:

'... the competition between schools and colleges and private training providers for post-16 provision inhibits the capability of education and training provision to meet the skills needs of the economy. GNVQ provision in schools tends to focus on those areas which can be most easily afforded and provided. In contrast the more resource intensive manufacturing and technology routes are frequently unavailable. All too often young people are encouraged to stay on in school pursuing traditional academic courses when that might not be their best option.' (page 14).

The Group notes that - uniquely for Wales- Parliament has given the Secretary of State (and thus the Assembly) powers to ensure that schools and colleges can work in partnership to provide further education post-16, through the Schools Standards and Framework Act 1998. Accordingly it recommends that the National Assembly establish a network of *Community Consortia for Education and Training* (CCETs) throughout Wales. These should be established with a new institutional framework of collaboration between schools and colleges described in the following terms:

'We recommend that the Assembly should secure formal Local Authority-College Partnerships by inviting all local authorities, schools and FE

*institutions to prepare plans to share facilities and improve provision; to build
on specialisms; and to deliver a broader range of choice for students post 16,
area by area.*

*We suggest that the Secretary of State should consider establishing a pump
priming **Partnership Incentive Fund** during the course of the Internal Review
in 1998 (see Chapter 4 for a description of the Review). We envisage that such a
fund should be available for the Assembly to administer **from financial year
1999-2000 onwards**. We recommend that initial provision should amount to
between £1m and £2m ...*

*... The Partnership Plans should be approved by each participating school and
FE institution; by the relevant local authority and the Further Education
Funding Council for Wales. We think that the Funding Council should be
responsible for taking TEC advice prior to submitting the plans to the Assembly
for approval, and then funding. The resulting local authority-College
Partnerships could themselves prepare the way for the formal introduction of
Community Consortia for Education and Training (CCETs). Indeed, in a sense
they could be embryonic CCETS.*

*We urge that this option be pursued forthwith, and endorsed by the Assembly,
so that **the first Partnerships can be implemented in the academic year
1999-2000**.'* (page 40).

The Education and Training Action Group proposed a radical shake up of post-16
education and training in Wales, with one institutional structure to embrace the
following functions:

- Schools sixth forms
- Further education institutions
- Local authority adult education
- Training and Enterprise Councils, in so far as they relate to training
  provision in colleges and with private providers.

Combining these functions, the Group argue, would yield significant benefits for
the development of skills within the Welsh economy, for mainstreaming equality of
opportunity, improving careers guidance, and promoting access for the socially
excluded. The Group considered whether the functions should be combined
directly under the Assembly's administration, under four new organisations based
on the four economic regions of Wales, or under a new all-Wales institution. On
balance it favoured the last approach and recommended the creation of a new

Council for Education and Training in Wales, accountable to the Assembly:

> 'This would have a wholly new remit. It would have a Board reflecting the major stakeholding interests and capable of taking balanced and impartial judgements about investment across Wales. We envisage that it would work through four regional offices and be responsible for assisting LEAs, further education institutions and the training sector to form CCETs to meet local skills needs and other educational needs. At this level as at every other it is vital that there should be arrangements to engage employers' guidance to shape education and training in support of a business friendly enterprise culture - not least through the 29 FE College Boards themselves' (page 44).

The Group estimated that rationalisation of post-16 education and training along these lines would produce savings in the range of £8m to £12m a year, which could cover the costs of transition to the new system in the first instance and later be re-invested in education and training.

CHAPTER 18

EDUCATION

Eirlys Pritchard Jones and David Reynolds

Education will be one of the Assembly's largest areas of spending and should be regarded as the greatest field of investment in Wales' future. Policy should not only include those in traditional education establishments but should embrace society as a whole. Attracting all into learning, ensuring quality in all learning experiences and facilitating high standards of achievement must be seen as the key priorities. If these are effectively pursued Wales will achieve economic confidence and cultural development as well as international competitiveness.

The Assembly should have the confidence to think creatively about education. The last decade has already seen a growing distinctiveness in our educational policies. The inclusion of Welsh as a national curriculum subject and the difference in knowledge content within some subjects, have been followed by policies distinct from those in England in such areas as:

- The absence of any publication of primary school performance tables.

- A decision not to adopt the highly prescriptive English literacy and numeracy strategies.

- The absence of the harsh rhetoric about school performance that has emanated from Ministers at the Department for Education and Employment and from the Office for Standards in Education.

- The continued emphasis within Wales on the need for schools to be in the 'driving seat' of change through processes such as school review contrasts with the use of market pressures as the 'driver' of change in England.

The National Assembly can of course build upon these differences in policies, but in a more positive way by initiating developments rather than merely failing to implement policies that are operative across the border, or by making modest adjustments. In this it will be aided by the separate organisational infrastructure that already exists. In addition we have a high degree of collaboration between different educational bodies. Developing these within an effective and efficient structure should be a major objective. The Welsh education system is now probably self-confident enough to welcome change. In the past it may have been one 'schooled for failure' and rooted in traditional approaches to curriculum and pedagogy. Today, however, it is on a steep curve of modernisation and improvement. Outcomes in such areas as the proportion of pupils gaining five GCSEs or more at grades A-C have improved rapidly over the last five or six years.

The recommendations of the Welsh Office Education and Training Action Group's draft report, published in October 1998 and described in part in the Appendix to the previous Chapter, underline many of the strands we draw out here. There are three important caveats to be made, however. First, there is an overwhelming emphasis in the Action Group's recommendations on the *vocational* side of education and training. This should be properly integrated with the academic and the most effective way of achieving this would be through revamping the post-16 curriculum. As we argue later in this chapter, this should be accomplished via the Welsh Baccalaureate (the *WelshBac*).

Secondly, the Education and Action Group's recommendations imply creating a free-standing tertiary sector in Wales. If this happened school sixth forms would be drawn out of the schools and merged into a single institutional structure with further education provision, local authority adult education, together with the training function of the TECs. Though we strongly believe, and recommend later in this chapter, that there should be much greater collaboration between the schools and colleges in Wales - collaboration that would be essential if the *WelshBac* were to succeed - this does not mean there should be a merger. Indeed, a merger would be harmful to pre-16 education provision in the schools. Further, it would fly in the face of another of the Education and Training Action Group's recommendations:

> We are certain that no institutional or other change should be made if it does
> not offer a compelling prospect of improving educational and training outcome.
> We regard it as essential that provision in schools pre-16, and that for
> education and training post-16 should be treated as a seamless whole (page 6).

Thirdly, the education and Training Action Group's report lays to much emphasis on institutional change rather that the underlying culture of the delivery of education and training. Making our institutions work effectively, and if necessary changing them, is important. More important, however, is the success of the education process at the chalk face. This is the emphasis we prefer and to which we turn in the following section.

TEACHING AND LEARNING: CORE PRINCIPLES

A number of core principles should underpin all consideration of Welsh education policy. Most of these cannot be legislated for as such but should be a matter of custom and practice within schools and colleges. However, in its policy-making the Assembly should be informed by them and do what it can to ensure that they become an essential part of our educational culture. They can be summarised as follows:

- The learner is the key. Past education policies have aimed to create systems of advice and inspection before first examining the educational and training needs of learners as individuals. This priority should be reversed.

- Learning, the process that happens at the interface between learner and teacher, is the crux of educational success. All the available evidence suggests that the classroom teacher is a much more powerful determinant of outcomes than the school level, yet the current discourse is about schooling, not teaching.

- Sound early years' provision is of principal importance. All the evidence suggests that educational quality between the ages of five and ten has more impact on development than between the ages of ten and fifteen. Children without basic skills such as literacy and numeracy by age seven or eight are likely to be in grave danger of subsequent educational under-achievement.

- Enlightened leadership is the essential ingredient for success. Good headteachers and college heads should define clear, shared aims and objectives, and a common vision as a basis and framework for a strong learning community where young people feel they 'belong'.

- High but realistic academic and vocational goals should become part of educational culture.

- Strong links between schools and colleges with parents are essential as is a culture of partnership with other organisations in society, especially the local business community.

- Generally, school is less important than society, since every available study shows that the influence of learners' backgrounds is greater than that of education organisations. Educational change needs to be underpinned by wider economic, social and structural change.

- Policies should vary with local context. The type of school regime and organisation that might 'work' in the Valleys may not 'work' in north Wales, or the policies appropriate to a sparsely populated rural area may not be appropriate for a large city.

More generally, the curriculum should be designed specifically for Wales, encompassing both breadth and depth, and taking the bilingual context of Wales as a natural part of its provision, with its focus on skills rather than on a know;ledge base. As knowledge in many areas is obsolete in maybe five to ten years, the conventional role of the educational system is one of knowledge transmission is increasingly irrelevant. Skills to access information, together with broader conceptual understanding, are the required priorities.

Finally, the distinctive character, culture and language of Wales should be a foundation for providing education in Welsh, as both a subject and as a medium of instruction as appropriate, to all pupils in Wales. The *Cwricwlwm Cymreig* should be used as the way of providing cultural roots, which enable people to look confidently at an international perspective. All research proves the importance of establishing firm cultural roots to enable young people to fulfil their educational potential and develop self-esteem.

THE GOVERNMENT'S POSITION

In its 'new economic agenda for Wales' *Pathway to Prosperity*, published in July 1998, the Welsh Office administration placed improving education and training at the centre of its economic project. The document declared.

> '*We need greater coherence between our education and training systems and institutions. For too long they have been viewed as being in competition - we must change competition into collaboration where the needs of employers and the aspiration of the individual are paramount*' (para. 6.1).

To come up with a practical agenda the government has established an Education and Training Action Group which has seven priorities:

- Help improve school performance to ensure that all pupils reach satisfactory standards by the end of compulsory education.

- Achieve more efficient and cost effective delivery of education and training by the further education colleges, TECs, local authorities, and other providers.

- Focus education and training more purposefully to deliver the skills needed by the Welsh economy.

- Tackle social exclusion.

- Realise the potential of the new technologies to expand access to learning.

- Ensure that indigenous small and medium sized enterprises are assisted to train more effectively and to develop better links with further and higher education.

- Maximise the benefits of the University for industry.

These are all highly desirable objectives. However, beyond stating them the administration so far has come up with little in the way of concrete policies on how they will be achieved. The same is true of an equally important educational aspiration, set out in *Pathway to Prosperity*. This is 'to create parity of esteem across all 16-19 education and training' (para. 6.3). The government is equally committed to broadening the post-16 curriculum, from the present narrow concentration of just three A-levels, and often only two if students judge that is all they need to gain entry to higher education. *Pathway to Prosperity* declared that the Government

> '... *intends to broaden the 'A' level and GNVQ curriculum to give greater choice and flexibility for sixth formers and to upgrade vocational qualification, including the introduction of a new Key Skills qualification in communication, number and information technology'* (para. 6.6).

However, the Government has failed to explain how it intends to broaden the curriculum, and neither has it come up with practical policies to ensure this will happen. Instead, for example, in its response to a year-long consultation around its *Qualifying for Success* document on the future of post-16 qualifications, published in 1997, it relied on voluntary initiatives by schools and colleges to increase the range of subjects taught, and offered no new resources.

The Assembly will need to mobilise a determination within Wales to come up with practical policies for an educational agenda whose content in principle has achieved wide agreement but so far no effective policy response. In what follows we offer an outline of an effective approach to the education challenge that will be central to the Assembly's agenda.

GOVERNANCE ISSUES

A single Education and Training Committee working under the guidance of the Education 'Minister' should direct the planning and resourcing of education, supported by the proposed Regional Committees of the Assembly.

At present the following organisations are among those sharing responsibility for different aspects of education and training, each taking its own slice of the budget: the Welsh Office, 22 local education authorities, the Higher and Further Education Funding Councils for Wales, the Welsh TECs, the Qualifications, Curriculum and Assessment Authority (ACCAC), the Welsh Joint Education Committee (WJEC), the Schools Inspectorate (OHMCI), the Welsh Local Government Association, and the Welsh Language Board.

Many of these organisations need to be rationalised. For instance, the remits of ACCAC and the WJEC overlap to such an extent that they should be reconstituted into a single Council for Education and Training in Wales (as is already the case in Northern Ireland). This follows closely the recommendation made by the Welsh Office's Education and Training Action Group, detailed in the Appendix to the previous Chapter. In addition to its recommendations, the Council for Education and Training in Wales should also be made responsible for the advisory and INSET functions that the 22 local authorities are struggling to deliver, some of them by means of ad hoc partnerships with each other. Delivering these at the all-Wales level, but of course locally according to need, would give important economies of scale and very usefully integrate them with the curriculum and assessment functions. Management of the Council for Education and Training in Wales should remain in the hands of representatives of the local authorities to ensure it worked in close liaison with them, within the strategic direction laid down by the National Assembly. The role of the Council for Education and Training in Wales should also include:

- Working with all education institutions to help to raise standards, encouraging and sharing good practice, recognising success and linking with appropriate partners – being an enabling and supporting mechanism without diminishing the autonomy of schools.

- Providing resource centres for support materials, disseminating effective resources and successful teaching strategies.

- Working with schools to raise the status and morale of teachers and encouraging career development.

- Providing a data base of information and practical help for other financial support, for example, sponsorship.

- Creating a successful publicity mechanism to create and encourage a culture of success in schools and in the community.

- Co-operating with schools to broaden international links and opportunities for pupils.

- Maximising partnership and development opportunities for schools with their communities; and strengthening relationships between governors, pupils and parents.

- Building partnerships with other sources of learning and resources such as museums and libraries.

- Encouraging opportunities to build positive images of schools and encourage young people to take a positive part in their communities.

- Supporting the role of parents in their child's education - for instance, family learning initiatives.

The role of the Training and Enterprise Councils (the TECs) should be split between the Further Education Funding Council for Wales and the Welsh Development Agency. This would allow funding to be directed where it is most needed, at the place of learning, be that in classrooms or in a different venue. The 'Enterprise' function of the TECs should be handled by the WDA as part of its business services remit. Training initiatives should be based on collaboration between the Further Education colleges and industry, basing provision on the local labour market needs and identification of the needs of individuals. Learning and training in the workplace should be a right for all, especially low skilled and disadvantaged groups. Widening participation in learning should be deliberately planned and should recognise the different reasons for previous under-achievement, providing learning in accessible places in attractive, relevant ways.

WELSH-MEDIUM EDUCATION

Welsh medium schools have grown substantially over thirty years and the sector is constantly developing. In 1997-8 30.2 per cent of Welsh school children were receiving Welsh medium education. One recent survey showed that 50 per cent of parents would choose Welsh-medium nursery education for their children if it were available to them.

Recognition of the quality of the Welsh medium and bilingual education sector and its value in Wales is long overdue. In many Welsh-medium schools, over 90 per cent of the pupils come from non Welsh speaking homes, which means that pupils are taught in what is actually their second language. The only place where most of them have a chance to speak Welsh is in school. This has resulted in particular features, which can be recognised as acknowledged characteristics of good schools, and which combine in those schools to contribute to a successful education. Language is at the heart of the curriculum; schools provide a 'family' atmosphere and traditional values - respect, co-operation, and consideration - as well as cultural identity. The cultural ethos creates a sense of belonging, of identity and unity in the schools.

Welsh medium provision is successful because it is seen to produce high standards of achievement, a strong sense of identity, breadth of experiences and the advantages of bilingualism. While many parents perceive these advantages, some LEAs appear to be reluctant to prepare proactively and adequately to meet parents' wishes. In many areas, the demand for Welsh medium schools far outstrips the available provision. This option should be available everywhere in Wales where parents wish to make this choice. Parents need a choice from a variety of provision - Welsh medium and English medium with some Welsh - in all areas of Wales.

Many schools are now using the modular curriculum to enhance a bilingual teaching strategy. Different modules can be taught in each language, thus ensuring comparable language and subject skills in both English and Welsh. Extending this kind of provision in some subjects in schools where English is the main teaching language would provide an excellent opportunity to make use of Welsh language skills presently taught in a vacuum as a second language.

By the year 2002, all 16 year old pupils in Wales will have received 11 years' education in the Welsh language as part of the national curriculum and so would be well equipped to use Welsh within parts of other subjects. Bilingualism enhances learning and achievement and, moreover, facilitates the acquisition of other languages.

THE CURRICULUM

The curriculum in Wales should be designed for Welsh schools and colleges, and not follow slavishly the model pursued in England. At the same time it must not be forgotten that our students will be competing for places in Higher Education and in the labour market with those who follow a different pattern.

The curriculum in Wales starts from a different basis. Wales' bilingualism leads to a situation that is common in most areas of Europe, where at least two languages are studied as norm throughout a school career. Different learning needs should be recognised. Experiences and skills should be the basis of the framework for learning rather than knowledge. Transferable skills reflecting personal development should be emphasised. The goal of developing well-rounded individuals who become valuable members of society should not be lost within the need to achieve high standards. Both are achievable.

The curriculum in Wales should be attractive and meaningful to students and permeating every part should be a balance between the *Cwricwlwm Cymreig* and an awareness of global, international issues. Vocational education (GNVQs) have a valid role in the curriculum for all students, in developing skills and processes of working which will be a basis for further, more specific training later. It is vitally important that parity of status be given to high levels of achievement in this area so that Wales can produce highly skilled technicians, engineers and craftsmen for the new technologies.

The value of encouraging young people to become adventurous in their attitudes, to be ready to take some risks in different contexts, to extend their experiences and learning must not be under-estimated. It is a disadvantage that traditionally in Wales, creativity is associated with the arts and culture generally, but not with business or economic development. Traditional suspicion of financial success has led to a general reluctance to take responsibility for our own and others' economic health. Our rural communities, the traditional backbone of our language and heritage as well as the steady spine of Wales' economy, need an infusion of positive attitudes in order to ensure their economic and cultural survival.

Initially, the curriculum should be based on the current core - Language (English and Welsh), Maths and Science but should develop to include wider elements of breadth as children's needs become apparent and their abilities mature. At all stages, the use of information technology should be developed as a basic skill for the future. Using the Digital College and distance learning techniques can add to the choices of available learning experiences and resources. Proficiency and confidence in new media should be part of everyone's skills.

The development of proficiency in several languages is easily achieved in other European countries. Using the base of Wales' bilingualism, a third and even a fourth language should become part of the useful learning of most children. It would require a change of attitude from the misplaced conception that acquiring another language is too difficult for all but the few. Yet experience in different countries shows that, properly taught, several languages can be mastered by most. By 1999 all pupils will have received Welsh from age 5 to 14 and will continue to 16. After eleven years' study, all pupils should have achieved some fluency. This should make the current, often artificial, distinction between 'first language' and 'second language' superfluous. Progress should be seen as movement along a continuum of linguistic development. This will give all students the basis for extending their use of the language into other contexts and use it as a medium for learning within parts of other subjects also.

Certainly, it is time to move away from a curriculum that is knowledge based, as information is now instantly available at the touch of a button. A greater emphasis of learning skills and processes, of being able to distinguish between the significant and the trivial, would be a more valuable use of the time spent in schools and colleges. In this debate sight must not be lost of the value, the essential need, for people to be well-rounded, civilised human beings, considerate and tolerant of others, able to communicate, having learnt from the past and aware of the need to conserve the future. The relevance of the subjects in the curriculum to the future of our young people in their daily lives and work is crucial - how well do we prepare them for living? Developing basic skills needed in life, such as parenting and cookery, should be considered fundamental in everyone's education. Society can no longer depend on the family to pass on the traditional skills. Good guidance on these issues will prevent problems later. A curriculum needs to be more than a list of subjects. Personal development, social awareness, moral/cultural and artistic knowledge and sensitivities play their part.

Drastic changes to the curriculum should be avoided and research and consultation should replace the recent series of knee-jerk reactions to perceived difficulties. A broad, balanced curriculum which is soundly based on educational experience and relevance for young people's future should be the aim.

In the state of flux that exists in this area at the moment, there is an opportunity to establish a curriculum framework designed for Wales, established on good practice and an awareness of needs, especially for the post-16 cohort. The Dearing recommendations emphasised the need for a broad curriculum at this stage of education. The Welsh Baccalaureate (the *WelshBac*) offers a framework which has been carefully developed by the Institute of Welsh Affairs to include all the elements of breadth and depth to provide the currently sought 'over-arching' cohesion of a balanced curriculum. Its main features are as follows:

- It is aimed at 80 per cent of the cohort.

- It includes in its structure choices that encourage students to take vocational qualifications as an intrinsic part of its diploma award. It gives parity of status and value to both academic and vocational qualifications.

- It includes an opportunity for all students to enhance their knowledge either of the Welsh language or of their country.

- As with the International Baccalaureate, all students follow a Core Skills programme, a study of theory of knowledge, global concerns and an element of community services as essential requirements before the diploma is awarded.

- It provides a broad and flexible field of study, which enables students to compete internationally.

- Its modular structure enables credit accumulation at different times and will provide a basis for later development; it sets a sound foundation for lifelong learning.

The *WelshBac* would produce well-equipped and well-rounded people with an awareness of the part they can play and the contribution they can make to their communities. Opportunity to develop every talent, to reach a high standard of achievement and skills would be available through the balanced range of learning experiences combined within a coherent framework. The *WelshBac* provides a practical way of achieving the Government's twin aim of broadening A levels and upgrading vocational qualifications. As the following section elaborates, it would also provide the means of unifying the schools and colleges of Wales into a cohesive system. Further, it would provide an educational and cultural underpinning of the emerging civic character of the new Wales. And, if all this is not enough, it could be achieved without significant budgetary consequences. All these are powerful arguments which should make the *WelshBac* an early priority for the National Assembly's agenda.

FURTHER EDUCATION

Colleges in Wales are a growing and dynamic part of the education sector, providing vocational education and training for approximately 195,000 students over the age of 16, mostly on a part time basis. The Government has pledged to increase the student population by 500,000 in the UK. Further Education Colleges will educate the majority of these, and in Wales it is expected that an extra 26,000 students will receive vocational education and training at an FE college early in the new millennium.

Since colleges became independent in 1993, standards have continued to improve. Colleges have become far more diverse, competing for students by supplying courses that suit student demand. Currently, funding from the Further Education Funding Council for Wales follows student recruitment and attainment, and there is general recognition that FE has been seriously under-funded over the last few years.

Further Education has a vital role to play in the economic regeneration of Wales. Colleges will be relied upon to deliver the government's agenda in terms of achieving a skilled and flexible workforce, lifelong learning and training the unemployed for work. In Ireland, vocational education and training has played a key part in achieving a highly skilled and flexible workforce. Wales could learn a lot from Ireland.

Further Education has reached a cross-roads. There are more requirements upon it now than ever before. The government sees it as a vehicle for achieving many of its policies, not just in terms of skills and lifelong learning, but as a means of tackling social exclusion as well. Increasingly, colleges are becoming the stepping stone for people to go on to higher education and are providing more and more diverse ranges of courses and qualifications.

More fundamentally, however, post-16 education needs to be viewed as a whole, linking schools and colleges together in a single system. As the current Welsh Office administration itself has said, in its economic policy document *Pathway to Prosperity*, quoted earlier, 'We need greater coherence between our education and training systems and institutions. For too long they have been viewed as being in competition'. In our view the way to achieve collaboration is through co-operation in a new curriculum. This is another great virtue of the *WelshBac* proposals which are based on offering every student both academic and vocational disciplines, and giving them parity of esteem. This could only be achieved effectively if neighbouring schools and colleges worked closely together in offering subjects each could deliver best - in general the colleges vocational courses, and the schools academic. We need a single system to deliver effective post-16 education. A single 'overarching' curriculum, which is the *WelshBac*, is the way to achieve it.

Additionally, in its first term the National Assembly should:

- Recognise the key role that FE has to play in economic development.

- More closely match economic demands with supply of skills.

- Secure a level playing field for the funding of post-16 education and training and quality assurance.

- Improve accountability in the management of FE.

- Ensure that FE can deliver the government's agenda on Lifelong Learning, widening participation, tackling social exclusion, improving the national skills base and the delivery of higher education in further education institutions.

- Assist in the development of tertiary arrangements to facilitate local planning of post-16 education provision.

- Ensure that there is FE sector representation, as a matter of course, on regional economic forums and other key decision–making bodies.

- Develop further and implement a post-16 credit framework to deliver all academic and vocational qualifications and be at the forefront of managing the impact of new technology.

HIGHER EDUCATION

Major changes in the approaches to Higher Education in recent years have extended access to people who previously would not have considered it appropriate. However, 70 per cent of young people in Wales still do not progress to HE. Increasing numbers of mature students, both part and full time, are taking up opportunities to study. 'New Universities' have illustrated that standards can be and are maintained by using different strategies and routes of access into high level qualification. Initiatives such as those taken successfully by several Universities in Wales in the field of outreach strategies - 'Community Universities' and various franchise arrangements and partnerships with other colleges - enable a wider range of students to develop their talents and achieve success. These initiatives have helped to create a climate of positive attitudes to continued education and training among employers, business communities and industrialists.

Building partnerships between Higher Education and Further Education to enable people to progress and continue education and training should be encouraged; some good examples already exist between colleges, universities and schools. Policy should be aiming for a continuing process of developing individuals through education and training, breaking down artificial divisions between different stages.

Links between the HE sector in Wales and industry, commerce and the public services should be promoted. One example is the £100,000 being invested by the Welsh Office during 1998-9 to support the Wales Electronics Forum in improving the employability of graduates for the electronics and semiconductor industries. The Assembly should extend such initiatives to every industrial sector in Wales.

What is the future of the University of Wales? The conflict between the original collegiate structure and the modern aspirations of individual colleges has been rumbling for some time. Will the greater independence of post-Assembly Wales foster a culture that will seek a greater degree of separation in individual institutions or will the original vision of a national institution prevail? The established reputation of the national university with 'federal' colleges should be promoted in the context of stronger national identity. The University of Wales should be encouraged in understanding that it has a role in serving both the educational and the economic needs of the country.

LIFELONG LEARNING

The development of the culture of lifelong learning should be seen as a priority within a Wales where disaffection and social exclusion are at higher levels than elsewhere. A general acceptance needs to be made in communities and throughout society that learning, education and training do not belong to only one period of life.

Mutual awareness of the need for concurrent skills and recognition of progress by employers and educators will promote public understanding of the value and validity of vocational qualifications. Constantly up-dating and improving qualifications should be seen as the norm within the patterns of work and career development. This will be assisted by the increasing modularisation of courses in a recognised framework, already a feature of many qualifications. People will be able to achieve parts of relevant and highly regarded qualifications in different places and at different times.

Employers should be encouraged to allow accessibility to appropriate courses for their workforce and be prepared to validate skills acquired in the workplace as a part of this cumulative process. As far as is practical, including employers in discussions on qualifications to ensure relevance and value would encourage their co-operation. Flexibility is important to allow systems to meet different contexts, aspirations and needs. Extending the provision of Welsh medium courses, linking with the increasing use of Welsh in the workplace, would reflect the needs of local communities and the growing recognition of the country's bilingualism.

The inclusion of all, particularly disadvantaged groups and those previously under-represented in our learning opportunities, will require many strategies and resources. The *Learning is For Everyone* Green Paper offers many valuable approaches, including accepting and promoting different points and methods of access for different groups. It is important that all people in Wales see themselves as a part of the Learning Society. Those previously most disadvantaged, including those with learning difficulties, should be targeted for appropriate personal learning development.

The accessibility of learning within communities is a key factor for bridging the skills and learning deficiencies that exist in Wales at several levels. Family learning strategies, the Basic Skills Agency, the Youth Service and Community Education all have crucial but different roles to play in widening participation in the developing Learning Society.

The potential contribution of the Digital College, the University for Industry, the Welsh Information Society and Community Universities should be used fully to reach and include potential students. No-one should feel excluded. Using familiar and non-threatening venues, accessible approaches to learning and offering relevant, positive guidance and counselling on the value of courses and qualifications should help boost low self-esteem and overcome perceived obstacles.

RESOURCES

Significant discrepancies exist in the levels of funding currently provided by the different LEAs to their schools. Similarly, the proportionate amounts kept centrally for administration vary greatly. Ring fencing the education budget would ensure that *at least* the minimum levels of funding provided from central sources were allocated directly for education. Since the inception of local management, schools have enjoyed their ability to use resources in accordance with agreed priorities; and pupils have benefited from this financial autonomy. Maximum funds delegated to schools and used wisely have positive outcomes in raising standards. Access to information about the internal methods of allocating funds within Local Authorities, along with transparency of all Authority accounts, would help to prove that resources are used cost-effectively.

The Assembly needs to address the inherited backlog of essential capital investment in buildings. The dilapidated condition of schools does not provide a conducive environment for effective study. Current LEAs are too small and too inadequately funded to do so, but the issue of inadequate facilities and antiquated buildings should be addressed as a matter of priority. Strategic planning for capital building and adequate resourcing of schools on a countrywide basis would meet this problem most effectively. If the current mode of private funding for capital development is pursued, consideration should be given to the industrial/financial situation of the area and the influence of that on what funding may be available. A poor industrial base could prevent development in some rural and economically deprived areas of Wales.

Priorities should be defined. Early years' education is the major resource priority as it has the greatest beneficial effect in raising standards. Within schools, the development of modern technology is essential to prepare young people for the workplace. Computers should be regarded as an essential part of school equipment, immediately available to pupils throughout their school lives. Links with industry could ensure that investment is made in the latest, relevant hardware, possibly using short-term hiring agreements to ensure the availability of the latest models. Attractive, relevant bilingual software should be available across the curriculum. The use of CD-ROMs, networks, the Grid for Learning and The Digital College should be a normal part of students' experience so that they hone their skills to appropriate levels and see ITC as a normal mode of communication and access to information and learning. Using the Welsh language in these developments should be promoted as a normal part of educational provision in a bilingual country.

Effective computerised administrative systems should simplify documentation and record keeping, minimising bureaucratic overload, and allowing teachers to spend their time on teaching, preparation and marking. The data assembled would be available as a management tool to focus on areas needing attention or recognising areas of success.

The National Grid for Learning will provide an excellent opportunity in Wales to overcome some of the particular resource problems and communication difficulties due to geography and topography. Proper use of the grid will enable good educational resources to be shared and maximise cost effectiveness. Information technology and its impact on society via The Digital College, The University for Industry and the Welsh Information Society will be essential planks in the daily life of the near future. Equipping and encouraging students of all ages to accept modern technologies as normally as books should be an integral part of the learning offered by all institutions. This involves not only the ability to use technology but also an awareness of what can be accessed through the technology and how to make sensible choices.

CONCLUSION

As is remarked throughout this volume, the National Assembly will have competing demands on its attention and resources. However, by virtue of its very large budget allocation alone, education is bound to be a major preoccupation. And, as has been argued in this chapter, education - together with training, as discussed in the previous Chapter - provides one policy area where, if it chooses, the National Assembly could make a substantial difference to the economic prosperity and civic culture of Wales.

CHAPTER 19

CULTURE AND THE ARTS

John Barnie

During the 1990s the arts in Wales have flourished in ways that could hardly have been predicted in the previous decade. Not only have established artists consolidated earlier achievement, new talent has emerged across the art forms, making this one of the most exciting periods in our cultural history.

To take some examples: thanks in large part to the research of Peter Lord, we have finally disposed of the old canard that Wales has no tradition of visual art. At the same time that he has been publishing the results of his research, there has been something of a renaissance in Welsh painting. During the 1990s, artists like Kyffin Williams, Peter Prendergast and Ernest Zobole have enhanced their reputations within Wales and beyond. Perhaps more significantly, a new generation of artists has come to the fore including painters such as Iwan Bala, Eleri Mills, Catrin Williams, David Tress and Catrin Webster who are experimenting in a wide variety of styles and media. They have ideas about Welsh art and where it is, or ought to be, going. Their views have spilled over into debate and polemic and provided an essential feature of a vigorous artistic culture.

It is no coincidence that a similar pattern emerges with film. David Berry's *Wales and Cinema* (1994) was another act of rediscovery and reclamation of a Welsh art form that had previously hardly been thought to exist. At the same time, a new generation of film-makers, stimulated to a large extent by the possibilities opened up by S4C, has created a contemporary Welsh cinema which is beginning to be taken seriously abroad as well as at home. The success of films as diverse as *Hedd Wyn* and *House of America* are examples. In film, too, a recovered history, and the emergence of new talent, have coincided with renewed debate about the nature and direction of what we can now call, with justification, the Welsh film industry. Annual events such as the Welsh International Film Festival (recently relocated from Aberystwyth to Cardiff) provide a showcase for the industry.

There has likewise been a distinct upturn in the profile of Welsh theatre, with companies like Brith Gof winning an international reputation for their experimental, avant garde productions, and with the emergence of playwrights of the calibre of Ed Thomas, and Simon Harris. Here again, the convergence of new talent and innovative productions spills over into debate about theatre in both English- and Welsh-language cultural magazines.

It is not possible in the compass of a short chapter to give an account, however brief, of all the art forms, so I will conclude with the current status of literature. Once more, there are signs of new developments, new ways of thinking about poetry and fiction, in both languages, although the process seems in many ways more hesitant, and less fully realised than is the case with the other art forms so far discussed. Perhaps the most promising trend has been the breakdown of the barrier of suspicion, if not outright hostility, that characterised the relationship between the two literatures earlier this century.

Younger Welsh-language writers, for example, are far more open to the translation of their work into English (and other languages) than were poets and novelists of even a generation ago. So we have Menna Elfyn publishing her latest collection, *Cell Angel*, in a dual text with translations by prominent English-language poets and translators with Bloodaxe, one of the leading poetry publishers in England. Wiliam Owen Roberts, whose successful experimental novel *Y Pla*, met with equal success when published in English as *Pestilence* by a mainstream London publishing house. And there is the phenomenon of Gwyneth Lewis who writes poetry with facility in Welsh and English.

Bilingual readings, and reading tours, are becoming far more common than they were even a few years ago, facilitated in part by the fact that perhaps a majority of younger English-language writers have a knowledge of Welsh and some of them a high level of fluency. This process seems to me not a sign of the weakness of Welsh-language literature vis-à-vis English, but an indication of the confidence younger writers feel in themselves and their Welsh-language literary culture, despite the real threats that still exist for the language from the powerful presence of English.

It is true that there is not the same sense of a ferment of ideas, of impassioned debate (at least in English) about the arts of poetry and fiction, as there are in visual art, film and theatre, but there is a sense of a stirring, of undercurrents, shifts and realignments that I suspect presage exciting new developments in the next few years. The work of literary historians such as M. Wynn Thomas is already changing our perception of the historical balance and interrelationship of the two literatures this century.

ENGLISH LANGUAGE WELSH CULTURE

Having sketched such a buoyant picture of the contemporary scene, it may seem almost perverse to suggest that the arts in Wales are also in a state of crisis but that is the situation that presents itself. It is not, as I hope my brief account has shown, a crisis due to any lack of native talent or achievement, but a crisis at the level of what has to be called arts management, precipitated by the steady squeeze on funding for the arts by central government at Westminster since the late 1980s.

In a country like Wales the economic superstructure of the arts is bound to be precarious. The population base that supports our culture is small in comparison with that of England, and it is reduced still further by the fragmented nature of our society. For the artist or artistic entrepreneur working within the medium of the Welsh language there is a notional audience of half-a-million speakers, though of course this in no way reflects the true size of a realisable audience, since Welsh-speaking Wales, like any other complex culture, is fragmented in all kinds of predictable ways. Audiences for anything beyond the most broadly popular, and that means, in effect, most artistic enterprises, have to be measured within a few thousands, not the tens of thousands that would be necessary for commercial success. For this reason alone, most Welsh-language art depends and will continue to depend on patronage; and in the kind of democratic society we live in, that patronage will come inevitably, and rightly, from the state.

Superficially, things might seem to be different for artists working through the medium of English, since the population base of English speakers is greater, and English offers the allure of reaching a far larger audience in England and the English-speaking world beyond. While this is true, it is only true to a degree. Within Wales, in fact, the situation of the English-language artist is in some ways less favourable than that of his or her Welsh-language opposite. The audience for Welsh-medium culture may be circumscribed, but it is also committed, to a fairly high degree. After all, if your language is Welsh there are no other alternatives, no one apart from the resources of your own artistic community to interpret and celebrate your Welshness to you.

For English-speakers the situation is very different. In the first place, English-speakers are far more vulnerable to the allure of English-language culture across the border in England, and in America. It is, in fact, impossible to avoid the inroads of the powerful English media, and the Anglo-American publishing hegemony with all the means for advertising and hype that it has at its disposal. And it would be foolish not to take the best of what this dominant culture has to offer.

There is a pay-off, however, which puts English-language culture in Wales at a severe disadvantage. In the first place, the English-speaking community is far from homogeneous. There is a large section of the population, comprising the immigrants of the 1970s and 1980s and a heavily Anglicised element within the indigenous Welsh population itself, whose culture is entirely orientated toward England, and for whom the English-language culture of Wales holds no interest whatsoever. It is a segment of Welsh society that might be won over eventually, it is true, but under present conditions, it is fair to say that it is more or less beyond the reach of English-language artists. Consequently, the true audience base for the English-language culture of Wales is probably not that much larger than its Welsh-language equivalent.

The result is that those aspects of Welsh culture that are mediated through English tend to have a low profile, even within Wales. This is exacerbated by a number of factors, the most important of which is the lack of a high quality daily and Sunday press. Such a press is the essential medium in a complex modern society for the propagation and dissemination of information and critical opinion about the contemporary cultural scene. Serious consideration of drama, film, music, literature, art, takes place there, far more so than on television, or even radio.

However, as is well known, the only broadsheet with pretensions to being a national newspaper is *The Western Mail* whose fortunes and circulation have been unstable for some time. In order to keep itself afloat in present conditions, *The Mail* has had to try to appeal to so broad a cross-section of its perceived potential readership that it has ended by backing itself into what seems an increasingly awkward middle-brow position.

One result of this is the comparatively low level of its coverage of the arts, notably in its Saturday supplement, The Magazine, where reporting on arts events is preferentially packaged as a human interest story, and where book reviews tend toward an ad hoc mishmash of pop paperbacks sent in by English publishers, with only limited attention being paid to the literary culture of Wales. Most of the reviews, too, are in-house, a sign that the paper cannot afford to employ a cadre of substantial independent outside reviewers; and while the reviews of the ubiquitous Mario Basini are of a consistently high standard, the same cannot be said for most of what passes for reviewing in The Magazine. The result is dispiritingly provincial.

People who are particularly committed to the arts and who expect a higher level of cultural debate, can turn to the quarterly and bi-monthly literary and cultural magazines, but the only way to broaden interest and commitment to the arts in Wales is through high-profile exposure in a large-circulation daily, or preferably dailies, which we do not have.

This is why an earlier generation of writers and artists before and after the Second World War migrated, temporarily or permanently to London, and why the metropolitan press has traditionally been seen as the essential mirror in which the English-speaking Welsh have had to look in order to see themselves. However, during the 1960s and through to the present day, that mirror has become somewhat tarnished due in part to increased opportunities for artists to express themselves here (through, for example, the Arts Council-sponsored magazines), which drew exiles back to Wales and persuaded others not to leave, diminishing in the process the Welsh artistic presence in London.

It has also been due to a downgrading of Wales in metropolitan eyes (a downgrading not unconnected with the failure of the devolution referendum in 1979) which has found expression in an amused contempt and the use of the Welsh as the butt for mildly racist jokes which for various reasons would no longer be considered appropriate if directed at the Scots, the Irish, or blacks. All of this is tedious, but its impact in terms of the dearth of serious coverage of the arts in Wales should not be underestimated. Even today any Welsh publisher will tell you that a prominent review in a London daily is worth half-a-dozen reviews from within Wales itself, in terms of sales, and how difficult it is to get such reviews for Welsh books.

For all of these reasons, the English-language culture of Wales is as heavily dependent on patronage for its continued existence as is its Welsh-language counterpart. This could change given the larger potential population base, but it does not seem likely in the short or medium term.

THE ARTS ADMINISTRATORS

Since the main source of patronage for the arts is the state, the attitude of government to the arts, and the founding ideas and assumptions of the professional élite of arts administrators, who nowadays mediate that patronage, are of crucial importance to the present and future achievement of the arts in both languages.

The attitude of central government can at best be described as disappointing. We live in a society where money is the measure of everything, and successive administrations from Thatcher to Major, to the Christian Democrat Blair, have treated the arts, through their meagre funding policies, with a scarcely veiled contempt. The present government recently announced a standstill grant to the arts at 1996-7 levels until the year 2001. This will mean, in real terms, a drop in the value of revenue grants to clients of around 13 per cent over this period. At the same time, New Labour confirmed their support for their own special 'Folly', the Millennium Dome, costing nearly three-quarters of a billion pounds. On a recent visit to Washington, Prime Minister Blair vied with President Clinton to sport the best populist credentials by inviting Sir Elton John to sing for them at a command performance (the President's choice was Stevie Wonder).

But if the arts cake is small and getting smaller, dished up by a succession of governments who probably wish that the arts would go away, what of the administrators, the men and women whose profession it is to slice it up? Here we approach the world of an intriguing élite (using that term in its descriptive, not its pejorative sense) which has, so far as I know, been little studied in its own right. This is a shame, since it is increasingly clear that arts administrators not only influence the arts through their overt decisions as to who gets, or does not get, funding, based on a judicious assessment of the merits of individual projects and assisted by a cadre of outside experts. More crucial in many ways is the deep structure of their thinking which is sometimes visible in the decision-making process, and sometimes so buried that it is difficult for an outsider to come at. This élite, in the Welsh context, comprises in part the officers of the Arts Council of Wales (formerly the Welsh Arts Council), the increasingly important Lottery Division of the ACW, and, for example, the consortium fronted by the Welsh Academy which holds the newly created franchise to administer an array of arts activities traditionally at the core of the Arts Council's own administrative role.

I should say at this point that I have a great deal of admiration for the Welsh Arts Council and its successor. The kind of florescence in the arts that I began by describing cannot take place without a phalanx of artists with vision and energy. However, the work of the artists can be consolidated by the right kind of patronage at the right time, and there is no doubt that the Arts Council's policies over the past thirty years underpin in many ways our current achievement in the arts.

Arts administrators at this level are thus not mere conduits for central government patronage but enablers, and how they think about the arts affects how, and what, they enable. In the early years of the Welsh Arts Council many of its officers were amateurs in the sense that the concept of the arts administrator was a new one and there was no cadre of professional administrators to draw on. At the same time, subject committees were set in place, establishing the principle that the persons best qualified to decide how funding should be dispersed to the artists were eminent practitioners themselves and critics of proven worth.

Times change, however, and organizations like the Arts Council of Wales change with them. In keeping with the increased bureaucratisation of life that took place under Thatcher (despite her régime's declared aim of freeing society from the trammels of government), the ACW itself became a more entrenched bureaucracy as individuals were recruited for whom arts administration offered a recognisable career path on a par with administrative careers in other areas of government and business.

This trend was confirmed by the Thatcherite crusade to endow our lives with the business ethos, encouraging us all to become small-time investors in the privatized utilities, urging us to think of ourselves and society at large in terms of the entrepreneurial spirit, in tune with the accountant and business manager, and with all achievement expressed as a balanced account of profit and loss. The late 1980s were a period that preached a vigorous kind of Darwinian capitalism with a bullying vigour and assurance which cowed many into acquiescence, in the age-old hope that compromise and complicity with a dogmatic, authoritarian regime would ensure survival. This state of affairs continued under Major in the early 1990s and continues today in a superficially softened version under New Labour.

At the time, some kind of accommodation with Thatcherism seemed to have the force almost of historical necessity. Whatever the truth of this, in the face of successive governments' covert hostility to the arts and their insistent preaching of the ethics of business, and with the dominant mentality of the accountant and the PR manager, the ACW chose what must have seemed the pragmatic course of compromise. And it has of course survived, though at what cost to itself and the health of the arts is a question that now needs to be asked.

One result of all this has been a growing tendency for the ACW to justify itself and the arts in business and accounting terms. In reports and promotional material (for PR now looms large in the arts world), it is frequently stressed that the arts are an important employer and that arts activities generate a significant revenue turnover. It was £38.5m in 1995-6 according to a recent ACW statement. What is rarely mentioned is that most jobs in the arts are poorly paid, short-term, and highly insecure, placing them on a par with that other much hyped growth area in the job market, tourism.

It is not that the Arts Council is not intimately, and in important ways, still heavily committed to the development of the arts in Wales. Of course it is. The point is that it is seriously in danger of losing sight of the true meaning and function of art in a viable culture. The ACW now issues 'corporate plans'. It has a 'portfolio' of clients. In the period 1998-2001 it will be seeking, among other things;

> 'to develop sources of earned income and public funding by enhancing the
> business capability of arts organisations and encouraging innovation in
> business practice, looking at the arts in terms of economic development and
> investment ...'

Roll over, Dylan Thomas, Saunders Lewis, Ann Griffiths, Dafydd ap Gwilym, your time is past. Except of course it isn't. Because great art in the end will always win out against the choking vine of bureaucracy and bureaucratese, even when that bureaucracy holds the purse strings and the arts, as they are now, are dependent on its disbursements.

In the face of this kind of language and its attendant attitudes, emanating not from some Thatcherite think-tank but from our premier arts funding body, it needs to be said again and again that, although there is a business element in the arts and more obviously in some such as theatre and publishing than others, artists themselves are first and foremost artists. While it makes sense for them to establish good business practice, the end result of their activities, art, cannot be measured by accountants, and cannot be subsumed in the ethos of business. Art in fact, by its very existence, exposes the lie at the heart of Thatcherism and is an act of resistance to it, standing for perceptions of beauty and truth in the world around us and in our own humanity, which offer a different set of values to those of the men in suits.

THE CULTURE OF GIGANTISM

Related to the business ethos so powerfully promoted by Thatcher in the 1980s is the phenomenon of populism. Apart from profit the only other acknowledged standard for success in Thatcherite thinking is appeal to the public in its homogenised form as the people or the mass. Here politics, business and mass culture merge. The best pop music is that which makes it into the Top Ten, grosses millions and makes the singers household names. The same is true of the best films, the best TV shows. There is a spiralling of superlatives, of records broken, of fortunes made. In the culture of gigantism that this breeds, individuals are propelled into the unreal sphere of stardom overnight, validated by the fact that millions have bought their records, watched their films; while beyond the glitz the individuals who make up the general public are manipulated by the international media companies who second-guess (usually successfully) our taste, and manipulate our patterns of enjoyment by means of multi-million dollar hype.

Politicians are alert to the power of mass culture. Thatcher conducted her election campaigns toward the end of her reign with the aid of Saatchi and Saatchi, and Tony Blair, a self-confessed admirer of the Baroness, has learned from her example. No opportunity is lost to associate himself and his government with the magic world of gigantism, from photo-calls with Liam Gallagher and Sir Elton, to plans for the Millennium Dome which will boast the biggest, brashest model of the human figure ever known in history.

The corollary is that whatever is not popular on this massive scale, which needs subsidy for its very existence, is suspect. Modernist music, experimental theatre, dance, poetry, much fiction, are loss makers, their existence unknown for the most part to the general public. The populist mentality is at a loss to know how to deal with such phenomena. Art of this kind is, in its terms, a failure and ought to go under. Yet people insist on producing it, and insist against the evidence that it is important. And the populist mentality, because of a residual suspicion that culture in this other sense perhaps indeed does matter, grudgingly feeds it crumbs.

At the same time, it pushes home relentlessly its message that success is really all to do with numbers, with appeal to a notional mass public. The élite of arts administrators are trapped here by a dilemma. In Wales they know that very few activities they promote will ever have appeal of this kind, but the pressure on them is to provide evidence to the contrary to justify their own existence. So the ACW has to play the numbers game, compiling figures not only for turnover (£38.5m in 1995-6) but also for attendances 2.51 million in the same year, comprising 40 per cent of the population according to recent ACW figures. Statistics of this kind have a certain impressiveness (and they are, I think, quite healthy) but they mask the reality that attendance figures for many events are, by populist standards, absurdly low; and every year the ACW has to set itself new targets, present new statistics, in a relentless treadmill.

Moreover, anyone who thinks about it knows that there is (usually) an inverse relationship between the size of an audience and the experimental or complex or simply new and therefore unfamiliar nature of a work of art. Yet it is precisely this art which needs, and has always needed, the lifeline of patronage. Moreover, there is no need to be apologetic for this or to seek to justify it in anything other than its own terms. There are two important riders: one, that a culture is ultimately judged by how it enables and integrates the achievements of such minority-interest art into the fabric of its self-image; two, that art which seems difficult and is limited to a coterie now may end by transcending both, influencing the broader culture in ways that are not imaginable at the time. (This influence may operate both ways, of course, with, for example, the Beatles experimenting with forms derived from American minimalism in some of their later compositions; and Philip Glass reversing the process by reworking the music of David Bowie and Brian Eno in works such as *Heroes*).

All artists want an audience, and all artists would like as big an audience as possible, but the nature of much art places a limit on the size of that audience. The function of an Arts Council should be to promote contemporary art with that understanding; to help make it popular in the truer and more modest sense, rather than in the inflated, unstable terms of gigantism. Most arts administrators, I think, know this, though they are increasingly afraid to say it. For in the past two or three years the ACW has suffered what can only be called a crisis in self-confidence, a doubting of those aims in the face of the bullying tactics of successive Westminster governments.

This loss of confidence has not been helped by the massive (and byzantine) restructuring of its own organization forced on it by the Welsh Office in order to cut administrative costs. Seen from the outside, the ACW appears to be in a state of disarray, its new slimmed-down structure weighted towards the business/accounting/PR side, while the arts themselves are bundled into one art-form division, with specialist officers effectively demoted, and the specialist committees retained in an advisory role only.

ARTS FOR ALL

The initial fruits of this are not promising. At one level the ACW, in order to strengthen its populist credentials, is more and more heavily committed to an arts-for-all policy, especially through its Lottery Division. What it means by arts-for-all is made clear in its corporate plan for 1998-2001, for although this catch-all certainly includes the aim of creating a climate which will be more receptive to the arts, it means above all participation: 'The success of the Lottery in opening up opportunities to scores of amateur, community and education initiatives is a demonstration of the huge potential of the arts to reach into every community, *particularly in terms of participation in activity*' (my emphasis).

What needs to be said about this is that amateur drama, music, painting and writing are all worthwhile activities, but they come under the rubrics of education and leisure, and that no matter how much they mean to the individuals who engage in them they have, for the most part, little to do with art. Moreover, there is little evidence that attendance at, for example, creative writing classes, encourages amateur poets and short story writers to read, to explore more widely or deeply, what contemporary Welsh literature has to offer. (If the opposite were true, publishers' sales figures in Wales would have soared a decade ago and would now be more than healthy.) Participants in such classes are encouraged, however, to think otherwise, to view their writings automatically as art, resulting in a bad confusion of poetry as art and poetry as therapy or self-expression. (Anyone who has waded through the entries to any of the hundreds of poetry competitions that have sprung up to support this illusion will know what I mean.)

At the same time as the Arts Council has committed itself ever more deeply to its arts-for-all policy, there is a real danger that it is beginning to look askance at more experimental ventures which by their nature have a limited appeal, no matter how much critical acclaim they may garner. The fate of the theatre company Brith Gof is an ominous example. Despite a justifiably high reputation for its innovative productions at home and abroad, the ACW cut back its grant in early 1998 to such an extent that the company could not survive. No specific reasons for the cut were given at the time. There was no suggestion that Brith Gof had failed to meet any of its targets, whether artistic, financial or in terms of audience quotas. Brith Gof lodged an appeal against the cut on procedural grounds and an independent panel appointed by the ACW found for the company. As a result, in May Brith Gof's grant was reinstated in full for 1998-99. On the surface, this was good news for the company, but the delay in confirmation of the grant seriously disrupted its programme, including essential long-term planning with promoters abroad. Moreover, according to an ACW press release, 'the Council remains concerned ... about Brith Gof's artistic programme and will monitor [its] progress over the coming year in accordance with an agreed plan'. These are hardly the best conditions under which to work. Instead of nurturing one of Wales's most radical and vital (but inevitably not widely popular) theatre companies, the ACW seems intent, in the eyes of many, on getting rid of it.

THE ASSEMBLY'S RESPONSE

This is the situation, confused and volatile yet full of possibility and excitement, that the Assembly will shortly inherit. What will, or should, the Assembly's response to the arts be? At present it is next to impossible to predict. So much depends on the composition of its members after the first election, not so much in the division along party lines, but in the calibre of the Assembly men and women, and especially whether they are drawn primarily from the existing cadre of politicians with local government experience who can be expected to proceed from entrenched positions, or whether there will be a predominance of new voices, politically perhaps relatively inexperienced, but with the vision and the will to see Wales whole and see it new.

It will depend even more on the calibre and commitment of the minister responsible for the arts, especially as the arts will only figure as a subset of his or her responsibilities.

What can be said is that as the Assembly has no tax-raising powers, and as it will face immediate and far-ranging problems in areas such as welfare, education, housing and transport, it is unlikely that the arts will rank very high on its list of priorities either in terms of finance or the time it can afford to devote to them.

What the Assembly can do in its first term is to indicate strongly its commitment to, and confidence in, the arts in Wales. In doing so it should acknowledge the true function of the artist, and the arts in society, by coming out forcefully against the attempt to subsume them within the Thatcherite business ethos, or drown them in the outreach of a populist arts-for-all programme that understands neither art nor its contribution to our culture.

In this context, the minister and committee responsible for the arts will have to consider as a matter of urgency its relation to the Arts Council of Wales and the future role of the Council. At the seminar held by the Institute of Welsh Affairs to discuss a draft of this essay, there was a call, especially from some of the artists present, for the abolition of the ACW on the grounds that it had signally failed in recent years to show any coherence or vision in its policy for the arts. Direct control by the Assembly was felt in these circumstances to be a better option, and one which might in fact be inevitable since arts organisations were likely to bypass the ACW and lobby Assembly members directly.

Lobbying of this kind is already going on in the run-up to the first election. However, sidestepping the ACW to catch the ear of a minister is one thing, abolishing the Council in favour of direct political control of the arts is another. The record of British politicians vis-à-vis the arts is, to say the least, poor. They tend to share the British predisposition to view art as a kind of charity to be supported grudgingly, rather than a vital component in the well-being of the nation, as in most continental European countries. We may be lucky, but there is no *a priori* reason to assume that the Assembly will be any different, and no guarantee that an enlightened minister will not be replaced by someone who looks on the arts with indifference in the power struggles and trade-offs that are at the heart of democratic politics.

If the Arts Council were abolished, as some advocate, something very like it would soon have to be reinvented. The Assembly can and should set the wider parameters for the arts within which the ACW will need to operate, but the day-to-day administration of arts subsidy needs a separate, and to a large degree, an independent body.

Plainly, however, the current structure of the Arts Council and the general drift of its policies will have to be reviewed by the Assembly. In the eyes of many, the ACW has not shown itself capable of effective internal reform, and the crisis of confidence which this has produced within the arts themselves needs to be addressed as a matter of urgency. In this context, there should be a reinstatement in one form or another of the specialist subject panels from their present demotion to an advisory role.

These panels have come under attack in recent years in England as well as in Wales, but *someone* has to make decisions about who gets funded and who does not, and a panel comprising leading artists and critics is more likely to get this right than administrators acting under advice, or politicians. Whatever the system, there will be those who will claim that it is biased. However, the specialist panels worked well in the past and could do so again given the right conditions.

As I write this, the ACW has published a consultation paper, *Building a Creative Society*, as the first stage in the preparation of its own strategy for the arts in Wales for the period 1999-2004. The future of the arts and the ACW is likely to hinge on the quality and vision of the final strategy document.

At the IWA seminar there was considerable support for a wide-ranging cultural policy, to be drafted by the Assembly, which would act as a framework for strategic initiatives within the arts. There is certainly a case to be made for such a policy, and again, it should be among the initial concerns of the minister and committee of the Assembly responsible for the arts. In framing it, I hope the voices of the artists will be heard. For too long in Wales such issues have been the domain of administrators and what might be termed cultural entrepreneurs, who come to the arts with very different assumptions from the artists themselves who are, after all, the primary producers in this area.

The problem is that artists tend to be individualists, working of necessity in isolation from one another, or in small groups, and concentrating to a high degree on their art. This does not mean that they do not have ideas about art in general, and often ideas that have been refined and validated in the crucible of their own practice. When the Assembly committee takes soundings as to what our cultural policy should be, the voices of the artists, those most deeply and passionately engaged in art, should be given particular attention. Mechanisms should be set in place which will make it possible to access those views. In the whole debate about the arts and the Arts Council in recent years, the artists too often have been sidelined. They have tended to be infantilised as the needy poor at the receiving end of charity hand-outs, whose thinking is done for them by others who know best. This is typical of the British near-contempt for the arts and can readily appear to be true if nobody challenges it.

And now is the time to do so. Recent achievements in the arts, teetering though they are on the edge of a disastrous reversal, have gone hand in hand with Wales' new-found political confidence. Clear thinking and good will can lead to an enlightened policy on the part of the Assembly, which will consolidate these achievements and give the arts the solid basis within a wider cultural and social framework that they so desperately need.

CHAPTER 20

HEALTH AND SOCIAL POLICY

Gareth Jones, John Wyn Owen, Jan Williams,
Mike Ponton and Chris Hawker

The Government has developed a new approach to the social policy agenda for Britain in which the key themes are:

- Empowerment, through promoting work and income.

- Community, which is less well defined but relevant to the 'social exclusion' concept.

- Family (though not necessarily the nuclear family) and the support and development of children.

Our health care system has historically focused on treating ill-health. Now there is a renewed interest in extending this to become more pro-active in regard to public health. A person's social situation should be considered alongside their health needs. According to this perspective social factors contribute to a person's health status, and by changing them, their health can be improved. Plainly this is not a substitute for the work of doctors and hospital clinicians. Repair work will always be needed. But it does raise the question whether or not improved public health might mean that less physical maintenance was needed for the large social group whose life-styles and living conditions appear to contribute to damage their physical health.

For this reason, expenditure on the health service is closely linked with expenditure on the social services. Indeed, given the correlation between ill-health and low incomes and poor housing, the health service should not be considered in isolation from other areas of expenditure.

THE INTERNATIONAL CONTEXT

Although the National Assembly will have Welsh health issues as its prime concern, it will need to be aware of world influences which are having an increasing impact on health policy. Health has become a global issue. Populations are living longer and there is increasing commonality of health concerns:

- Western diseases have been exported.

- There is greater mobility of people world-wide.

- The growth of international commerce is accompanied by potential transfer of health risks as infectious diseases and contaminated foodstuffs.

There are three particular reasons for adopting a global outlook towards health:

- Increased co-operation is necessary to combat threats to health that do not stop at national borders. These are being reinforced through increased population mobility and global markets - be it new and re-emerging infectious diseases, or AIDS, drugs and the tobacco epidemic.

- Co-operation is also necessary in view of such common challenges as ageing and urbanisation, problems that all societies are facing with increasing speed and urgency.

- To ensure that, in comparison with countries elsewhere, the highest quality health service is available in the most cost-effective manner.

In 1986, the World Health Organisation's Ottawa Charter identified three basic ingredients for health improvement:

- Advocacy to create the essential conditions for health.

- Enabling all people to achieve their full health potential.

- Mediating between the different interests in society in the pursuit of health.

The 1996 World Health Organisation Ljubljana Charter argued for health care systems which are:

- Driven by values of human dignity, equity, solidarity and professional ethics.

- Targeted on protecting and promoting health.

- Centred on people, allowing citizens to influence health services and take responsibility for their own health.

- Focused on quality, including cost-effectiveness.

- Based on sustainable finances, to allow universal coverage and equitable access.

- Orientated towards primary care.

The World Health Organisation adopts a life-cycle approach to health improvement:

- Infants and young children - healthy growth in a nurturing environment.
- Older children and young people - skills for healthy choices and fulfiling roles.
- Working age - coping with life's challenges, enjoying a satisfying life.
- Latter days - healthy and happy.

To achieve this, the World Health Organisation's 1997 Jakarta Declaration proposes:

- Promoting social responsibility for health
- Increasing investment in health development
- Consolidating and expending partnerships
- Increasing community capacity and empowering the individual
- Securing an infrastructure for health improvement

OVERVIEW OF HEALTH IN WALES

Welsh health is at the 80th percentile of the European average. Life expectancy in Wales is about one year less than in England. The death rate from heart disease is 18 per cent higher in Wales than in England, and from cancer 10 per cent higher.

There are substantial differences in death rates and ill-health between different communities in Wales. Death rates from coronary heart disease, from lung cancer in men, and breast cancer in women, are one and a half to two times greater in the most affected unitary authority areas compared to the least.

The urban slums of our cities and in the Valleys where there has been little success in attracting new industries, pose special problems. In both areas the needs lie with young families. In the Valleys they also lie with the 'left-behind' elderly who often suffer the triple jeopardy of poverty, industrial disease/illness and poor housing.

Rural areas are in decline for a range of current economic reasons. Here there are families trapped by location and low value properties who do not have the confidence or experience to get out and try another environment. Much is hidden in the official statistics as the extremes are buried in the averages of relative affluence. A key task for the National Assembly, therefore, must be to consider ways of addressing:

- Severe inequalities in health status amongst the people of Wales.

- Existing inequities in access to health care.

INNOVATION IN THE WELSH HEALTH SERVICE

In 1989, the Welsh Health Planning Forum published its pioneering *Strategic Intent and Direction for the Health Services in Wales*, as a response to the World Health Organisation's strategy *Health for All by the year 2000*. Its motto was: 'To add years to life and life to years'. Consideration should be given to re-establishing a 'Think Tank' of this nature, appropriate to the current health needs of Wales and the priorities of the Assembly.

Wales' learning disability strategy was a major breakthrough in Europe and Wales' mental health strategy is patient and community orientated rather than institutionally driven as elsewhere in the UK.

The Medicentre at the University Hospital of Wales is a centre of excellence for the wider commercial application of research at the University of Wales College of Medicine.

A few years ago Wales led the world in the application of informatics and tele-medicine in the rural, more remote communities. However, as other regions have seen the potential of tele-medicine, Wales is in serious danger of falling behind. Informatics and tele-medicine should be significantly developed to its full potential.

When Professor Archie Cochrane was Director of the Medical Research Council in Wales in the early 1970s, he wrote his monograph on *Effectiveness and Efficiency* and changed perspectives on medicine and health care across the world. The National Assembly should absorb and implement his message.

CURRENT GOVERNMENT HEALTH POLICY

PUTTING PATIENTS FIRST (JANUARY 1998)

The Welsh White Paper *Putting Patients First* set out the Government's agenda for rebuilding the NHS and restoring it 'as a genuinely public service of high quality, delivered in co-operation with others to protect and improve health as well as respond to illness and disability'. The NHS and social services departments were encouraged to work more closely together. More specifically the Government declared its intention to achieve its aims through:

- Developing local responsiveness through the establishment of Local Health Groups which will bring together GP practices, other health care professionals, representatives of social services departments and voluntary organisations. They will work with the local Health Authorities and Trusts in developing the services to meet local needs and priorities.

- Reducing health variations across Wales and tackling inequalities in health and in access to health care.

- Continuing to develop evidence-based services through focused research and development.

- Ensuring that the NHS is health gain focused, seeking to reduce the number of premature deaths in Wales and improve the quality of life. Health improvement should be a responsibility at all levels, involving partnerships and collaboration.

BETTER HEALTH, BETTER WALES (MAY 1998)

This consultative 'Green Paper' sets out some key new principles in the future health policy for Wales. There is a strong emphasis within it on the need for individuals to take greater responsibility for their own health and well-being - that is to say, the accent is on *personal empowerment*. In the first place it emphasises health and well-being:

*'Good health may not be possible at every stage in our lives. There will be times when we are more vulnerable, perhaps in the early years of life, or as older people. We cannot always avoid ill-health or disability. However, we can aim for **well-being**, that is to live life as we choose. When we are ill, we may need access to health and social care services'* (para 1.5).

Secondly, it emphasises **sustainable** health and well-being:

'... sustainable health is achieved when people and communities can take control of their lives and are able to live their lives to the full. The factors which contribute to a state of well-being include feeling safe, having the security of a home and enough to live on, satisfying relationships, interesting and varied activities, and having a sense of moving forward' (para 3.1).

'Long-term action is needed to tackle the root causes of health economic inequality. This may mean a new approach to maintaining health and to using health and social care services as a community resource. The introduction of health impact assessment, health promotion that addresses the pressures of multiple disadvantage in some communities, and refocused professional responsibilities may all be needed. A major priority is to recognise the importance of sustainable health in economic and social regeneration' (para 3.4).

The document aims to:

- Set a strategy for national, regional and local action which will be taken forward by the National Assembly.

- Prevent disease and substantially improve the health and well-being of the people of Wales.

- Bring the level of those with the poorest health up to the level of those with the best health.

- Improve the health and well-being of children.

- Encourage individual responsibility for health.

- Improve the health and safety of people at work.

However, there will be no additional funding for these initiatives.

RESOURCES AVAILABLE

There are 146 hospitals in Wales with 16,000 beds. Only 16 hospitals have more than 300 beds. More than half have fewer than 50 beds. Wales has more than 1,800 general practitioners. In total, the NHS in Wales employs 58,000 staff.

There are considerable variations in Wales on expenditure per head of population by health authorities. There are also significant differences in access to specialist care. For example, parts of south Wales have the greatest access to accident and emergency services, and Bro Taf and Dyfed Powys have the poorest access to local longer term care facilities.

Expenditure on the Health Service in Wales accounted in 1998-99 for £2.4bn, or 34 per cent of Welsh Office expenditure. This is 13 per cent more per capita than in England.

In April 1996 the number of health authorities was reduced from sixteen to five - Gwent, Bro Taf, Iechyd Morgannwg, Dyfed-Powys and North Wales. In April 1998 the five ambulance trusts were reduced to one. The Government intends to reduce the number of acute and community trusts from April 1999.

HEALTH SERVICE PRESSURES 1999 - 2003

The Health Service faces new pressures each year arising from:

- Demographic trends

- Year-on-year increases in activity

- New drug costs

- Genetic advances
- Continuing care
- Medical technology

In addition to these, social attitudes towards, and expectations of the health services are changing. People are becoming more demanding, thereby creating additional pressures. Within the health service itself, there are changes occurring which will result in further pressures. For instance, over half the medical under-graduate entrants now are women and the retirement age for GPs is falling.

When the National Assembly comes into existence in May 1999, the Health Service in Wales will have undergone – and still be undergoing – significant change:

- A new pattern of Health Trusts will have been established with effect from 1 April 1999.
- Local Health Groups will, for the first time, be in process of being established.
- The new Public Health Strategy, arising from consultations on the 1998 Green Paper *Better Health, Better Wales*, will be in place.
- A new Corporate Plan for the NHS in Wales will be taking shape.
- Health Improvement Programmes will be in preparation.
- A new Patients' Charter will be in its first year.
- New National organisations - NICE (the National Institute of Clinical Excellence) and CHIMP (the Commission for Health Improvement) will be starting to take effect.
- A new national framework for NHS performance will be in place.

There will be a need for some stability for the Service to absorb the implications of all these changes. Further major changes would be counter-productive and even destructive of morale.

POLICY PRIORITIES FOR THE ASSEMBLY

Nevertheless, action should be taken on a number of fronts if the Assembly is to be responsive to the challenges of improving the nation's health. Some key principles that the Assembly might wish to adopt are:

- Health care reforms should take place as a coherent part of an overall policy for health in line with World Health Assembly policies and consonant with the socio-economic condition of Wales. Indeed, the Assembly should be international in outlook, playing its part in the work of the European Union and the European Regional Office of the World Health Organisation.

- Major policy, including operational policies, should be evidence-based and any reforms should be capable of being monitored and evaluated. Wales needs 'evidence-based politics'.

- The Assembly should lead the public debate on the equitable distribution of resources within Wales, involving the public in discussion of the issues involved.

- Services will need to be developed to achieve the right balance of self-care, family care and other informal care. The right balance is also needed in the provision of the most appropriate settings for care - hospitals, community care, primary care in the GP surgeries, day care or home care.

- The basic aim of health care and health services should be to produce health. As the Welsh Office Green Paper *Better Health, Better Wales* puts is, 'Health is a state of complete physical, social and mental well-being and not merely the absence of disease: it is something positive, a joyful attitude towards life and cheerful acceptance of the responsibilities that life puts on individuals'.

One over-riding issue is the level of funding of the NHS in Wales and its share of the total cake. 'Demand' will argue for a greater proportion of public expenditure to be spent on health services, for example, to reduce waiting lists and waiting times. On the other hand, the Assembly will have competing pressures from other services. However, any major and precipitate shift in the allocation of resources to the health service would, in effect, 'bankrupt' the system. The implications of this are that every effort needs to be made to ensure that all the large £2.4bn, or so, budget is effectively spent.

Other key issues and questions for the Assembly to consider include:

- No health service in the world systematically evaluates the 'outcomes' of health interventions and whether the monies spent were effective in bringing about genuine 'health gain'. The Assembly should adopt a 'health gain', targeted approach to this difficult problem.

- There are differences in the performance of general medical services across Wales. As the general practitioner is the main gate-keeper to hospital services, strengthening GP services where they need strengthening would represent a positive step forward in the treatment of illness and improved cost-effectiveness. Primary care should include provision embracing much of that now provided in institutions) for people who require a long-lasting broad range of health and social support, such as the elderly and chronically ill. Can a convincing case be argued for the introduction of salaried GPs?

- There are inequalities across Wales in access to appropriate care, particularly in the more rural areas. How can this be best addressed given that it would mean the reallocation of resources between Health Authorities?

- A clear, long-term strategic framework for the NHS in Wales needs to be discussed and, once agreed, adhered to over a 5-10 year period. How best can the Assembly achieve this longer term strategic response to the problems of health in Wales?

Further specific approaches and ideas for the Assembly to consider include:

- It would be dangerous in the complicated field of health care to rush to conclusions too quickly.

- It is essential that the Local Health Groups proposed in the White Paper *Putting Patients First* are encouraged to work well and become effective as quickly as possible.

- It is highly desirable to 'depoliticise' health and social services as far as possible so that there can be broad all-party agreement on the strategy and the best way forward for the health and related services in Wales.

- The over-riding focus should be on an international perspective. Parochial issues should not dominate thinking and discussions.

- Involvement of the public in discussions of future health policy in Wales should be encouraged.

- Public Health issues cannot be resolved by the Health Service alone: the problems with which it deals are too broad and far-reaching. It will require the closest working relationships with a range of other organisations to begin to resolve problems which have become endemic in Wales for many, many years.

A suggested four-year action programme for Health and Social Policy might look like the following:

Year One: Listen and learn from the Health Authorities, Trusts, Community Health Councils, local authorities, and voluntary organisations. Revive the Welsh Health Planning Forum in an appropriate form and with terms of reference consonant with the priorities of the National Assembly.

Year Two: Digest the information from Year One and establish provisional priorities and objectives.

Year Three: Evaluate options for the future of the service.

Year Four: Formulate the ten-year strategic intent for the health service in Wales and the new Health Policy and Social Care Agenda.

CHAPTER 21

SOCIAL SERVICES

Ian Butler, Mark Drakeford, Andy Pithouse

The term 'social services' is often used narrowly to refer to the activities of local authority social services departments. The term is most frequently used to describe direct services delivered to identified groups or individuals either at times of crisis or at key transition points in their lives. For example, council-run residential accommodation for children in trouble is recognised as a social service in a way that primary school education or mortgage tax relief is not.

There is often an implication in the way that the term is understood that social services are somehow residual services, operating at the margins of our society, for the benefit of those who have exhausted their own means or capacities. In short, social services are sometimes thought of as 'poor services for poor people'. In practice, neither the identification of social services with local state provision, nor the boundaries around what constitutes personal as opposed to universal social services, nor the inferences made about those who benefit from them are easily sustained.

The complexity, interdependence and diversity of social services provision in Wales can be seen from the following summary of its main roles. For example, social work with children and families covers services to abused infants as well as to teenagers in trouble, offering both protection and family support and taking place in people's own homes, foster homes and family centres. Such work may involve a major national childcare charity, a local community or voluntary group as well as several local authority departments working together.

Services for older people may include residential care provided through the independent sector and paid for by a combination of the person's own means, central government funds and local authority contributions. It may involve domiciliary care provided by a combination of health and welfare professionals including the district nurse and the home help.

Services for people with a physical or a mental illness might be delivered by a mixed team of social care and health professionals and could integrate acute hospital care and nursing home provision as well as day centres and other forms of care in the community such as hostels or drugs counselling services. The criminal and civil courts require the provision of social as well as legal services whether in relation to pre-sentence reports or in relation to divorce court welfare.

The extent of social services provision is perhaps best indicated by reference to some key statistical indicators. In Wales in March 1997, 4,672 older people were living in local authority residential homes. A further 8,073 people lived in homes operated in the independent (that is, voluntary and private) sector and another 10,121 people aged over 65 were living in private nursing homes. On the same date, local authorities offered 204 places in 28 homes for people with mental health problems. Another 51 homes offering 516 places were available in the private and voluntary sector.

The same pattern of a public/private mix is to be found in services for people with learning disabilities. One third (480) of the residents of homes for people with learning disabilities in Wales are living in local authority run homes while two thirds (1,028) are living in private or voluntary organisation homes. The level of provision in this area across Wales varies from none in Flintshire to over 20 places per 10,000 under 65 in Denbighshire, where all of the provision is in the private or voluntary sector. In contrast in Blaenau Gwent there is a provision of five places per 10,000, all in local authority run homes. (Source: *Digest of Welsh Local Area Statistics* 1998).

There were 1,016 children on child protection registers in Wales at the same period, distributed amongst the different local authorities according to a highly variable pattern, as set out in Table One on the following page. Levels of activity in other social service spheres are similarly high. More than three million 'meals on wheels' are provided during the course of a year in Wales and that local authorities provide over ten million home care hours. In 1995/96, on average, almost 40,000 people per week were in receipt of social services from local authorities alone at a total net expenditure for Wales of £436,892,000 (sources: Welsh Office *Digest of Welsh Local Area Statistics* 1998 and CIPFA Statistical Information Service *Personal Social Services Statistics* 1995-6).

Provision on this scale requires considerable staffing and financial resources. Indeed, local authority social services employees have increased during the middle years of the 1990s, as local authorities were required by government to take on increased responsibility for the provision of care in the community, as shown in Table Two (overpage).

Service provision and related expenditure differs markedly from authority to authority. Table Three provides details of revenue and capital expenditure amongst the local authorities in Wales, and indicates the proportion of such spending devoted to the personal social services (PSS). The variability across Wales is striking. In revenue terms, Pembroke allocated 15 per cent of its budget to social services, while Wrexham devoted 22.5 per cent. Neither Flintshire nor Neath Port Talbot recorded any capital expenditure in this area during 1997/98, while Newport and Swansea both undertook capital works valued at more than a million pounds.

TABLE ONE

Child Protection Registrations

	NUMBER *		RATE **		CHANGE
	31.3.96	31.3.97	31.3.96	31.3.97	
Isle of Anglesey	16	17	10.2	10.8	0.6
Gwynedd	51	82	19.7	31.6	11.9
Conwy	38	54	16.7	23.7	7.0
Denbighshire	30	37	14.7	18.1	3.4
Flintshire	33	31	9.8	9.2	-0.6
Wrexham	25	31	8.6	10.7	2.1
Powys	45	43	16.6	15.8	-0.8
Ceredigion	32	33	22.9	23.6	0.7
Pembrokeshire	81	73	30.5	27.5	-3.0
Carmarthenshire	104	125	28.4	34.1	5.7
Swansea	134	123	26.2	24.0	-2.2
Neath Port Talbot	126	158	39.5	49.5	10.0
Bridgend	48	37	15.9	12.3	-3.6
The Vale of Glamorgan	98	108	33.7	37.1	3.4
Cardiff	380	462	50.1	61.0	10.9
Rhondda,Cynon,Taff	111	135	19.5	23.7	4.2
Merthyr Tydfil	55	68	37.0	45.7	8.7
Caerphilly	43	152	10.2	35.9	25.7
Blaenau Gwent	23	50	13.1	28.5	15.4
Torfaen	23	39	10.4	17.6	7.2
Monmouthshire	40	45	20.7	23.3	2.6
Newport	113	126	33.3	37.2	3.9
WALES	**1649**	**2029**	**24.4**	**30.0**	**5.6**

*   per 1000 of population under 18

** per thousand of the population under 18

Source: Child Protection Register: Statistics for Wales, 1997

TABLE TWO

Local Authority Staffing

	1992	1993	1994
Social Services: Manual staff	8,600	8,500	8,800
Social Services: Non-Manual staff	7,300	7,400	8,100

Source: CIPFA Local Government Comparative Statistics 1997

TABLE THREE

Unitary Authority Revenue and Capital Expenditure: Total and Personal Social Services 1997-8

	NET REVENUE EXPENDITURE			CAPITAL EXPENDITURE		
	Total	PSS		Total	PSS	
	£m	£m	%	£m	£ '000	%
Isle of Anglesey	67.4	12.3	18.3	15.8	142	0.9
Gwynedd	127.6	25.4	19.9	25.4	457	1.8
Conwy	94.9	18.6	19.6	18.4	92	0.5
Denbighshire	89.7	18.5	20.7	13.5	27	0.2
Flintshire	124.2	24.5	19.7	28	0	0
Wrexham	106	23.8	22.5	16.7	585	3.5
Powys	127.2	21.9	17.2	22.5	450	2
Ceredigion	73.6	12.2	16.5	14.8	207	1.4
Pembrokeshire	109.7	16.5	15	23.3	0	0
Carmarthenshire	172.8	29.9	17.3	36.9	111	0.3
Swansea	214.5	43.3	20.2	30.5	1,079	1.6
Neath Port Talbot	141.2	30.0	21.3	27.5	0	0
Bridgend	120.6	24.0	19.9	14.9	373	2.5
The Vale of Glamorgan	100.1	18.2	18.2	15.3	77	0.5
Cardiff	290	58.4	20.1	63.5	445	0.7
Rhondda,Cynon,Taff	235.5	47.7	20.2	50.6	911	1.8
Merthyr Tydfil	62.6	13.0	20.8	12	96	0.8
Caerphilly	156.3	28.9	18.5	36.4	510	1.4
Blaenau Gwent	71.3	15.6	21.8	15.1	921	6.1
Torfaen	81.9	16.8	20.5	12.8	0	0
Monmouthshire	68.5	13.9	20.3	7.4	7	0.1
Newport	130.1	27.5	21.1	33.2	1,162	3.5
WALES	**2765.6**	**540.8**	**19.6**	**540.6**	**8,109**	**1.5**

Source: Digest of Welsh Local Area Statistics 1998

The National Assembly will encounter a well established and intricate network of services operating at full stretch and under growing stress. With what are widely perceived to be inadequate human and material resources in relation to demand, services are straining to meet the needs of a wide range of vulnerable people. In an era of rapid change in the organisation and nature of government and against a changing demographic and economic background, the Assembly will have much to do in preserving the best of social services in Wales as well as in identifying new directions for the future.

ISSUES INSIDE THE SOCIAL SERVICES

REORGANISATION AND FRAGMENTATION OF SOCIAL SERVICES DEPARTMENTS

Local government reorganisation has had the effect of fragmenting eight former county social services departments amongst 22 new smaller units. The debate which surrounded reorganisation highlighted childrens' services in particular. In the House of Lords in February 1994, a series of speakers rose to question the difficulties which might arise through problems of co-ordination (Lord Henderson), the level of consultation with children themselves (Baroness David) and, in the words of Lord Prys-Davies, the 'destruction, disorientation and reshuffling of officers brought about by reorganisation' (*Hansard*, 28 February 1994 col. 828).

The impact of the reorganisation on social services has been to produce a plethora of often small-scale organisations in which co-ordination and achievement of equity between authorities has been elusive. The notion that any citizen should be able to rely upon a similar standard and range of core services unrelated, for example, to income or geography, has been a traditional aim of social policy. Yet it is one which has shifted lower down the order of policy priority during the last fifteen years. If, however, the long-established political affiliation patterns of the Welsh electorate are reflected in the selection of National Assembly members, then demands of equity are likely to command a more important place in policy formulation. The Assembly will face a set of policy challenges exacerbated by reorganisation and budget restraints which will only be met through an informed and innovative use of scare resources.

NEW ALIGNMENTS

Whereas social services departments have traditionally been free-standing, and have reported via a social services committee, that pattern is now far more diverse. In a number of Welsh local authorities social services share a common administrative structure with housing, including joint directorates and shared committee arrangements. There are proposals for further co-location, in which housing, social services and education might all be brought together under one division. There is a debate too, about the efficiency savings or integrative benefits which such changes bring about. Inevitably, the Assembly will have to deal with a more complex pattern of administration in which issues of accountability may appear more diffuse than tangible.

The fragmentation caused by local government reorganisation coincides with a number of recent policy thrusts which add to the sense of instability across much of social services delivery in Wales. The Conservative agenda for public services placed a major emphasis upon privatisation and the injection of market forces into the social as well as the economic sphere of government. The extent to which this was successful depended, to a large extent, upon the political character of local government. In Wales, the wholesale transfer of buildings, staff and services from the public to the independent sector simply did not take place in a way which was characteristic of some local authorities in England. Rather, Welsh councils were more likely to resist the sale of assets and loss of function. They tended to oppose by passive inaction market-orientated policies such as compulsory competitive tendering and provider/purchaser splits.

Yet any government which has almost twenty years at its disposal is in an immensely powerful position to make progress with its own agenda, whatever sources of local resistance might be encountered. The National Assembly will therefore inherit a social services pattern in which diversity (to use a term favoured by its supporters) will be more firmly embedded in patterns of provision than the political instincts of many members will find palatable. Even those who find the claims of diversity and choice convincing cannot ignore the instability which such fragmented patterns have engendered in the day-to-day operation of social services departments.

REBALANCING PREVENTION AND PROTECTION

A pressing and topical question for the Assembly will be the prevention/protection debate concerning child and family services. Briefly, there is a depressing familiarity about the stressful events, personal histories and social circumstances of those parents who come to social services departments for help with bringing up their children. Social workers have available a range of effective responses to help head off such problems before they become of more urgent concern. However, at present by far the greater part of social workers' time and energy is invested in the much smaller number of families where abuse is alleged or has been proven. Whilst there are significant differences between those families in which child abuse takes place and those which are experiencing specific difficulties in bringing up their children, strategies which aim to change the context in which child rearing takes place can help both groups of families. There is scope for harnessing the creativity and resourcefulness that is the hallmark of all good parenting. This would include an emphasis on:

- Easier and earlier access to services
- Provision of services to children in their own homes
- Flexible responses that take into account fast changing patterns of local need,
- Inter-departmental initiatives that look at services to children and families 'in the round'

Plans that embrace these principles might include neighbourhood-based work, family centres and children's forums whereby children themselves can provide first-hand accounts of what growing up is really like. Taken together, these would create a range of provision which acknowledges that prevention really is better than care.

SCANDAL, SENSITIVITY AND RISK MANAGEMENT

Social services may appear, at first glance, to be relatively tranquil political territory. Arguments may divide the parties in terms of service delivery, but few politicians suggest that social services ought not to be provided for the major client groups, including children, older people, and those with problems of physical or mental health. It may be something of a surprise, therefore, to suggest that one of the major components of the social services brief for the new Assembly will be scandal and risk management. The following three problems illustrate the extent to which this dimension of public policy can cause significant headaches for practising politicians:

- As one of its earliest challenges, the Assembly will inherit the report (and its aftermath) of the independent Waterhouse Inquiry into the abuse of children in north Wales. This is only one of such scandals. The care and protection of vulnerable children will always be matters of acute public concern. A sensible and sensitive response to revelations and proposals contained in forthcoming reports will be a significant test of the Assembly's strategic capacity and political will to improve services for children and families.

- The abuse of older persons is also gaining greater recognition as an issue which requires attention. New systems of regulation in residential, home and day-care settings will be in place by the end of 1998 and will impose a fresh set of challenges upon already hard-pressed services.

- The modern era of mental health service scandals may be traced to the Geoffrey Howe report into conditions and treatment of patients at the Ely hospital in Cardiff in the 1960s. Contemporary mental health scandals arise more often in relation to the community care of the mentally ill and, in particular, the incidents of violence which appear to be linked to discharged patients of mental health institutions. In England, homicides by such individuals are automatically and statutorily followed by an independent and public inquiry. The rules in relation to Wales are more permissive, and do not place the same level of obligation upon health authorities or hospital trusts to behave in a similar fashion.

The National Assembly will inherit the aftermath of one particular incident which has brought to the surface such policy problems in a particularly graphic way. It involves the actions of the Dyfed-Powys Health Authority in the case of Andrew Cole. On 2nd May 1996 Cole murdered William Crompton and Fiona Ovis at Llandrindod Wells, having been discharged from the Mid Wales Hospital on 30th April. The Authority resisted, for many months, pressure for an independent inquiry, only conceding the case for one in the early weeks of 1998.

The Assembly will therefore need to be prepared for some early encounters in the field of social services which will provide greater and more general testing of its political and policy mettle than might traditionally have been associated with this area of responsibility.

TRAINING AND LANGUAGE ISSUES

The Assembly will also face other issues which are primarily of significance within the social services world, but whose resolution will demand skillful and knowledgeable handling. The first concerns the demise of the Central Council for Education and Training in Social Work (CCETSW), the organisation which for more than a quarter of a century has been responsible for the training and professional accreditation of a range of social welfare professionals. While its reputation generally has been variable – and undoubtedly contributed to the decision by the last Conservative administration to have its functions redistributed to the new National Training Organisation – the Wales office of CCETSW has a far stronger place in the development of social services. In particular, CCETSW Cymru has been in the forefront of the development of linguistically sensitive services, and a workforce capable of delivering them, within the terms of the 1993 Welsh Language Act. Replacement arrangements will have to be developed.

The changes which the present Government has announced make it clear that there will be a General Social Services Council through which the regulation and training of the workforce will be shaped. Welsh Office Ministers have already moved to ensure that Wales will have separate and distinctive arrangements within this field. The success of this new body will depend upon clear objectives in the construction of standards, processes and administration across a range of provider bodies and sectors. Responsibility for the practical achievement of this ambitious project will fall to the Assembly.

Furthermore, there are particular reasons why a fully bilingual service is a necessity, rather than a preference, within the social services sphere. The proportion of monolingual Welsh speakers amongst social service users, in young children and older people for example, is higher than in the population as a whole. The nature of social services, dealing so often with matters of personal sensitivity and distress, also places a premium upon the ability to discuss such questions in the language which is most comfortable and familiar to the person in need. Such issues become particularly acute in those areas where social welfare workers have legitimate but seriously intrusive powers, such as in child protection or in committing people with a mental illness against their will to an institution where treatment may be imposed upon them. Evidence exists in Wales of the disadvantages which arise for individuals in such circumstances where, for example, linguistic confusion – through having to use English because that is the language of professional workers, rather than Welsh – may sometimes be interpreted as mental confusion and as evidence of mental illness (Davies, E. 1994, *They All Speak English Anyway*, CCETSW/Open University Press).

YOUTH JUSTICE

Youth justice represents another challenge, and opportunity, for the National Assembly. Indeed, it may well have implications for the development of the institution itself, far beyond the social services sphere. The difference between youth justice and almost all other social services responsibility lies in the extent to which the discharge of the function depends upon relations with other public bodies and government departments outside the direct control of the Assembly. While other social service dimensions will require co-ordination and co-operation between different professional groups and services – education, in the case of children, health services in relation to older people – these areas will all lie within the Assembly's control. The major players in youth justice, by contrast, almost all lie outside its direct sphere of influence. The police and probation services are set to remain relatively autonomous organisations. The Home Office will remain responsible for criminal justice policy. The Lord Chancellor's department will retain control of the Crown Prosecution department and the judiciary.

During the second half of the 1980s, and into the early years of the 1990s, both the Welsh Office and Welsh local authorities took a particular interest in youth justice matters, publishing Welsh-specific information and policy documents and placing an unmistakable emphasis upon policies of diversion and decarceration. However, the advent of the Michael Howard régime at the Home Office and the competition between political parties to appear ever tougher than their opponents in criminal justice policy, brought these initiatives to an abrupt end.

The National Assembly will therefore inherit a policy area which is both contentious in itself, highly politicised in character and where its scope for decisive or distinctive action will be heavily circumscribed by the actions of other organisations. It is because of this that the area might develop a significance over and above the salience of youth justice issues themselves. The whole question of powers and responsibilities has been amongst the most contentious in the establishment of the National Assembly. It would be naive to expect that these issues will not continue to be developmental, in the sense that in its operation the Assembly is bound to give rise to new information and new views in relation to the practical organisation of its powers and functions. Youth justice, combining substantial contention and insubstantial powers in equal measure, may well provide a testing bed for some of the most acute of these questions.

THE INTERFACE BETWEEN SOCIAL AND HEALTH CARE

In the last decade local authority social services have seen constant change via key legislation around child care and community care, local government reorganisation and major reforms in health care delivery. Such change has taken place during a period of growing and complex care demands. This has further occurred against a background of cash limits and a tightening of eligibility criteria making community care a typically residual service for those most in need, based on charging policies that vary across Wales. Health services, too, operate in a climate of cut backs and scarcity and at a time of growing public concern over related issues, for instance the environment, agri-business, and water quality. All this is in a period when we are witnessing in the UK some of the widest health inequalities in Europe. Accordingly, an issue for the National Assembly will be how the interface of primary health care and social services can be improved to offer more effective services, particularly for older people and those with continuing health and disability needs.

More change can be anticipated as a result of the 1998 Welsh Office White Paper Putting Patients First. The changes anticipated there assume considerable realignment of local government, health authority and regional government boundaries in order to deliver services that promote a more community-based preventive, rehabilitative and maintenance role for care providers. It is possible that some of these boundaries will require considerable adjustment if not removal in order to achieve the aims of the White Paper, a point we return to shortly.

In any event, the White Paper implies a long term commitment from the Assembly to a process of organisational and cultural change. This will take time, will threaten if not undermine professional/occupational territories and traditions, and will only succeed if trust can be developed among key participants. The start of this process will be the government's plans to establish Local Health Groups (likely to be headed by GPs) which can combine the main players and unify resources by creating a partnership approach to community-based services. However, current social services community care is typically dominated by budgetary constraints and incremental forms of expenditure. Change here will require highly effective joint mechanisms at a local and strategic level to:

- Allow greater professional and financial collaboration.
- Unlock investments in institutional care that can be used to create new service routes in integrated health and social services provision in the community.

When Local Health Groups have been established, ideally they will be in a position to deliver a 'whole system' approach to primary and social care. They will be funded by transfers from secondary care – assuming there will be no 'new' money. At the same time this should not assume that care in the community is always less costly – 24 hour home care, for example, is not necessarily a cheap alternative to hospital.

Much progress has been made throughout Wales in generating good liaison between providers of social and health care. There is now much greater joint planning at operational, locality and strategic levels over hospital admissions and discharges. But there is no obvious blueprint for the way in which such shared planning and practice should be undertaken. In a time of considerable organisational, financial and cultural change in health and welfare it is unlikely that a uniform approach will emerge, nor is it self-evident that this would be feasible or desirable. More change seems inevitable as we move towards the creation of Local Health Groups. It is likely that GPs will play a lead role in developing these groups, but we are yet to see if they possess the management capacity to create new service systems that will take the pressure off secondary care. It will be crucial therefore that services are properly monitored and evaluated against accepted standards.

The role of health authorities remains critical. A scenario of health authorities simply holding the ring between parties while Local Health Groups accrue greater influence in health commissioning and acquire more staff and resources is an issue creating some unease. Some believe it might fragment the NHS and leave vulnerable groups at the mercy of whatever priorities, interests and managerial capacities these local bodies may possess. In such circumstances hospital discharge and continuing care arrangements might reflect the negotiations made by local players about (perceived) user priorities and needs. It could not be assumed this would augur well for all patient groups. Indeed, the present system is already in need of occasional unifying edicts from government, as can be seen from recent circulars from the Department of Health on continuing care. It is likely therefore that a clear strategic framework will be needed that will allow local interpretation but in the context of overall clarity around accountability.

Collaboration stands as a major organisational issue in the future of health and social care in Wales. To save money, health authorities may wish to pursue the closure of long stay beds, increase patient throughput and seek an extension of community provision. Social care via statutory provision offers means-tested and budget disciplined services to the most needy. This division is bridged by good collaborative arrangements in many areas but there remain serious difficulties when agencies cannot resource or agree a balance of provision providing the right palliative, rehabilitative or maintenance care. The result can be a breakdown in care and disputes about financial responsibility. Both sectors may see themselves as victims of cost shunting by the other – the health providers believing that social care agencies are bed-blocking to reduce expenditure, with the social care side believing that health are 'dumping' patients to achieve higher throughput.

SOCIAL INCLUSION

The idea that local authority social services alone can somehow apply its resources to promote social inclusion through the regeneration of socially deprived communities is implausible. The term social inclusion is, in any case, in danger of dilution to the point where it will join or supplant 'community' as what is sometimes called a 'spray-on' term - a word attached to an otherwise-questionable concept, in order to deodourise it of unpleasant or problematic connotations. New Labour, in some of its dimensions at least, has a distinctly social authoritarian approach to policy. The Crime and Disorder Bill, for example, contains an Anti-Social Behaviour Order which will allow for the imprisonment of individuals whose problematic behaviour occurs in essentially social spheres - such as housing tenancies - rather than the criminal. The Secretary of State for Education informed teacher union conferences in Easter 1998 that the state will be 'hard as nails' with parents who fail to measure up to new responsibilities to be placed upon them. The Minister responsible for mental health services announced in 1998 new powers for the compulsory treatment of the mentally ill and a moratorium upon the closure of mental institutions.

These developments expose a certain contradiction within the social exclusion debate for they suggest that there are significant elements within the population to whom the inclusionary embrace is not to be extended. From a social services perspective such a contradiction would be particularly significant because social welfare work so often involves engagement with just such groups and individuals - the troublesome, as well as the troubled. At the very least, inclusion in these circumstances is not an unambiguous policy goal which can be unproblematically pursued. However, to deny some the opportunity of playing a full life in society by reason of illness, disability, immaturity or poverty is divisive and wasteful. The cost of such exclusion is borne not only by the individual who is denied any sense of personal achievement but also by the wider community. Given this degree of reciprocity, a strategic approach to social services that is premised on a sense of social justice, equality of opportunity and active citizenship will maximise the potential contribution of *all* the people of Wales.

This is not to argue for universal services necessarily, but it is to argue for inclusive, participative and responsive services that will contribute to the general well being and collective welfare of the nation. For while many of the users of social services may occupy marginal positions in society, it should be recognised that their capacity is determined by forces which extend beyond their sphere of influence. This requires social services to be actively redistributive in terms of both resources and power. The users of social services represent the greatest constituency of vulnerable people in our society. Yet their experience has not been gained without the acquisition of particular skills and knowledge. This understanding needs to be sensitively reflected in service planning and delivery.

Social inclusion should mean the creation of initiatives to allow people to participate in a range of life chances available to most of us. It should be related closely to economic and social development which entails a comprehensive response from all the key players – the National Assembly, local government, community involvement, and partnership with the private sector. Within a strategy agreed between these partners social services does have a prominent role linked to its mainstream activity around social care for groups most in need. The key principles of social and economic development are listed briefly below and will be followed by some outline suggestions on the possible contribution from social services within a broad strategy of community renewal.

The first objective should be to improve the absolute standard of living as well as improving the quality of life of the most vulnerable groups. Three elements should be recognised throughout: social needs, ecological awareness and economic sustainability.

Policies should be judged against criteria such as:

- Does the policy improve the attractiveness of an area in social and economic terms
- Do amenities and services benefit all social groups
- Is action complementary across several sectors

Effective economic and social regeneration requires the right balance of bottom up and top down involvement. Here, the National Assembly will have a key role in encouraging the development of local partnerships within a national framework, ensuring a coherent and stable organisational and policy framework and in providing financial incentives to promote partnership.

Social inclusion as social and economic development is unlikely to be effective without a concentration of resources to achieve critical mass. Similarly, effective leadership that is confident, inspiring and innovative is essential, particularly in respect of the most vulnerable. The involvement of communities at all stages is critical and while this may assume participation by local people it also would include organisations within the voluntary sector that are community-based and often able to meet a wider range of local needs than either the public or private sectors. Lasting change will be best achieved by involving the local community with the public, private and voluntary sectors. Residents and agencies should be encouraged to participate at all levels of the development process.

There is a growing interest among city regions in particular in a more strategic generation of area-based economic development through local and community partnerships. The area-based approach highlights local development capacity that can work towards lower costs, developing technical expertise, co-ordinating services between different levels of government and the voluntary and public sectors. The private sector can offer financial help but just as importantly, business leaders can use their management skills to help local communities in the task of regeneration. Business methods have advantages in that they are likely to be founded upon an analysis of strengths and weaknesses, will have clear objectives, and be realistic in terms of resource availability. The involvement of business leaders can assist the integration of measures designed to address infrastructure as well as training and business support. In addition, ensuring a private sector stake in local success will encourage a clear vision for the future of the area to be developed and will help promote a shared voice and common purpose.

Considering social inclusion within a framework of social and economic development, social services could make a number of useful contributions:

- Their role as provider of social care to the most needy places them in a unique position to identify with some precision groups and communities which have little opportunity to participate in the opportunities enjoyed by most of us and to link these to a vision of change.

- Social services are often located in and are certainly familiar with the neighbourhoods they visit and will know something of the relative strengths and capacities of residents to engage in development strategies.

- Social services have a strong record in partnership working at the individual and group level and this could assist in developing the skills that residents will need for effective participation. Here, the growth of user/carer groups in recent years bears testament to a social services capacity for involving local people at different organisational/policy levels. Such know-how may have relevance for other forums such as those engaged in development planning and decision making.

- While social workers are trained to communicate, engage, assess, plan and intervene (all transferable skills in the social development context) they also advocate on behalf of their clients. That is to say, they give voice to the needs of service users, a skill that could find new expression in development strategies.

Though there are few social workers in the statutory sector in Wales who might be described as 'community workers', there are many who work at the community level in designing services that are needs-led wherever possible. Furthermore, while most workers have good local knowledge of the community they also typically operate in a multidisciplinary and inter-agency context, and therefore have experience of interlinking their activities within a wider network of providers. In short they are community oriented and corporate minded, two qualities of direct relevance to development strategies. Lastly, social services management has a long record of joint strategic planning and commissioning which would add considerably to the skill mix essential for sound leadership in development initiatives.

The commonality of the above themes lies in the realm of process rather than in the substance of their development. Social services could play an important *facilitative* role: sharing information, promoting new relationships, training, brokering interests, servicing resident groups, giving voice on behalf of the most vulnerable or those least able to articulate their interests, and perhaps co-ordinating development strategy at various levels. Such roles would have costs in respect of staff time. But such a role would not fundamentally disturb the broad structure of local government social services as currently configured around child protection, family support, adult social care.

However, should there be the view that somehow social services can by itself act as the leading edge of community regeneration then this would assume a transformative capacity within these departments that have not been revealed before. It would also assume that statutory duties could still be met whilst doing something fundamentally different with social services provision. That would be a dubious if not high risk assumption given the current level of resources committed to community care and child protection.

In brief, if the National Assembly wishes there to be a social inclusion role for social services that shifts practice and resources in some fundamental sense away from individuals and families in need, and towards communities in need, then this will have profound consequences for policy, training and management. It will also have serious political consequences if the present imperfect levels of response to vulnerable clients are threatened by such a re-focusing of social services. It is likely that social services, as but one key player in a social inclusion strategy, are best seen, at least in the medium term, as having an intelligence, representative and perhaps leadership function rather than as an entity in need of wholesale reconstruction as a social development agency.

CHAPTER 22

HOUSING

Jane Carpenter

Welsh housing problems are not generally different to those England, except in the scale of their severity. This is characterised by:

- A large proportion of our housing is very old – in 1991 37 per cent was built before 1919.

- Unfitness and disrepair is unacceptably high – 150,000 homes (13 per cent of total stock) were recorded unfit in the 1993 House Condition Survey.

- High levels of owner occupation, recorded at 71 per cent in the 1997 Welsh Housing Statistics.

- Average income of households in Wales is lower than the rest of the United Kingdom.

- The lack of Welsh Office guidance on the future dwelling requirements and other aspects of housing need in Wales, and the difficulties of ensuring adequate provision through the planning system.

- The need for housing organisations to reorganise and restructure, and ensure that future policy development involves tenants and other voluntary groups and the private sector.

- The need for housing organisations to produce and implement housing programmes in Wales to respond directly to specific Welsh problems.

INSTITUTIONAL CHANGES

The development and delivery of housing policy and programmes in Wales has changed substantially since the Labour Party gained power in May 1997. Prior to the election there was a division of power and responsibility between Whitehall, the

Welsh Office and Tai Cymru, and the local authorities in Wales. Other groups such as the Housing Associations were key players in the delivery of services, with influential roles played by bodies such as the Chartered Institute of Housing in Wales and the Centre for Housing Management and Research at Cardiff University on the direction of housing policy and programmes.

Whitehall was, and remains responsible for primary legislation, much of which impacts on housing provision and housing management such as Right-to-Buy, Private Finance Initiatives, Housing Benefits and Council Tax. However, the Welsh Office and Secretary of State for Wales have control of secondary legislation, which enables them to take account of specifically Welsh circumstances. The Welsh Office funds all agencies delivering housing services, including local authorities and voluntary groups. Local authorities, as enablers rather than providers are responsible for local housing strategies, setting local priorities for projects and funding, while simultaneously managing their own stock of homes. New social housing development has been carried out by individual housing associations.

The relationships between these players has not always been harmonious, with struggles for the balance of power constantly occurring. Criticisms before the 1997 general election were that housing issues had become more centralised, with Westminster having too much influence while local authorities lost responsibilities. Before it was absorbed into the Welsh Office in October 1998, Tai Cymru faced prolonged criticism for being unaccountable. Even local authorities were criticised for failing to develop truly participatory forms of democracy.

The Labour Party manifesto pledged many changes to the institutions of Wales. Once in power, these promises quickly began to be implemented. The White Paper *A Voice for Wales* outlined the Governments proposals, not only for establishing a National Assembly, but on the reorganisation of the Quangos. Early action was initiated on the merger of the Welsh Office Housing Division and Tai Cymru. The aim of creating one body responsible for all national housing issues in Wales gained the general support housing interest groups.

The new Welsh Office Housing Department was operating in a shadow form from October 1998 with the full process due for completion by January 1999. The new department is made up of three divisions - Policy and Resources, Operations, and Performance. It will advise the Secretary of State until the National Assembly begins work in May 1999. Meanwhile, the Department has established the National Forum for Housing in Wales with representatives from the key agencies. The Forum is working towards a National Housing Strategy for members of the Assembly to consider. Many other groups, such as the Social Landlords Forum, the Housing Research Group and the Housing Needs Assessment Working Party have also emerged to develop advise on specific areas of housing policies and practice.

One member of the Assembly's Executive Committee or Cabinet will have housing included within his or her portfolio, probably together with other responsibilities such as health and social services. The Assembly Secretary's work will be scrutinised by a relevant Subject Committee. The National Assembly Advisory

Group suggests that there should be six subject committees with corresponding Assembly Secretaries, grouped around the three themes of social, economic and environmental issues. The precise formulation will have to await the allocation of portfolios to Cabinet members once the first Welsh government is formed.

Despite this uncertainty there are some general policy issues that can be expected to emerge as a result of the creation of the Assembly. Most notably, these will be the balance of power between Whitehall and the National Assembly in relation to primary and secondary legislation and the issue of resources for housing matters.

It can be expected Assembly members will want primary legislation framed in as broad a way possible, to allow them fullest opportunity to develop appropriate secondary legislation to take account of the Welsh situation. Many in Wales consider that too much primary housing legislation has been passed based upon situations and experiences of London and the South East of England. These have little relevance and in some cases adverse consequences for housing in Wales. As Gareth Hughes, Director of the Welsh Federation of Housing Associations, has put it:

> Apart from establishing Tai Cymru there has been no piece of housing legislation that has not been framed for an English purpose, and then applied to Wales, whether relevant or not ... The Government see their housing policy through English eyes. Wales' needs are an afterthought' (A Parliament for Wales, Gomer, 1994, page 223).

Furthermore, there is unlikely to be any additional money for housing once the Assembly is established. Indeed, some expect a reduction in the monies available. The housing budget for 1998-99 stood at £500m (see Chapter 4 for a break-down of the Welsh Office budget). Those with an interest in housing may find it necessary to fight harder for retaining the proportion of the overall Assembly budget for housing use in future years, as other responsibilities such as health and education vie for additional resources.

The real possibilities for change will be the allocation of monies for different priorities and new schemes within the overall housing budget. The Assembly should review current spending on existing projects against new priorities in an effort to achieve best value. However, such a reassessment will need to be well researched and properly justified. It is within limited and possibly contracting financial resources that the development of future housing policy formulation and the delivery of services will lie.

A NATIONAL HOUSING STRATEGY

It is important that the National Housing Strategy is put in place at the earliest possible opportunity, but without compromising the required research and consultation that will be an important component of its preparation. The Assembly Committee responsible for the preparation of the National Housing Strategy will need to:

- Establish the parameters of the strategy including content, timescales and consultation arrangements.

- Prioritise housing programmes and subsequently allocate resources to them.

- Ensure the strategy (and individual schemes) comply with the broad corporate agenda of the Assembly. For example, housing policies should be consistent with the Assembly's strategy for Sustainable Development (see Chapter 11).

- Ensure that the strategy is properly implemented.

ESTABLISHING THE PARAMETERS

In establishing the parameters, the National Assembly will be essentially determining the procedures it will follow during the preparation of the strategy. It is an important stage in the process, as it will provide an opportunity for the Assembly to promote dialogue and develop confidence in its housing work at a very early stage. In addition to the strategy's content, the Assembly should make clear the timetable for the strategy's consultation arrangements and adoption target date.

The Assembly will have a statutory duty to consult with local government, voluntary groups and businesses on its activities. All three sectors include agencies involved with housing and housing related services, and are currently extensively involved in Welsh Office activities. Such bodies will welcome an increased opportunity to participate in housing issues, and would be unlikely to accept any reduction in current levels of involvement. It would be fair to say that all agencies are looking to the Assembly to fulfil the promise that it will operate in the spirit of partnership and inclusivity. Members of the Assembly should therefore consider the benefits of embracing this wealth of knowledge and experience, albeit with an appreciation that many of the key groups have conflicting or at least divergent ideas on policy development and priorities.

It is important that in encouraging maximum participation in policy development the Assembly does not compromise speedy decision making. The two objectives must be reconciled. Business groups such as the CBI have advocated a system where full and thorough consultation on an annual national strategy takes place, after which day-to-day decisions are left to Assembly members. This proposal could easily and effectively apply to the preparation and implementation of the National Housing Strategy.

Furthermore the National Housing Forum for Wales has the potential to become an excellent line of communication between the Assembly, the civil service, local authorities, voluntary organisations, business and other groups with legitimate housing interests. The Forum should therefore be retained by the Assembly.

PRIORITIES AND RESOURCE ALLOCATIONS

The Assembly will inherit the Welsh Office's 1999/2000 housing programme. To assist in examining future alternatives Assembly members should be furnished with proper research into the operation and achievement or failures of existing programmes and the potential of new (and perhaps previously discarded) programmes. At the same time it is inevitable that the Assembly will build on existing programmes.

COMPATIBILITY WITH WIDER AIMS AND OBJECTIVES

The housing strategy should be prepared with due regard for the work of the other Subject Committees and Regional Committees of the Assembly. For too long, at both the Welsh Office and local authority levels, housing policies have been prepared in isolation of the work other policy areas. Policies have been weakened by conflicting or at least deviating, policies operating elsewhere within the same or other organisations.

The National Housing Strategy must at least be prepared with the assistance of Assembly members and the relevant civil servants responsible for health, social services, economic development and planning. Similarly, the role of housing must be considered in the work of these other topic committees. How such matters relate to each other, or dovetail together for mutual benefit, including potential cost savings, should be explored. A corporate approach in co-ordinating the overall aims, objectives and strategies of each Subject Committee within the corporate vision or plan is an essential requirement.

The government's wider political agenda should also be embraced within the National Housing Strategy. The development of sustainable communities and promoting urban regeneration can be assisted through social housing grant allocations and land use policy. Furthermore, the use of local labour or encouragement of training through New Deal or Welfare-to-Work can be a requirement of large capital (maintenance or development) projects funded by an Assembly housing grant.

IMPLEMENTATION

The Assembly will be accountable for any failure in the delivery of its policy even though actual delivery will be through a plethora of housing bodies on its behalf. To ensure that the delivery of programmes and policies to the standard required is properly carried out, the issue of monitoring and regulating the activities of these agents is one the Assembly must address and this is dealt with in more detail below.

DELIVERY OF THE STRATEGY

While the Assembly will ultimately be accountable for the delivery of housing policy, the implementation of programmes will be delegated to other bodies. Local authorities have been promised an enhanced role in the delivery services in their areas. While the precise nature of this enhanced role is not clear, local authorities will be the key players in translating the National Strategy into local policy and ensuring its delivery either themselves or by enabling other agencies to do so. These include housing associations, tenant and resident groups, the voluntary sector, and the private sector. For the best possible results the various sectors must work together in partnership, assisted by the overall guidance provided by the Assembly's housing strategy.

Under the present system by the Welsh Office tends to deploy blunt instruments too late against agencies failing in their service delivery commitments. This will not be sufficient for the Assembly. It will need to assess how it will regulate the bodies delivering services. This is likely to prove one of the more difficult issues facing the Assembly in its early days. It will need to decide:

- What should be regulated.
- Whether targets or minimum standards should be established.
- What action should be taken against those who do not achieve the desired standard, or deviate to an unacceptable degree from the national policy.

REGULATION

In determining the need for regulation and at what minimum level standards should be set, the Assembly must be satisfied that the criteria for achievement is reasonable. At the same time there should not be a resort to the 'lowest common denominator'. The aim should be to raise standards.

There are 22 local authorities and 28 working housing associations in Wales. Examples of good and bad practices can be detected in most agencies. An early review of existing performance should be carried out to identify the factors affecting service delivery, with the aim of promoting good practice throughout all agencies.

The Assembly will need to establish targets for achievement and minimum standards for performance. These should relate to value for money, technical standards, and administrative practices and procedures. They should be included within the National Housing Strategy, clearly indicated against the relevant programme and stating which agencies will be expected to comply.

Some regulation currently exists. Tai Cymru used to regulate the activities of the Housing Associations in Wales, a role now absorbed within the Welsh Office Housing Division. Indeed, Tai Cymru's record in improving the performance and efficiency of Housing Associations was commendable. Similarly through their housing strategy operational plans local authorities currently monitor their own performance. In the main, therefore, the Assembly will be standardising control over all agencies to agreed minimum levels, although new aspects of regulatory control may emerge as a result of the overall process.

Certain bodies are advocating that the Assembly should enforce minimum standards across all the housing service providers. Others, mainly those who would become regulated, are arguing in favour of maximum autonomy at the local level, and minimum interference by the Assembly. Disagreement should be expected amongst potential consultees about the levels at which minimum standards should be set. It would be reasonable to expect those who are to be regulated to argue for lower standards and increased levels of autonomy for their agencies. On the other hand, those who could be described as the 'users' or 'consumers' of the services or the system, such as tenants groups or the private sector, would argue in favour of high minimum standards. It will be for Assembly members to resolve what should be the acceptable standards.

MONITORING

A system of monitoring the effectiveness of the National Housing Strategy and the delivery of its programmes will need to be established. The system must be capable of picking up the failings, either of the programmes themselves or the individual agencies.

It will be important, in the first instance to understand why failures may be occurring. Perhaps the programmes are unworkable or unpopular. Perhaps the expectations of performance are too high. Alternatively, an agency may not be achieving due to its own internal problems. Where such constraints exist, the Assembly should seek either to review the strategy or programme or to assist the particular agency or service provider in overcoming its difficulties.

There may be occasions when a service provider is identified either as a persistent poor performer or as promoting policies that are consistently at odds with the National Housing Strategy. Again, the Assembly must resolve what action has to be taken to improve or refocus such an agency. Sanctions, financial or otherwise, for the worst cases should be considered.

PRIORITY ACTION FOR THE FIRST THREE YEARS

Individuals and agencies involved in housing and housing related services have been active in preparing for the impact of the National Assembly. All believe that, because our housing problems are so acute, they should achieve a higher profile within the Assembly compared to their current position.

It would not be considered sensible for new Assembly members to revamp the existing housing policies and programmes too quickly, and certainly not without the necessary research and consultation. At the same time the Assembly will be under pressure to make a difference in a relatively short time frame. Before making any substantial and meaningful changes, the Assembly should take stock of existing practices and review any new proposals and their implications. A three-year housing programme could look like the following:

YEAR 1: 1999/2000

- The Assembly will inherit a predetermined housing programme, which will be implemented throughout this financial year.

- The Assembly develops its Corporate Vision and Plan, and its procedures for ensuring that all plans and strategies produced by its various committees will be properly integrated.

- The Assembly Secretary, relevant Subject Committee and civil servants begin the preparation of the National Housing Strategy. Work on reviewing current policies and programmes, performance of service delivery, and evaluating alternatives, also begins.

- Dialogue with housing interest groups begins, to ensure the Assembly's statutory duty to consult local government, voluntary groups and businesses is fulfiled.

- The 2000/2001 Housing Programme is determined – in the context of existing practices, the Corporate Vision and early conclusions from the Assembly's review work.

YEAR 2: 2000/2001

- Implement the 2000/2001 Housing Programme.

- The Assembly concludes its initial research, and publishes for consultation a draft National Housing Strategy.

- The draft strategy and consultation responses are used to guide the development of the 2001/2002 Housing Programme.

- An 'adopted' National Housing Strategy, including a system of monitoring, regulation and sanctions, is in place by May 2001.

YEAR 3: 2001/2002

- Implement the 2001/2002 Housing Programme.

- First Review of National Housing Strategy.

- Begin a system of formal monitoring and regulation of housing service providers.

- Develop 2002/2003 Housing Programme.

PART THREE

RELATIONSHIPS

CHAPTER 23

FINDING OUR VOICES

Graham Day, Martin Fitton, and Margaret Minhinnick

Wales is not unique in experiencing new pressures and new opportunities, which point towards the need for greater public participation and involvement in government. In a variety of publications, policy statements and presentations, the government has made clear its intent to revitalise local government at every level. An important change is occurring in the political culture of Britain, which presents us with an opportunity to move forward in Wales with the development of new forms of genuinely local participatory democracy. This connects, too, with *Local Agenda 21*, the series of environmental initiatives which emerged following the 1992 Earth Summit.

At the same time, there is a need to follow this through with an equally radical reform of the connections between local communities and their elected representatives. At present we rely too heavily on small, and frequently closed, circles of individuals and organisations to speak and act 'for' their communities. Often there is little proof that they are sufficiently in touch with the full range and variety of local opinions. This is a missing link in the chain of democratic governance. It needs to be put in place if the 'democratic deficit' is to be adequately addressed. Only then will the 'democratically disinherited', including the disadvantaged, the poor, the unemployed, the marginalised and excluded, be brought meaningfully into the decision-making process.

The National Assembly should take early action to foster and sustain the energies of decision making at local and community level. We are convinced that by engaging a greater proportion of the population in decision processes, and bringing power nearer to its appropriate level, the Assembly can create a strong foundation for sustainable communities. Local ownership of policies, and local control over the implementation of services, will help to realise the aims of *Local Agenda 21*, including its commitments to a 'lean' use of resources at local level. Ideally, too, these new arrangements for involvement will themselves acknowledge the importance of 'absent generations', that is to say those from which we inherit, those to which we bequeath (Roger Scruton, 1998). In short, we need to re-emphasise our role as 'custodians'.

DEMOCRATIC DISINHERITANCE

As a means of making the views of people at local level count, local government has not been working well. During the past 20 or so years, local authorities in the UK have been stripped of many of their powers. Even in those areas where they retain formal responsibilities, they have had their freedom of action curtailed. Local democracy has been squeezed by the transfer of powers to non-elected agencies and Quangos, and by the expansion of the role of the market as a replacement for public control and decision-making. The impact of deregulation, privatisation, and the introduction of new systems of management across the whole range of service delivery, including health, education and welfare, has eroded if not dismantled much of local government's traditional role. It has undermined the transparency of decision making, and made those in charge less answerable to the general public. Increasingly the management of services such as education and health has come to be seen as a job for the 'experts', those with management training and qualifications, and therefore beyond the reach and control of ordinary people for whom they are intended.

These processes have contributed to the growth of apathy, confusion and distrust among voters. Public knowledge of political institutions is also weak. The turnout for local elections in Wales is low, and decreasing. About a fifth of local councillors are returned unopposed, and no elections are held at all in a quarter of local authority wards. Isobel Lindsay, a leading member of the Campaign for a Scottish Parliament, crystallised our concerns: 'Apathy and the lack of belief in change work in the interests of established structures of power and privilege ... and when fewer people take an active and informed interest in politics, the vulnerability to manipulation is greater' (*Welsh Democracy Review*).

It has yet to be seen whether the reorganisation of local government into a system of unitary authorities will do much to remove the sense of distance that has arisen between local people and what should be their most immediate levels of effective governance. Examples such as the breakdown of trust between local government officers and voters in Ynys Mon in 1998 hardly encourage optimism in this respect. Elsewhere we find people viewing their local authorities with suspicion or even hostility, regarding them as obstructing the achievement of local aims and wishes as often as they serve them. This is not a healthy state of affairs.

However, participation in local elections offers only limited public involvement in the political process. Only a tiny minority are prepared to go a step further by putting themselves forward for the onerous role of elected representative, or even to become actively engaged with organised local political life. No more than two in every hundred people belong to a political party. Even fewer play an active part in their workings.

With limited competition for seats on councils, members of the local authorities form a less than representative cross-section of the general population. They are predominantly male, rather elderly, and under-represent a number of significant social groupings. The same applies to representation at local community and town council level. Although Wales has a system of community councils which could act as a significant vehicle for expressing local needs and aspirations, these vary greatly in the effectiveness with which they operate. They do not cover the whole of Wales and where they exist many are lacking in dynamism. At times they can deploy their statutory powers in ways which do as much to impede local wishes and developments, as to assist them. Previous efforts to inject greater energy and accountability into community/town councils have proved ineffectual (Welsh Office, 1992). Yet as the Campaign for the Protection of Rural Wales has commented, 'Community and town councils are a much under-estimated and under-utilised layer of local government. They offer great scope for enhanced powers and responsibilities' (CPRW, 1991).

INVOLVING THE PUBLIC

The failings of the present system are widely acknowledged. The need for officials, elected and non-elected, at all levels, to consult local opinion, as a way of improving the delivery of services is a theme of numerous government publications. Such documents contain repeated pledges to 'promote more well-informed and effective participation by citizens in decision-making' or 'to strengthen the co-operation between statutory, voluntary and community sectors and to respond to communities' own perceptions of their needs and priorities' (*Sustainable Communities in Wales*, HMSO, 1998). In *Opportunities for Change*, the UK's strategy for Sustainable Development, the case is put overtly:

> *'Decisions need to be taken at the right level whether national, regional or local in ways which make the best use of the energy, ideas and commitment of the British public. We aim to devolve decision making to country, regional and local levels where possible so that those people best placed to take the decisions are able to do so and that decision makers are more accountable to local people'* (paras. 53/54).

Listening to, and involving the local community in decisions are seen as key principles of action to achieve local sustainability, as in the implementation of Local Agenda 21 action plans. The duty to consult extends beyond elected authorities to such bodies as Health Trusts and School Management Boards. In particular, the March 1998 Green Paper on local government reform endorses the importance of finding innovative systems for identifying local needs as a way of improving the democratic process. Here the Government's proposal to reconsider the role of community councils and to use them 'as points for gathering and then projecting the views and concerns of those they represent' provides a welcome way forward (*Modernising Local Government* 4.3.1).

Although there is much that is rhetorical in these commitments, if acted upon they could provide the opening for creating governmental processes that are far more accessible, and accountable, than has generally been the case in the past. If properly pursued, this should mean considerably more than a managed, 'top-down', delegation of powers. It could create the space for the promotion and expression of genuinely grass-roots opinion and organisation 'from below', capable of challenging and revitalising local politics.

The Welsh Office has committed itself to reviewing and strengthening the powers and role of community councils. This should be carried on by the Assembly as a signal of its readiness to endorse public participation. There is a need to establish what part councils will play in giving people enhanced control over local affairs.

BUILDING ON EXISTING COMMUNITY SKILLS

Local democracy in Wales does not have to be rebuilt from scratch. Apart from existing community councils, there is also substantial popular involvement in other forms of local and voluntary action. The Wales Council for Voluntary Action estimates that there are 23,000 voluntary organisations in Wales. They boast an annual turnover of £675m. The monetary value of involving 700,000 formal volunteers and 1.6 million informal volunteers is estimated to be £2bn annually. These people vastly outnumber the activists within political parties (see also Chapter 27, on *The Voluntary Sector*). Yet it might be said that the variety of volunteering is also its great weakness. There is little common cause shared by volunteers, spread as they are over every interest and activity.

Volunteering also might be said to take away the energetic and the talented from local politics. Indeed, certain forms of volunteering – especially in the Green movement – represent a response to the failures of conventional politics. For instance, direct action and pressure group work has been seen as more effective in achieving environmental aims than working within the traditional political system.

Yet even if traditional politics are viewed with scepticism, participatory democracy is alive and well within Wales. Indeed, there is much to celebrate with respect to the enthusiasm and inventiveness that has been shown by people at local level in expressing their aspirations and finding ways of acting upon them. Example after example could be provided of local interventions that have had direct effects upon policy outcomes and decisions. More generally, local organisations such as Community Enterprise groups, rural LEADER groups, and Local Agenda 21 Fora, demonstrate that there is a thriving participatory culture in Wales (Adamson 1998).

What is needed is that this enthusiasm, energy, and expertise should be plugged in, regularly and systematically, to the higher levels of government and decision-making, so that local participation comes to form a permanent, established and comprehensive component of the democratic system. Ideally, this would shift public involvement from reactive towards more proactive engagement, that is from a position where people merely respond to initiatives, often in a negative or blocking fashion, to one where they are able to take the initiative themselves in bringing about the developments that conform most closely to their own aspirations and values.

Yet, a revitalised system of community councils will not be enough in itself to create a wholly participatory democracy. Partly this is a question of the style of working. Ways need to be found of stimulating and maintaining processes of active involvement among both individuals and community organisations, as a regular and continuous feature of local life. Meetings need to be structured in ways which encourage participation, and make attending them a rewarding experience. Ideally, these meetings will come to be seen not just as talking shops, but as occasions where effective decisions can be made. The right kinds of structures and mechanisms need also to be created. There has to be a variety of 'junction boxes' through which participation can be built into government in Wales.

Means should be found to ensure the inclusion of grassroots organisations which have shown that they can provide vitality and enthusiasm, yet which are now frequently alienated from the existing power structures. They can provide the energy to sustain the necessary integration between the political process and the voluntary sector.

COMMUNITY LINKS WITH LOCAL AUTHORITIES

A number of suggestions have already been made as to how the voluntary sector as a whole might achieve closer integration with the Assembly and the local authorities. Indeed, Community Voluntary Councils, which work in each unitary authority, are developing a structured strategic partnership with local government, whilst promoting and providing support to the voluntary sector. They, along with the Welsh Local Government Association, have agreed to establish this initiative at an all-Wales level. The membership is to comprise in equal numbers, elected members, nominated by the local authorities and voluntary sector representatives, nominated by the Community Voluntary Councils. Among the subjects they will consider are community-led initiatives, volunteering, national organisations, social welfare, environment, and leisure and culture. In their document *Achieving Shared Aims - Working to a Common Agenda* the following objectives are listed:

- Ensure that the broad range of voluntary and community activity in each area is effectively represented.

- Enhance the capacity of local communities to participate in the planning and policy formation of the local authority.

- Facilitate and maintain a structured relationship which will help the local authority to communicate effectively with a broad range of local voluntary activity.

The Welsh Local Government Association undertakes to:

- Develop structures and processes which facilitate the sharing of decision-making and responsibility with voluntary and community groups.

- Develop criteria which will put the community at the centre of activity and demonstrate in a transparent way that communities really are involved in the design, implementation, and evaluation of programmes.

- Raise the benefits of a productive partnership with all kinds of voluntary action, not just those with which the local authority has a financial relationship.

While welcome, such initiatives only tend to involve types of people who already participate. Channels of communication are needed for the 'disinherited'. Linkages will also need to be made at the community level since the unitary authorities are often too remote to energise local concerns and commitments. Periodic joint meetings between the different levels of government could then be effective. For example, unitary authorities could convene meetings of their community councils to ensure that joint initiatives are properly considered and dealt with. At present they are reluctant to do this.

A WALES CIVIC FORUM

Another proposal has been for the formation of a Wales Civic Forum, located above the unitary authorities, to bring the Assembly directly into contact with voluntary bodies and Welsh civil society generally. Its members would come from the whole spectrum of society such as trade unions, religious bodies, business, professionals, academia, artists, farmers, community and voluntary organisations. The aim is to operate at an early stage in decision-making to:

- Foster wider participation in the National Assembly.

- Improve the quality of information and therefore of debate.

- Develop an advisory role, passing recommendations, where there is consensus, to the Assembly, Unitary Authorities and other public bodies.

- Undertake a monitoring role.

Scotland, Northern Ireland and the Republic of Ireland have already established such bodies. The Scottish Civic Assembly does not involve political parties, whilst the National Economic and Social Forum in the Republic of Ireland does include representatives of government and opposition parties. The Easter 1998 Irish Peace Agreement states that a

> '... consultative Civic Forum will be established ... The First Minister and the Deputy First Minister will by agreement provide administrative support for the Civic Forum and establish guidelines for selection of representatives to the Civic Forum'.

It also states that consideration will

'... be given to the establishment of an independent consultative forum
appointed by the two administrations, representative of civil society, comprising
the social partners and other members with expertise in cultural, economic and
other issues'.

Exploratory meetings to consider how a civic forum might work in Wales were held during 1997 at the instigation of the Wales Council for Voluntary Action. Those involved in the discussions included representatives from the TUC, CYTUN (Churches Together in Wales) and the Institute of Welsh Affairs. The conclusion at that stage was that attempting to establish formal structures would be premature. The view was taken that any initiative should come from the bottom up. A top-down approach, led by existing well-established organisations might end up trying to second guess the outcomes of the Assembly's deliberations.

In late 1998 a renewed initiative was made, this time led by the Church in Wales and CYTUN, aimed at raising awareness of the Assembly and linked to the first elections. An all-Wales conference together with constituency meetings are planned during the first Assembly election campaign where community concerns can be voiced. It is hoped that some kind of Welsh Civic Forum might emerge from the church-led constituency groups that will undertake this initiative. However, any all-Wales initiative should be informed first by views relayed from the grassroots and then amplified upwards to the Assembly by whatever kind of Civic Forum emerges.

AN INCLUSIVE ASSEMBLY

It is proposed that the Regional Committees which are to be established in the Assembly will be the main link between the Assembly, the Unitary Authorities and the communities they serve. Currently, the role of these committees remains unclear, apart from their having an advisory and representative role (see Chapter 25). What is needed is a clear structure that will allow communities direct access to the Assembly so that their concerns are reflected in its policies.

One possibility is for the Assembly to be peripatetic from time to time and meet as a whole at a regional level to make it easier for communities to become involved with its work. The example of the Swedish Rural Parliament which meets every two years and brings grassroots decision makers together with their national equivalents on a face-to-face basis might also be explored as a way of providing access.

In their document *Agenda for the National Assembly - The Welsh Language in the next Millennium* Cymdeithas yr Iaith Gymraeg suggest that permanent county-based youth forums should be established. These would provide an opportunity for young people to engage in decisions of importance to their communities and young people.

The Government of Wales Bill places a duty on the Assembly to set out a scheme for working with the voluntary sector. The establishment of a Compact – a mutually agreed working partnership between the Welsh Office and the voluntary/community sector – will recognise respective roles, agree shared values and common goals. This is a welcome step. However, it does not cover the practical arrangements for the Assembly's committees to meet with the voluntary sector representatives. This is still to be considered and agreed by the Assembly members and the Welsh voluntary sector. The Wales Council for Voluntary Action has suggested a joint liaison group which would report to the Assembly's Executive Committee.

Community participation is not only about the linkages. It is also about the working style of the Assembly. It is expected the Assembly will operate procedures and practices which will involve 'those who have previously faced barriers in participating in Welsh political and community life' (Equal Opportunities Commission, 1998). This document reminds us that Westminster style politics, with its adversarial, aggressive point scoring is 'alienating for many women, people with different cultural backgrounds and, indeed, many men. To promote inclusiveness it will be important to set a style that listens to views, seeks to find solutions to problems and allows for development of constructive argument and debate. This can be achieved through Standing Orders ...'.

It must be stated, however, that Welsh local politics, if not adversarial, are often dominated by power-broking cabals – parties within parties – from which not only the public but many elected members are excluded.

A PROGRAMME APPROACH

Today's government departments have been compared (by Alan Clark in his *Diaries*) to a series of isolated pillars, great vertical structures between which there is little connection. This is a powerful image of the type of governance we are seeking to avoid in Wales. The National Assembly Advisory Group has proposed that a programme approach be adopted to achieve integration. It suggests that committees might be set up on a 'task and finish' basis in a process that should involve expertise from outside groups.

Action programmes for community involvement should operate 'horizontally' as well 'vertically', in a holistic manner. This means they encompass all service provision areas, and also equality of opportunity, environmental protection, cultural diversity and anti-poverty measures. To encourage these developments, we believe the Assembly's plan for community participation should include steps to ensure that participation becomes embedded as a key principle and requirement of its action programmes. The implementation of such a plan would require a commitment of long term funding, including an appropriate educational and media strategy.

Achieving participatory democracy at all levels of Welsh governance, from the

Assembly to the Community Councils, will require detailed consideration of structures and procedures. The Wales Association of Community and Town Councils suggest that a first step towards making community councils more effective would be for the National Assembly to ensure that all areas of Wales, including the large conurbations, are serviced by a community council. The Association says that repatriation of the local business rate is also long overdue, and that this, at a stroke, would restore local interest whilst encouraging a greater range of people to become councillors. A transfer of power and resources would not require primary legislation. It is within the existing scope of the Assembly and could be carried out early in its existence. The aim would be to encourage a positive climate for local partnerships in coordinating and monitoring the provision of local services.

There also needs to be direct input from town and community councils into the committees of the Assembly, to ensure that their concerns and interests are incorporated into the agendas. The Assembly's Regional Committees could provide the structure for this to happen. If local authorities are to be effective, they will need greater resources. In addition there will be a training requirement, to familiarise councillors with methods and processes of consultation and involvement.

A range of techniques to facilitate community participation are already available and there is a growing expertise in their use in Wales. For instance, 'Jigso' has encouraged over 200 communities, mostly in rural areas, to undertake local appraisals which are self-administered questionnaires that enable communities to identify their needs, resources and aspirations. On the basis of such appraisals communities can draw up their own action plans. Other techniques being developed include: Community Visioning, Community Planning Weekends, Planning for Real, Village Design Statements, Parish Maps, Roundtables, Forums, Citizen's Juries, Community Arts, Referenda, Open Space Technique, and Consensus Building (Graham Day et.al., 1998). At the same time, there is awareness that abuse of such techniques, or the failure to connect them to real and desired results, can lead to frustration, disappointment, and to people turning away from involvement.

Consideration needs to be given to who should be the trainers. For example could/should community councillors become the facilitators for participatory community involvement throughout Wales? The Wales Association of Community and Town Councils are not opposed to this idea.

Other questions to address are how should we train our local authority councillors to be more responsive to community participation? Obviously, there will be resistance, especially in areas where power has been wielded for generations by particular political and social groupings. But if we are to move towards more genuinely participatory systems, a rearrangement of power is needed. Training in consensus building is important here because it serves to promote a sense of ownership of local decisions, rather than alienation and discontent with unmet needs.

Alongside this, the planning system must also be reviewed. It is over planning issues that the public most often encounters its elected representatives and enters into dialogue with them. However, according to the Campaign for the Protection of Rural Wales the planning system is less open and accountable than it was 20 years ago (*Rural Wales*, Summer 1998). The Assembly will need to give particular attention to the way in which the devolution of planning powers might encourage a sense of local ownership and responsibility for planning. The Assembly may excite public debate and encourage participation, but if expectations of influence grow, while planning decisions take little heed of public opinion, then the Assembly itself might suffer in terms of public perception of its capabilities.

The National Assembly Advisory Group has proposed that the Assembly establish an information and education facility to help people understand and become involved in the Assembly. This could be expanded into a section that would promote civic education and promote participatory techniques. The Government's current interest in a 'Life Long Learning' programme could also support this type of initiative. Civic studies might be taught in schools, leading to a better understanding of active citizenship. With such backing community decision-making can provide the energy to inform the Assembly's policies and agendas.

The role of the media is crucial in drawing attention to both participatory techniques and new citizen roles. For instance, we should see more positive news about the myriad of community, social, cultural and environmental initiatives now underway. Appropriate, but comprehensive coverage by the media of the Assembly's committees and debates is also needed. Those debates could at times be mirrored locally, and covered by the local papers and stations. If handled well this would provide a tremendous chance for interactive dialogue and discourse on important issues of the day between citizens, communities and the Assembly. This is not a matter of using the new digital technology to operate simple yes/no referenda. There is nothing instant or slick about democratic participation. Overall the media should inject a sense of excitement and commitment into involving the whole community in running Wales.

Whilst civic forums at neighbourhood, community/town, unitary authority, regional and all-Wales levels would be desirable, at present they could prove as alienating as political structures. For this to change, the voluntary sector must get its own house in order. It needs to break down the barriers of self-interest, foster links, and encourage integration within its own constituency. New coalitions need to be established which manifest the connections between socio-economic, health, cultural and environmental concerns. This would allow voluntary effort to be at the heart of helping to create sustainable communities. The ground rules entailed in the effective operation of Local Agenda 21 programmes could serve as the mechanism to achieve the necessary restructuring.

CONCLUSION

The establishment of the National Assembly, if really inclusive, could be the most important challenge for all of us as we move into the millennium. The Assembly can create the structures for fostering genuine participation. The voluntary sector especially, can better integrate to make wider and lasting partnerships. The media could promote participation in a way that will make future politics exciting and relevant. It is possible for people in their communities to enjoy the challenge of setting their own agendas for a community-based sustainable Wales. With political will and commitment it can be achieved.

References

National Assembly For Wales. 'NAAG Consultation Paper'.Para 7.6/7.8

David Adamson, *Social and Economic Regeneration in Wales: the role of community development in community enterprise*, Community Enterprise Wales, 1998.

Roger Scruton, *Absent Generations*, Philosophy of Environment Conference, King's College, London April 1998.

Campaign for the Protection of Rural Wales, *The Structure of Local Government in Wales*, 1991.

Cymdeithas yr Iaith Gymraeg, *Agenda for the National Assembly - The Welsh Language in the next Millennium*, 1998.

Graham Day et. al., *Where Do We Go From Here? A Review of Community Participation Methods*, University of Wales, Bangor/ Jigso/WCVA, 1998.

Equal Opportunities Commission, Commission for Racial Equality and Disability Wales, *Mainstreaming Equality: The National Assembly*, 1998.

Stewart J and Stoker G 1988. 'The Future of Local Government'.

Tewdwr-Jones M, *Rural Governance and Community Participation*, Journal of Rural Studies, 1998.

Wales Council For Voluntary Action and Welsh Local Government Association, *Achieving Shared Aims - Working to a Common Agenda*, 1998.

Wales Council for Voluntary Action Policy, *Briefing The National Assembly - A Framework for Strategic Development*, 1998

Wales Association of Community and Town Councils paper to IWA community participation seminar group. June 1998.

Welsh Democracy Review, No. 3, Parliament For Wales Campaign, 1998

Welsh Office, *The Role of Community and Town Councils in Wales: a Consultation Paper*, 1992.

Welsh Office, *Modernising Local Government in Wales: The Agenda*, 1998.

Welsh Office, Modernising Local Government In Wales: *Local Democracy and Community Leadership*, 1998.

Welsh Office, *Sustainable Communities in Wales for the 21st Century. Why and How to Prepare an Effective Local Agenda 21 Strategy*, 1998.

CHAPTER 24

LOCAL GOVERNMENT

Sue Essex

The relationship forged between the National Assembly and local government will be one of the most, some would say *the* most, important indicators as to whether the new governance structure will work. The Assembly and local government are intrinsically wedded together. Both are the creation of central government and they have a common duty to the electorate of Wales.

At the same time the Assembly will have strong controlling powers over local government, not least in terms of distributing essential finances. It could easily assume hierarchical control and an attitude of supremacy. If this occurred the Assembly would lose a significant opportunity to create a new synergy of governance in Wales.

It is important therefore, at the outset, to establish the equal validity of both the Assembly and local government in the total governance structure of Wales. They need to reach a working accommodation and relationship that allows them both to respond to their own democratic mandates and to operate effectively together. At the very least this will be necessary to avoid confusion and duplication. Delivering a new political agenda in Wales will depend on the strengths of all forms of government working together as harmoniously as can be achieved.

CO-OPERATION OR COMPETITION?

Despite these aspirations, there are many who still have severe reservations that such a positive relationship can be achieved in practice. Indeed, such doubts were in the minds of the electorate during the referendum campaign. Many voters did not understand the need for more government in Wales, particularly following on the new structure created by the local government reorganisations of 1996. 'Do we need an Assembly as well?', 'Is there room for both?' These were frequent questions that did much to reduce the Yes vote in the referendum.

Many of these concerns were directly voiced from within local government itself. An important matter for Ron Davies as Secretary of State for Wales in the period leading up to the referendum was keeping local government on board. The support of Welsh local government leaders in particular was crucial. Antagonism and open opposition would have seriously reduced the chances of winning a Yes vote.

It is perhaps surprising that he should have been so worried, considering the Labour Party's long standing commitment to the Assembly. In fact, in 1989 the document on devolution agreed at the Wales Labour Party Conference that year, presented an Assembly as an initiative that would be supportive to local government, responding to a democratic need in Wales. Subsequent to that in the early 1990s the need for an Assembly as a strategic tier was frequently quoted by the Labour Party when opposing the then Tory Government proposals for local government reorganisation in Wales. The Labour approach was that Unitary Councils should only be delivered within the framework of an Assembly. However, despite this public position, in private many Labour Party members involved in local government expressed fears and misgivings about the Assembly.

Welsh devolution is about transferring powers from an appointed Secretary of State to an elected Assembly. On the face of it this should not present a threat to the integrity of local authorities. Nevertheless, there are fears that in practice, the role of local government will become downgraded and subservient to the Assembly. Paul Griffiths, of the Welsh Local Government Association, has stated, 'if an Assembly were perceived as a means of centralising power in Wales, imposing top-down standardised answers to local problems, then support for that Assembly would rapidly dissipate' (*Welsh Democracy Review*). The Constitution Unit's 1996 Report *An Assembly for Wales*, which provided much of the bedrock of thinking for the Assembly, acknowledged that the relationship between the Assembly and local government might be 'difficult'. The report identified four areas of potential friction:

- Finance
- Further local government reorganisation
- Strategic direction
- Raising standards

The Report suggested ways of achieving a better relationship, many of which have been followed through in the legislation – a legal recognition for local government, a protocol or compact with local government, the ability for co-option on Assembly committees and a joint liaison committee (which has emerged in the legislation as the Partnership Council).

A COLLABORATIVE APPROACH

Relationships between central and local government in Wales have significantly improved since the election of the Labour government in 1997. A concordat between central and local government has been signed, and a close working relationship has developed between the Welsh Office and the Welsh Local Government Association achieving considerable progress in joint policy development.

This change of approach must also be seen alongside the new Government's intention to modernise local government, expressed in a series of consultation papers published separately for Wales, signalling a different way forward. The Government's viewpoint is that active democracy, quantified by increasing electoral turnout at local elections, is central to giving local councils greater legitimacy. Poor turnout figures undermine local democracy - a consistent theme of central government politicians. It could also be argued that the 50 per cent turnout for the Assembly referendum suggests that apathy may be a problem for the Assembly itself. Consequently there should be an interest common to both the Assembly and local government in encouraging greater electoral participation.

The modernising local government documents also set out alternative arrangements that could be operational in local government. Considerations on the role of the executives, committees and backbenchers mirror the debates that have taken place in regard to the internal working of the future Assembly. One question that arises is whether there will be a movement towards compatibility of internal management styles between the Assembly and local councils? Would such a move help in promoting collaborative working arrangements between the two arms of government?

A central issue will be the way the Assembly undertakes the operational management of local government. Much of current Government thinking emphasise 'Best Value' concepts. Whatever form these eventually take, they will impose new disciplines on local government. Alongside the inevitable tensions that will accompany the dissemination of the block grant by the Assembly, such matters will test any 'entente cordiale' between the two tiers.

Above all, the Government is expecting local authorities to take on a stronger role of community leadership, thereby strengthening local identity and accountability. If the thrust of the recent consultation documents is followed through, there will be greater expectations of local government in terms of standards and effectiveness. However, in turn, local councils will have an opportunity to play stronger roles within their own areas.

THE ASSEMBLY'S POLICY APPROACH

The Assembly will come on stream three years after the upheaval of local government reorganisation in Wales. It will also inherit the new bargain on offer from central government to local councils, where effective service delivery and accountability is rewarded with more local autonomy. Co-operation between the

Assembly and local government will be determined by prevailing legislation, the attitude of the Westminster government and the new political culture and agenda in Wales itself. If words are to be believed the Assembly will be operating within the frequently quoted milieu of 'inclusivity'. With this in mind, the following considerations should be taken into account:

SUBSIDIARITY

To avoid confusion and instill some clarity in defining the role and responsibilities for the Assembly and local government, the principle of subsidiarity should be applied. This would allocate a clear duty of local government to its locality, endorsing the role of community leadership for the elected unitary council. The role of the local elected member should be enhanced and greater emphasis given to local government responding to community needs. In line with the consultations on modernising local government, this principle should result in more freedom and discretion at the local level for Councils.

At the same time the strategic direction of Wales should be the prime responsibility of the Assembly, setting both overall policy direction, for the Quangos and other agencies that remain as much as for local government. This critical division between strategic and local, based on the principle of subsidiarity should be used to counter the frequently voiced concern that an Assembly without primary legislative powers will inevitably encroach on local council business. In practice, however, strategy needs to be informed by what happens on the ground at the local level and there needs to be workable mechanisms established for this to happen. Subsidiarity should also be a critical principle for defining the role of the Assembly vis à vis the Westminster Parliament.

EQUAL PARTNERS

This twin approach must be based on a partnership of equals between local authorities and the Assembly. The recognition of the special relationship between local government and the Assembly was, as the Constitution Unit suggested, included in the legislation. The Assembly has a duty 'to promote local government'.

However, this does not make for an automatic partnership of equals, especially when one partner holds the purse strings and the purse. On the other hand the Assembly is dependant on local government delivering its policies on the ground and this dependency will be a strong card in the hand of local government. In reality a marriage of convenience is likely to emerge between the Assembly and local government, perhaps a marriage of necessity. Both partners have a vested interest in making the marriage work, not least because the public will not thank either side for a quarrelsome relationship.

MAKING THE STRUCTURES WORK

Defining the respective relationship of strategic and local responsibilities inevitably touches on some murky interfaces between the two which will have to be addressed. The Partnership Council laid down in the legislation is the obvious formal mechanism for effective liaison. Equally, the operation of the Regional Committees and the Subject Committees of the Assembly will also be extremely significant in terms of collaborative working between the Assembly and local government.

The role of the Regional Committees remains uncertain ahead of the establishment of the Assembly. On one hand, there is a concern that they will undermine a 'Wales wide' approach and work against integration. On the other hand, regional structures may well provide a useful spatial context for agreeing strategic priorities and co-ordination.

When the Regional Committees are set up by the Assembly, existing regional structures, like the North Wales Economic Forum, which links local government and other agencies, particularly the WDA, will already be well established. There is concern that the Assembly might simply absorb such existing institutions. This could prove one of the most difficult areas to negotiate. But it is important for public and business confidence that there is a consistent approach to the regional spatial structures if confusion and tension are to be avoided. The solution is likely to come from co-operation rather than coercion. Above all, Wales has suffered for many years from a lack of constant governmental cross-boundary structures at the regional level. One way or another, effective collaborative mechanisms should be established in a clear and accountable way.

So far as the Subject Committees are concerned, the Assembly should set up the mechanisms for local government involvement and dialogue. It is essential that local councils are involved in developing and setting policy with an avoidance of the client/contractor style of working relationship. The Assembly should take forward many of the precedents of joint working already established by the Welsh Office and the Welsh Local Government Association and also the collaboration that has been established with the voluntary sector and other agencies in Wales.

The need for an integrated (programme) approach has been advocated in the report of the National Assembly Advisory Group, to reflect the way that issues need to be tackled on the ground in Wales. In many councils this kind of corporate, problem-orientated approach, has been working over a range of issues for some time. However, they may not always match with the Assembly's priorities. For the programme approach to work, there needs to be a harmonisation and agreement at the outset between the Assembly and all its partners, particularly local government.

A NEW POLITICAL MODEL

Much has been made of the new approach the Assembly will need to take, to be listening, open, inclusive, and so on. It is likely that the public will be hard to convince of this new way unless their experience of government changes substantially. Although there is no evidence of high public dissatisfaction with local council service delivery, the referendum campaign showed there was no great enthusiasm for existing local government ways of working.

This has led to calls for a new political model in Wales. This would mean greater public involvement through dialogue and participation, which if it worked effectively, could infuse a new-style democracy. It is an exciting vision. Yet, throughout the current debate and stated enthusiasm for change, the role of the elected representative has been given comparatively little attention. Despite the Government's attempts to induce a modernising culture into local government, key questions around elected representation have passed by with little debate.

There is a genuine problem with the recruitment of councillors. There is generally an inadequate representation of the mix of population, and, not least, there are difficult questions concerning councillor renumeration. In Wales we have a culture where many local council seats are uncontested, where women councillors are considerably underrepresented, and where councillor renumeration frequently ends up as local newspaper headlines. All these issues need to be addressed if a working partnership of equals is to be established between the Assembly and local authorities.

CONCLUSION

Despite the newspaper headlines, and certainly during the early days of the Assembly, local government will be in a strong position. Three years after massive structural reorganisation it has survived, has continued to deliver local services, and for the most part councils have worked together well. In many areas local government has established reasonable working relationships with agencies such as the WDA together with civil servants and Ministers. It is also beginning to address, hopefully with some degree of determination, the key tests of local accountability set by the government, according to the 'Best Value' criteria.

Local government should therefore be in a strong and confident position in May 1998, in contrast with the newly elected Assembly members who will be finding their feet in an unproven political environment. Contrary to the popular local government fear, it could just be, assuming that it shows the right maturity, that local government can take the lead, show its new-born sibling, the Assembly, that being friends from the start is much better than competing aggressively. If co-operation does not happen, the public is unlikely to discriminate between the two. It will blame both.

References

Constitution Unit, *An Assembly for Wales*, 1996.

Sue Essex, *Does it have to be them or us?* Red Kite, September 1997.

Paul Griffiths, *A Welsh Assembly and Welsh Local Government*, Welsh Democracy Review, Issue No.2, 1996.

Local Government Information Unit briefing, *Modernising local government*, March 1998.

Welsh Local Government Association, *Local Democracy in Wales: The Implications of a Welsh Assembly*, 1997.

Welsh Office consultation paper, *Modernising Local Government in Wales*, March/April 1998.

Welsh Office, *National Assembly Advisory Group Recommendations*, August 1998.

CHAPTER 25

THE REGIONS OF WALES

Ioan Bowen Rees

The National Assembly has a unique opportunity to consider regions on the small scale which is endemic to Welsh historical geography. The four or five region approach adopted by the Quangos towards the end of the Tory regime, and substantially adopted by the Welsh Office for its four-region super-Quango (the new WDA), should not be allowed to pre-empt either the Assembly's advisory regions or the development of local government.

Neither should the Assembly's Regional Committees be allowed to take over the Economic Forums within which unitary authorities liaise with the Quangos. Any executive decentralisation of Assembly functions should use the unitary authorities as agents and pave the way towards subsidiarity within Wales. The role of the Regional Committees will be to influence the Assembly Cabinet and Subject Committees and press for a certain regional balance, especially within the Cabinet. Regions should therefore be chosen so as to facilitate consultation with grass roots bodies such as community councils and local voluntary bodies, as opposed to official bodies which already have channels of influence in their own right. This process will in itself enhance the claim of the new 'western and valleys' area for European Objective One grants.

Seven regions is the minimum compatible with a more inclusive view of Wales. Based on socio-economic criteria adapted to unitary authority boundaries, and open to further variation by local demand, these would reflect the growing divide between east and west. This has supplanted the traditional stand-off between north and south both linguistically and economically. Seven regional committees would help to focus the Assembly upon social justice and sustainability as opposed to the convenience of the Welsh establishment inherited from the Tories. By acting jointly where appropriate, they could help to stem the over-development of Greater Cardiff and question such 'eggs in one basket' coups as the £220m invested in the Korean LG plant near Newport. Regional Committees may not be crucial to the future of the Assembly but the choice of region will signal the extent to which it can attempt to redress the present imbalances and revive Wales from within.

THE SUPER-REGIONAL THREAT TO LOCAL GOVERNMENT

If any deep-seated feeling of belonging is the criterion, Wales probably has more regions than it has counties. If, as in Germany and Switzerland, we were to include one or two cities amongst our potential Länder or cantons, it would certainly be difficult to make do with less than twelve to fifteen. Most British-trained bureaucrats, and most big businessmen, are uncomfortable with the small scale which this implies. Yet it is, in fact endemic to the Welsh condition, as determined by geography, and confirmed by a history in which small units remained sovereign for centuries after England had become a single unitary state.

Well before the recent Tory reorganisation of Welsh local government – carried out without the benefit of either an expert commission or genuine public consultation – some of us expressed alarm that, far from bringing government closer to the people, the Local Government (Wales) Act 1994 was designed to group weaker local authorities into four or five sub-regions, dominated by the Welsh Office and its Quangos. According to the White Paper which preceded the Act imposed on Wales by the Conservatives, 'one of the main objectives' of the reorganization was 'to create a structure which removes unnecessary duplication' and which was 'capable of delivering services cost effectively and of offering the potential for efficiency gains'.

This was the very policy invoked by the Home Office in favour of larger police and fire authorities, and by the Welsh Office itself to justify amalgamating health authorities and Training and Enterprise Councils. With so many of the new local authorities in dire financial straits, we might well have seen a Conservative Secretary of State relying on the powers granted him by sections 33 and 34 of the new Act – perhaps the most draconian ever to threaten local government in Britain – to create new joint boards for services like education, or even new councils 'for all purposes'. The coming of the National Assembly may well spare us that but the Welsh establishment – frantic in every sphere in its efforts to pre-empt democracy – has touted hard and victoriously for a regional division within and under that Assembly which bears the hallmarks of Hunt and of Hague, and of a public service which has inherited eighteen years of humiliation.

The four-region division has now been adopted, not only by the Welsh Office for the super-Quango, but also by the National Assembly Advisory Group (NAAG) for the Assembly's statutory Regional Committees. It appeared in NAAG's Consultation Paper as Option A, which does not reflect a late decision to move the former district of Meirionnydd from north to mid Wales[1] (see Figure 1 overleaf). Apart from mid-Wales, each of the four regions is dominated by conurbations which have prospered in comparison with their hinterlands (Cardiff/Newport, Swansea, Wrexham/Deeside) while even in mid-Wales, the unemployment figures reveal a decidedly eastern bias. During the last financial year, the Newtown travel-to-work area - the location of the Rural Wales Development Board's headquarters - had the lowest unemployment figure in Wales, while Welshpool and Brecon were

FIGURE 1

The Four WDA Regions

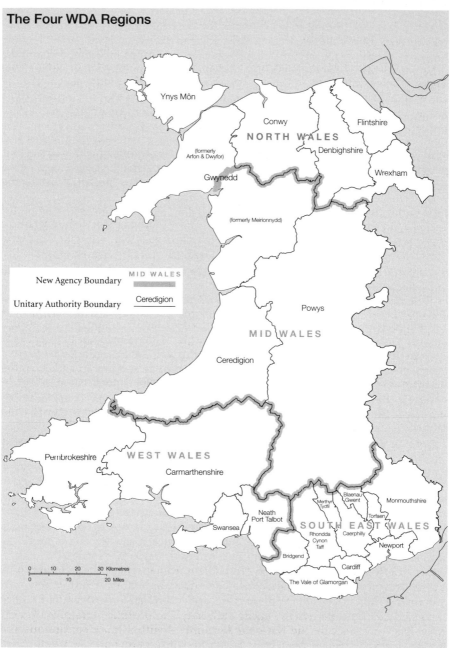

Ynys Môn

Conwy

Flintshire

NORTH WALES

Denbighshire

(formerly
Arfon & Dwyfor)

Gwynedd

Wrexham

(formerly Meirionnydd)

MID WALES

New Agency Boundary

Unitary Authority Boundary

Ceredigion

Powys

MID WALES

Ceredigion

Pembrokeshire

WEST WALES

Carmarthenshire

Blaenau
Gwent

Monmouthshire

Merthyr
Tydfil

Torfaen

Neath
Port Talbot

SOUTH EAST WALES

Swansea

Rhondda
Cynon
Taff

Caerphilly

Newport

Bridgend

Cardiff

The Vale of Glamorgan

0   10   20   30 Kilometres
0   10   20 Miles

Base map derived from digital data supplied by Lovell Johns Ltd., Oxford

the next lowest. Machynlleth and Ffestiniog, on the other hand, were ninth and tenth worst out of 34[2].

One cannot deny that, in the most difficult economic climates, any bureaucratic development agency will tend to concentrate on the easier, eastern options which share the attractions of Severnside, or Cheshire (the only English county outside South-east England which compares with that region in prosperity) or Shrewsbury. Equally, there is little point in having a Welsh agency at all if it cannot act on behalf of the west and the Valleys, not only as a matter of justice, or long-term sustainability, but as a matter of identity. It is in the west that, in spite of emigration and lack of opportunity, Welsh is still a community language (Figure 2 overleaf shows these areas within which the majority speak Welsh as heavily shaded or, where the proportion is over 70 per cent, black). It is the Valleys, their English just as glorious as their reviving Welsh, which created the city of Cardiff. All over Wales, it was the people of the regions who created a country which could, in all its variety, be identified.

One of the pleasant surprises of the White Paper *A Voice for Wales* which preceded the Government of Wales Bill related how the Assembly was expected 'to promote and foster local government in line with the European Charter on Local Government', a Charter which the United Kingdom has at last signed in spite of its supposed incompatibility with parliamentary sovereignty. If only in pursuit of subsidiarity, another, more legitimate, reorganisation of Welsh local government will be necessary sooner rather than later. This one must emphasise functions, finance and freedom to act, as opposed to boundaries[3]. Eventually, it is strong new local authorities which should take the lead, from the Community Council and, one hopes, Ward Council, upwards in determining – through the National Assembly – any regional level which may still be required within Wales.

In the meantime it is vital that, in creating the Regional Committees required by clause 61 of the Government of Wales Act, the Assembly neither damages the existing local authorities nor entrenches the recent regionalisation imposed upon Wales by the Tories and their Quangos, and now sadly adopted by Labour. According to the Act, the Assembly's Regional Committees will be purely advisory in character: they will not be competent to take over the existing regional forums or to develop regional executives themselves. Any regional administration which the Assembly finds necessary should be delegated to the local authorities as agents. In the case of some services like the maintenance of trunk roads, hospital and police administration, or liaison with the Development Agency or Arts Council regional tiers, the local authorities could well be grouped, for the time being, and act through one lead authority.

Agency of this kind is the norm in most liberal democracies. It helps to give local authorities certain economies of scale, to give the citizen a single point for information on a wider range of services, and to promote coordination between tiers. Agency both boosts the agent authority's importance and provides the principal – in this case the National Assembly – with a more continuous and realistic source of information and influence than inspection pure and simple.

FIGURE 2

Percentage of Welsh-Speakers, 1991

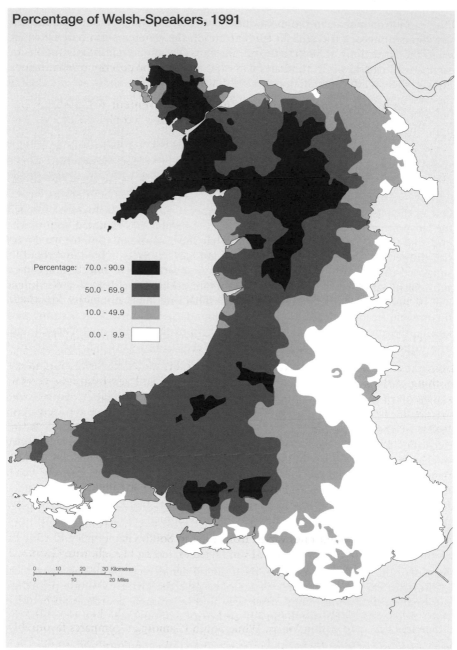

Percentage: 70.0 - 90.9

50.0 - 69.9

10.0 - 49.9

0.0 - 9.9

0   10   20   30 Kilometres
0   10   20 Miles

Source: Census of Population, Office of Population Censuses and Surveys.   Base map derived from digital data supplied by Lovell Johns Ltd., Oxford

'THE OTHER WALES':
THE WEST AND THE VALLEYS

Ideally, the National Assembly should have been given power to determine its own regional committee structure, if it felt that a body of sixty members needed them at all. There is certainly an argument for having as few as possible. While the WDA pattern will appeal to tidy minds, it takes experience on the ground to ruffle minds enough to comprehend the untidiness of reality.

The four-region option is probably the most convenient for professional administrators and party whips alike. It is certainly the sycophantic option. But was it for this that we created an Assembly? Did we not create it to be inclusive, and to bring succour to the neglected and the less fortunate? And at the same time to enhance and celebrate the variety within Wales? In delineating regions for advisory committees, is it not the most marginalized and deprived entities which should be given a voice first? According to a geographer as eminent as David Harvey, the problem in delineating regions is 'to design a form of spatial organization which maximizes the prospects of the least fortunate region'. He warns us against 'boundaries ... placed so that the least advantaged groups are so distributed, with respect to the more advantaged groups ... that whatever the formula devised for the allocation of resources the latter always benefit more than the former'[4]. What comfort is it to Amlwch or Aberdaron that the WDA has created another 200 jobs 'in north Wales', if north Wales usually means Wrexham or Deeside?

All over Wales, in terms of social justice, the east/west dichotomy is now far more important than the traditional north/south division. The later division stemmed from ancient history and became less relevant with the Industrial Revolution, to say nothing of the post-1945 rise of Cardiff as a cultural and administrative capital, and the steep decline of Liverpool. But it is not only the west which has been losing out. Or the 'Green Desert' between Llangadfan in Montgomeryshire and Defynnog in Breconshire. The south-eastern Valleys vie with the western peripheries for the worst unemployment and poverty record. In 1991, GDP per head was 92.5 per cent of the UK average in Clwyd, but only 76.4 per cent in Gwynedd; 88.3 per cent in West Glamorgan but only 75.5 per cent in Dyfed and Powys; and also 110.9 per cent in South Glamorgan, but only 69.4 per cent in Mid-Glamorgan[5].

Such differences are typical of at least the preceding decade or so, and they continue. In April 1995, for example, the average gross weekly earnings of full-time male employees on adult rates varied from £354 in South Glamorgan and £352 in Clwyd East, to £278 in Powys and £313 in Dyfed excluding Llanelli, with Gwynedd on £314. (The differences in female rates are much less striking but give a Welsh average of only £247, as opposed to £331.4 for males). According to Stephen Drinkwater, author of the latest Statistical Profile to be published in *Contemporary Wales*, a constant theme running through these annual profiles has been the vast differences that exist within Wales. While South Glamorgan 'compares favourably with the UK in most cases', Mid-Glamorgan's GDP has, as a proportion of the UK's 'reached an all-time low and is declining rapidly'. Low earning and high unemployment in west Wales is 'another area of growing concern'[6].

Why labour the point when Kevin Morgan and Adam Price's IWA July 1998 report *The Other Wales* concluded that 'the case for re-classifying Wales into a west-east configuration is unanswerable' – while 'west Wales and the Valleys bring together areas which may appear different in conventional terms but which suffer from the same extensive structural problems'[7] – and the Welsh Office itself accepts this grouping in seeking Objective 1 assistance?

Regional Committees able to focus on such differences will help but neither should we forget the immense differences within, for example, Cardiff (Ely and Cyncoed) or the old Gwynedd (Holyhead and Deganwy). As Raymond Williams so often argued, particularly *in The Country and The City* (1973), the urban and rural poor – together with the environmentally aware, and the Welsh language community as a whole – have a common enemy in the minority which uses severely restricted criteria in deploying capital investment. But only the west and the Valleys have the regional will to question both the conventional market philosophy of the Welsh economic establishment, and the orthodox urban Socialist view of the country, and enable the Assembly as a whole to see, in Williams' words, 'the country and the city within a single tradition'.

Our crachach have been thriving on comparatively easy investment successes on the eastern peripheries of Wales, and on the penchant of Secretaries of State to turn each major success into a spectacular public relations coup. One recalls that John Major himself found it convenient to cash in on the South Korean LG investment outside Newport. This was helped by a massive £220m WDA contribution which a National Assembly might well have chosen to put in more than one basket on account of the vagaries of international finance, the arms race in the Far East, and the skills shortage in south-east Wales, to say nothing of regional justice. It has been argued that more than the expected 6,000 jobs could have been created by an equal investment in small indigenous firms all over Wales[8].

The proliferation of committees in a small Assembly is generally to be deplored but Wales is simply too complex to be content with the four WDA regions. There is great potential for undue conflict or peripheral neglect within a unitary north Wales. Large regions could also facilitate isolation, or a tendency to look to Manchester and Birmingham ('north Wales' and 'mid-Wales') or dominance by one region (a monolithic 'industrial south Wales'). By way of analogy, a single French-speaking region in the west would probably have destroyed Switzerland, especially if there was a single German-speaking region to the east. There is little doubt that the existence of 26 small cantons (with more powers than Scotland will have) has helped to distribute growth. To consolidate the unity of the new Wales, we need a number of inter-locking regions, each looking in more than one direction, rather than three or four which can make some pretence to forgetting the rest.

During the 1980s, the author was involved in obtaining over £100m net of European Objective 5b funds for the Gwynedd, Dyfed and Powys Integrated

Development Operation. This Gwynedd County Council initiative faced byzantine obstacles at first and owed little to the Welsh Office and the development agencies until the later stages of the bid. From the point of view of Brussels, it cannot be helpful for the present government's long-term aspirations for European aid that its own recently announced super-Quango regions cut across the Objective 1 areas in the west and the Valleys. After all, in making decisions, the European Commission will be looking, not only for evidence of deprivation, but for decentralised management, 'integrated regional and social development strategies' and active, creative involvement on the part of the assisted areas themselves[9].

The traditional central government method of devolution within Wales was to quarter her, with Montgomeryshire in the north-east and Brecon and Radnor in the south-east, but that now seems too simple and too dangerous. Swansea is too powerful to be in the south-west proper and would, if assigned to the south-east, either make that region even more dominant or tear it apart. The size of Powys is still greatly resented in Montgomeryshire, at least, but 'mid-Wales' runs almost from the foot of Snowdon to the foot of Pen-y-fâl (the Sugar Loaf) above Abergavenny. Even so, the Development Board for Rural Wales, whose public relations purse and social fund virtually created the concept of mid-Wales, actually excluded the most deprived parts of rural Wales. It did no more economically for Meirionnydd than the WDA (which lacked PR as well as social powers) did for Arfon and Dwyfor.

Before 1974, most Dolgellau addresses were described as being in 'North Wales'. Since 1994, however, Meirionnydd has been destabilised by losing its district council without having its original county council restored, and that contrary to an explicit promise by the Conservative government. Different parts of the old county sometimes look different ways for different services. To the extent that Gwynedd as a whole is having to succumb to the north-east and the 'A55 corridor', Meirionnydd can indeed be forgiven for flirting with Newtown. Basically, however, as a high official confided in me, 'Meirionnydd had to be in mid-Wales to make up the numbers, which are small enough as they are'. As one might expect of a society which supported a county of its own from 1284 to 1974, and which has more than once led the way in Welsh politics, Meirionnydd nevertheless retains its identity. Politically, it has from time immemorial been a basic constituent of north-west Wales. Its people deserve greater recognition from the Assembly than they received from the Tories. In this, they symbolise those western and Valley communities which led Wales to devolution.

On the scale of British central government, there is simply no rational solution for central Wales. However, a single Powys/Dyfed unit could only have been conceived by the more primitive kind of accountant. Powys has a much bigger population than ten of the 26 Swiss cantons. It is large enough physically, and different enough, to have a Regional Committee in its own right. With no executive powers envisaged for the Regional Committees, the accountant is not involved in this decision. A Powys Regional committee would be small but a committee of three or four is often inferior only to a committee of one or two. In any case, clause 61(5)b of the

FIGURE 3

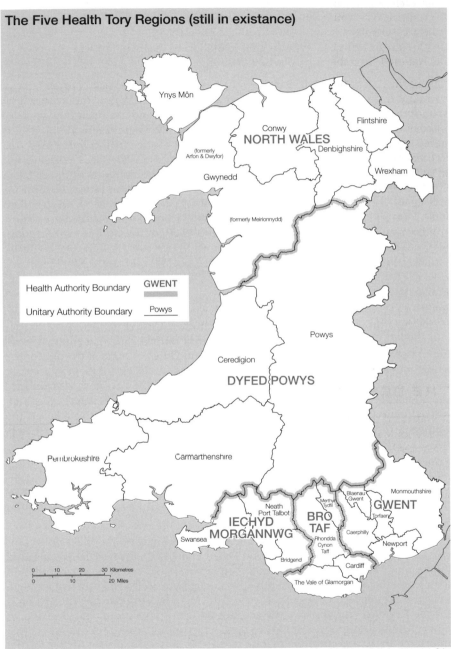

The Five Health Tory Regions (still in existance)

Ynys Môn

Conwy
NORTH WALES
Denbighshire
Flintshire

(formerly
Arfon & Dwyfor)

Gwynedd
Wrexham

(formerly Meirionnydd)

| Health Authority Boundary | GWENT |
| Unitary Authority Boundary | Powys |

Powys

Ceredigion

DYFED POWYS

Pembrokeshire
Carmarthenshire

Monmouthshire

Neath
Port Talbot
Merthyr
Tydfil
Blaenau
Gwent
GWENT
Torfaen

IECHYD
MORGANNWG
BRO
TAF
Caerphilly

Swansea
Rhondda
Cynon
Taff
Newport

Bridgend
Cardiff

The Vale of Glamorgan

0   10   20   30 Kilometres
0   10   20 Miles

Base map derived from digital data supplied by Lovell Johns Ltd., Oxford

Government of Wales Act empowers the Assembly to add up to four list members from each relevant European constituency to the basic membership of a Regional Committee. The south-eastern committee could include no less than half the 60 Assembly members. Even without a single list member, it would have a minimum of 18, enough to negate any lobbying by the other three committees proposed by the National Assembly Advisory Group.

One of the difficulties in devising regions within Wales is the lack of experience of so many influential parties of more than one part of Wales, the hold which stereotypes take in the absence of such experience, and the declining sense of history in the public service[10]. Before dealing with Glamorgan, perhaps it is necessary to state that two of the author's children were born in Splott and that another (Haverfordwest born but brought up mainly in Bethesda, Gwynedd) has lived in Cardiff for some years. A relative of mine was Lord Mayor of Cardiff in 1908-09 and the first Chairman of the City Education Committee. He and his colleagues expected to see the Assembly come to Cathays Park sooner rather than later. I am not sure how either the Lord Mayor or my Cardiff-based Super Furry Animal would sub-regionalise industrial south Wales today. Does one base regions on Cardiff, Swansea (where I used to visit my grandparents) and Newport, like the Health Authorities [see Figure 3], or just divide the Valleys from the coast (on one side, my forebears also ranged across the Valleys from Blaenau Gwent, via Merthyr and Aberdâr, to Ystalyfera), or do both? Will an inner south-west based on Swansea and Neath, and one Valleys region suffice to balance a south-east region based on both Cardiff and Newport? As in the past, a local government joint body will doubtless continue to consider strategic matters relevant to industrial south Wales as a whole.

THE DEMOCRATIC ALTERNATIVE

It looks as if the only choice lies between at least six regions and several more, and there should therefore be provision for joint meetings of Regional Committees, and cross-border observer membership (the lack of correlation between regional and constituency boundaries may give some Assembly members a seat on more than one: see Figure 4 overleaf). This would encourage alliances, not only between adjoining regions (the north-west and north-east pushing for railway electrification; the north-west and Powys taking the lead on rural issues)[11], but between distant regions with mutual interests (deprived Valleys plus deprived north-west and south-west).

Such alliances are vital to prevent Cardiff from concentrating as much relative power as London and Dublin. The example of Dublin – which included 35 per cent of the Republic's population by 1985, as opposed to 17 per cent in 1926 – is indeed alarming. In Europe only Athens has expanded to a similar relative size. According to Joe Lee's brilliant volume on recent Irish history, this owes much to administrative forces, for public administration in Ireland continued to be 'centralised to an extreme degree' after self-government, while local government

FIGURE 4

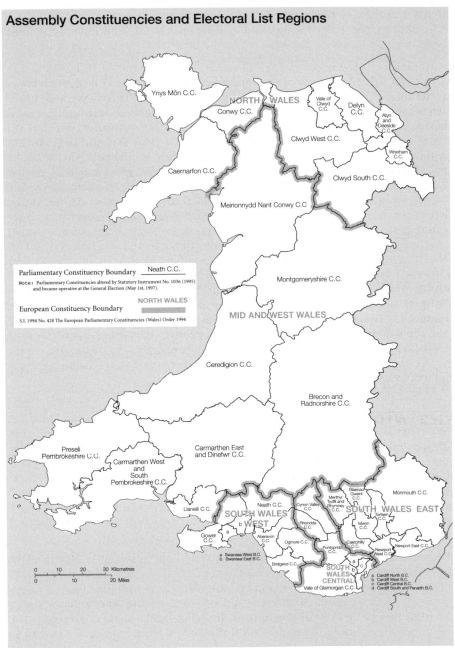

Assembly Constituencies and Electoral List Regions

Ynys Môn C.C.

NORTH WALES

Conwy C.C.

Vale of Clwyd C.C.

Delyn C.C.

Alyn and Deeside C.C.

Clwyd West C.C.

Wrexham C.C.

Caernarfon C.C.

Clwyd South C.C.

Meirionnydd Nant Conwy C.C

Parliamentary Constituency Boundary _Neath C.C._

Note: Parliamentary Constituencies altered by Statutory Instrument No. 1036 (1995) and became operative at the General Election (May 1st, 1997).

Montgomeryshire C.C.

NORTH WALES

European Constituency Boundary

S.I. 1994 No. 428 The European Parliamentary Constituencies (Wales) Order 1994

MID AND WEST WALES

Ceredigion C.C.

Brecon and Radnorshire C.C.

Preseli Pembrokeshire C.C.

Carmarthen East and Dinefwr C.C.

Carmarthen West and South Pembrokeshire C.C.

Blaenau Gwent C.C.

Monmouth C.C.

Merthyr Tydfil and Rhymney C.C.

Llanelli C.C.

Neath C.C.

Cynon Valley C.C.

SOUTH WALES EAST

SOUTH WALES WEST

Rhondda C.C.

Islwyn C.C.

Torfaen C.C.

Gower C.C.

a

Aberavon C.C.

Ogmore C.C.

Pontypridd C.C.

Caerphilly C.C.

Newport West C.C.

Newport East C.C.

b Swansea West B.C.
b Swansea East B.C.

Bridgend C.C.

a

SOUTH WALES CENTRAL

b

a Cardiff North B.C.
b Cardiff West B.C.
c Cardiff Central B.C.
d Cardiff South and Penarth B.C.

| 0 | 10 | 20 | 30 Kilometres |
| 0 | | 10 | 20 Miles |

Vale of Glamorgan C.C.

© Crown copyright 1997

Base map derived from digital data supplied by Lovell Johns Ltd., Oxford

continued to be very restricted, as I have observed in my own dealings with the City and County of Dublin[12]. Civil servants are disproportionately located in Dublin and the role of the state has increased to an unprecedented extent since 1970. All this has 'helped foster further the dependency syndrome throughout society'.

In an article on the impact of the Thatcherite experiment on Wales, Jonathan Morris and Barry Wilkinson of the Cardiff Business School recently divided Wales on the socio-economic basis shown in Figure 5[13] overleaf. This division into four rather more 'urban', and three rather more 'rural' regions, provides a useful starting point for a regional map, but is based on the former district council areas. Figure 6 adapts it to the present unitary authorities. However,one suspects that putting the comparatively rural new Monmouthshire in with any part of Powys (rather than the 'urban south-east') depends, if it is in any sense a starter, on Montgomeryshire joining the 'rural north'. Once one concedes departures from the present counties, however, Llanelli could go east, rather than west. In the 'urban south-east', it could be argued that natural centres are being cut off from their hinterlands. Unless the special problems of the Valleys are separately recognised, however, a very large south-eastern committee could, under strong leadership, prove a pain in the neck to a Welsh Cabinet even of the same party. Regions like the north-west and south-west are, on the other hand, microcosms in their own right, with their own small-scale urban centres. There is little point in forcing them into shot-gun marriages with partners from the east, for the sake of the illegitimate regional offspring of Tory ministers who could only mate with Quangos. In any case, the western regions and the Valleys are stronger runners from the point of view of European regional aid and, probably, sustainability. The sustainable region may be an elusive concept, but its proponents always emphasise the involvement and welfare of the population concerned[14].

THE WIDER AGENDA

Are we making heavy weather of all this? In my experience - particularly in Lancashire, when even the administrative county had a bigger population than Wales - regional or divisional committees tended to be served by the third team, to attract little interest, and even to wither away. On the other hand, ad hoc joint bodies tended to work when confined to a specific project to which all concerned were more or less equally committed. One example was the Gwynedd, Clwyd and Cheshire group which gained the support of British Rail, the European Commission and the Irish – if not, alas, the British – Government for a specific, costed, scheme to electrify the railway from Crewe to Holyhead.

The Assembly's choice of regions could nevertheless be much more significant than the purely advisory nature of their committees might suggest. At its worst, it could pre-empt the future of local government. It will certainly signal to all concerned how much difference the Assembly will really make from the point of view of the ordinary people of Wales.

FIGURE 5

Morris and Wilkinson's Seven Socio-Ecomomic Regions

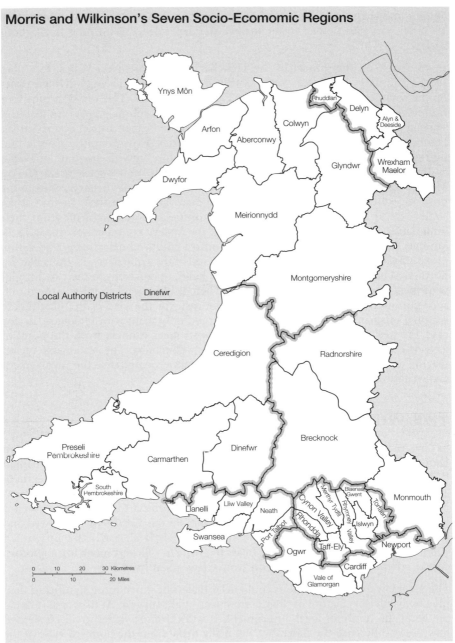

Local Authority Districts   Dinefwr

Base map derived from digital data supplied by Lovell Johns Ltd., Oxford

FIGURE 6

Seven Socio-Economic Regions Adapted to Unitary Boundaries

Ynys Môn

Flintshire

Conwy

Denbighshire

(formerly
Arfon & Dwyfor)

Wrexham

Gwynedd

(formerly Meirionnydd)

Unitary Authority Boundary   Powys

Powys

Ceredigion

Pembrokeshire

Carmarthenshire

Monmouthshire

Blaenau
Gwent

Merthyr
Tydfil

Neath
Port Talbot

Torfaen

Rhondda
Cynon
Taff

Swansea

Caerphilly

Newport

Bridgend

Cardiff

The Vale of Glamorgan

0   10   20   30 Kilometres
0   10   20 Miles

Base map derived from digital data supplied by Lovell Johns Ltd., Oxford

In spite of its immense majority, the new Labour government is finding great difficulty in shuffling off, not merely the mechanisms of its Tory predecessor, but its mentality. All over the world, governments which preach social cohesion are having to adapt to the hire-and-fire practices of the Washington consensus[15]. Even Mandela – like Mugabe before him[16] – is being attacked for making so few inroads into economic, as opposed to political, apartheid. Even the university sector is being gradually adjusted to the global market in services demanded by GATS (the General Agreement on Trade and Services), the World Bank and the OECD. This is a market in which it will become more and more difficult for universities to project unique identities and cultural values, to probe the weaknesses of the economic élite or to promote activities valuable in themselves [17].

One accepts that steering a ponderous state with an immense committed budget in a new direction is as awesome and delicate a task as steering a huge tanker into Milford Haven. One has to accept too that commercial globalisation has impinged upon the power of states to a degree which outlaws many socialist options. The doyen of European socialist thought, Jürgen Habermas, claims to be at a loss 'as we confront the destructive consequences of a worldwide capitalism whose productivity we do not want to give up'[18].

And yet the Washington consensus does include democracy amongst its tenets, the European treaties do emphasise subsidiarity, Habermas continues to stress that the legitimacy of the democratic constitutional state does give it a certain moral power, if 'only to the extent that all groups find access to the political sphere, that they all speak up, that they are able to articulate their needs, and that no one is marginalized or excluded'[19]. For many, this is the whole point of having the Assembly, and the Subject and Regional Committees which channel the views, not merely of Quangos and unitary authorities which already have access to government, but of community councils, local voluntary bodies, and Mrs Jones, Llanrug ... (see Chapter 23).

We must not let them governmentalise these committees in the way in which the executive will be governmentalised, to say nothing of the enlarged Welsh Development Agency and the officers of most political parties with a chance of office. There must therefore be at least seven, including the north-west, the south-west, Powys and thc Valleys, not in spite of the super-Quango set-up of four, so much as because of it. Regional Committees will, after all, advise on the whole Assembly agenda, including social policy, health, education in its proper broadest sense, the arts and, above all, the environment.

References

1

    a   According to Clause 61(3) of the Government of Wales Act, its Standing Orders must specify the regions and it is, in effect, the Secretary of State who will make the first Orders. A Standing Order can nevertheless be changed at any time by two-thirds of those voting on the point in the Assembly (Clause 46(4)).

b   Meirionnydd is used to being part of the area of the Development Board for Rural Wales - the devil it knows – but this is a demeaning precedent for education authorities, further education colleges, health authorities and Trusts and National Parks (the super regions split the Snowdonia Board, Meirionnydd's main planning authority and tourist asset).

2   Kevin Morgan and Adam Price, *The Other Wales, The Case for Objective 1 Funding Post 1999*, Figure 3.1, Institute of Welsh Affairs, July 1998.

3   See the the Cardiff University Devolution Group's Memorandum to the Welsh Affairs Select Committee Inquiry into Devolution, paras. 366 and 367. Also Ioan Bowen Rees, 'The Restoration of Local Democracy in Wales', *Transactions of the Honourable Society of Cymmrodorion*, 1993, 139-181.

4   David Harvey, *Social Justice and the City*, London 1973, 110-11. On Harvey, see Chambers Biographical Dictionary, 5th Ed..

5   'An annual review of economic and social research', *Contemporary Wales*, Vol.8, Cardiff, University of Wales Press 1995,Table 11.1, p.219.

6   'The Welsh Economy: A Statistical Profile', *Contemporary Wales*, Vol.9, Cardiff 1997, 170-90, esp. Table 10.15 and 'Overview.'

7   Morgan and Price, op. cit., pp.3 and 25.

8   According to Mark Atkinson in the Guardian, Gordon Brown has received reassurances in Seoul about investment in the UK but political unrest is causing a tumble in shares in Korea, while 'the economic downturn is only just beginning' (5 May 1998). See also Sion Barry, Business Correspondent of The Western Mail (6 May, 1998) on a recent University of Glamorgan Business School report.

9   Morgan and Price, op.cit., pp. 20-1, but the opinion about the Brussels viewpoint is my own.

10   See the warnings of as eminent and unromantic a historian as Eric Hobsbawm at the beginning of his masterpiece, *The Age of Extremes, The Short Twentieth Century*, 1914-1991, London, 1994, p.3: 'Most young men and women at the century's end grow up in a sort of permanent present lacking any organic relation to the public past of the times they live in. This makes historians ... more essential at the end of the second millennium than ever before'. Is this not particularly true of the public past of Wales?

11   See the Cardiff University Devolution Group Memorandum, op.cit., para.343 i and ii.

12   Joe Lee, *Ireland* 1912-1985, pp.559/62.

13   *Contemporary Wales,* Vol.8,Table 2.1, p.32.

14   See, for example, Paul Selman, *Local Sustainability*, London 1996, pp.35-6.

15   See Martin and Schumann, *The Global Trap*, English version, London 1997; and John Gray, *False Dawn: The delusions of global capitalism*, London 1998.

16   See Deborah Potts with Chris Mutambirwa, 'Basics are now a luxury: perceptions of structural adjustment's impact on rural and urban areas in Zimbabwe', *Environment and Urbanization*, Vol.10/1, April 1998, which confirms how World Bank policies have wrecked the comparative success of Zimbabwe's first decade.

17   See Jane Kelsey's article, 'Privatizing the Universities', based on the comparatively extreme experience of New Zealand but published in *The Journal of Law and Society*, Vol.25, 1, pp 51-70, March 1998, which is edited by Philip A.Thomas at the Cardiff Law School, though published in Oxford and Boston.

18   *Dio Normalitat einer Berliner Republik* (1995) trans.Steven Rendall as *A Berlin Republic, Writings on Germany*, Cambridge 1997, p.141.

19   Ibid. p.150.

CHAPTER 26

THE ROLE OF
THE WELSH CAPITAL

Phil Cooke

What is the role of a capital city? For a long time it has been said of Cardiff that it was never a real capital because to deserve such a designation it would need to house the national parliament. As Wales didn't have one, consequently Wales itself did not have a real capital, despite Cardiff officially being given the royal accolade as such in 1955.

The complications surrounding this last achievement bear examination because of the echoes that have resonated down to the present day concerning where the capital of Wales should be located and what its role should be. History repeats itself, said Karl Marx: the first time as tragedy, the second as black farce. He wasn't thinking of Cardiff at the time, but he might as well have been. We need to learn from this experience and try to ensure that history doesn't repeat itself a third time as something worse.

The first section of this chapter will summarise some key points about Cardiff's achievement of capital city status. Second, we will look at how Cardiff measures up against other capitals, particularly in Europe, where many other 'regional' capitals have interesting political histories and equivalent contemporary functions. Finally, we will explore some issues concerning the future, and the functions Cardiff needs to consider once the National Assembly is housed in Cardiff Bay.

CARDIFF: CAPITAL OF WALES

Wales continues to suffer from the effects of the Act of Union in 1536. While most of the Welsh and some of the Marcher English of the time spoke no language other than Welsh, the territory defined as Wales was annexed to England. So, to the outside world Wales was established, administratively and in terms of external perception, as a western promontory of England. The latter's royal and governmental capital was London.

Even the 'regional' governance body of the time, the Council of Wales and the Marches – given legal status by the 1542 Act of Union – met in Ludlow, Shropshire. One of the reasons for this, according to modern historical interpretation, is that Ludlow was geographically convenient for all parts of Wales. And although Ludlow was not among the bids to house the National Assembly, we shouldn't forget that, until the last couple of decades, the Football Association of Wales used to meet in nearby Shrewsbury for the same reason. Wales may well be unique in global and historical terms in having had its most convenient meeting place outside its borders. It has lacked a centre, and some still think Cardiff is a poor substitute, historically or culturally, for such a centre.

Again, perhaps uniquely, the cultural centre of Wales, the National Eisteddfod, is peripatetic. This makes us rather like a microcosm of the Holy Roman Empire,whose capital under dynastic heads like Charlemagne could, temporarily, move around as he did when he was on the road, governing.

Cardiff only became a city in 1905, but leading up to that event its breakneck expansion as the biggest coal exporting port in the world had given it a leading position amongst the urban centres of Wales. The optimism of its commercial class and the largesse of the Third Marquis of Bute led to Cathays Park being designed as a civic centre of world-class, with space reserved to house a Welsh parliament building on the site subsequently occupied by the Welsh Office. The City Hall, the Law Courts, the National Museum of Wales (now quietly and curiously advertising itself as the National Museum of Cardiff) and University all lent an air of splendour to the grimy city of commerce, perhaps despite rather than because of the will of Cardiff's cosmopolitan bourgeoisie. Martin Daunton's history of Cardiff stresses the abiding political antagonism between Cardiff's 'shopocracy' and Cardiff Castle in local politics[1].

On receiving city status, it was *The Western Mail* that suggested, unusually perhaps, given its imperialistic outlook, that Cardiff's recent commercial and even historical roots made it a logical choice to be the Welsh capital. This was echoing the views beginning to be expressed by Liberal politicians that Wales needed to see itself, like Ireland, as a nation, to seek Home Rule and, as a consequence, to think of an appropriate location for a capital to house its projected government buildings. After the Great War, *The South Wales Daily News* organized a ballot among Welsh local authorities asking: Should there be a Welsh capital? If so, where should it be? Ninety per cent answered yes to the first question, but although Cardiff received the highest number of votes, Caernarfon and others, such as Aberystwyth, also received strong support.

Following the vote, Cardiff's Lord Mayor put his foot in it by requesting the Home Secretary to designate Cardiff the capital of Wales. This produced a storm of protest, especially from Swansea, and the matter was shelved, leaving Cardiff temporarily wary of taking any more such cavalier initiatives. After the war, though, history repeated itself when Cardiff Corporation responded to an official request to Westminster from Caernarfon to be designated capital by pressing, once again, its own claims. Aberystwyth and Machynlleth piled in, drawing, like Caernarfon, on cultural and historical argument.

In 1951 the new Minister of Welsh Affairs, Sir David Maxwell-Fyfe made it clear to George Thomas, that he wouldn't recognise anywhere in Wales as a capital until there was a consensus from Wales as to where it should be. Cardiff and Caernarfon negotiated and, through a conference of Welsh local authorities whose association met in May 1954, a vote was taken with 90 per cent of the delegates, representing two million people, favouring Cardiff. This led to the official announcement on 20 December 1955. Gwilym Lloyd George, by then Minister for Welsh Affairs made the announcement and only Jim Callaghan sounded a discordant note: 'Dockworkers would be more excited if Mr. Lloyd George had announced that two more ships a week would be sailing into Cardiff to discharge their cargo'[2].

Outside Westminster there was resentment at Cardiff's stridency in making its claims. John Morgan, a native of Swansea, wrote in *The Observer* that 'Within Wales, Cardiff is not greatly loved ... it is an alien place to many Welshmen (sic) where Welsh is seldom heard'. Typically, however, and with a London editorial perspective, he went too far in questioning whether a nation without power needed a capital at all[3]. Such dissenting voices were drowned in the celebrations which brought 700 guests to City Hall, including the mayors of all the boroughs in Wales, chairs of the county councils, Welsh MPs and representatives of all the main Welsh societies and organizations. Harmony had broken out nearly everywhere and Cardiff's new rôle was represented in the letters patent from the Queen authorising changes to Cardiff's coat-of-arms. Thereafter Cardiff's heraldic supporters, the mountain goat and the sea horse, would display a gold chain and the royal badge of Wales.

CARDIFF AS THE WELSH CAPITAL

Cardiff has undoubtedly benefited from its capital status, but a key question is whether it has benefited Wales in the same way. With echoes to the present day, it is no coincidence that only three years after receiving capital status Cardiff was able to host the Empire Games in 1958. This advertised, at least to the English-speaking world, the fact that Wales had a capital even though the Empire Pool was the only lasting memento in the built environment.

The Games made a profit of £30,000 largely by using the Arms Park dog-track for the athletics, the Sophia Gardens ballroom (a converted air craft hangar) for the boxing and Maindy Stadium for the cycling. Still, the success of the Games built confidence. The city, unlike others of much greater size, was learning the responsibilities as well as the opportunities that come with capital city status.

By the 1960s, and with the arrival of a Labour government at Westminster, two very different kinds of opportunity presented themselves. Labour was committed to establishing a Welsh Office in Cardiff, something which had been boiling away for almost as many years as the question of the capital city for Wales. The offices of the Welsh Board of Health, built in 1938, became the home of the Welsh Office in

Cathays Park. Over the years it was greatly extended on the site originally proposed for the Welsh parliament, to employ more than 2,000 civil servants to administer the country. The Welsh Development Agency followed in 1976 and at its peak employed a further 500 well-paid public servants. Public administration for Wales was being concentrated more and more in Cardiff and large scale health and higher education facilities were also becoming major employers.

In the early years of the Welsh Office, a plan for economic development *Wales: the Way Ahead* (1967) was produced which advocated, amongst other things, urban renewal to offset the rundown of old industries in south Wales, for example, Llantrisant New Town, and mid-Wales, the expansion of Newtown. Most of its projections were wrong and the Welsh Office never repeated the exercise. However, the proposals also encouraged Cardiff to become a 'real capital city' by seeking to plan its urban environment in a modern way, with a major new city centre. It is an interesting sign of those times that to be a 'real capital city' meant having urban motorways and a massive indoor shopping centre rather than a parliament. These were the days of the Wilsonian 'technocrats' with grand plans for the development of 'Severnside'.

But although most of what was planned, such as Llantrisant New Town and the Cardiff Hook Road never got built, mainly due to popular opposition from those who would have to move or be moved to achieve their realisation, Cardiff did benefit from the development of the city centre as a high class shopping area, with the St. David's concert hall included. Cardiff, which lagged behind (many would say thankfully) modernising cities elsewhere in Britain, had begun to respond to Hook Road consultant Sir Colin Buchanan's sombre 1968 assessment that, 'Much of the city is either obsolete or likely to be so before the end of the century'[4].

The1960s and 1970s marked a shift in Cardiff's collective mentality as to what was involved in being a 'real' capital city. In the 1950s a civic-minded and inclusive attitude towards matters Welsh had been relatively pronounced. Now, however, the

TABLE 1

Jobs, GDP and Spendable Income, 1995

	Cardiff	Swansea	Next Highest	
Jobs*	157,000	76,000	57,000	(Newport)
GDP, 1995	£4.1bn	£1.92bn	£1.95bn	(Bridgend/Vale)
Spendable Income	£2.5bn	£1.2bn	£1.2bn	(Bridgend/Vale)
GDP (Wales=100)	125	99	112	(Wrexham)
GDP Share 1982	15.4	9.2	7.2	(Rhondda, Cynon, Taf)
GDP Share 1995	16.7	7.8	7.9	(Bridgend/Vale)

* full-time equivalent

Source: Welsh Economic Research Unit, Cardiff Business School [5] city turned more to providing commercial facilities that would draw shoppers, and theatre and concert-goers, at the expense of other urban areas within its hinterland. Cardiff also had its own commercial ambitions to satisfy and problems to deal with: in particular, the continuing decline of the docks and the closure of East Moors steelworks. It had become an administrative centre, providing services and leisure-related activities. To survive and develop it had to compete with other cities outside Wales, especially Bristol.

This led Cardiff through the 1980s and into the 1990s, to look abroad at other European cities with regional or small-country national capital city status. Cardiff is not a large city. Following local government reform, it is only marginally larger demographically, by some 16,000, than Swansea. This may not be unconnected with the verve Swansea showed in mounting a serious challenge to Cardiff as the location for the Assembly. But Cardiff dwarfs Swansea and all other Welsh unitary authorities on many economic indicators. Swansea does not always even come second, as the statistics in Table 1 show.

These Gross Domestic Product comparisons with the Welsh average and share of the Welsh total in 1995 are revealing. What is significant, in line with the earlier analysis, is that Cardiff's prosperity as a capital city has given it an even greater share of Welsh income since 1982. On the other hand, the relative prosperity of

TABLE 2

City Indicators, 1991

	City Population (000s)	Employment (000s)	University Places (000s)	Banks	Hotel Nights (000s)	International Conferences	Air Passengers (000s)
Amsterdam	703	320	38	66	4,024	45	16,147
Barcelona	1643	680	134	87	NA	41	8,280
Bologna	404	204	59	46	1,392	2	1,270
Cardiff	**306***	**190+**	**25±**	**18**	**547**	**6**	**638**
Copenhagen	553	391	77	45	2,515	27	13,059
Edinburgh	435	243	31±	35	4,050	6	2,610
Manchester	447	273	45±	51	3,980	2	10,146
Seville	680	310	52	41	1,700	3	NA
Valencia	753	319	85	52	980	NA	1,280

N.B   * 1997 figure   + includes part-time   ± 1995 figures

Source: Cooke, partially updated [7]

TABLE 3

Cultural Facilities

	Museum	Opera	Auditoria	Orchestra	Theatre
Barcelona	14	1	1	1	7
Birmingham	3	1	1	1	5
Cologne	20	1	2	1	10
Valencia	3	-	1	-	5
Seville	4	1	1	1	2
Copenhagen	15	-	1	1	3
Manchester	3	1	1	1	7
Edinburgh	3	-	3	1	6
Bologna	20	1	1	1	8
Cardiff	**3**	**1**	**1**	**1**	**2**

Source: RIR-WS Atkins (8)

Swansea has declined, so that it now contributes marginally less than Bridgend and the Vale of Glamorgan combined to the wealth of Wales. It is thus undeniable that Swansea would have benefited more in relative terms from the injection of investment associated with hosting the Assembly. In absolute terms, however, Cardiff is probably in a better position to retain income generated, because it already has more of the support services needed to enable day-to-day Assembly functions to operate smoothly.

It is when we look at the European comparisons in various regions and small countries that Cardiff is placed in a less prominent position. Table 2 summarises some key city indicators for selected European regional and smaller national capitals. In some respects, Cardiff's small population size affects its lower scores on many indicators except employment. Here, as Cardiff's evidence to the Welsh Affairs Select Committee on Devolution stated, Cardiff services a larger labour market than the city's population alone could sustain[6]. Thus, in 1991 54,000 people travelled into Cardiff each day from surrounding areas and, according to the same source, some 36 per cent of Cardiff's workforce now commutes daily from beyond the city's boundaries. So Cardiff depends on its neighbours and they, perhaps increasingly, depend on Cardiff, for employment. But on international measures, Cardiff's performance in attracting tourists, conferences and air passengers is weak, even compared with, for example Edinburgh or Manchester.

To continue the comparison with respect to cultural facilities, Table 3 shows how Cardiff compares with some cities from the previous table and some others. Again, Cardiff is revealed to be thinly provided with cultural facilities though, of course, the data are somewhat old and, with developments to occur in Cardiff Bay, Cardiff's position will improve for opera and has already for auditoria. Also the Chapter Arts Centre was missed by the Atkins survey and with its announced expansion into Cardiff Bay, may help improve the theatre statistics even further. Nevertheless, for a capital city with European pretensions, Cardiff really has a long way to go to compete in the all-important cultural stakes. To the extent capitals show the best a country has to offer while integrating the country by representing its diversity in cultural and other affairs, Cardiff and Wales clearly need to develop an ambitious future strategy for achieving this.

In the brutally honest results of a study commissioned by the Institute of Welsh Affairs from Coopers and Lybrand in the mid-1990s, a French government study which classified cities into eight categories was deployed (9). London and Paris were placed in category one; Milan two; Madrid three; Greater Manchester four; Birmingham five; Bristol six; and Cardiff seven, with Aberdeen representative of category eight. Cardiff's classification was based on size, but with less cultural or commercial and administrative attributes than cities in higher categories. The key indicators which helped it were possession of better than expected media and telecommunications functions upon which a future strategy could be built. For these indicators Cardiff ranked category four. An expert panel concluded that:

- Cardiff was perceived as small and peripheral with poor international links. The airport had inadequate scheduled services.

- Cardiff lacks corporate HQs and research and development activity while services are mainly public administration and back-office in nature.

- Cardiff is known for the Welsh National Opera and Cardiff Arms Park but its culture and arts strengths were citizen rather than tourist-focused.

- Cardiff's retail offer was seen as local and city-regional rather than having national or international appeal.

- Cardiff enjoys a positive image for quality of life.

The overall conclusion of the Coopers and Lybrand report was that Cardiff should seek development as a high quality city, with European significance in specific specialist areas. These included

- Development of arts, culture and media activity through WNO, Chapter, media/multimedia, developments in Cardiff Bay and enhancement of traditional architectural attractiveness.

- Development of higher education, innovative University-industry networks, upgrading of skills and qualifications. This will attract high value inward investment and jobs.

- Physical renewal to provide high quality sites and infrastructure, for example, Cardiff Bay, light rail, airport. 'Environmental City', and a coordinated strategy for the whole city region.

- Develop 'social justice' in the city by tackling crime, unemployment, skills shortages, urban regeneration and other social pathologies existing in pockets in Cardiff.

It would be churlish not to note that some progress has been made on many of these headings and Cardiff now has one of the UK's leading (top twelve) research universities and a strong medical school, both with industry networks. The arts and cultural assets of the city will improve with developments in the pipeline in Cardiff Bay as, to some extent will physical renewal with the development of the media/multimedia cluster in Mount Stuart Square. But non-road infrastructure and transport links to the airport have not improved, there is no city-regional strategy and Cardiff still has major pockets of social deprivation. As Wales' capital, Cardiff still has a long way to go to be the shining example of Wales and its best assets that a capital city normally aspires to be. Maybe now, with the arrival of the National Assembly, is the time for Cardiff to look not only inwards at its own needs and problems, and, perhaps, enviously outwards to gaze on the splendours of Barcelona or Bologna, but towards the country of which it is at last to be truly the capital, Wales.

THE FUTURE OF WALES' CAPITAL CITY

What is the role of a capital city? Eight features come to mind:

- A capital should *integrate* the diverse parts of its country. So Cardiff should be proud to demonstrate itself as capital to two main cultures, Anglo-Welsh and Welsh, and should strive to represent also its minority cultures, whether Asian, Afro-Caribbean or southern European. It could start by having a representative street-naming policy in new developments. It could promote, in its restaurant quarter, diverse cuisines as Madrid has Galician, Basque and Andalusian restaurants around the Plaza Major. It could aim to establish, in partnership, a Museum of Contemporary Welsh Art.

- A capital should be able, in a flexible way, through fairs, exhibitions and expositions to *represent* the best of Welsh inventiveness, creativity in business, craft-skills and produce, through hosting events which bring the outside world regularly to Cardiff and beyond into Wales to help Welsh businesses to further broaden their markets.

- A capital city should thus be a *gateway* into the country for tourists and business visitors who having tasted what Cardiff has to show, will wish to return again and again, to take advantage of the attractions both Cardiff and Wales have to share.

- A capital must be a *showcase* of all the best cultural facilities and talents the city and country have to offer in sport, opera, theatre, galleries, media and in terms of conferences on internationally-relevant themes.

- *Leadership* is expected of a capital city on initiatives, issues, problems and opportunities relating to the country of which it is the leading city, for example on north-south infrastructure links in Wales, and on light railway networks to nearby communities. It must try in consultation with others, to ensure not only that 'all roads lead to Cardiff' but that they also lead outwards from Cardiff.

- A capital should act as a *focus* by developing a talent for hosting national and international events such as special festivals, and local but not parochial celebrations of an artistic and cultural nature.

- It should, in many respects, seek to '*repay*' its constituent regions for the privilege of being the capital city with all the benefits that brings. Cardiff, as capital, could support, sponsor or subsidise local events in each county on a recurring basis – agricultural shows, eisteddfodau, minority cultural or administrative activities on a small, but locally important, scale.

- A capital city should, in all ways that can be thought of and as appropriate, express the *identity* of its country. It should display its differences from other countries but also its versions of common experiences with others in the past and for the present and future.

All this, of course, is a challenging agenda and calls for an associative, partnership-minded and even magnanimous mentality very different from that of the entrepreneurial, competitive outlook that has developed in the last decades. That is not to say Cardiff should not strive to be better but that it should seek to be co-operative with its fellow Welsh cities and counties.

Recently, Cardiff submitted evidence to the Select Committee on Welsh Affairs on how it saw the role of the capital city.[10] The 'gateway', 'showcase', 'leadership' and 'focus' functions were all mentioned and well-expressed. So, in different ways, were the aspiration for Cardiff to maximise the benefits to Wales from having a dynamic and energetic capital. The capital, their evidence says, plays a leading role in restructuring a country's economy. It may even have, as Cardiff seems to have developed of late, a potential 'locomotive' function in relation to its country.

So, for the present, Cardiff scores 50 per cent on the 'capital indicators' list. Understandably, it still shows signs of the old inward-focus which can leave the rest of Wales bemoaning Cardiff's stridency or 'selfishness'. Plenty of Cardiff institutions from the National Museum and University to the rugby club, let alone the County Council show signs of not wanting to lead the whole nation. Now is the time for Cardiff to set an example by offering a friendly, helping hand to all parts of the capital's domain.

References

1   M. Daunton, *Cardiff: Coal Metropolis*,1977, London, Arnold

2   D. Morgan, *The Cardiff Story*, 1991, Cowbridge, D. Brown.

3   John Morgan, The Observer, 25 December 1955.

4   D. Morgan, op.cit., p.241.

5   Welsh Economic Research Unit, *Local Prosperity in Wales: GDP Estimates for Welsh Unitary Authorities*, University of Wales, Cardiff, 1997.

6   Welsh Affairs Committee, *The Impact of the Government's Devolution Proposals on Economic Development and Local Government in Wales*, Vol. II, London, HMSO, 1998.

7   Cooke, P. (1992) *Cardiff, Making a European City of the Future*, a Report to South Glamorgan County Council, Cardiff.

8   Coopers and Lybrand, *Cardiff Eurocity, Cardiff's Potential as a European City*, Institute of Welsh Affairs, 1994.

9   WS Atkins, *Superlative European Capital*, South Glamorgan County Council, Cardiff, 1992.

10   Welsh Affairs Committee, op. cit.

CHAPTER 27

THE VOLUNTARY SECTOR

Peter Bryant and Jane Hutt

As a result of representations from the voluntary sector, the Government of Wales Act includes a measure requiring the National Assembly to have a scheme setting out how it will promote the interests of voluntary organisations. This chapter sets out the contribution made by the voluntary sector, the working relationship it should have with the Assembly, and the measures needed to ensure it is able to play a full and constructive part in the Assembly's work.

Voluntary action and volunteering arise out of the tradition of self help that is firmly grounded in the diverse communities of Wales. It forms an intrinsic part of the fabric of local communities, underpinning much of the activity and organisation that binds communities together. It provides a vital channel by which disadvantaged groups and communities can get their voice heard, and through which local community leadership can grow. It provides opportunities for people to come together to address society's challenges collectively and develop innovative approaches to providing the services society needs.

As pointed out in Chapter 23, the size and scope of the voluntary sector in Wales is formidable. There are an estimated 23,000 organisations engaged in some form of volunteering or community activity, involving one in three of the population. Together they have an annual turnover of around £675m. The Wales Council for Voluntary Action estimates that just over a million adults in Wales, that is about half, undertake some form of formal volunteering each week. Formal volunteering is defined as being carried out through an organisation or group. Once the figures take into account informal voluntary activity, that is individual activity taking place among friends and neighbours, around 1.8 million adults (83 per cent), do some voluntary activity every week This unpaid effort is valued at £2bn annually. Voluntary and community organisations touch on every sphere of public service, as advocates for improvement, engines for change and innovation, tackling social exclusion and promoting equal opportunities as well as providing sources of independent advice and mainstream services.

Voluntary organisations have been at the forefront of important campaigns such as disability rights, homelessness, domestic violence, environmental issues and AIDS, raising public awareness and providing objective analysis of the issues and potential solutions. Hundreds of community groups play a vital role in combating deprivation and regenerating their local communities. Over 400,000 enquiries are handled annually by independent advice services. More than 46,000 affordable homes are provided by the housing association movement. It can be seen, therefore, that voluntary organisations are an indispensable resource for policy formation and service delivery.

We now have a unique opportunity in Wales to create a strategic approach to public policy, one that addresses the needs of Welsh communities, builds on the best experience of representative democracy and incorporates the participation of local people through the organisations of civil society. In order to achieve a new framework for inclusive governance in Wales, fresh thinking is required regarding the Assembly's structures, and new ways of developing integrated policy programmes.

THE ASSEMBLY AND THE VOLUNTARY SECTOR

There has been a strong emphasis on inclusiveness, participation and equality of opportunity running through the proposals for the Assembly. The voluntary sector has a long history of tackling disadvantage and discrimination. It has been at the forefront of challenging the barriers which have excluded individuals and groups from influencing the process of government. It acts as a channel by which many otherwise disenfranchised and marginalised groups in society can get their voice heard.

The promotion of equal opportunities and openness across the Assembly's operations will create an expectation that people will be able to have access to the decision-making process in ways they have not been able to before. However, for this to work in practice people will need to come together and organise to put their case across. For many, this will mean engaging with the Assembly through voluntary and community organisations. Consequently, the National Assembly will have profound implications for the future of the voluntary sector in Wales. The Assembly will:

- Determine policy and priorities in the majority of areas of concern to the voluntary sector.
- Control, directly or indirectly, most of the public funding for the sector.
- Oversee or influence the activities of most of the agencies with which the sector works.
- Provide scope for a more strategic approach to the development and implementation of policy.

- Provide opportunities for voluntary organisations to inform policy and engage in constructive partnerships with the public sector.

- Create the potential for greater public involvement in the operations of government.

There are considerable potential benefits for both the Assembly and the voluntary sector in working together to achieve common goals. Voluntary organisations can help the Assembly to meet its objectives of participation and openness and contribute its experience to the development of policies and services. The Assembly can assist voluntary organisations by providing opportunities to represent their interests, influence policy and work in partnership.

In order for any of this to happen, there need to be robust and workable arrangements that enable the Assembly and the sector to engage with each other. It is vital that they agree the values and principles that will underpin their relationship and that this is based on a common understanding of the voluntary sector's role and contribution. It is essential that the Assembly has coherent and constructive policies for working with the sector and that these are implemented consistently across the Assembly's committees. There needs to be common agreement on what is good practice in working with the voluntary sector, for example:

- Voluntary organisations need to be involved in policy formulation from the outset.

- There needs to be objectivity, consistency, fairness and clarity in the administration of funding programmes.

- Partnerships need to be founded on the basis of equality and shared responsibility.

THE VOLUNTARY SECTOR SCHEME

For these reasons the Wales Council for Voluntary Action worked to secure an explicit measure in the Government of Wales Act for a Voluntary Sector Scheme. This requires the Assembly to set out 'how it proposes, in the exercise of its functions, to promote the interests of relevant voluntary organisations'. It goes on to state that the scheme should specify how the Assembly will provide assistance to relevant voluntary organisations, how this will be monitored, and how it will consult with voluntary organisations. The scheme will be drawn up in consultation with voluntary organisations and will have to be approved by the whole Assembly. In addition there will be an annual report on its implementation.

There is a parallel initiative on government-voluntary sector relationships arising out of Labour's Manifesto commitment to develop a Compact setting out how it will work with the voluntary sector. In Wales the Compact covers:

- Recognition of the respective roles of the voluntary sector and Government.
- Policy statements on volunteering and community development.
- Procedures for consultation, partnership working and funding administration.

The Compact will therefore provide a framework for the Assembly to build its working arrangements with the voluntary sector. It will not cover the practical arrangements by which the Assembly engages with the voluntary sector. These will have to be worked out once the Assembly is in being. However, the following will be essential for the effective operation of the Voluntary Sector Scheme.

A NATIONAL ASSEMBLY-VOLUNTARY SECTOR LIAISON COMMITTEE

The Government of Wales Bill states that the Voluntary Sector Scheme has to be agreed by the whole Assembly and cannot be delegated to a sub committee. To have credibility it will also have to gain the approval of the Welsh voluntary sector. There is therefore a need for a joint body to oversee the implementation and working of the Voluntary Sector Scheme.

It is proposed that this should be undertaken by a joint liaison committee made up of members of the Assembly and elected representatives of the sector. The liaison Committee should report to the Assembly's Executive Committee and the Executive Committee of the Wales Council for Voluntary Action.

There should be an Assembly Secretary with responsibility for the voluntary sector and this person should chair the liaison committee jointly with a nominated voluntary sector representative.

It is essential that the joint liaison committee comes under the auspices of the Assembly's Executive Committee if the scheme is to be owned and implemented consistently across the Assembly's structures. Any other arrangement would not carry sufficient authority within the Assembly, nor would it command credibility within the voluntary sector in Wales.

The joint liaison committee would also act as a point of contact on broad issues of policy and practice that affect the voluntary sector in general. In this respect it would succeed the Voluntary Sector Forum that has been set up as an interim measure to draw up the Compact and discuss policy issues. The voluntary sector representation on the liaison committee will need to cover the broad spread of subject interests within the sector.

WORKING WITH THE ASSEMBLY SECRETARIES AND COMMITTEES

In order to implement the Voluntary Sector Scheme effectively, the Assembly Secretaries and Subject Committees will need to set out how they will develop constructive working relationships with the voluntary organisations that have an interest in their areas of responsibility. Recognising that the secretaries and committees will have a heavy work load it is important that these arrangements assist them in their tasks and are not overly cumbersome.

This would be assisted by a programme approach to key issues that would benefit from the combination of strategic thinking across policy areas and dedicated funds to produce more effective decision-making, greater cooperation between agencies and more efficient use of resources. Programme committees should be set up to plan and implement strategic programmes, reporting directly to the Executive Committee with dedicated budgets and involving the relevant Subject Committees and other sectors.

As a first step it is proposed that each Assembly Secretary and Subject Committee meet with the relevant voluntary sector networks and umbrella bodies and agree practical arrangements for dialogue and co-operation in line with the Voluntary Sector Scheme.

These should cover:

- Exchange of information and views on developments in Assembly policies and priorities.

- Informing the Assembly of developments and concerns identified by voluntary organisations through their work.

- Participation in working groups to develop new policies and strategies.

- Consultation on policy and new strategic programmes.

- Agreeing on co-operation in implementing programmes.

- Dealing with administrative arrangements for funding programmes.

- Agreeing an approach to monitor the results of joint action.

It is the voluntary sector's responsibility to develop the structures it needs to relate to the Assembly committees. Several parts of the sector already have a national umbrella organisation to represent their interests. Others have less formal forums that serve a similar purpose. Significant parts of the sector have no such structures as yet and new arrangements may have to be created where they do not already exist. A significant proportion of voluntary organisations will relate to more than one Assembly committee.

It should therefore be possible to build on existing voluntary sector structures and identify a voluntary sector constituency to relate to each policy portfolio. Whatever arrangements emerge it is essential that they incorporate the principles of fair and open access and equality of opportunity.

PANELS OF ADVISORS

The Assembly Secretaries and Subject Committees will wish to take advice and evidence from outside experts and to involve them in working groups to advise on policy and strategy. The voluntary sector should respond positively to this by setting up panels of advisors covering a range of expertise that can be called on as needed and chosen according to equal opportunities criteria reflecting the diversity of Wales.

These individuals would have a responsibility to keep abreast of voluntary sector developments and perspectives and feed back to the sector on their discussions. Advisors might offer advice on a regular or occasional basis to the whole committee, or they might be chosen for time limited but intense pieces of work on a task group.

The membership of the panel should be reviewed annually and there should be safeguards to ensure that the independence of the advisors is maintained. Such an arrangement has the advantage of being able to respond quickly to calls for advice or membership of working groups. It also creates a cadre of people in the voluntary sector familiar with the working practices and developing policy agenda of the Assembly.

A VOLUNTARY SECTOR CENTRE

The creation of a National Assembly presents the voluntary sector with opportunities for greater influence on policy as well as greater scope for collaborative ways of working. For this to be realised voluntary organisations will need effective communication links with the Assembly to keep informed of forthcoming business and to brief members, secretaries and committees on issues they wish to raise.

In reality relatively few organisations will have the resources to employ dedicated Assembly officers or to engage professional lobbyists to undertake these tasks. If the Assembly is to fulfil its objectives of participation and inclusiveness it will be necessary to put in place accessible arrangements to assist voluntary and community organisations, irrespective of their size, to access the Assembly's machinery. To achieve this a voluntary sector information and support centre should be established close to the Assembly building. It would:

- Provide an information service on the work of the Assembly, tailored to the needs of voluntary organisations and alerting them to the potential impact of Assembly policies.

- Provide briefings and advice for voluntary organisations on how the Assembly operates and how best to take their issues through the system.

- Provide Assembly Members with information about the sector, briefings on its key issues and priorities and relevant contacts in the sector.

- Provide a convenient and informal setting for Assembly Members and voluntary organisations to meet.

- Assist in arranging meetings for voluntary groups when needed.

- Work with the key voluntary sector networks and umbrella organisations to put in place the liaison arrangements necessary to implement the Voluntary Sector Scheme.

It is important that such a service is located close to the Assembly building if it is to develop the contacts and relationships necessary to make it work. From a purely practical viewpoint, busy Assembly Members and officials will not want to leave the area to attend meetings elsewhere. This Centre would meet all the criteria necessary to ensure it is fully accessible according to the guidelines set by Disability Wales. The Wales Council for Voluntary Action, on behalf of the sector, is seeking the funding for the operation of this facility.

CHAPTER 28

THE ASSEMBLY
AND WHITEHALL

Ivor Lightman

As in many other areas, it is impossible to prescribe with any certainty the ways in which relations between the Assembly, its civil servants and their colleagues in Whitehall might develop. The Government of Wales Act provides little guidance in terms of detailed arrangements. Such material as is available so far emerges primarily from the White Paper *A Voice for Wales*; from statements by Ministers in reply to Parliamentary Questions; from points made during the debates during the Committee Stage of the Bill in the House of Commons; and from internal guidance to Welsh Office civil servants that was circulated in early 1998. Of course, once it is established the Assembly itself will have to grapple with its relationship with the central government machine in a situation which will be new and untried for both.

This chapter considers what is known in advance of the Assembly's first meeting and moves on to areas in which the foundations for a constructive set of relationships can be laid. The first questions are who will constitute the 'civil service' (in inverted commas at this stage at least) of the Assembly and what will be the formal and informal basis of their influence on behalf of the Assembly with Whitehall.

THE CIVIL SERVICE

The White Paper states that the staff of the Assembly will be members of the Home Civil Service, and this is repeated in clause 35 of the Act in terms of status, pay systems and management. The large majority will be transferred from the existing Welsh Office simply because this is where the expertise and experience currently lie. But this need not be a continuing requirement, and no doubt more staff will move across from the Agencies. Others will be recruited from other bodies and perhaps directly as time passes, both for political reasons and in order to enlist skills and experience that may not exist within the civil service. As for their status, it is worth repeating here some of what is said on the matter in the *Guidance to Civil Servants* that was issued to staff of the Welsh Office in February 1998 and copied to all Welsh MPs by way of further elaboration on what was in the White Paper. In addition to matters concerning salaries and conditions of service, this describes their relations with Whitehall in the following terms:

Inter-departmental mobility

Mobility between Whitehall and the National Assembly for Wales will be encouraged. Indeed, a more active programme of inter-departmental mobility, at all levels, than currently exists is likely to be needed to sustain the unity of the Home Civil Service. Similarly, the role of the Senior Civil Service in promoting cohesion, sustaining key values and developing staff will become increasingly important.

Constitutional, political and propriety considerations

The Civil Service Code says that civil servants 'owe their loyalty to the duly constituted government'. In practice, their day-to day loyalty is to their departmental Minister. Constitutionally, the position of the Civil Service will be unchanged by devolution. While the ultimate loyalty of civil servants will remain to the Crown, in practice the loyalty of individual civil servants will be to whichever administration they are serving. Individual civil servants will continue to take their instructions from the Assembly as a whole, or from its Committees or Assembly Secretaries, to the extent that the Assembly has delegated powers to them.

The document goes on to comment on the resolution of disputes between civil servants in Whitehall and Wales, thus:

'Close co-operation between civil servants in Whitehall and Wales will minimise the risk of disputes between them. But it is inevitable that differences will arise from time to time. For example, Westminster may dispute the legal competence of the devolved body to take a particular action. Assembly members may adopt policy positions within their legal vires that create difficulties for the UK government, and vice versa. The civil service will need to adapt to the fact that the power-sharing nature of the constitutional settlement is likely to add a more public and political dimension to the conduct of government.

There will be formal, statutory procedures for dispute resolution between the UK Government and the Assembly. In the event of dispute about the legal competence of the Assembly which cannot be settled by agreement between the

Assembly and the UK Government, the Attorney General and the Assembly will each have the power to refer the matter to the Judicial Committee of the Privy Council for decision. Guidance will be issued at the appropriate time about how Assembly officials should handle disputes such as these'.

That is the relevant part of the official guidance issued so far. None of it, however, appears in the Act as it has emerged from Parliament. Nonetheless, it is established that the staff of the Assembly will be classed and employed as Home Civil servants and will be subject to the same rules of conduct as their peers in the rest of the Service. This leaves to be made clear the detailed working relationship between the Assembly's staff and their counterparts in Whitehall. It also leaves less than entirely clear how the Assembly's civil servants will view themselves in relation to their counterparts in Whitehall. In particular, it begs the underlying question, which is whether they will see themselves in reality as being part of a single structure with a common set of loyalties, or whether instead they will see themselves as part of an organisation which is politically quite separate from 'the government' in Whitehall and may indeed on occasions be in conflict with it. If so, this might have the effect of making the exchanges described as being desirable rather more difficult in practice for people expected to move freely between the two 'sides'.

This official advisory material seems to reveal a 'closed shop' attitude, implying that recruitment to the Assembly's civil service will be confined to the ranks of the existing Home Civil Service. But given the inevitable desire of elected Assembly members to be masters in their own house, it should be recognised that the question of divided and perhaps conflicting loyalties can be expected to become increasingly real as time passes.

Indeed, this issue was raised during the Commons Report stage of the Bill. Not only will civil servants themselves feel the push-pull of their disparate traditional and new obligations, but it must be anticipated that Assembly Secretaries and Members will expect their staffs to be single-minded in their loyalties to them. When this gives rise to strains, the Assembly must surely be expected to decide to augment – or even replace – some of its 'old civil service' staff members by people meeting its own specifications and coming from what might be considered to be more appropriate backgrounds.

The task of accommodating such people within the requirements of Home Civil Service status will not be easy. It may be that the distinct nature of the Assembly's civil service will, over time, come to be more formally recognised along, perhaps, the lines of the independent Northern Ireland civil service. Ted Rowlands, MP for Merthyr, identified this issue during the Report stage debate when he referred to officials coming to Whitehall from the Welsh Office or the Assembly not having a common allegiance, but having separate relationships and loyalties, and reflecting the different priorities and political interests of their new masters.

CONCORDATS

Leaving that very wide issue aside, it is clear that in any event a single framework applying equally to all Whitehall Departments is not a practical proposition. There will need to be developed a 'tailored' relationship between the Assembly's civil servants and their opposite numbers in each Whitehall department. The Assembly will have no experience (and few precedents of any value) to draw upon and will need, within the framework provided by the Act, effectively to make up the rules as it goes along. So indeed will Whitehall, and it would be unsurprising to find that those involved are already finding it necessary to adapt and adjust to what they see approaching on the horizon.

Here enters the concept of 'concordats', and since these will be critical to the effective development of a constructive and mutual set of understandings it is worth repeating here the reference to the matter in paragraph 3.40 of the White Paper *A Voice for Wales*, thus:

> *'The Assembly will need to work in close partnership with those Whitehall departments that are responsible for developing policies or preparing secondary legislation on matters which, in Wales, will be dealt with by the Assembly. The Assembly's officials and their counterparts in Whitehall will consult each other on the timing and content of secondary legislation. The basis of these consultations will be set out in concordats'.*

Now these concordats appear nowhere in the government of Wales Act and will therefore be non-statutory. It follows that although the Welsh Office has issued guidance about the basis on which they are to be framed, it will be for the Assembly itself to agree the terms of each concordat (for signature, except in particularly difficult and politically contentious areas, by its civil servants). That said, the basis of the concordats has been set out in a Parliamentary Reply in February 1998 which is annexed to this chapter. No doubt this will be the text upon which the actual concordats, as they are negotiated, will be based once the Assembly is in being (see also Keith Patchett's discussion of concordats in Chapter 7).

A question that emerges is whether the officials in Whitehall and Cardiff who have to form this close relationship will be prepared, or allowed by their political masters at both ends of the M4, to speak as freely to one another as they do at present within the Whitehall 'family' of which both are an integral part. Will they, in short, be regarded as 'one of us' or will they be seen, as is suggested above and especially in difficult and contentious areas of policy, as representing an outside body operating very much at arm's length?

One says nothing at this point about the distinct possibility that even at the outset, the Assembly may have something of the character of a coalition, with the Labour party not being in a position to govern Wales without support from a minority party or parties. The political divide may of course be even wider at some point in the future. To illustrate the variety and range of policy areas in which the relationship will have to develop, Figures 1 and 2 below appear in House of Commons Research Paper 97/132, which is in turn based on a paper by Keith Patchett which appeared in the Institute of Welsh Affairs journal *Agenda* for winter 1996/7. These indicate the activities that will require a variety of levels of consultation and collaboration between Cardiff, Westminster and Whitehall as the new regime comes into operation.

As has been said, the concordats will have no legal force, and there is no reference to them in the Act. Nevertheless, they will reflect the complex and varied pattern of links between, under the present dispensation, the Secretary of State, the Welsh Office and their Whitehall counterparts over the whole range of activities. These extend from primary and secondary legislation to other policy issues affecting both sides but not necessarily involving legislation at all. In future, there will be an equally complex and in many respects unpredictable pattern of links between the

FIGURE 1

Wales' influence in Whitehall under the Welsh Office

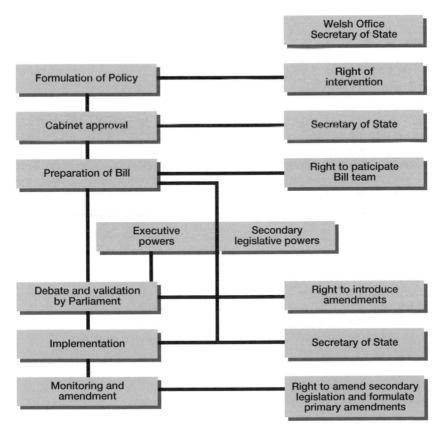

FIGURE 2

Wales' influence in Whitehall under the National Assembly

Assembly itself and Whitehall. The basic elements, as far as they can be discerned at this point, were outlined by the former Secretary of State, Ron Davies, during the Second Reading Debate on 8 December 1997 (*Hansard*, col 682), in the following terms:

> *'Once the Assembly is established, the Secretary of State will have a continuing role to represent Wales in the Cabinet, to liaise with the Assembly, and to develop the important non-statutory concordats that will be the foundation of the relationship between Government Departments and the Assembly. In addition the concordats will set out the role of the Assembly in the policy discussions that settle the UK line for European negotiations on matters in*

which it has an interest and, beyond that, its participation in relevant meetings of officials or politicians, including the Council of Ministers ...

' ... The Assembly First Secretary or the appropriate Assembly Secretary will be able, with the agreement of the lead UK minister, to take part in the UK delegation and relevant meetings and will be able to speak on behalf of the delegation according to the previously agreed UK line'.

If, then, the concordats are indeed to be the foundation of the Assembly-Government relationship, it is clearly of the highest importance, in terms of developing mutual confidence, that as experience develops, those at both ends of the spectrum - Whitehall and Cardiff - should know, in the clearest terms, what the words of the concordats mean and should be able to assess whether, in practice, they are being honoured or not. This may smack of an atmosphere of mutual suspicion, but unworthy as that might be, it would be unwise to ignore reality. Be that as it may, the task of drafting concordats in the absence of practical experience will be difficult.

It is essential that the Assembly should be able to scrutinise each of the concordats in detail before they are signed to ensure that their extent – and their limitations – are fully understood and accepted. This was acknowledged by the former Secretary of State Ron Davies during the Committee Stage debate, and he added that,

'... there will not be one great concordat ... but there will be one for each Department. There will be a series of concordats'.

The point he was making was that the concordat for each department, while following the same general principles, will have to reflect the area of policy with which that Department is involved so that, for example, the concordats with the Treasury, the Department of Trade and Industry, and indeed the Foreign Office will be substantially different from one another and will no doubt have to be modified as experience develops. In the process, Ministers and Assembly Secretaries as well as civil servants will be involved, since the concordats will embody political balances as well as working relationships within and between bureaucracies.

THE SECRETARY OF STATE

All this was said, of course, before the decision was announced that the Assembly should be constituted on the Cabinet system. Leaving that aside, it is clear that the role of the Secretary of State will be a subject of contention and debate between him and the Assembly. The right of the Secretary of State to participate directly in the deliberations of the Assembly may well give rise to a jockeying for position between the two during the Assembly's formative months. The Secretary of State's position as a member of the UK Cabinet, together with his pre-existing links with colleagues in Westminster and Whitehall during the period when the Assembly will not have had time to establish itself firmly on the wider political scene, will ensure his continuing power and no doubt exacerbate the inevitable tensions within the Welsh political scene. To cite the Institute's December 1997 publication *Making the Assembly Work*, 'there is a danger that in the formative years functions and procedures may be arrogated from the Assembly to the Secretary of State' (para. 4.3). While he is unlikely to have a large staff after the bulk of the Welsh Office's functions have been transferred to the Assembly, this is a temptation that will need to be watched and the separation of powers jealously guarded.

The question of the role of the Secretary of State is of great significance. The critical proposal in the *Voice for Wales* White Paper was that the Secretary of State should be able in his own right to attend meetings of the Assembly and participate in its debates, but not to vote (para 1.18). Yet despite the acknowledged case for a close relationship during the formative period, it is essential that the autonomy of the Assembly should be established, and clearly seen to be established, from the first day of its existence. If the Assembly were seen to be led by a senior member of the Westminster government, for however short a period, it is difficult if not impossible to imagine how he could avoid being seen to dominate the Assembly's policy in the interests of the government of the day. In its report *Making the Assembly Work* the Institute's Constitution Working Group discussed this matter and concluded that the Secretary of State's role should be confined to being invited to attend and address the Assembly rather than having the right to attend and participate in its activities (para 4.16). The same point was made repeatedly during the final debate before the Bill received Royal Assent. It was suggested that even if the government were not prepared in principle to accept the objections to the dual mandate, they should formally limit the transitional period during which the Secretary of State could also serve as Leader of the Assembly to a matter of a few months. This would help avoid the danger, referred to above, of arrogation of authority resulting from the Secretary of State's powerful dual role, which would give entirely the wrong message to the Welsh people about the position of the Assembly as an expression of a distinct element, within the United Kingdom, of Welsh identity.

In the medium term, which may be sharply contracted, the emergence of the Joint Ministerial Committee within the UK Cabinet Office, discussed in the following Chapter, must throw a large question mark over the continuation of the office of Secretary State. As John Osmond asks, at the end of his Chapter, will there be room for both the Assembly's First Minister and the Secretary of State as members of the Joint Ministerial Committee?

SECONDARY LEGISLATION

To turn to the volume of work that is currently the responsibility of the Welsh Office and will transfer to the Assembly in the first days after it comes into being, one can at least see something of the legislative load that the Welsh Office carries at present in terms, at least, of secondary legislation. The Welsh Office explains, for example, that in 1995 the Secretary of State made 93 Statutory Instruments, and that other Secretaries of State made a further 274 on matters that could be transferred to the Assembly under the new regime.

While the past pattern has been for most secondary legislation emerging from the Welsh Office to depart from the English pattern in terms of little more than the signatures at the end of the documents (and this may continue for many areas in the future). However, it must be expected that the areas of difference, so to speak, will widen over time. Much secondary legislation may be made by the Assembly itself on matters of exclusive concern to it. On these matters, therefore, there will be little involvement by Whitehall despite consultation with and the provision of information to Whitehall at one level or another, under the terms of the relevant concordats.

More problematic is the area where English Departments will be preparing primary legislation which may involve Welsh consequences, for example by necessitating Welsh-only secondary legislation. But in both cases – primary and secondary legislation – and indeed in respect of matters where legislation may not be involved, the need for collaboration is nonetheless clear. It is obvious that a relationship, not between equals perhaps, but certainly between independent partners with a common interest in good administration, the closest links through consultation, collaboration and contacts at every level will be more than ever necessary.

CONCLUSION

This chapter has been written, if not in a vacuum, then at a point when the National Assembly has yet to be elected. The Act has established the statutory framework within which the Assembly will be presented with its powers. However, its duties and the limitations on its powers, its working arrangements and relationships with Whitehall, with the Agencies, with Europe and with the myriad interests in between, have barely been sketched in outline. Nevertheless, the Act does offer a starting point, and whatever follows will have to be understood and progressed against its provisions. Devolution will, indeed, be a process rather than an event.

APPENDIX

On 27 February 1998 the former Secretary of State for Wales, Ron Davies, made the following statement in the House of Commons on the concordats that would be drawn up between Whitehall departments and the National Assembly:

'The White Paper *A Voice for Wales* noted that the Assembly would need to work in close partnership with those Whitehall departments responsible for developing policies or preparing secondary legislation for England, on matters which in Wales, would be the responsibility of the Assembly. It also noted that the Assembly's officials and their Whitehall counterparts would need to consult each other on a range of issues; the basis of the consultations would be set out in concordats.'

The Government has produced guidance setting out the principles which might govern the concordats, as follows:

CONCORDATS

Purpose

This note explains the basis of the non-statutory concordats which will set out certain key aspects of the working relationships between, on the one hand, the National Assembly for Wales and, on the other hand, Government Departments in Whitehall. The aim and purpose of these agreements is to preserve the good working relationships which currently exist and ensure that the business of government in Wales and at the UK level is conducted smoothly and efficiently after devolution takes effect. Their purpose is **not** to create legal obligations or restrictions on any party; rather, they will set the ground rules for administrative co-operation and exchange of information.

Concordats are not necessarily the only way to regulate these relationships in future. Other, less formal, arrangements will be appropriate in many cases, and in others there will be no need for any standing arrangements at all.

Why are concordats needed?

There are currently good working relationships between the Welsh Office and other Departments of Government. Such relationships are vital to the effectiveness of government and serve the interests of the public. Following devolution, the need for co-ordination will remain to take account of the programmes for implementing new legislation and shared interests in matters such as EU business. The basis for the Government's approach to concordats was set out in paragraph 3.40 of the White Paper *A Voice for Wales*.

General approach

The need for a concordat should arise from the particular circumstances of the policy area, which will also largely drive the nature of any agreement. In general, concordats will set out the principles on which working relationships will be based rather than prescribe the details of what those relationships should be. They will set down common processes and the main features of good working relationships, rather than specify substantive outcomes. They will need to meet two key aims:

- to provide the National Assembly for Wales and Whitehall Departments with the confidence that working relationships will be conducted properly and in accordance with agreed processes such as adequate consultation;

- to avoid constraining the Assembly or Whitehall Departments in their actions within their fields of competence.

Common provisions

A number of topics are likely to be common to many concordats. This list is not prescriptive and it will ultimately be a matter for the National Assembly and the UK Government to decide what should be covered by the agreements. The likely common topics include:

- Consultation arrangements in relation to proposals for legislation and executive action, including advance notification. The aim on both sides should so far as possible be 'no surprises'. There should also be arrangements for the voice of the Assembly to be heard on cross-cutting subjects such as women's issues and social exclusion'

- Exchange of information, including policy papers, analysis and statistics;

- Joint working including participation in working groups, official committees and so on;

- Confidentiality within these arrangements;

- Arrangements for liaison on EU and international matters;

- Any financial arrangements;

- Access to research, research budgets and specialist advice;

- Liaison between chief professional officers;

- Consultation about appointments including those to UK/GB public bodies; the exercise of Ministerial functions relating to such bodies, such as giving directions or approving corporate plans; and the relevant mechanisms of accountability and financial arrangements. It may be necessary to have a separate memorandum of understanding for each body;

- Operation of agency arrangements whereby matters are administered by the UK Government on behalf of the National Assembly on an agency basis or vice versa.

- Arrangements for resolving disagreements about any matters related to the concordat;

- Arrangements for renewal and review of the agreement. In some cases an official committee might be set up, perhaps with a rotating chairmanship, to report at intervals to Assembly Secretaries and Ministers on the operation of the concordat; but in many others this ought not to be necessary.

Who signs concordats?

Normally, concordats would be signed at senior official level, but if concordats concern politically sensitive issues they might be signed by UK Ministers and Assembly Secretaries.

Legal form

Concordats will be non-statutory and are not intended to be legally enforceable contracts between the parties. Any necessary statutory provisions are included in the devolution legislation and it is not intended that duties and liabilities should be imposed indirectly through concordats.

Publication

In accordance with the proposals in the Government's White Paper *Your Right to Know: Freedom of Information*, all formally agreed concordats should be published unless publication would cause substantial harm on one of the clearly defined grounds set out in that White Paper. In practice, this means that all concordats are likely to be published.'

CHAPTER 29

THE JOINT MINISTERIAL COMMITTEE AND THE BRITISH-IRISH COUNCIL

John Osmond

There is a fundamental instability at the heart of the constitutional change underway in the United Kingdom. While rapid developments are taking place around the edges of the system – in Wales, Scotland and Northern Ireland – the centre is being left relatively untouched. The assumption has been that things will 'settle down', that political life in Westminster and Whitehall will continue much as before, with maybe a few odd adjustments here and there.

At the centre constitutional change is slowing down. Hereditary peers may be stripped from the House of Lords, but its essential character and functions are likely to remain much the same. The probability is that the previous built-in Conservative majority will be replaced with a more equitable Labour representation based at least in the first instance, on appointed Life Peers. Wholesale reform of the second chamber, to take account of the devolution settlement, seems unlikely. This would entail it being made representative of the nations and regions of the United Kingdom. More likely is some kind of mix of direct election and appointment. Again, it is likely that the monarchy will be reinforced through partial (slimming down) reform. An element of proportionality in the voting system is likely to be introduced following the proposals of the Jenkins Commission in October 1998. However, implementation may be put back, to beyond the next general election. Otherwise, to borrow a phrase, the periphery will change so the centre can stay much the same. This outlook was summarised by the Lord Chancellor Derry Irvine, himself, when he declared in early 1998, that though the Government was embarking on the most radical programme of constitutional change since the 1832 Reform Act, essential British sovereignty would remain untouched:

'Our proposals have been designed to preserve the Union, the sovereignty of Parliament, and the separation of powers'.[1]

According to this outlook, devolution within Britain is merely following what has become a normal pattern within the European Union, with states like Germany and Spain having successfully decentralised to regional institutions. What the perspective fails to take into account, however, is that both these states have elaborate written constitutions making provision for devolved institutions at the centre. As Tom Nairn has pointed out, Britain has gone about reform in the reverse order - periphery first, and the centre at some unspecified later date: In Spain for instance, the nearest comparable country to Britain in devolution terms, he notes that:

'... a massive political and juridical machinery was constructed for the centre simultaneously with the concession of self-rule in the two problem-populations, the Catalans and the Basques. It was understood from the start that 'home rule' for the latter demanded radical reform and democratisation at the centre, and indeed for everybody else. Unfortunately, the most basic conditions for this democratic success story to be imitated by the United Kingdom are lacking. Blairism has gone about reform exactly the other way round - periphery first, the centre later, and all too probably, never'.[2]

THE JOINT MINISTERIAL COMMITTEE

The lack of institutions to ensure effective liaison and the resolution of disputes between the centre and the periphery was acknowledged very late in the day during the passage of the Scotland Bill through the House of Lords. It was always realised that establishing a separate legislature within the United Kingdom might lead to arguments over which matters were devolved and which retained. In the last analysis there was provision for disputes to be referred to the Judicial Committee of the Royal Privy Council. How robust such a procedure was likely to prove was always questionable. At the very least, it was likely to result in protracted, not to say expensive, legal wrangling.

What was needed was a political mechanism. And at the last minute, at the fag end of the passage of the devolution legislation, the Government came up with a response. This was a top-table Committee administered through the Westminster Cabinet Office, where the leading Ministers from Scotland, Wales, Northern Ireland together with the British Prime Minister could meet on a regular basis. The new institution will be hugely important in the future governance of the United Kingdom. It will be the forum where the key relationships are worked through, where grievances are dealt with, and disputes resolved. As a senior Cabinet Office official put it,

'Its purpose is to head off trouble before fires break out and end up in the rafters, or in constitutional terms, in the law courts. It will enable proper negotiations to take place before the UK government has to use the 'nuclear option' of overriding a decision by a devolved Assembly'.[3]

It is hoped the new institution will achieve the squaring of the circle of a political contradiction at the heart of the devolution exercise. That is to say, it will enable the UK administration to engage at the highest level with the leadership of the devolved Assemblies in a situation where there is no shared collective responsibility. Plainly it will be an innovation of some magnitude in British political governance. It is likely to become much more than the fire-fighting emergency service intimated by the Cabinet Office official quoted above. Rather it is likely to develop into an essential gear box at the core of the emerging devolution machine within the new United Kingdom polity. For example, it could well become the place where Welsh efforts to influence the Westminster primary legislative agenda are exerted to most effect, resolving some of the issues raised by Keith Patchett in Chapter 7.

The Joint Ministerial Committee emerged in a typically low-key British way, its significance under-stated and its birth unremarked by the Press and media. It came in response to a hostile amendment during a late stage of the passage of the Scotland Bill through the House of Lords. The announcement, in the early hours in late July 1998, was made by a junior Government whip, Baroness Ramsey of Cartvale, in the following terms:

'The Government intend that all the devolved administrations should be as fully involved as possible in discussions with the UK Government about the formulation of their policies on all issues which touch on devolved matters. Indeed, a great deal of thought has been given to how the UK Government and the devolved administrations should interact on matters of communal interest.

The Government intend that there should be standing arrangements for the devolved administrations to be involved in UK Government at ministerial level when they consider reserved matters which impinge on devolved responsibilities. It is envisaged that his would be achieved through the establishment of a joint ministerial committee of which the UK Government and the devolved administrations would be members. The joint ministerial committee will be an entirely consultative body, supported by a committee of officials and a joint secretariat ... Where there is agreement between the parties that it should do so, the JMC could also discuss the treatment of devolved matters in the different parts of the UK.

These standing arrangements will run in parallel with and underpin the bilateral concordats between the Scottish executive and departments of the UK Government. These arrangements would be non-statutory. The Scottish executive cannot, of course, be committed in advance to any particular form of liaison. That said, however, the UK Government believe that there will be strong mutual benefits from such liaison arrangements and we would expect the devolved administrations to recognise this also. The Government believe that these non-statutory arrangements together with the provisions in the devolution Bills, will enable the United Kingdom to work more effectively in future, giving due and appropriate weight to each of its components ... There will be one joint ministerial committee [but] representation will vary according to the specific issues under consideration. Fisheries ministers would be involved on fisheries matters, for example ...' [4]

This last reference to a range of ministers participating according to subject matter only emphasises the analogy with the Council of Ministers in the European Union. The implication is clear. Structures are being put in place at the centre of the United Kingdom polity that will enable, perhaps hasten, the whole creaking structure to move in a federal or quasi-federal direction. As the Cabinet Office official quoted earlier also put it:

'The dynamics are something that London cannot dictate. They will be determined very largely by the devolved institutions. We envisage that the JMC will be particularly important in EU affairs. Of course, these are uncharted waters. So far we've been chugging along the coast in sight of land. Very shortly we'll be heading out to sea ...'

And it is EU affairs that will provide the choppiest waters. An agenda is not difficult to compile. Disputes over money are likely to loom large, with complaints that the Treasury is refusing to match European funding to which Wales, Scotland and Northern Ireland are entitled. This may well turn out to be the first area of serious dispute between the National Assembly and Whitehall, in the event of EU Objective One status for western Wales and the Valleys being secured. Agriculture will be another area of contention. So, too, will be the handling of Britain's entry into the single European currency.

Yet the tone of the House of Lords statement is controlling. As the Cabinet Office official said, the Joint Ministerial Committee is regarded as a fire-fighting device, put in place to dampen down sparks before they flare out of control. But as he also observed, the devolved institutions will have a hand in shaping the agenda and the direction that policy change take. If Wales, Scotland and Northern Ireland can agree a common line their influence within the Joint Ministerial Council will be all the stronger. And co-incidentally, as a by-product of the resolution of the conflict in Northern Ireland, another institution is being erected which will provide an opportunity for the leading Ministers from Wales, Scotland and Northern Ireland to meet on a regular basis.

THE BRITISH-IRISH COUNCIL

Quite independently from the processes of devolution in Wales and Scotland, the pressures of reaching agreement in the Irish peace process spawned a new institution that may prove highly influential in shaping the course that devolution takes. The British-Irish Council was designed to assuage Unionist fears that they were being dragged into a process of all-Ireland unification. It was a trade-off against the North-South Ministerial Council which was established

> 'to bring together those with executive responsibilities in Northern Ireland and the Irish Government, to develop consultation, co-operation and action within the island of Ireland ...' [5].

This was Strand Two of the Agreement. Strand One established the Northern Ireland Assembly itself. Strand Three created the British-Irish Council and the British-Irish Intergovernmental Conference. All three strands have to be triggered simultaneously before the Agreement as a whole can be implemented. This is why although the Northern Ireland Assembly elections took place in the summer of 1998, the Assembly will only operate in 'shadow' form until all the interlocking institutions are in place.

The Agreement is sketchy on the make-up of Council, its character and functions. In typically British fashion constitutional change was made up on the hoof, with little consideration about wider implications beyond the demands of the immediate moment. So, for instance, the Isle of Man and the Channel Isles are involved, as well as Wales and Scotland. There is little evidence that they were consulted about their participation, however. On the other hand the new Assembly in London, whose establishment was shortly to confirmed by a referendum, is left out. It seems that the British Government regards the London Assembly as a tier of local government, and therefore not eligible. Whether this will be the case if elected regional government in other parts of England emerge, for example in the North East, seems unresolved. The Agreement refers to their being involved 'if appropriate'. In any event, the role of the Council is described in the following terms:

> 'The BIC will exchange information, discuss, consult and use best endeavours to reach agreement on co-operation on matters of mutual interest within the competence of the relevant Administrations. Suitable issues for early discussion in the BIC could include transport links, agricultural issues, environmental issues, cultural issues, health issues, education issues and approaches to EU issues'.[6]

There seems little here that will be outside the interests of the National Assembly and the Scottish Parliament. A Cabinet Office Paper on the working of the Council, reported in the Irish Republic newspaper *The Irish News* in September 1998, remarks, 'There is no theoretical limit to the matters which could be put forward for discussion' [7]. Moreover, and crucially from the point of view of the operation of the Joint Ministerial Committee, the Agreement goes on to say:

> 'In addition to the structures provided for under this agreement, it will be open to two or more members to develop bilateral or multilateral arrangements between them. Such arrangements could include, subject to agreement of the members concerned, mechanisms to enable consultation, co-operation and joint decision-making on matters of mutual interest; and mechanisms to implement any joint decisions they may reach. These arrangements will not require the prior approval of the BIC as a whole and will operate independently of it' [8].

Here, ready-made so to speak, is the institution, or 'mechanism' as the Agreement has it, for Wales, Scotland and Northern Ireland to jointly negotiate positions prior to meetings of the Joint Ministerial Committee.

REFORM AT THE CENTRE

The creation of the British Irish Council, together with the late emergence of the Joint Ministerial Committee, are unconsciously pushing the United Kingdom towards a quasi-federal constitutional settlement. An issue that will have to be addressed sooner or later is how the developing institutions at the periphery will interlock with institutions at the centre. The creation of the Joint Ministerial Committee is one response. However, it will not be transparent. The meetings will be held behind closed doors.

There is a danger that the UK will develop along the lines of the heavily bureaucratic German federal system. In Germany the power of decision-making rests largely with the executive rather than with the respective legislatures. So much so that the German system can accurately described as 'executive' rather than 'democratic' federalism[9]. Most laws are passed at the federal level, while the administrative competence for the execution of most of the legislation rests with the Länder state governments. The salient feature of the system is the dominance of the executives in the intergovernmental process, with a marginal role for the parliaments, and in particular the state legislatures. Co-operation, co-ordination and joint policy-making are the almost exclusive preserve of the executive. At the top of the joint policy-making system are regular meetings among the Länder Minister-Presidents, amongst them and the federal Chancellor, together with institutionalised conferences between the state ministers – usually with federal ministers also present – organised along departmental lines. The analogy with the United Kingdom's newly fledged Joint Ministerial Committee is clear.

Beneath this top political level in Germany, there is a vast network of administrative committees of different status as well as ad hoc meetings, staffed by public servants. This is a formidable bureaucratic, co-ordinating machinery which not only prepares top-level political decisions, but, perhaps more importantly, serves to harmonise and synchronise the development and implementation of public policy. Little wonder, therefore that not only the Länder state parliaments, but the Federal lower house itself, the Bundestag, often finds it difficult to exercise effective influence, let alone control, over this intergovernmental policy-making activity.

A United Kingdom response to democratic dangers of this kind would be to use reform of the House of Lords as the way to inject democratic transparency into the relations between the nations and regions and the political centre[10]. The House of Lords is in the frame for constitutional change, but the government is unsure what direction it should take. Apart, that is, from removing the hereditary peerage and converting it into a completely appointed, but still undemocratic and unrepresentative chamber. A Commission is being established to consider the options, including the impact that devolution will have. In this context the British Irish Council suggests the kind of new central institution that is needed within the newly emerging polity of the British Isles – one that represents its constituent parts. Wales is to have its National Assembly, Scotland its Parliament, and Northern Ireland a legislative chamber. All that leaves is England.

But England is already moving in a regional direction. London is to have its own elected mayor and authority, confirmed in the recent referendum. The Government is committed to creating development agencies for the English regions which may well be followed by English regional assemblies, referendums permitting. All experience elsewhere, and especially in Spain, shows that once a centralised state starts devolving in some directions, a movement begins in which everywhere is anxious to catch up and compete on equal terms.

The sensible approach therefore, is to start thinking of a reformed Second Chamber at the centre which can hold together and mediate between the constituent parts. Within such a framework the British Irish Council could sit quite comfortably, as the Second Chamber operating, so to speak in its international mode, embracing Wales and Scotland as well as the North and South of Ireland.

This is a process that would continue the change of the United Kingdom's political culture in a civic direction, It is a process in which the people are becoming European English, Welsh, Scots and Irish citizens, rather than British subjects. This is not to argue that 'Britain' will simply dissolve as an idea or level of governance. Rather it will change and the role it has always sustained will become transparent. This is to be a focus for certain political, constitutional loyalties and for civic values that are held in common between peoples who come from quite different cultural and national backgrounds. Beyond this there are a number of instrumental advantages to a regional reform of the House of Lords, which can be summarised as follows:

- It provides increased justification for democratic decentralisation and an enhanced role for the new regional and national institutions, as well as for the Second Chamber itself.

- It provides a completely different democratic foundation for the Upper House from the House of Commons, so distinguishing clearly between the two.

- The Second Chamber would not be seen as a competing legislative chamber. This would be emphasised if the national and regional assemblies were represented in the Second Chamber. The membership of the Upper House would then be made up of members appointed by the national and regional assemblies, thereby being indirectly elected.

- The Second Chamber would provide a forum for negotiation between the centre and the regions and nations of the United Kingdom, especially so far as the resolution of financial differences and conflicts are concerned. The advent of the British-Irish Council serves to underline this constructive dimension.

- It locks one part of the constitutional reform agenda closely with another and emphasises the underlying change in political culture that is involved.

- Because the central legislative processes will be umbilically linked to the geographic and historic regions of the country, the system will create a natural counter-weight to the instinctive centralising tendencies of the Whitehall administrative machinery.

- It makes the point that democratic decentralisation, far from threatening 'the Balkanisation of Britain' – as some of its opponents allege – holds out instead the prospect of a new and more constructive partnership between the nations and regions and the centre.

- It would bring the evolution of British democracy into line with common constitutional practices around the world, and especially continental European, democratic constitutions. It would make it easier for Britain to participate effectively in European Union institutions, especially the Committee of the Regions and the European Parliament.

CONCLUSION

The three developments discussed here – the emergence of the Joint Ministerial Committee, the advent of the British-Irish Council, together with the developing debate around the reform of the House of Lords – are combining with devolution itself to move Britain in a quasi-federal direction. Where and when this process will stop is difficult to predict. However, it cannot be denied that we have embarked on a process of radical change. And inevitably this will be an important dimension of the National Assembly's political agenda.

Depending on how quickly this particular part of its agenda develops is likely to decide the future status of the Secretary of State for Wales. Will there be room for both the Assembly's First Minister and the Secretary of State to be members of the

Joint Ministerial Committee, assuming the same person does not hold both positions? This is a question that is sure to be raised in the early sessions of the National Assembly.

References

1   Lord Irivine, speech in Cambridge, 17 January 1998.

2   Independent on Sunday Review, 20 September 1998. A full analysis of this author's views on the future constitutional direction of the UK is cointaining in his *After Britain*, Verso, 1999 (forthcoming).

3   Interview with the author, September 1998.

4   House of Lords debates on the Scotland Bill, Hansard, 28-29 July 1998, cols. 1488-9.

5   Agreement Reached in the Multi-Party Negotiations, Strand Two, Clause 1, 10 April 1998.

6   Ibid., Strand Three, Clause 5.

7   Irish News, 14 September 1998.

8   Irish Agreement, op. cit.. Clause 10.

9   Klaus H. Goetz, *German Federalism and European Integration: Compatibility and Adjustment*, paper presented to at the ESRC Research Seminar 'Intergovernmental Relations in the European Union', London School of Economics, December 1993.

10 For a full discussion of the case for reforming the House of Lords along regional lines see John Osmond, *Reforming the Lords and Changing Britain*, Fabian Society, August 1998.

CHAPTER 30

LINKS WITH BRUSSELS

Sir John Gray

The relationship between Wales and the European Union will be at least as important after devolution as before. It is therefore essential that the Assembly creates structures which will ensure that the ability of Wales to influence decisions taken within the EU increases, and certainly that it does not diminish. In seeking to achieve this goal, the Assembly will find that devolution presents both positive and negative opportunities.

The relationship between Wales and Europe is a complex one which takes place on broadly two planes. One plane consists of institutions - special interest groups, local government authorities, regional governments, member states, the institutions of the EU. The other plane consists of stages in the development of EU policy - preparation, negotiation and implementation. The two planes interact in various ways but for the purposes of this paper those interactions are most easily considered in geographic terms - in Wales, in London and in Brussels.

IN WALES

At present Welsh views on European issues are passed to a variety of interlocutors (the Welsh Office, Whitehall departments, the EU Commission) from a variety of sources, including special interest groups, local government authorities, and the private sector. The result is a cacophony of often conflicting or parochial views which lack both coherence and the power that coherence confers. The advent of the National Assembly provides an opportunity to remedy that situation by creating mechanisms for considering the interests of all concerned, balancing them against each other and reaching compromise solutions in the wider Welsh interest.

To do this the Assembly will need to establish a European Committee, as the National Assembly Advisory Group has recommended. This should hear evidence in public from all concerned with issues as they arise - local government authorities, public sector, private sector, voluntary bodies and individuals.

It should report to the Assembly. It would be for the Assembly Cabinet to decide whether and if so how to relay the Committee's conclusions to London or Brussels. But the fact that the Committee's deliberations would be both public and inclusive would give those conclusions considerable authority.

It is rumoured that the UK government is opposed to the creation of a committee on European affairs, preferring to see each Subject Committee separately responsible for the European issues within its competence. This would not be a wise move. The risk of committees adopting conflicting conclusions on similar issues could not be ruled out and the incoherence which would result would be even more damaging than the present unstructured free-for-all. More acceptable would be a cross-cutting committee with representatives of all Subject Committees concerned with the issues under discussion sitting on it – what the NAAG calls a 'programme' committee. In order to extend the authority and influence of the European Committee, the right should be given to Wales' MPs, MEPs and representatives in the Committee of the Regions (CoR) to attend its meetings but without the right to vote.

IN LONDON

Devolution notwithstanding, the UK will remain the member state representing Wales in the EU on all matters whether or not devolved to the Assembly. The preparation of 'the agreed UK line' and its modification if necessary in the light of negotiations in Brussels will continue to be done in London through the operation of official and ministerial committees as at present. Indeed, as discussed in the previous Chapter, late in the day the Government has resolved to establish a Joint Ministerial Committee within the Cabinet Office to bring together the UK Prime Minister and the lead Ministers from Wales, Scotland and Northern Ireland. It is here that we can expect difficult EU issues, in particular, to be resolved.

Despite such opportunities for pressing the Welsh case within prior United Kingdom discussions provided by the Joint Ministerial Committee, at the end of the day it will be as representatives of the UK promoting the agreed UK line that Assembly officials and ministers will sit on the appropriate working bodies in Brussels. It will therefore be essential for the Assembly, working through its representatives, to have the right to participate in the development and possible modification of policy and its promotion in Brussels. At the same time those representatives must also have the discipline to stand by any policy (or its subsequent modification) to which they have agreed.

At present Welsh Office participation flows naturally from the fact that its officials are part of the Whitehall system and its political head is a member of the UK Cabinet. Devolution will change all that. The Assembly will have its own political leadership, perhaps one day at odds with that in London. Moreover, its officials will have a problem of loyalty. The need for a mechanism to resolve these difficulties is recognised; and the solution proposed is that of 'concordats'. These would be agreements between the Assembly and Whitehall departments, usually at the level of officials. They would have no force in law but would hopefully acquire over time that sanctity which the uncodified British 'Constitution' bestows on most long-established customs.

Nevertheless, this is a shaky basis on which to build a lasting and constructive relationship, as Ivor Lightman argues persuasively in Chapter 28. This is particularly the case in relation to European affairs, where many of the subjects covered by concordats would include issues which under UK law have been devolved to the Assembly. At the very least this would seem to require an over-arching concordat between the Assembly and the Cabinet Office.

It also implies an active role for the Secretary of State for Wales (for so long as that post remains in existence) in ensuring the effective negotiation and implementation of the necessary concordats. This will be particularly important for the first Labour leader of the Assembly, not least for the credibility of his own party's commitment to devolution. A similar commitment should be encouraged in Wales' MPs. Even so, the Assembly will have to tread a fine line between being too aggressive in promoting its rights (and risk provoking a backlash from London) and being too relaxed (and risk seeing Wales taken for granted). It is difficult to escape the conclusion that in the long run some more constitutional arrangement, that is to say, a legal framework incapable of being easily set aside by Whitehall or the UK Cabinet, will be required.

Consequently, the Assembly should negotiate as quickly as possible concordats with the Cabinet Office and other Whitehall departments binding the latter as closely as possible to a commitment to give Assembly officials and Secretaries meaningful access to the development and modification of the agreed UK line on EU matters. The Assembly should then seek to use the the Secretary of State (and, to the extent possible, Wales's MPs) to promote and defend the strict application of these concordats by Whitehall and the Cabinet. At the same time the Assembly should remain conscious of the possible need at some future date to put the arrangements on to a sounder constitutional basis.

IN BRUSSELS

In seeking to promote and safeguard Welsh interests in Brussels the Assembly will need to establish links with a wide variety of bodies: the Council of Ministers, UKREP (the Office of the UK Permanent Representative to the EU), the EU Commission, the European Parliament (EP), the Committee of the Regions (CoR), a number of special interest groups and representatives of other member states and regions. The Regional dimension will be considered in the next Chapter.

The Council of Ministers is, to all intents and purposes and notwithstanding recent advances by the EP and the CoR, the supreme legislative authority in the EU. It is composed of the member states, advised as necessary by the Commission. It is not, of course, a monolithic body. The Council meets with a varying membership according to the subject under discussion - industry ministers for industry subjects, agriculture ministers for agricultural matters, and so forth. Alliances and compromises are nearly always necessary if conclusions are to be reached. This means that negotiating positions may have to be changed between Council meetings or even at them.

If the Assembly is to increase Wales' ability to monitor and influence events in the Council and its subordinate bodies at official level then it will have to be confirmed in the right of the pre-devolution Welsh Office to be represented at Council and it must exercise that right assiduously on issues of major importance to Wales. There is even an argument for Wales or Scotland occasionally leading the UK delegation where the balance of interest lies with the devolved authorities rather than the central government. There are plenty of precedents for this in other EU states where powers are devolved.

UKREP receives its instructions from Whitehall and reports to Whitehall. Its job is to gather information on the intentions of the Commission and the representatives of other member states, and to present the British Government's thinking to them in return. It takes an active part in the development of the agreed UK line on any issue. With this array of duties, allied to a formidably well-qualified staff and privileged access at home and in the Commission, it is little wonder that UKREP enjoys a powerful position in the development and promotion of UK policy.

It will be important for the Assembly to get on to terms with UKREP. There are a number of ways in which this can be done. These include pressing for a senior member of the Assembly's staff to be given a post at UKREP sensitive to Welsh interests - in regional development, for example. This would not only have intrinsic value but it would ensure that a Welsh voice was heard in UKREP's highest councils. There would also be value in placing UKREP under the obligation of keeping the Assembly regularly informed of developments on issues notified as being of major concern to Wales. The Assembly should also promote an active policy of seeking out and encouraging potential Welsh candidates for the European Commission's staff - again so that a Welsh point of view might be heard.

More importantly, the Assembly's relations with UKREP could be exercised through two institutions, one of which is already in existence. This is the Wales Europe Centre, a body largely funded by the WDA and the local authorities but also drawing support from a wide variety of Welsh public sector bodies. At present the Centre derives no funding from the Welsh Office. Its ability to promote Welsh interests in Brussels, though considerable and ably done, is to some extent limited by Welsh Office constraints on its freedom of action. If those constraints were removed and the Centre placed under the control of the Assembly, it would be ideally placed to act as an interlocutor for Welsh interests with UKREP. It would also provide a base for the second instrument which the Assembly should seek to establish in Brussels, namely a Representative of its own. This post would obviously bolster the Assembly's ability to alert UKREP to Welsh concerns.

Both the Centre and the Representative would also be useful in establishing closer links between the Assembly and the Commission. Nearly all EU policy initiatives begin in the Commission whose grip on the development and implementation of EU legislation is enormous. To influence the Commission at an early stage of its thinking on issues which might affect Welsh interests should be an important priority of Assembly action on European affairs. Effective exploitation of the Centre and the Representative would go far to achieving this, backed up by targeted contacts between Assembly Secretaries and senior Commission figures.

The same two institutions, the Centre and the Representative, should be one of the channels through which the Assembly might seek to influence the EP and the CoR. The other, of course, would be through cultivating Wales's representatives in those two bodies, not least by encouraging them to participate in the Assembly's European Committee and to use the facilities of the Centre. Finally, the Centre and the Representative should be used to develop relations with the more important of the special interest groups active in Brussels. These are often among the best informed and most successful lobbyists in that city.

In summary the Assembly should ensure that any concordats with Whitehall on European affairs give it the right to have representatives on all Councils and their subordinate bodies at which issues of major interest to Wales are discussed, and in certain circumstances to provide the leader of the delegation. The same concordats should require UKREP to take in a senior member of the Assembly staff, to maintain close contacts with the Wales Europe Centre and the Assembly's Representative in Brussels, and keep the Assembly informed of developments of interest to it.

Further, the Assembly should assume responsibility for the Centre's finances and work programme, which should include close monitoring of the Commission's intentions and activities and liaison with the EP, the CoR and special interest groups. Finally, the Assembly should appoint a Representative in Brussels who would head the Wales European Centre there.

A WELSH AGENDA

The implication of much of the above, and particularly the section on Brussels, is that the Assembly might need to cultivate a different agenda from Whitehall and the UK Cabinet. That is not an implication which should be universally applied. Within Wales there is clearly no reason why the Assembly should not use the consensus-building framework of its European Committee to establish a popular mandate for the elaboration of possible European policies different from those being followed in London. Nor is there any reason why, armed with that mandate, the Assembly's representatives in Whitehall committees should not argue for a change in the agreed UK line at any time. But the development of an agreed line will almost always require compromise and the weighing of interests. It would be to the long term advantage of Wales, at least while the present devolutionary régime lasts, to work within the disciplines which compromise requires - from all parties, including those in Whitehall.

Similarly in Brussels, the Assembly's representatives should be careful not to provoke resentment in London by arguing publicly against policy lines which they have previously agreed. This should still leave plenty of room for legitimate lobbying of the Commission to ensure that Welsh interests in the initial stages of developing new policy areas or the implementation of old ones are made clear. Equally it would allow for a robust defence of Welsh interests in any delegation discussion to change the agreed UK line during Council negotiations for tactical reasons. Nor would it bar the Assembly and its representatives from insisting that any grant for a specific purpose in Wales by the EU should not be taken into account in determining the amount of the Block Grant.

CHAPTER 31

THE ASSEMBLY'S INTERNATIONAL ROLE

Stephen Thomas

In European Union parlance Wales is a 'Region' since it is the administrative unit next down from the nation state. With the setting up of the British-Irish Council (see Chapter 29) we should also perhaps be thinking of Wales as a Region within a British context. Much has already been done by elected representatives and officials from Wales in Brussels, Strasbourg and elsewhere to maintain a significant Welsh profile within the EU since the UK's accession in the 1970s.

The Assembly's creation in 1999 should prove to be good timing for Wales - a historic nation within Europe at last obtaining its own elected body. With greater powers officially to be handed over to regional authorities by the EU, for developing new agricultural and regional development policies, Wales has the opportunity to influence some of the future shape of the Union at a crucial period.

Enlargement of the EU to include up to ten central and eastern European countries and related revisions to the EU's structural funds and to the Common Agricultural Policy will play a large part in taking the 'European project' to its next stage. The Assembly can perform the key co-ordinating and cementing role that Wales has so far lacked in mobilising the diverse parts of Welsh representation in Europe to act together on these issues. The Assembly can also start planning constructively for a more concerted, official Welsh presence on the wider world stage.

THE NEW REGIONALISM

The National Assembly has great potential to improve Wales' standing in relation to its neighbours, both within the European Union and in the wider world. However, a note of caution should be struck. In his book *The Search for Peace* in 1997, former UK Foreign Secretary Douglas Hurd called nation states 'both immortal and incompetent'. It is important that we accept both of these concepts concerning Wales' relations with the outside world.

A greater degree of decentralised autonomy within the British state may add to the Assembly's competence in coming years, but the UK body politic will remain 'immortal' for a considerable time to come. And a change of political persuasion in the corridors of power is not enough to call this viewpoint into question either. Current Foreign Secretary Robin Cook put forward in August 1998 the idea of a second parliamentary chamber in Europe made up of nation state MPs, as a check to power based in the European Commission in Brussels. Potential for influence certainly exists with the Assembly, but it needs to be well channelled and focused in order to be effective.

The new Regionalism, like devolution, is a process not an event. The high water mark for the concept of a 'Europe of the Regions' was about a decade ago. Then even Chancellor Kohl and President Mitterrand were using it as a catchphrase, accepting that the relationship between nation states and their constituent parts was being radically altered by the European dimension of policy. In that respect the creation of the National Assembly for Wales has come rather late to the party. However, there are signs that the trend towards regionalisation continues - not least in eastern Europe, where Poland with its 12 'super regions', and the Czech Republic and Hungary have accepted the concept as an important part of their new constitutions. Indeed it is part of the EU's drive for greater cohesion that has encouraged them to embrace the principle of regionalism, so as to better prepare for EU membership.

Though there is no legal and uniform definition of 'Regions' in Europe - they can be historical, administrative, economic or ethnic in their composition - a sense of cultural identity or empathy with a geographical unit is a prevailing feature. They have become integral parts of the EU's fabric as they form a rung of the subsidiarity ladder, between the nation state and local authorities. Their role in making and implementing economic decisions in particular is important, reflected in the existence of Directorate General XVI on Regional Policy and Cohesion within the European Commission (DG XVI in EU terminology). Regional structural funds, motor regions, maritime regions and inter-regional funding from the EU show how regional policy has been closely linked to money. Subsidiarity being the taking of decisions at the most appropriate level closest to the people, this decentralisation of economic power has gone hand in hand with attempts to popularise the EU through the Regions. The objective has been to make it more relevant to people and to build bridges between citizens and the EU.

WALES IN EUROPE

If Wales is to have an effective voice and and impressive image within the corridors of power in the EU, it must start by utilising what already exists and build upon it. Below are the six key institutions on which Wales is already represented, or structures that have already been created that the National Assembly needs to capitalise upon if it is to leapfrog effectively over the UK nation state level and have direct influence in Europe.

COMMITTEE OF THE REGIONS

The Committee of the Regions has had a somewhat downbeat existence since first convening in March 1994. Put in place by the Maastricht Treaty as a recognition of the increasing importance of Regions within the EU, it is a consultative forum rather than a decision-making one. It enables Regions to articulate their views, send opinions and lobby the European Commission on policy matters from a regional viewpoint. The acceptance by the EU that 'Regions know best', in economic policy in particular but also increasingly on other policy matters, means that the Committee's remit is likely to develop further. Whether it will actually reach the stage where it becomes a second chamber of the European Parliament as predicted by some is questionable. Nonetheless it is the most significant step yet in institutionalising the presence of Regions in the EU, and therefore a forum to be utilised supportively by the National Assembly.

The Assembly will inherit a position whereby the Welsh Local Government Association (WLGA) is the body that nominates members to the Committee of the Regions from Wales. In 1998 Wales, like Scotland, saw its number of full and alternate Committee members reduced (from 6 to 4). This was the result of redistribution of the seats available to the UK, in which English Regions gained seats based on population figures. The reduction went ahead despite a rearguard action by the former Secretary of State for Wales, Ron Davies. However, the structure of commissions that the Committee uses ensures that Wales continues to be represented on four of the six commissions within its system.

ASSEMBLY OF EUROPEAN REGIONS

Based in Strasbourg, the Assembly of European Regions has a similar policy-shaping brief to the Committee of the Regions. However, it has a lower profile as it is not a formal part of the EU's structure. It has the potential advantage, however, of having a remit beyond the boundaries of the EU, to include other European countries. With the enlargement of the EU in coming years this may prove to be a significant place for input, prior to the formal accession of central and eastern European countries as EU member states.

LINKS WITH THE 'FOUR MOTOR' REGIONS

Another form of official link with other European Regions instituted in Wales since the late 1980s is the memoranda of understanding with the 'Four Motor' Regions – Catalunya in Spain, Rhône-Alpes in France, Lombardy in Italy and Baden-

Württemberg in Germany. Bilateral trade and cultural agreements have been negotiated and signed with all four by the Welsh Office in a series of inter-regional partnerships. They are called 'Motor' Regions because they are economically strong and among the most advanced in Europe in terms of technological change, political democracy and social systems. Hence they serve as excellent role models for Wales to seek to emulate.

The links have had positive spin-offs in raising awareness of Wales elsewhere and providing insight into how others have developed their regional structures, though the tie-in with Rhône-Alpes has been less developed than with the others. The advantages have been largely in unquantifiable fields such as the exchange of personnel and ideas between civil servants and business people, cultural performers and academics. The potential certainly exists for further development of these links under the Assembly's aegis.

LIAISON WITH REGIONAL DEVELOPMENT AGENCIES

The Welsh Development Agency has been instrumental in promoting innovative regional economic links with partners in Europe. These have frequently been on the basis of a network of 'Intelligent Regions' - regions with sound business and institutional links, both private and public, capable of appraising their economic and social strengths and weaknesses and keen to network effectively with others on an international level. The infrastructure needed for such innovative Regions is based on good education, business support services, skills development and training, the involvement of universities, technology transfer and firms supporting each other by passing on experiences. The best current example of this is the EU's Regional Technology Plan project, based in eight European Regions including Jutland in Denmark, Macedonia in Greece, the Basque country in Spain and parts of Austria, as well as Wales. The creation of the new Welsh Development Agency, in October 1998, uniting the old WDA, the Development Board for Rural Wales (DBRW) and the Land Authority for Wales, will assist the Assembly's work in extending these regional links.

MEMBERS OF THE EUROPEAN PARLIAMENT

Wales has been well served by its Members of the European Parliament (MEPs) since 1979. Many of them have had high profiles and brought lustre to Wales, though largely on an individual basis. It is therefore a positive step that as from the European Parliamentary elections in June 1999 a system of proportional representation will be used to elect the five Welsh MEPs, with Wales as a single electoral unit. This will ensure a fairer representation of the electorate's views among those elected and will create a coherent bloc of people who see themselves as representing the same territory that the Assembly will also be fighting for within Europe.

UKREP IN BRUSSELS AND THE WALES EUROPEAN CENTRE

There are two important Brussels-based institutions as far as Welsh issues are concerned. As discussed in the previous Chapter, the UK Permanent Representation in Brussels (UKREP) is the key British institution. Representation for the Assembly in UKREP - presumably at officer level - is proposed by the National Assembly Advisory Group (NAAG), together with a formalised relationship with the Wales European Centre in Brussels. Established in 1992, the Wales European Centre performs an important lobbying and representational role for Wales, one of more than 150 such centres lobbying on behalf of their Regions. As Sir John Gray argues in the previous Chapter, the Assembly should assume responsibility for the Centre's finances and work programme, to ensure its effectiveness is enhanced.

KEY EUROPEAN POLICY ISSUES

European Monetary Union is, in public perception and quite likely in reality, the most important issue facing the EU in the near future. The National Assembly will have little direct say on the UK's policy towards it. Given that those involved with inward investment to Wales are on the whole favourable to the Euro currency's introduction, the Assembly view should also be broadly in favour. In so far as it will take monetary policy decisions out of the hands of member states, thus reducing their economic control, it can be construed that EMU will enhance the economic role of the Regions over time.

Three other significant European subjects will have a more direct bearing on the Assembly's agenda.

ENLARGEMENT

The impending enlargement eastwards of the EU will bring inevitable reforms in the financial obligations of member states. Regional policy will be a significant part of this reform, as it will help achieve the integration of the new member states and the cohesion that is deemed such an important concept within the EU. Expansion will potentially enlarge the EU's population by 24 per cent, but increase its GDP by only four per cent. This has already created a mathematical urgency for reform that is reflected in the *Agenda 2000* proposals for change that the European Commission has drawn up in the late 1990s.

It is not as extreme a situation as some analysts make out. Countries such as the Czech Republic, Poland and Hungary are comparatively economically stronger than were Greece or Portugal when they became members of the EU. The timescale for full integration of the first wave of states will take at least until 2003, and probably longer. And since the EU's structural funds have to be matched by national or regional funding in order to be released, the ability of eastern European countries to absorb large amounts of such funds is limited. The extra costs for existing member states are therefore likely to be spread over a considerable period of time. The enlargement issue is nevertheless an important one and will need to be addressed by the National Assembly in terms of how Welsh interests can best be maintained in the reformed and expanded picture that emerges.

STRUCTURAL FUNDS

The current regulations that govern use of the EU's structural funds expire on 31 December 1999. Wales will have received approaching £1bn in grants from those funds by then. Partly driven by the enlargement process noted above, there will be wholesale changes in structural funds. *Agenda 2000* proposes that the current seven Objectives covered by the structural funds be reduced to three, to increase efficiency and to simplify their running. These aims are intended to be achieved by creating a stronger partnership between the European Commission, member states and the Regions. The priority for the Assembly is how to negotiate the best possible coverage of structural funds for Wales from 2000 onwards.

This is particularly relevant for Objective One money, which is the most favourable potential tranche for Wales. Work to secure Wales' status for this has begun and important victories already achieved, namely the re-drawing of the deprivation map of Wales for acceptance by the EU and the support this has won in Whitehall. The next crucial step is to press the case that the newly defined, most deprived areas (north-west Wales, west Wales and the Valleys) should be entitled to Objective One status for the next round of European funding, from 2000 to 2006. The criterion is that an area must have per capita gross domestic product below 75 per cent of the European average - something that the new area achieves according to the July 1998 IWA report *The Other Wales: The Case for Objective 1 Funding Post 1999*. The funds will be concentrated on a smaller proportion of the EU's population than before (35-40 per cent) and the lobbying must begin with the UK government in the first instance, to convince it of the priority of the Welsh case. Objective Two will be available for declining industrial and rural areas that are undergoing economic change, and Objective Three will cover regions outside the range of the other two, to help modernise their systems of training, education and employment.

The Welsh Office has created a task force, headed by Hywel Ceri Jones, who has been a European civil servant for 25 years. The task force includes a mixture of public, private and voluntary organisations which will draw up a list of projects within Wales that would help sell the Welsh case for Objective One status, and the money that would stem from it - estimated at as much as £1.8bn over six years. The Assembly needs to mobilise its forces from the start to support these endeavours, at a British level as well as within Europe. Lobbying at the British level is especially important since, even if Objective One Status is achieved, funds can only be drawn down in so far as they are matched by home funding. In this area there may be scope for the National Assembly to make common cause with the new Assembly in Northern Ireland and the Parliament in Scotland.

It is with regard to this subject that the maturity or otherwise of Welsh democracy within the Assembly will perhaps be best measured. Not all parts of Wales can benefit from priority funding. But for some parts to obtain it, a united rather than a fractured (and fractious) front is required to put the case. The demand for consensus therefore might never be as pressing as here. Competing claims for Objective One status for Cornwall, parts of North West England and Yorkshire, as well as the Highlands and Islands of Scotland, are also likely. It would prove injurious if Assembly members resorted to narrow geographical interests to create competing claims within Wales as well.

COMMON AGRICULTURAL POLICY REFORM

As part of the package following enlargement the notorious Common Agricultural Policy (CAP) will be reformed as well, with the emphasis being on higher priority for integrated rural development and more sustainable, environmentally sensitive farming methods. Policy objectives under *Agenda 2000* are:

- Improved competitiveness through lower prices.

- Stable incomes and a fair standard of living for the agricultural community.

- Integrated environmental goals included in the policy.

- The creation of alternative income and employment opportunities for farmers and their families.

Cereals, beef and milk are the main products to be affected by the reforms. There will be cuts in intervention, support prices and price guarantees. Compensation for losses of income will be through direct payments instead – yearly payments for dairy cows for example. Funding for conservation and good environmental practice will be incorporated. Simplification is one of the overall objectives, coupled with decentralisation in the way the CAP is managed. Member states and Regions will be given more responsibilities for implementation - once again an opportunity for the Assembly to seize influence for itself. (This issue is explored in some depth by Terry Marsden in Chapter 15.)

Welsh agriculture is heavily subsidised by the CAP and dairy and cattle farms in particular will be affected by these changes. A comprehensive rural development strategy for Wales is needed and the Assembly should make it a priority to provide it.

DEBATING EUROPEAN REGIONAL ISSUES IN THE ASSEMBLY

The NAAG report recommends that one plenary session each year be set aside for a debate on the Assembly's handling of matters relating to the EU. European issues will be dealt with on a weekly basis by a standing Programme Committee of the

Assembly (as distinct from a Subject Committee). This will be a cross-cutting body, a suitable means of accommodating the broad spectrum of issues with European dimensions that will impinge on the Assembly's work. NAAG recommends that:

- The European issues Programme Committee should have a balance of political representation.

- Each Subject Committee elects one member to be on the European Committee.

- Assembly Members who are not members of it can make representations to the European issues Committee.

In addition, NAAG recommends that each Subject Committee appoint one of its members to act as European co-ordinator for that Committee, reporting monthly on events in Europe affecting the Committee's fields of responsibility. Overseeing the administration of the structural funds will be delegated to relevant Subject Committees.

This is a useful framework for integrating work on European issues, but does it go far enough? In order to achieve the much vaunted ambition of consensus building and inclusivity within the Committee, it is important that its members accept from the outset that it will need input from outside the confines of the Assembly itself. The NAAG report also states that it believes it would be beneficial for the Assembly to arrange meetings with relevant representatives of certain other bodies. As argued in the previous Chapter, to become truly representative of the various levels of Welsh representation within Europe, the Committee should go further and co-opt members from other tiers of government and relevant bodies:

- Members of the European Parliament

- Members of the Committee of the Regions

- Members of the EU's Economic and Social Committee

- Representatives from the Wales European Centre

- Welsh Local Government Association representatives

More than the mere taking of occasional advice from such people is needed to ensure the Committee is effective. It may be appropriate to include officials in this process as well. Furthermore, since the commissions on which Welsh members of the Committee of the Regions sit are likely to correspond to certain Subject Committees of the Assembly (education, rural affairs and agriculture, economic development, social affairs) it would be appropriate for those Committee of the Regions members to report back direct to the equivalent Assembly Committee.

In terms of the Committee of the Regions, the Assembly should use the Partnership Council that is to be formed between it and local government in Wales to come to an agreement on how the next set of Welsh members to the Committee is elected. The current full members (two) and alternate members (two) were elected for a four year term starting in February 1998. It would be appropriate to utilise the experience that these individuals already have (some of them now nearing five years in post) by re-affirming their position to the end of their stay in early 2002.

Thereafter, it would be logical for the Assembly, as the next tier of government downwards from the UK government, to have the authority to nominate the replacements to the Committee. Ideally they should be Assembly members, so that the disparity that exists at present between a Regional President from one of the German Länder or Spanish Autonomous Communities sitting on the Committee of the Regions next to a local authority representative from Wales can be narrowed, if not totally overcome. It should also be a target for the Assembly to re-negotiate the representation of Welsh interests on the Committee of the Regions back to its former status of three full and three alternate members.

THE WIDER WORLD

Some have talked of a foreign policy stance for Wales being possible through the Assembly. This is wishful thinking, given the limited remit that is available. In October 1998 Ireland opened a consulate in Cardiff in recognition of the increased status that Wales will have from 1999 onwards, but Ireland is a sovereign state. The possibility of Wales returning the complement, however symmetrical and apposite, is not for the short term. It is likely that the only Welsh 'consulate' will remain the Wales European Centre in Brussels, whatever its future form, for some considerable time.

The international links that exist between Wales and the wider world are nevertheless many and disparate. On a commercial level, the raising of Wales' profile abroad has been achieved by the WDA and DBRW obtaining inward investment from a wide range of countries and by formal agreements between the Welsh Office and New South Wales in Australia, Ontario in Canada and Oita in Japan. Some links are localised or community-based, such as town or school twinning arrangements. Others are artistic. The creation of Wales Arts International by the British Council in Wales and the Arts Council for Wales has been an important recent development in that field. Sport, too, is an important international connector that has played a role in strengthening Wales' image overseas. And there are numerous academic departments in Welsh universities that have strong overseas links and specialisms but which do not necessarily have a framework through which to make a decisively Welsh input.

There is a case for saying that the Assembly should review international Welsh interests in the round and give a lead where necessary. The concept of regional/national links is just as valid for Wales beyond Europe, but there has not been a formalised structure on which to hang them in the same way. There already exists in Dolen Cymru, the Wales Lesotho Link, a body that has taken on international co-operation and development issues directly. The experience of groups such as the Wales Nicaragua Solidarity Campaign, Cymru Cuba and smaller local groups that have established links with Haiti, Cape Verde, South Africa and other countries and which provide a distinctively Welsh context to their work can be used to help create a more formalised agenda.

In the ethnic minority communities in Wales, particularly in the well-established and quite large Somali community, there exist connections with developing countries that are already diverse in terms of the work of their voluntary and community groups here. Given the Assembly's avowed remit of catering for minorities and giving them a voice, the creation of formal links – possibly through a form of overseas aid – is an option to investigate. Some indications of the way things might develop are already visible. The UK Department for International Development (DFID) has acknowledged the separate status of Cyfanfyd (the development education association for Wales) by providing it with financial support to employ a co-ordinator and to manage its own grants fund for development education in Wales. DFID is also considering establishing a Welsh presence for itself. A feasibility study by the Assembly to look at the various international strands mentioned here would be a useful beginning.

An international context for Assembly members is important for their understanding of the interrelationships that exist in an increasingly globalised world. The United Nations, the structure of international human rights agreements and conventions, and the work of UN agencies should all have a bearing on the Assembly's agenda, however domestic it is in essence. Sustainable Development, explored in Chapter 11, is the most truly global of all the matters with which the Assembly will be concerned. It is therefore correct that it should do so within the framework that is provided by the UN *Agenda 21* programme, created by the Rio Earth Summit in 1992 and the Kyoto follow-up meeting in 1997.

ACTION POINTS AND PRIORITIES

- The Assembly should build on the efforts of the Welsh Office and the other bodies in the Welsh European equation.

- A positive commitment to the concept of a 'Europe of the Regions' by Assembly members will give the Welsh image in Europe a boost and should help in securing a good financial deal for Wales from European reform.

- The Assembly should build upon the experience and links already formed between Wales and the 'Four Motor Regions' and with regional economic development agencies to create more vibrant alliances and new Regional groupings in Europe.

- There should be a permeable membership of the Assembly's European Programme Committee and Subject Committees to tap into expertise already accrued elsewhere in Europe by Welsh officials and representatives and to build the all-important consensus across party divides and interest groups that is needed in dealings with outside bodies.

- Responsibility for election of members of the European Committee of the Regions should be taken over by the Assembly by the time of the next nominations for members, and a case made for increasing Welsh membership on that Committee from four to six.

- A feasibility study should be instituted, separate from the Assembly's European Committee, to look into the international links and concerns that the Assembly needs to consider in the future, beyond the limits of the European Union.

CHAPTER 32

WALES AND
THE GLOBAL ECONOMY

Dafydd Trystan

Economic success is increasingly defined in relation to the operation of the global economy. But what does the globalisation of the economic sphere mean in real terms for Wales? What can and should the National Assembly do to promote Welsh interests in an increasingly competitive world-wide market place? The first task facing the National Assembly is to understand the relationship between the Welsh and global economies, a relationship about which there is little consensus. *Pathway to Prosperity - A New Economic Agenda for Wales* (Welsh Office, 1998), offers some analysis of the current state of the Welsh economy, but there is much work to be done to ensure that Wales takes full advantage of the changes currently occurring at the international level.

There is a widespread perception that the world economy is now different from anything that we have seen in the 75 years after World War One. And the shorthand term for this new economic world order is 'globalisation'. The distinguishing characteristics of globalisation are large and rapid flows of capital around the world and a reorganisation of production in many industries, making them much more footloose than before.

Capital can flow around the world more easily for two reasons, one political and the other technological. The collapse of communism and the relative success of liberal capitalism in the third world have opened up more areas of the globe to foreign investment. The information revolution has facilitated the transfer of funds. Moreover, it has enabled many industrial and commercial processes to be broken down into their component parts. Whereas in the 1950s to the 1970s much production tended to take place in large vertically integrated firms, now the so-called 'value-chain' can be split up. Processes like research, design, and component manufacture can be outsourced to a greater extent than before. Often this outsourced activity can take place anywhere in a different county or even continent from the rest of the process. So, for example, European airlines can put computer facilities in southern India and German banks can get clerical and administrative functions carried out in Ireland.

This has changed the balance of power within and between countries and classes. Workers find themselves competing with other, often lower-paid workers, across the globe. To provide jobs, countries compete for footloose capital for 'overseas investment'. Wales has been an energetic player in this game.

Capital is not the dominant factor in this world, however, although it has gained at the expense of low-skilled labour. Equally, or more important, are key skills that remain in scarce supply and attract capital to work with them. Enterprise, the ability to bring together skills and capital is also of the first importance.

Wales has been relatively successful in attracting capital, generally to set up manufacturing establishments. The appeal has often been labour that is very cheap by European standards and proximity to large affluent markets in the European Union. But assembly of goods is now often not the part of production which adds most value or generates most wealth. The design, financing and marketing of goods often accounts for a larger part of their price. And all too often these functions are carried out elsewhere, even for goods 'made in Wales'. To increase its prosperity, Wales has to be able to undertake more of the higher value-added parts of production. Not only will that result in higher incomes but it will give greater robustness to the economy. Marginal production facilities can easily be closed or move away when there is excess capacity in the world economy.

The context of Wales's interaction with the wider world economy is increasingly set at the European level. From the Single Market Programme to the development of Economic and Monetary Union, Europe continues to be a key factor in the success or otherwise of Welsh economic linkages, not only with fellow European countries, but further afield. The achievement of Objective One status for western Wales and the Valleys would greatly enhance the scope of the Assembly's potential action (Morgan and Price, 1998). What influence therefore can the National Assembly have on the patterns of linkages between the Welsh economy and the global economy? How can it set targets and direct more effectively the activities of the enlarged Welsh Development Agency?

THE CURRENT POSITION

The media coverage of such flagship projects such as the LG development in Newport, Sony in Pencoed, and Ford in Bridgend might lead one to conclude that Foreign Direct Investment (FDI) plays a central role in the Welsh economy. And at one level it is undeniable that foreign direct investment has had a significant impact, particularly during the very difficult transition period from when the economy was largely based on coal and steel to the more diverse pattern of industry at the turn of the twenty first century. On the other hand one should note the amount of jobs created in Wales by foreign owned firms. Table 1 illustrates the ownership of new manufacturing plants in Wales between 1966 and 1994:

TABLE 1

	Number of factory openings between 1966 and 1994	1994 Employment
New branch plants of UK owned firms from Outside Wales	151	17,400
New branch plants of Welsh owned firms	136	17,400
Total (branch plants)	287	34,800
Transfers into Wales	99	9,200
New Enterprises	676	28,500
Total UK Investment	**1,062**	**72,500**
Overseas Investment		
First time investment	141	25,000
New branch plant of company already in Wales	27	2,700
Plant transfers to Wales from other parts of the UK	20	4,700
Total Overseas Investment	**188**	**32,400**
Total	**1,250**	**104,900**

Source: Welsh Economic Trends, 1006: 63

Considering the media attention lavished on new foreign owned firms, it may be surprising to learn that only 30 per cent of new investment in manufacturing in Wales has come from outside the UK. And employment in overseas owned manufacturing plants in Wales only accounts for five per cent of Welsh employment (*Welsh Economic Trends*, 1995-96)[1] The pattern of ownership of these overseas owned companies is also illuminating. The evidence indicates that most originate in the USA and elsewhere in the EU, rather than the Far East, as Table 2 below illustrates.

Over 40 per cent of the overseas enterprises in Wales are owned by American firms,

TABLE 2

Area of Origin	Number of Plants	Number of Companies	Employment 1996 (000s)	Percentage of Wales total in overseas owned plants
USA	139	116	30.9	41.0%
Japan	38	28	16.9	22.4%
EU	141	123	20.2	26.8%
Other European	18	15	1.9	2.5%
Canada	14	12	3.0	4.0%
Other	31	20	2.5	3.3%
Total Overseas	**381**	**314**	**75.4**	**100.0%**

Source: Digest of Welsh Statistics, 1997: 153

whilst a quarter are owned by EU firms[2]. Only 22 per cent of overseas owned manufacturing plants are owned by Japanese firms. Thus it may well be said that the Welsh economy remains embedded within the Atlantic economy, a pattern which replicates the situation in the earlier part of the century when Wales was highly dependent on coal and steel.

Wales has undoubtedly been very successful in attracting foreign direct investment, both within the UK and on a global basis. World-wide in 1996 the UK was third in terms of FDI inflows, behind only China and the USA. Within the UK Wales was particularly successful, attracting 22.1 per cent of FDI (WDA, 1997 : 2-3). Thus not only was Wales the amongst the most attractive locations world-wide, but we also ranked amongst the top global Regions for attracting FDI capital expenditure[3] on a per capita basis as well.

However, considering the data on foreign owned firms in Wales and FDI inflows, is only a part of the equation of Wales' relationship to the global economy. One must also consider the outflows of investment. In this instance the record of the Welsh economy is far less successful. Phil Cooke in a recent article comparing Wales to Baden-Würtemberg remarks that:

'... while Baden-Würtemberg possesses foreign direct investment - IBM, Hewlett-Packard, Sony - this is dwarfed by the presence of indigenous multi-nationals such as Daimler-Benz and Robert Bosch. Moreover Wales has nothing to compare with the often world-class **Mittelstand** sector and the dense supply-chain systems of automotive, electronic and machinery firms'
(Cooke, 1997).

Whilst Wales has an undoubted weakness in the lack of domestically-owned multi-nationals, notwithstanding the recent international growth of Hyder plc's activities (Hyder, 1998), there is also an acknowledged reluctance for companies to export. This reluctance is particularly acute amongst the small and medium-sized enterprise (SME) sector, and has led the Welsh Development Agency to institute its *SAGE* (Strategic Approaches to the Global Economy) programme, to deal with this perceived weakness. The challenge faced is a significant one and is underlined by data on the exporting patterns of SME's across the UK. Some 100,000 small and medium sized enterprises across the UK export their products, yet only 500 are Welsh SMEs (*SAGE*, 1997:1). This figure represents only 10 per cent of the expected total if one were to consider a proportional population based figure for Wales. Welsh SMEs are far less likely to export than their counterparts in the rest of the UK.

Wales has been amongst the most successful countries world-wide in attracting foreign direct investment in manufacturing enterprises. These now employ around 25 per cent of the Welsh manufacturing workforce. On the other hand, foreign-owned firms still only account for a small proportion of total Welsh employment, about eight per cent.

CURRENT PROGRAMMES

The WDA is seen as a model development agency within the UK and across Europe because of its many programmes linking Wales with European and global best practice. Examples examined here include the *SAGE* and *Intelligent Region* programmes. In recent years, too, the WDA has placed great emphasis on developing the soft-ware of the Welsh economy through networking initiatives such as *Team Wales* and *Source Wales*.[4]

'GLOBALIZATION' PROGRAMMES

The *Strategic Approaches to the Global Economy* (*SAGE*) programme, was developed with small and medium-sized enterprises (SMEs) in mind, to encourage them to develop a positive management outlook towards the global economy. Through workshops, seminars, videos and conferences the aim of the programme is to disseminate best practice examples and to offer practical advice for those companies wishing to develop an international market for their goods and services.

It is difficult to assess the success of the programme. However informal evidence suggests that a more positive attitude is being developed amongst companies involved in the project[5]. Having said this, the language of the programme does seem somewhat out of touch with the everyday business realities of the companies involved. The key message of the programme is that firms should develop a positive attitude towards 'going global'. Yet even the strategies of those companies held up as best practice examples reflect clear national and international targeting.[6] Companies tended to focus attention on particular foreign markets and develop strategic alliances in others.

The *Global Link* programme is described by the WDA as:

> '... *the WDA's international business development service facilitating profitable growth by identifying, selecting and presenting new business opportunities throughout Europe and the world.*'[7]

The programme claims the participation of over 400 companies and more than 250 successful deals. Undoubtedly the impact of the initiative will grow in importance as the networks of those companies wishing to become international players develops.

TECHNOLOGICAL INITIATIVES

Technology is increasingly seen as a key component of success in relation to the global economy. Industries and regions with a high technological and innovative profile are deemed to be amongst the most successful on a global level (Cooke, 1997, Morgan 1997). Though Wales has suffered traditionally from a lack of Research and Development expenditure (Welsh Office, 1998, 11), and still lags behind most UK regions in this regard, progress has been made in recent years.

Wales was amongst the first European regions to benefit from a Regional Technology Plan, and the associated initiatives which were spawned as a result of this plan. These have also been linked to the *Wales Information Society* and *Intelligent Region* projects, described in Chapter 13. Though it is too early to analyse the success of these initiatives, anecdotal evidence certainly points to a significant growth in the importance accorded to the related technology both in business and in public administration in Wales.[8]

Much of the debate surrounding economic development in Wales has emphasised the high-technology, high-skilled, high value-added aims of the agencies charged with economic development. The importance of high-technology industries, and in general the importance of technology to all enterprises will inevitably increase. In this there will be a central role for the Assembly and the new WDA to promote people-centred investments in technology.[9]

TEAM WALES AND SOURCE WALES

Team Wales has been pioneered by the WDA to create an attractive 'Team' for inward investors. The aim is to bring together public agencies, at both the national and local levels, private enterprises, and the TECs to provide a package of services to potential investors. It has been cited as a significant attraction and has certainly been a factor in the decisions of some major inward investors to come to Wales. LG is hailed as one of the latest 'success' stories of the 'Team Wales' approach.

The WDA's *Source Wales* initiative is described as:

> '... *a buyer-driven service helping businesses to find high quality suppliers and helping suppliers to reach the high levels of performance now demanded by the world's leading companies.*' [10]

The programme not only ensures high quality supplies for inward investors but seeks to develop the standards within Welsh businesses to be able to supply these companies. Its aim is to ensure that the benefits of inward investment are widely diffused within the Welsh economy.

It is worth considering other examples of 'globalization initiatives' from regional development agencies in other parts of Europe, for example ERVET the development agency for the Emilia-Romagna Region of Italy, and the Graz technology transfer plans in Austria.

ERVET

ERVET is the development agency of the Emilia-Romagna Region of Italy. Established in 1974 its activities may be summarised as:

- Promotion of the entrepreneurial fabric.

- Socio-economic development of the regional territory.

- Technical assistance to the Emilia-Romagna Regional Government.'
  (ERVET, 1998:3).

Its aim is similar to many RDAs across Europe. ERVET, however, places significant importance on its 'system' or network, and this has been crucial in delivering services to enterprises to deal with the challenges of the global economy. This is particularly relevant for those SMEs given advice by ERVET on productive reconversion, and at a more general level on diversification of industrial sectors. Within rural areas covered by the EU's current Objective 5b regions ERVET has conducted 14 workshops, seminars and meetings on the theme of internationalisation, providing information for rural SMEs on issues surrounding the development of the global economy.

A key lesson from ERVET is the promotion of regional socio-economic development. All too often in the recent past the Welsh Development Agency has sought to promote a particular form of economic development which has led to uneven geographical and sectoral growth, without due attention to the social dimension. Developing upon the practices of ERVET the National Assembly should define the appropriate framework for a holistic method of socio-economic development.

TECHNOLOGY TRANSFER - GRAZ

The aims of Graz's Technology Transfer programme are as follows:

> 'Competitive advantages are realised through advanced knowledge nowadays.
> In the future those regions will be successful that will be able to transfer
> information into knowledge.' (Mortlbauer & Schrittwieser, 1998:1)

The objective is to improve knowledge transfer within the Graz region, and thus enhance its competitive advantage. The strategic development plan is divided into three modules: awareness raising, targeted co-operation and networking between SMEs. (Mortlbauer & Schrittwieser, 1998:4) The scheme has moved from workshop-based awareness-raising sessions to developing links between economic enterprises and the educational sector. Links with the educational sector have included multimedia school-based programmes, and a programme specifically targeted at local polytechnics, to improve co-operation between regional enterprise and local polytechnics. Whilst focusing on SMEs, the Graz technology transfer programme has recognised the key role of education in promoting technological innovation.

The Graz example points to the central importance of public animation or leadership in developing an appropriate framework for regional innovation. As noted earlier, the WDA has developed several programmes related to this theme, but the crucial importance of innovation should be not be overlooked at any stage.

POLICY IMPLICATIONS FOR THE ASSEMBLY

EDUCATION - PARTICULARLY HIGHER EDUCATION

It is commonplace to assert the traditional importance of education within Welsh society. However, within the context of the changes in the global economy, the role of education and particularly higher education assumes even greater importance. Success in developing indigenous industries ready for the challenges of the global economy and in attracting high value investments from elsewhere, depends on a highly-skilled, flexible workforce[11].

Ireland, for example, has successfully prioritised higher education. As a result it has been able to offer high quality graduates to indigenous firms as well as those coming from overseas (Arnold, 1998). Such success may be contrasted with the mixed record of the provision of a highly skilled workforce to LG in Newport (Phelps, Lovering and Morgan, 1998: 133). If Wales is truly to benefit from the global economy, then more emphasis should be placed on education, providing adequate training and resources to equip the Welsh workforce to take advantage of the global economy (see Chapter 17).

All too often there is a tendency to unquestioningly believe the powerful discourse surrounding 'globalization', and to develop programmes based on this understanding. A detailed analysis of the **actual** impact of international pressures on the Welsh economy should be commissioned by the Assembly early in its existence.

Detailed analysis of the Welsh economy is a relatively new pursuit. With a few notable exceptions[12], the majority of the work has been conducted during the last decade. The most recent economic analysis has been the Welsh Office's economic strategy *Pathway to Prosperity* (1998), which whilst strong on analysis, does not focus primarily on the international realm. The Assembly should be wary about accepting uncritically the WDA's approach to the global economy. It should be subjected to rigorous, independent analysis, a task well suited to the economic development Subject Committee of the Assembly.

NEW DIRECTIONS FOR THE WDA PROGRAMMES

The Assembly should also consider whether a shift in emphasis is appropriate for several of the WDA programmes. For example with the *SAGE* Programme the emphasis on 'going global' should be reconsidered and enhanced. Programmes should be directed towards changing the management culture of enterprises to enable them to take advantage of opportunities in alternative markets. The focus should be on providing companies with the appropriate skills and training to analyse specific exporting opportunities and decide on the most effective course of action within the company in relation to international markets.

A FOCUS ON TECHNOLOGY AND INNOVATION

Technology and Innovation are increasingly becoming key determinants of success on a global scale. Throughout its workings the Assembly should build on the work of the *Wales Information Society* project to promote technological literacy amongst the people and enterprises of Wales, and a culture of innovation within the management structure of enterprises. Technological literacy should be prioritised within education.

The innovatory dimension is quite crucial in terms of the transformations that are occurring within the global economy. The pace of product development, technological change and market fluctuations has increased rapidly and shows signs of gathering even greater pace in future. It will be necessary not only to have a workforce trained in today's technologies, but a flexible and adaptive workforce that can deal as easily with new technologies and products. This will be a major challenge for the Assembly and the wider education system.

A SUSTAINABLE APPROACH TO THE GLOBAL ECONOMY

The National Assembly has a statutory duty to promote Sustainable Development. As discussed in Chapter 11, this duty is as relevant to the global economy, as any other component of its work. With decreasing transport costs and real opportunities for companies to set up operations in less developed countries, Wales will not succeed in the long-term by offering a low skilled, low waged workforce.

The Assembly should adopt a holistic approach to economic development. The promotion of indigenous industries is crucial and should not be ignored at the expense of large-scale inducements to foreign-owned firms, which still only play a relatively small part in the overall economic success of Wales. The key focus in this instance should be value for money. Whilst LG certainly attracts positive attention, questions that would have been debated if the Assembly had been underway would have been: Is this the most effective use of public funds for the promotion of economic development? Would have this amount of public investment been better directed to the less well-off western parts of Wales?

MADE IN WALES

The Assembly should develop the *Source* and *Team* Wales initiatives. The possibility of a Made in Wales programme should be given serious consideration - a programme backed by quality control, branding strategies and marketing back-up, for both goods and services. The Assembly could play a key role in ensuring that Wales becomes known as a producer and provider of high-quality and distinctive goods and services. Not only would the economic development of Wales be enhanced, but also Welsh enterprises backed by the Made in Wales brand would be in a stronger position in the global economy, and be able to deal more effectively with its competitive pressures.

CONCLUSION

The National Assembly has a key role to play in giving a strategic direction to the economic development of Wales. Over the past 20 years we have experienced the benefit that developments within the global economy can bring to Wales, particularly through the attraction of foreign direct investment. Whilst FDI is unlikely to continue at current levels, opportunities and challenges will remain. A range of Wales-specific 'global economy' projects, developed on a sustainable basis by the Assembly, will be important if we are to become a dynamic global Region at the turn of the twenty first century.

To strengthen the Welsh economy will require a Herculean investment in the skills of our people to equip them to compete on good terms in the global economy and to give them the wider perspectives required to create an enterprising culture. Sometimes the skills needed are misidentified. Not everyone has to be a rocket scientist. Italian prosperity, for example, is built on superior design and style in a wide range of consumer goods. Technology plays a part in this but the bedrock is a visually-sensitive culture and the artistic talents to which that gives rise. Microchips can be bought very cheaply, as LG workers know to their cost. However, a Gucci or Versace label commands a premium price. If we had developed a highly distinctive cuisine, for example, our tourist industry would be much more valuable.

The challenge is not only to train people to keep abreast of modern technologies, it is also to identify the incipient strengths of Welsh culture and to find ways to develop some of these for commercial prosperity. One of the traditional Welsh traits is a lively imagination and there is plenty of scope for applying this to the problem of making a good living in the modern world.

References

Arnold, Lyn (1997, in *Welsh Agenda*, Winter 1997-98, pp. 24-25.

Cooke, Phillip, (1997), 'Regions in a Global Market: the experiences of Wales and Baden-Würtemberg' in *Review of International Political Economy*, 4 (2), Summer 1997, pp. 349-381.

ERVET (1998), *ERVET's System - Description of Activities*, (Bologna: ERVET)

Hyder (1998), *Annual Review and Summary Financial Statement 1998*, (Cardiff: Hyder)

Lovering, John, (1998), 'Constructing the Welsh Economy: Changing Perspectives on Regional Economic Development', The O'Donnell Lecture 1998 delivered in March 98, at Aberystwyth, Swansea and Bangor

Mackay,. R. Ross et al., (1997), *The Economic Impact of the Welsh Assembly*, (Cardiff: IWA)

Morgan, Kevin, (1997), 'The Regional Animateur: Taking Stock of the Welsh Development Agency', in *Regional and Federal Studies*, Vol.7, No.2, Summer 1997, pp.70-94

Morgan, Kevin & Price, Adam, (1998), *The Other Wales: The Case for Objective 1 Funding post 1999*, IWA Research Report, (Cardiff: IWA)

Mortlbauer, Ursula & Schrittwieser, Walter, 'Networking and Partnership in an Intelligent Region - Regional Knowledge Transfer Graz (Austria)' paper presented at the Intelligent Region Conference, Cardiff, 18-19 May 1998

Phelps, Nicholas A, Lovering, John and Morgan, Kevin, (1998), 'Tying the firm to the region or tying the region to the firm?' in *European Urban and Regional Studies*, Vol. 5(2), (London: SAGE Publications), pp.119-137.

SAGE (1997), *Strategic Approaches to the Global Economy*, WDA booklet

Welsh Development Agency, (1997), *Investors Wales - A quarterly economic update of Wales*, Winter 1997-98, Issue No, 16 (Cardiff: WDA)

Welsh Development Agency Video, 'Strategic Approaches to the Global Economy'

Welsh Development Agency Web Site, global link section, http://www.wda.co.uk/business/global/index_fr.htm

Welsh Development Agency Web Site, Source Wales section, http://www.wda.co.uk/business/source/index.htm

Welsh Office (1995), *Welsh Economic Trends*, No.16, 1995 (Cardiff: Welsh Office)

Welsh Office (1997), *Digest of Welsh Statistics*, (Cardiff: Welsh Office)

Welsh Office, (1998), *Pathway to Prosperity - A New Economic Agenda for Wales*

Notes

1 Having suggested the relatively small part of the Welsh economy accounted for by 'foreign' owned firms, one should not discount the supplier-chain impact of such projects, particularly in light of the WDA's success through programmes such as the *Source Wales* in developing Wales-based supplier networks for many of the inward investors. At the same time the *Source Wales* programme has its limitations, as was noted by one analysis of the impact of LG in South Wales, where doubt is cast on the ability of Welsh suppliers to service the new LG plants (see Phelps, Lovering & Morgan, 1998:133).

2 Excluding the UK

3 Whilst Wales has been particularly successful in attracting FDI based on manufacturing industries and thus ranks highly in terms of FDI capital expenditure, it has a particularly poor record in terms of FDI in the finance and business services sector.

4 I have divided the programmes to be considered into those categories to facilitate analysis. In the broader sense the success of one programme is very much linked to another, and sight should not be lost of the holistic approach to analysing the WDA's package of programmes.

5 Informal interviews held with various company managers at the WDA's *SAGE* conference, held at the Park Hotel, Cardiff, March 18-19, 1998

6 This was clear during the presentation by DMM engineering, Llanberis, at the *SAGE* conference, where distinct market targeting, expanding in the UK first, then in Europe, and then further afield was described as the key to the company's success.

7 From the WDA web site, address - http://www.wda.co.uk/business/global/index_fr.htm

8 On the public administration side, there is now an acceptance of the importance of information technology within the structures of the National Assembly and the benefits that can come as a result.

9 This type of focus can be seen in the Welsh Office's economic strategy, where the emphasis is placed in Chapter two on developing a higher skills, higher wage workforce. (Welsh Office, 1998. 4-7)

10 Information accessed at the WDA web site, address - http:\\www.wda.co.uk/business/source/index.htm

11 In this instance the term flexible is used to denote a workforce which is adaptive and innovative with a wide range of transferable skills. In this context one must not only consider purely vocational training, but education in the broadest sense developing a wide base of knowledge and transferable skills.

12 For example, the work of the late Professor Edward Nevin on Welsh economy input/output tables in the 1960s and the *Economic Plan for Wales*, produced by the Plaid Cymru Research Group in 1970. See also the annual economic review in *Contemporary Wales*, and several reports produced by the IWA, including *Wales 2010* (1993) and *Wales 2010 ,Three Years On* (1996).

APPENDICES

I   NOTES ON THE CONTRIBUTORS

II THE IWA NATIONAL ASSEMBLY AGENDA CONFERENCE PROGRAMME 1998

III PARTICIPANTS IN THE IWA NATIONAL ASSEMBLY AGENDA SEMINAR PROGRAMME 1998

IV IWA PUBLICATIONS

APPENDIX 1

NOTES ON THE CONTRIBUTORS

DENIS BALSOM

Dr Denis Balsom is Warden of Gregynog, the University of Wales Centre in Powys. He was a Lecturer in Political Science at the University of Wales, Aberystwyth, 1974-95 and has recently served as a Specialist Adviser to the Select Committee on Welsh Affairs. A consultant to HTV Wales he is also Editor of the annual Wales Yearbook.

JOHN BARNIE

Originally from Abergavenny, Monmouthshire, John Barnie was Lecturer in English, at Copenhagen University from 1969 to 1982. He was Assistant Editor of the bi-monthly cultural magazine *Planet* from 1985 - 90, and is now its Editor. He is a poet, essayist and writer of fiction.

NIGEL BLEWITT

Nigel Blewitt became Research Officer with the Institute of Welsh Affairs in 1998 after gaining a Doctoral Degree in labour economics from Cardiff University. His research focused on unemployment and economic inactivity in Wales during the 1980s and early 1990s.

PETER BRYANT

Peter Bryant is Head of Policy at Wales Council for Voluntary Action where he has responsibility for co-ordinating the input on government policy affecting the voluntary sector. He is currently involved in drafting the Compact between government and the voluntary sector and preparing the sector for the National Assembly.

IAN BUTLER

Ian Butler is a Senior Lecturer and Research Fellow in Social Work at the University of Wales Cardiff. He was for many years a social work practitioner and manager in residential, field and day-care services for children in both the statutory and voluntary sectors. He is an Honorary Member of the Council of the NSPCC. Recent books include: *Getting into Practice: Social Work with Children and Families* (1997) (with Gwenda Roberts), London: Jessica Kingsley; *A Case of Neglect? Children's Experiences and the Sociology of Childhood* (1996) (Ed. With Ian Shaw): Basingstoke: Avebury; *Children Speak: Children, Trauma and Social Work* (1994) (with Howard Williamson), London: Longman.

JANE CARPENTER

Jane Carpenter currently works as Regional Planning Officer for the House Builders Federation in South Wales. Jane speaks on behalf of the housebuilding industry in Wales, principally on matters of housing policy, planning policy, technical matters and political issues. She is a Chartered Town Planner and previously worked for the Rhondda Borough Council.

PHIL COOKE

Phil Cooke is Professor of Regional Development and Director of the Centre for Advanced Studies in the Social Sciences at the University of Wales Cardiff. His most recent projects are the EU-Fourth Framework-funded studies of *Regional Innovation in Europe and Academic*

Entrepreneurship in Europe. Recent books are (with Kevin Morgan) *The Associational Economy* (1998) for Oxford University Press; *Regional Innovation Systems* (1998, UCL Press) and *Networking for Competitive Advantage* (1996) produced for the National Economic and Social Council of the Republic of Ireland. In 1995 *The Rise of the Rustbelt* (UCL Press), a study of innovation in older industrial regions of Europe and North America was published. In 1992 he published *Towards Global Localisation* (UCL Press).

BOB DAIMOND

Bob Daimond is surveyor to Gwynedd Council and heads the Highways and Engineering Department. Prior to re-organisation, he was Director of Highways with Gwynedd County Council. Since 1996 he has been advisor to the Welsh Local Government Association on transport and technical services.

GRAHAM DAY

Graham Day is a sociologist, and currently Head of Department of the School of Sociology and Social Policy at the University of Wales Bangor. He is joint editor of the journal *Contemporary Wales* and has written extensively on economic and social change in Wales, especially rural Wales. He has a particular interest in community participation and is the author of a recent review of participatory methods, *Where Do We Go From Here?*, published by the Wales Council for Voluntary Action.

MARK DRAKEFORD

Mark is a lecturer in Social Policy and Applied Social Studies at the University of Wales in Cardiff. His research interest lie mainly in poverty issues, social policy in relation to young people and social policy in Wales.

SUE ESSEX

Sue Essex has considerable local government experience as an officer and also as an elected member in Cardiff for the last fifteen years. She was the first woman to become Leader of the former Cardiff City Council and served on both the Council of Welsh Districts and the Association of District Councils. Currently she is a member of the Countryside Council for Wales and of the Welsh Office Transport Advisory Group. In her capacity as a Lecturer at Cardiff University, she has researched and written on local/central government relations and takes a prominent role in planning and environmental issues in Wales.

MARTIN FITTON

Martin Fitton is the Chief Executive of Brecon Beacons National Park, the Chair of Wales JIGSO which promotes techniques for encouraging public participation and Chair of Coed Cymru, the Welsh Woodland Project.

SIR JOHN GRAY

Sir John Gray joined the Diplomatic Service in 1962 and served in the Lebanon, Bahrain, London, Geneva (UN), Bulgaria and Saudi Arabia. Head of Maritime, Aviation and Environment Department in the Foreign Office and subsequently Ambassador to the Lebanon, the OECD and Belgium. Retired 1996 and moved to Wales. Consultancy posts with Hyder, WDA, Brecon Mineral Water Company, Generale Bank (of Belgium); Member of the Board, Cardiff Bay Development Corporation. Community work with the Welsh Centre for International Affairs, Wales Council European Movement, National Botanic Garden of Wales, IOD Wales, Commonwealth War Graves Commission and various British-Belgian and Middle East associations.

CHRIS HAWKER

Following work in and with the Third World, Chris Hawker worked in Community Development in both London and York before coming to South Wales to train as a Social Worker. He worked initially in research, development and training for the University of Wales Swansea on User Empowerment and a number of national agencies on projects as diverse as economic development in rural Europe, social development in rural Wales and the introduction of Community Care. He was recruited by Mid Glamorgan County Council to help implement the 1990 NHS and Community Care Act. He is now Assistant Director of Social Services (Policy and Performance) at Rhondda-Cynon-Taff County Borough Council.

STEPHEN HILL

Stephen Hill is Director of the Welsh Economy Research Unit at Cardiff Business School and has written widely on various aspects of the local economy, including economic strategy and industrial and labour market analysis.

JANE HUTT

Director of Chwarae Teg (Fair Play), an economic development initiative set up to expand the role of women in the Welsh workforce. She is responsible for the Welsh Office Under Fives childcare Initiative and the South East Wales TEC Out of School Childcare Initiative. Jane has worked in Wales for over 20 years, mainly in the voluntary sector and has been involved in setting up a number of women's initiatives. She is author of *Opening the Town Hall Doors* - an introduction to local government, and *Making Opportunities* - a guide for Women and Employers.

MARI JAMES

Mari James was a member of the National Assembly Advisory Group and is a member of Assembly Preparations Group. She was Co-ordinator of the Parliament for Wales Campaign and Vice Chair of the 1997 Yes for Wales umbrella referendum campaign. She is Research Project Manager at the Centre for Advanced Studies, Cardiff University. She was previously Vice President, Public Affairs with Olympia and York Canary Wharf Ltd and Account Director of Westminster Strategy Public Relations.

J. BARRY JONES

Director of Political Studies, Cardiff University. Publications include (with Michael Keating) *Labour and the British State* (1985); *Parliament and Territoriality: The Committee on Welsh Affairs,* 1978-1983; Editor (with David Foulkes and R A Wilford) *The Welsh Veto: The Wales Act 1978 and the Referendum,* (1983); Editor (with Michael Keating) Regions in the European Community (1985) and *Regions in the European Union* (1994). Secretary of the Wales for the Assembly Campaign during the 1979 referendum.

GARETH JONES

Dr Gareth Jones has been Chairman of the Nevill Hall & District NHS Trust since 1994. He was previously a non-executive director of Powys Healthcare Trust and Gwent Health Authority. He was Chairman of the group which produced the *Wales 2010 - Creating our Future* report for the Institute of Welsh Affairs in 1993 and author of *Wales 2010: Three Years On* (1996). He is a director of the IWA and chairs the Institute's Research Panel.

GARETH WYN JONES

Gareth Wyn Jones is Professor in the School of Biological Sciences at the University of Bangor and Associate Director of the Centre for Arid Zone Studies. Previously, he was Deputy Chief Executive and Director of Science and Policy Development for the Countryside Council for Wales. He has extensive experience of rural development and sustainable use of natural renewable resources in Wales and elsewhere. He is currently co-ordinating an EU project on Sustainable Rangeland Management in Southern Africa. He is Chair of the IWA North Wales Branch, recently Chair of Coed Cymru, and President of the Bardsey Island Trust.

EIRLYS PRITCHARD JONES

Eirlys Pritchard Jones was Headteacher of Ysgol Gyfun Cymer Rhondda from 1989 to 97 and was a member of Tony Blair's Education Summit on raising standards in Education. She is Executive Chair of Menter a Busnes, the Aberystwyth-based economic development company. She is Chair of the IWA Steering Group on research into Welsh medium education, a member of the Institute's *Welsh Baccalaureate* working group, and of the IWA's Research Panel.

IVOR LIGHTMAN

Ivor Lightman spent most of his career as a civil servant in Whitehall, serving in a number of Departments including HM Treasury and the Departments of the Environment and Trade and Industry; in the last he was the Under Secretary heading the Industrial Policy Division. In 1981 he came to the Welsh Office as Deputy Secretary (Health and Social Policy). Since leaving the civil service in 1988 he has been a member of the Parole Board, public affairs adviser to Touche Ross Management Consultants and Chair and Vice Chair of two Welsh Housing Associations. In 1995-96 he chaired the Constitution Unit's Consultative Group on a Welsh Assembly. He is a member of the Institute of Welsh Affairs' Research Panel and chairs its Constitution Working Group.

R. ROSS MACKAY

Professor of Economics and Director of the Institute of Economic Research, University of Wales, Bangor. His research interests include Labour Market Adjustment, Regional Economics and the Political Economy of Social Insurance. Author of the IWA report, *The Economic Impact of the Welsh Assembly* (1997).

TERRY MARSDEN

Professor of Environmental Policy and Planning in the Department of City and Regional Planning (CPLAN) at Cardiff University. He directs the Environmental Planning research unit in CPLAN and has written extensively on rural and environmental matters. These include *Constructing the Countryside* (UCL Press 1993), *Reconstituting Rurality* (UCL Press, 1995) and *The Condition of Sustainability* (Routledge. forthcoming 1998). He is a government adviser on rural and agricultural matters.

NICK MILLER

Nick Miller is a specialist consultant and researcher on labour market economics and skills issues. Through his own consultancy Miller Research and in association with the Welsh Economy Research Unit, he has worked for a wide range of clients in the public and private sectors, including a number of TECs, development agencies and local authorities.

MARGARET MINHINNICK

Founder and Director of *Sustainable Wales Cymru Gynhalol* which seeks to integrate environmental, social and cultural concerns and thus promote sustainable development. A former teacher, she founded and developed Friends of the Earth Cymru, directing campaign strategies from 1984-1994. She organised regular Wales-wide training days for the public on a range of environmental issues. In 1995-96 she was presenter and researcher for HTV's *Grass Roots* series. Board member of Prince's Trust, Bro and Groundwork Bridgend, Advisor to the Board of the Women's Environmental Network, Member of Council of Management, CYLCH.

BRIAN MORGAN

Director of the Small Firms Research Unit at Cardiff Business School. The main objective of the Research Unit is to develop an innovative programme of research into the business development needs of SMEs. Prior to joining the Business School in 1997 Brian was Chief Economist at the Welsh Development Agency. He joined the Agency in 1991 from the Civil Service where he was Senior Economic Adviser at the Department of Energy, running the section responsible for analysing the impact of world oil markets and energy developments on the UK economy.

KEVIN MORGAN

Kevin Morgan is Professor of European Regional Development in the Department of City and Regional Planning at Cardiff University. He has published extensively on regional development issues in Europe and he is the co-author of *The Associational Economy: Firms, Regions and Innovation* (Oxford University Press, 1998). In addition to his academic work he has acted as an adviser to the European Commission, the OECD and Regional Development Agencies throughout Europe.

GEOFF MUNGHAM

Geoff Mungham is Director of Development, School of Journalism, Media and Cultural Studies at Cardiff University. His main interests are in the areas of political communications, media policy and global communications. A former Cardiff City Labour Councillor, he also has a keen interest in Labour Party history and policy-making.

JOHN OSMOND

John Osmond has been Director of the Institute of Welsh Affairs since 1996. Formerly a freelance journalist, TV Producer and research consultant, he was Welsh Affairs Correspondent with *The Western Mail* during the1970s. He was a Producer with HTV in the 1980s, and Assistant Editor *Wales on Sunday* 1988-90. Chair of the Parliament for Wales Campaign 1991-96. Author of many articles and books on Welsh politics and culture, most recently *Welsh Europeans* (Seren 1996).

KEITH PATCHETT

Emeritus Professor of Law in the University of Wales; law consultant on legislation, law drafting and public law, principally for countries in the Commonwealth, Central and Eastern Europe and the Baltics; member of the Advisory Committee of the Constitution Unit and its Advisory Group on Welsh devolution; member of the Working Party on a Government for Wales Bill for the Parliament for Wales Campaign; member of the Constitution Working Group of the Institute of Welsh Affairs.

ANDREW PITHOUSE

Andrew Pithouse practised in social work and has taught and researched in welfare for several years at Cardiff University where he is Director of Social Work Studies. His research interests include child care, community care, organisational change, welfare economics, management and service evaluation. His published work is in the area of family services evaluation, sociology of social work, user involvement, community care. Recent books include *Engaging the User in Welfare*, with H Williamson, Birmingham, Venture (1997); *Family Support and Family Centres: Issues Research & Evaluation in the UK, US and Hong Kong*, with S Lindsell and M Cheung, Ashgate (1998); *Social Work: the Social Organisation Of An Invisible Trade*, Ashgate (1998).

MIKE PONTON

Mike Ponton started his NHS career in Cardiff. During the late 1960s and early 1970s he worked as Medical Records Officer and subsequently House Governor at St Mary's Hospital Paddington, before taking up the post of Deputy Hospital Secretary at Leicester General Hospital. He returned to Wales in 1974 where he was Sector Administrator, Swansea North, then Area Planning Operator to West Glamorgan Health Authority. In 1982 he became Assistant District General Manager in West Glamorgan and in 1985 returned to Morriston Hospital as Unit General Manage r to Swansea's North Unit. He became Associate District General manager with East Dyfed Health Authority and in 1993 was appointed Joint Managing Director to the Pembrokeshire and East Dyfed Health Authorities. Since 1993 he has been Chief Executive of Health Promotion Wales.

IOAN BOWEN REES

Dr Rees served public authorities in London and Lancashire and in the four corners of Wales, retiring in 1991 after eleven years as Chief Executive of the old Gwynedd County Council. As a young man he fought Conwy and then Merthyr on behalf of Plaid Cymru, served on the party executive and developed a taste for comparative government. His work on Swiss local government gained him the Haldane Medal of the Royal Institute of Public Administration,. In 1994 he was a European Union Observer at the South African General Election. In 1997 he was awarded an honorary doctorate of laws by the University of Wales and appointed to the National Assembly Advisory Group. His publications include *Government by Community* (1971), *Cymuned a Chenedl* (1993) and *Beyond National Parks* (1995)

DAVID REYNOLDS

David Reynolds is Professor of Education at the University of Newcastle. He has researched school effectiveness and school improvement for twenty years, first in the Rhondda and then in Gloucestershire. He has also carried out research on best education practices in other countries and has recently chaired the Government Numeracy Task Force. He is co-author of the IWA study *A Competitive Edge: Why Welsh Medium Schools Perform Better*.

ANNETTE ROBERTS

Dr Annette Roberts is a researcher at the Welsh Economy Research Unit, Cardiff Business School, specialising in modelling the regional economy.

PAUL SILK

Paul Silk is a Deputy Principal Clerk of the House of Commons, currently working in the House's Legislation Office. He is a former Secretary of the Study of Parliament Group, and is

Convenor of its Study Group on Westminster and the Welsh Assembly. He is the joint author of *How Parliament Works* (4th edition 1998) and a contributor to a number of other publications on parliamentary affairs. He lives in Powys.

TERRY STEVENS

Dr Terry Stevens is the head of Stevens and Associates, a tourism and leisure consultancy based in Swansea since 1986. He has more than 25 years experience in the planning, development and management of tourism, having held posts with the Wales Tourist Board,Cadw: Welsh Historic Monuments, the Pembrokeshire Coast National Park and West Glamorgan County Council. He was Dean and Professor of Tourism and Leisure Management at the Swansea Institute and is currently visiting Professor at Reading and Bournemouth Universities. He has worked for the World Tourism Organisation, the United Nations Development Programme, the World Bank, and the EU.

MARK TEWDWR-JONES

Dr Mark Tewdwr-Jones is Lecturer in Planning at the Department of City and Regional Planning, Cardiff University. He worked for a short period in local government as a planning officer in South West England before returning to Cardiff in 1992 to undertake teaching and research work. His main research interests are in the fields of national planning policy, the distinctiveness of Welsh planning, European spatial planning, community involvement in local government, and second home controls. A regular commentator in the media on Welsh planning matters, Mark has also undertaken research work for both the Department of the Environment and the Welsh Office. On 1 February 1999, he takes up the post of Senior Lecturer in the Department of Land Economy, University of Aberdeen, where he will be involved in comparative research looking at the impact of the Scottish Parliament and Welsh Assembly on future planning policy.

STEPHEN THOMAS

Stephen Thomas has been Director of the Welsh Centre for International Affairs since November 1996. He previously worked for the Save the Children Fund and for Comic Relief on the management and funding of development work in Africa. He has also lived in France and Malta.

DAFYDD TRYSTAN

Dafydd Trystan teaches Welsh Politics and Welsh Political Economy at the Department of International Politics, University of Wales Aberystwyth, and is currently completing his doctoral work on the relationship between the Welsh economy and the global political economy. His research interests include globalisation, international political economy and contemporary developments in Welsh politics.

COLIN H WILLIAMS

Colin Williams is Research Professor in Sociolinguistics in the Department of Welsh, Cardiff University. He has previously taught in Universities in Canada, England and the USA. His publications include: *Called Unto Liberty: On Language and Nationalism*, Multilingual Matters, Clevedon, Avon, 1994; and (Ed) *The Political Geography of the New World Order*, J Wiley, London, 1993. He has recently completed a Welsh Language Board-sponsored project on Community Language Planning and Policy, whose first major report was published as Williams & Evans, *Y Cynllun Ymchwil Cymunedol (The Community Research Project)*, Welsh Language Board, Cardiff, July 1997. Currently he is analysing the European

Parliament's language policy and undertaking comparative research in Welsh, Irish and Scottish perspectives on bilingual public service provision.

JAN WILLIAMS

Chief Executive, Iechyd Morgannwg Health, formerly Chief Executive Llanelli/Dinefwr NHS Trust 1992-1995. She joined the NHS as a National Administrative Trainee in 1979. Held a number of posts in all aspects of health services management at hospital, community and health authority level, prior to becoming the UGM and subsequently Chief Executive of the Llanelli Dinefwr Trust, a post she held for eight years. Now into her third year of being a Health Authority Chief Executive, Mrs Williams' special interests are in the field of organisational development and equality of opportunity. She was the Opportunity 2000 Commissioner for NHS Wales from 1994-1996.

KEVIN WILLIAMS

Kevin Williams is Senior Lecturer in the School of Journalism, Media and Cultural Studies at University of Wales, Cardiff, and was a Research Fellow at the Danish National School of Journalism in Aarhus, Denmark during 1998. His latest book is *Get Me A Murder A Day* published by Arnold, a history of mass communications in Britain.

JOHN WYN OWEN

Mr Wyn Owen took up the post of Secretary of the Nuffield Trust, UK, in March 1997. Prior to this he was Director-General of New South Wales Health and until 1994 was Director of the National Health Service in Wales. His career has spanned both public and private sectors and is based on a strong commitment to research, education and training as a foundation for effective management.

NEIL WOODING

Neil Wooding was appointed to the position of Equal Opportunities Advisor to the National Health in Wales in the spring of 1992. Prior to this he worked within local government as the first Equality Officer in Wales. His interests in the Equality field include British and European legislation and theories of Equality change. He is the author of *The Equal Opportunities Good Practice Guide and Flexible Working Practice*. For the past five years he has lectured at a number of Universities on European and British Equality Law to postgraduate students from a variety of professional fields. He is currently engaged in post-doctoral research at the University of Bristol predicting the future scope of equal opportunity policies inside 21st century organisations.

APPENDIX II

THE IWA NATIONAL ASSEMBLY AGENDA CONFERENCE PROGRAMME 1998

THE NATIONAL ASSEMBLY'S POLICY AGENDA: 13 MARCH

This Conference, at the Park Hotel, Cardiff, was attended by 121 people. Leading MPs and spokespeople from each of the four main parties participated. The morning conference was followed by an IWA tenth anniversary lunch, attended by 200 people and addressed by the former Secretary of State for Wales, Ron Davies.

THE NEW POLITICS AND THE OPERATION OF THE NATIONAL ASSEMBLY: 20-21 MARCH

This international conference was organised as a two-day event at the Cardiff Bay Hotel in association with Charter 88, the University of Wales Institute Cardiff, and the University of Birmingham Institute for German Studies. The conference was attended by 270 people.

EUROPE'S DEVOLUTION DEBATE: THE FUTURE OF REGIONAL GOVERNANCE IN THE EU: 7 MAY

This conference, attended by 90 people, was organised in association with the Philip Morris Institute and the Brussels-based *Europe of Cultures 2002 Foundation*. The venue was provided by the Welsh Centre for International Affairs at the Temple of Peace, Cathays Park, Cardiff, and assistance provided by the Wales Council of the European Movement.

A RESPONSE TO THE NATIONAL ASSEMBLY ADVISORY GROUP: 15 MAY

This conference, attended by 40 people, was organised in Wrexham by the IWA's North Wales Branch.

WEST WALES AND THE NATIONAL ASSEMBLY: 12-13 JUNE

This dinner and conference, attended by 70 people, was organised by the IWA's West Wales Branch in association with Carmarthenshire County Council.

THE POLICY AGENDA OF THE NATIONAL ASSEMBLY: 27-28 JUNE

This conference, attended by 138 people, was held over two days on the University campus at Aberystwyth. The Conference was opened by Welsh Office Minister Peter Hain, with sessions grouping together themes addressed individually in the National Assembly Agenda seminar programme (see overleaf). Plenary sessions were held on Economic Priorities, Delivering Services, An integrated Rural Strategy, World Competitiveness, and Communications. In addition, there were individual contributions on The Assembly and Whitehall, A New Political Culture, Working With the National Assembly Advisory Group, The Assembly and Europe, and the Assembly and the Political Parties.

APPENDIX III

PARTICIPANTS IN THE IWA NATIONAL ASSEMBLY AGENDA SEMINAR PROGRAMME 1998

HOUSING SEMINAR, 1 APRIL 1998
(IWA, CARDIFF)

Ceri Black, Institute of Welsh Affairs; Jane Carpenter, The House Builders Federation; Barbara Castle, Penywaun Enterprise Partnership; Mike Cuddy, Land Authority for Wales; Jane Davidson, Welsh Local Government Association; Bob Dumbleton, Welsh Tenants' Federation; Keith Edwards, Director, TPAS; Gareth Hughes, Director, Welsh Federation of Housing Associations; Maggie Ing, Chair, Housing Committee, Bridgend County Borough Council; John Osmond, Director, Institute of Welsh Affairs; Adam Peat, Chief Executive, Tai Cymru - Housing for Wales; Selwyn Runnett, Principal, Runnett Consultancy Services; Graeme Salt, House Builders Federation; Mike Shanahan, Assistant Secretary, Housing Division, The Welsh Office; Robert Smith, University of Wales Cardiff; Tamsin Stirling, Policy Officer, Chartered Institute of Housing in Wales; Mark Tewdwr-Jones, University of Wales Cardiff.

VOLUNTARY SECTOR SEMINAR, 27 APRIL 1998
(IWA, CARDIFF)

Ceri Black, Institute of Welsh Affairs; Peter Bryant, Wales Council for Voluntary Action; James Crowe, SCOVO; Noel Davies, Secretary General, CYTUN Wales; Graham Day, University of Wales Bangor; Mark Drakeford, University of Wales Cardiff; Jill Evans, NFWI Wales; Martin Fitton, National Park Officer, Brecon Beacons National Park; Carol Green, Swansea Council for Voluntary Service; Jane Hutt, Director, Chwarae Teg; Ruth Marks, Business in the Community; David Middleton, Family Planning Association; Margaret Minhinnick, Sustainable Wales; Lynne Neagle, Wales Labour Party; John Osmond, Director, Institute of Welsh Affairs; Suzanne Smith, Co-ordinator, MEWN Cymru; Stephen Thomas, Director, Welsh Centre for International Affairs; Catriona Williams, Chief Executive, Children in Wales / Plant yng Nghymru.

ARTS SEMINAR, 6 MAY 1998
(IWA, CARDIFF)

Elen ap Gwynn, General Manager, Radio Ceredigion; Michael Baker, Arts Council of Wales; Iwan Bala; John Barnie, Editor, Planet; Ceri Black, Institute of Welsh Affairs; Phil Clark, Artistic Director, Sherman Theatre; Dave Clarke, DCA; Sybil Crouch, Manager, Taliesin Arts Centre; Steve Garrett, Cultural Concerns; Phil George, Head of Arts, Music and Features, BBC Wales; Sue Grayson Ford, Cardiff Bay Art Trust; Tamara Krikorian, Director, Cywaith Cymru - Artworks Wales; Peter Lord; John Matthews, McCann Millman Matthews; Clifford McLucas, Brith Gof; John Osmond, Director, Institute of Welsh Affairs; Maldwyn Pate; Robin Reeves, The New Welsh Review; Alwyn Roberts; Elfed Roberts, Eisteddfod Genedlaethol; Rhian-Anwen Roberts, Wales Millennium Centre; D R Thomas, Welsh Office; Ned Thomas, Gwasg Prifysgol Cymru; M. Wynn Thomas, University of Wales Swansea; Michael Trickey, Planning & Public Affairs Director, Arts Council of Wales; Yvette Vaughan Jones, International Officer, Arts Council of Wales; Catrin Webster.

TRANSPORT SEMINAR, 8 MAY 1998
(IWA, CARDIFF)

Brian Bigwood, CPRW; Nigel Blewitt, Research Officer, Institute of Welsh Affairs; Joan Clark, FTA; George C G Craig, Transport Planning & Environment Group, Welsh Office; Neil Crumpton, Friends of the Earth Cymru; Bob Daimond, Director of Highways, Gwynedd Council; John Davies, DSW Rail Ltd; Richard Diment, Director and Chief Executive, British Road Federation; Mike Hollingsworth, Welsh Development Agency; G Iwan Huws, National Park Officer, Snowdonia National Park Authority; Gareth Jones, Institute of Welsh Affairs; Brian Kemp, Head of Engineering & Transport, Newport County Borough Council; Renee Martin, Kennedy and Donkin Ltd; Richard Ninnes, Countryside Council for Wales; John Osmond, Director, Institute of Welsh Affairs; Iain Skewis, The Development Consultancy; Victoria Winckler, Welsh Local Government Association; Julian Worth, General Manager Business Development, EWS Railways.

ECONOMIC DEVELOPMENT SEMINAR, 11 MAY 1998
(PENCERRIG COUNTRY HOUSE HOTEL, BUILTH)

Brian Ashcroft, Fraser of Allender Institute; David Blackaby, University of Wales Swansea; Nigel Blewitt, Research Officer, Institute of Welsh Affairs; Hilary Hendy, WDA International, Welsh Development Agency; Mike Hollingsworth, Welsh Development Agency; Gerald Holtham, IPPR; Grenville Jackson, Development Director East, Development Board for Rural Wales; David Jenkins, Wales TUC; Derek Jones, Head of Industry & Training Department, The Welsh Office; Gareth Jones, Institute of Welsh Affairs; Dylan Jones-Evans, Professor of Small Business Management, Business School; Ron Loveland, Director Business Services, The Welsh Office; R Ross Mackay, Director, Institute of Economic Research; Peter Midmore, University of Wales Aberystwyth; Brian Morgan, University of Wales, Cardiff; Kevin Morgan, City & Regional Planning, University of Wales, Cardiff; John Osmond, Director, Institute of Welsh Affairs; Adam Price, Menter a Busnes; Gareth Rees, University of Wales Cardiff; Geraint Talfan Davies, Chairman, Institute of Welsh Affairs; Gareth Thomas, MP for Clwyd West; Meirion Thomas; Nigel Thomas, Robert Bosch Ltd - Cardiff Plant; Yvette Vaughan Jones, International Officer, Arts Council of Wales; David Waterstone; Brian Willott, Chief Executive, Welsh Development Agency.

ROLE OF THE WELSH CAPITAL SEMINAR 12 MAY 1998,
(AGENCY OF THE BANK OF ENGLAND OFFICE, CARDIFF BAY)

Jeff Andrews, Assistant Director, Policy Department, Cardiff County Council; Cllr. Kevin Brennan, Cardiff City Council; Keith Bush; Phil Cooke, CASS; Norma Jarboe, Cardiff Marketing Ltd; Sally Medlyn, Director, Centre for Visual Arts; John Osmond, Director, Institute of Welsh Affairs; Kevin Pett; Huw Williams, Edwards Geldard.

EQUAL OPPORTUNITIES SEMINAR, 12 MAY 1998
(AGENCY OF THE BANK OF ENGLAND OFFICE, CARDIFF BAY)

Ceri Black, Institute of Welsh Affairs; Granville Brunt; Ivy Cameron, Cameron Woods Associates; Val Feld, Equal Opportunities Commission Wales; Anna Freeman, Comm Services & Policy Officer, Monmouthshire County Council; Aileen Haskell, Manager, Commission for Racial Equality; Colin Heyman, NHS Wales Equality Unit; Phil Jenkins, Equal Opportunities Commission; Howard John, Director, Disability Wales; Helen Mary Jones, Equal Opportunities Commission Wales; Judith Jones, Commission for Racial Equality; Paul Morrissey, General Manager, New Employ Wales Ltd; John Osmond, Director, Institute of Welsh Affairs; Susan Pritchard, Management Development Consultant;

Teresa Rees; Sara Reid, Welsh Women's Aid; Jennie Richards, Welsh Development Agency; Mary Ann Stephenson, Fawcett Society; Robert Taylor, Director, Age Concern Cymru; Charlotte Williams, University of Wales Bangor; H Wood, Nursing Group, The Welsh Office; Neil Wooding, NHS Wales Equality Unit.

ASSEMBLY COMMITTEES SEMINAR, 13 MAY 1998
(IWA, CARDIFF)

Phil Bird, Agriculture, Welsh Office; Jonathan Bradbury, Swansea University; Kevin Brennan, Cardiff City Council; Rosemary Butler, County Borough of Newport; Sue Essex, Dept of City and Regional Planning, Cardiff University; Martin Evans, Welsh Office Devolution Unit; Paul Griffiths, Head of Corporate Affairs, Welsh Local Government Association; J Barry Jones, University of Wales Cardiff; Ivor Lightman, Institute of Welsh Affairs; Richard Livsey, MP for Brecon & Radnor; Martin Mansfield, Wales TUC Cymru; John Osmond, Director, Institute of Welsh Affairs; Keith Patchett; Lindsay Runnett; Michael Rush, University of Exeter.

ELECTING THE ASSEMBLY SEMINAR, 14 MAY 1998
(IWA, CARDIFF)

Denis Balsom, University of Wales Gregynog; Ceri Black, Institute of Welsh Affairs; Andrew Davies, Welsh Context; Karl Davies, Chief Executive, Plaid Cymru; Russell Deacon, University of Wales Institute Cardiff; Tom Ellis, Welsh Liberal Democrats; Mike German, Welsh Liberal Democrats; Leigh Jeffes, Wales Conservative Party; J Barry Jones, University of Wales Cardiff; Ivor Lightman, Institute of Welsh Affairs; John Osmond, Director, Institute of Welsh Affairs; Huw Roberts, Welsh Office; Mike Tonkin, Nursing, The Welsh Office.

MEDIA SEMINAR, 14 MAY 1998
(CENTRE FOR JOURNALISM STUDIES, CARDIFF UNIVERSITY)

Leighton Andrews, Welsh Context; Ellen ap Gwynn, General Manager, Radio Ceredigion; Denis Balsom, University of Wales Gregynog; Ceri Black, Institute of Welsh Affairs; Bob Franklin, Sheffield University; Eurfron Gwynne Jones, Digital College; Clare Hudson, HTV Wales; Dylan Iorwerth, Y Cyfarwyddwr, Golwg; Gwyn Jones, Welsh Office; Gwyn Jones, Welsh Office; J Barry Jones, University of Wales Cardiff; Geoff Mungham, Centre for Journalism Studies; John Osmond, Director, Institute of Welsh Affairs; Huw Roberts, Welsh Office; Dai Smith, BBC; Nick Speed, South Wales Echo; Dafydd Williams, Media and Communications Executive, Welsh Development Agency; David Williams.

HEALTH AND SOCIAL POLICY SEMINAR, 15 MAY 1998
(TEMPLE OF PEACE, CARDIFF)

Cindy Adcock, Breast Cancer Coalition; Yvonne Apsitis, Daybreak Trust; Ceri Black, Institute of Welsh Affairs; Virginia Blakey, Health Promotion Wales; Carl Clowes, Medical Director, Powys Health Care NHS Trust; Jane Davidson, Welsh Local Government Association; Dewi R Evans, Consultant Paediatrician, Swansea Hospital; Elizabeth C Evans, General Practitioner; Hugh Gardner, Director of Social Services, The City and County of Swansea; Peter Gregory, Director, Welsh Office Health Department; Chris Hawker, Assistant Director, Community Care, Rhondda Cynon Taff County Council; Gareth Jones, Institute of Welsh Affairs; Margaret Knight, British Diabetic Association Wales; Dai Lloyd, General Practitioner; Siobhan McClelland, School of Health Science, University of Wales Swansea; John Osmond, Director, Institute of Welsh Affairs; John Wyn Owen, Nuffield Provincial

Hospitals Trust; Michael Ponton, Health Promotion Wales; John Saunders, Consultant Physician, Nevill Hall and District NHS Trust; Sally Stucke, Nevill Hall and District NHS Trust; Morton Warner, Director, WIHSC, University of Glamorgan; Colin Williams, Assistant Secretary, Welsh Office Health Strategy Division; Jan Williams, Chief Executive, Iechyd Morgannwg Health; Sue Wilshere, Chief Officer, Association of Welsh Community Health Councils.

Sustainable Development Seminar, 18 May 1998
(Brynafon Hotel, Rhayader)

Joan Asby, Co-ordinator, SPARC; Simon Bilsborough, Senior Economist, Countryside Council for Wales; David Philip Bown, Environmental Consultant; Cynog Dafis, MP for Ceredigion, Plaid Cymru; Elizabeth Wasteneys Dutch, Wales Rural Forum; Paul Finch, Forestry Commission; John Good, Institute of Terrestrial Ecology; Peter Harwood, Chairman, Ramblers Association in Wales; David G Jenkins, Director, Coed Cymru; Phil Jones, Welsh School of Architecture; Peter Midmore, University of Wales Aberystwyth; Margaret Minhinnick, Sustainable Wales; Brynmor Morgan, Brynmor Morgan Consultancy; John Osmond, Director, Institute of Welsh Affairs; R Elwyn Owen; Don Snow, Mandix; Merfyn Williams, CPRW; Gareth Wyn Jones, University of Wales Bangor.

Farming and Rural Economy Seminar, 21 May 1998
(IWA, Cardiff)

Susan C Balsom, Francis Balsom Associates; Nigel Blewitt, Research Officer, Institute of Welsh Affairs; Gillian Bristow, Cardiff Business School; Huw Brodie, Welsh Office; Peter Budd, Chief Executive, Welsh Food Promotions Limited; Gilli Davies, Gilli Davies Limited; Brian Edwards, Agriculture Business Advisor, Development Board for Rural Wales; Mark Goodwin, Professor of Human Geography, University of Wales Aberystwyth; Lynne Griffiths, The Welsh Office; Patrick Holden, Director, The Soil Association; Mary James, Director of Agricultural Policy, Farmers' Union of Wales; Clunie Keenleyside, Senior Agricultural Policy Officer, Countryside Council for Wales; Richard Knight, Country Landowners Association; Terry Marsden, University of Wales Cardiff; John Osmond, Director, Institute of Welsh Affairs; Chris Price-Jones, Project Director, Food Centre Wales; Malcolm Thomas, Deputy Director, National Farmers Union; Nia Williams, Development Board for Rural Wales.

Local Government Seminar, 22 May 1998
(IWA, Cardiff)

Mark Drakeford, University of Wales Cardiff; Sue Essex, Department of City and Regional Planning, Cardiff University; Martin Fitton, National Park Officer, Brecon Beacons National Park; Derek Griffin, Chief Executive, Wrexham County Borough Council; Paul Griffiths, Head of Corporate Affairs, Welsh Local Government Association; Margaret Minhinnick, Sustainable Wales; John Osmond, Director, Institute of Welsh Affairs; Jon Shortridge, Director, Economic Affairs, Welsh Office; Jacky Tonge, Chief Executive, Powys County Council; Eurig Wyn, a Gwynedd councillor and member of the European Committee of the Regions.

Education Seminar, 2 June 1998
(NCM Building, Cardiff Bay)

Colin Baker, University of Wales Bangor; Wynford Bellin, University of Wales Cardiff; Ceri Black, Institute of Welsh Affairs; Richard Daugherty, Department of Education,

University of Wales, Aberystwyth; John David, Institute of Welsh Affairs; Keith P. Davies, Director of Education, Carmarthenshire County Council; Alan Evans, Department of Education, Cardiff University; Steven Gorard, Education, University of Wales Cardiff; Roy James, former HM Chief Inspector of Schools; Colin Jenkins, Principal, United World College of the Atlantic; Philip Johnson, Nursing Division, The Welsh Office; Mike Jones, Chief Executive, Fforwm; Huw Lewis, Wales Labour Party; Margaret Morgan, National President, National Association of Headteachers; John Osmond, Director, Institute of Welsh Affairs; Gareth Pierce, Welsh Local Government Association; R T F Plaut, Chair, ACCAC; Eirlys Pritchard Jones, Institute of Welsh Affairs; Meirion Prys Jones, Bwrdd yr Iaith Gymraeg; W H Raybould; David Reynolds, University of Newcastle; Sonia Reynolds, The Quadrant Centre; Wyn Roberts, Welsh Joint Education Committee; Anne Robertson, Chair, Governors Wales; Phil Rogers, Parent Teacher Association of Wales; Paul Rowson, Director, Business in the Community Wales; Kim Ryley, Director of Education, Rhondda Cynon Taff CBC; Elizabeth Taylor, Welsh Office; Iola Thomas, OHMCI; Cen Williams, Director, Canolfan Bedwyr; John Williams, Head, Pen-y-dre High School; John Valentine Williams, Chief Executive, Curriculum and Assessment Authority for Wales.

SKILLS AND TRAINING SEMINAR, 2 JUNE 1998
(NCM BUILDING, CARDIFF BAY)

Ceri Black, Institute of Welsh Affairs; Nigel Blewitt, Research Officer, Institute of Welsh Affairs; Paula Brooks, BAMC; Jeffrey R Cocks, Pontypridd College; Jarmila Davies, School of the Built Environment, University of Glamorgan; Rhianwen Edwards, Director, Strategy, CELTEC; Steve Hill, Cardiff Business School; Robert Humphreys, University of Wales Swansea; Richard Keveren, Assistant Secretary, Industry, Training & Policy, The Welsh Office; John Osmond, Director, Institute of Welsh Affairs; Gareth Pierce, Welsh Local Government Association; Sonia Reynolds, The Quadrant Centre; Elen Rhys, ACEN; Annette Roberts, Welsh Economic Research Unit, Cardiff Business School; John Taylor, Chief Executive, South East Wales TEC; Len Taylor, South Wales Institute of Engineers; Gavin Thomas, Fforwm; Nigel Thomas, Robert Bosch Ltd - Cardiff Plant; George Watson, Welsh Policy Chair, Federation of Small Businesses Wales; Gwenda Williams, Resources Manager, Hyder Services; Iain Willox, Welsh Development Agency.

STRATEGIC PLANNING SEMINAR, 4 JUNE 1998
(IWA, CARDIFF)

K Cassidy, Management Planning & Review, Welsh Office; Mike Cuddy, Land Authority for Wales; Alun Davies, MD, Grosvenor Waterside Plc; Keith Davies, Senior Planner, Countryside Council for Wales; Jan Dominguez, Welsh Office; Graham Evans, Chief Planning Officer, Wrexham County Borough Council; Mike Flynn, Royal Town Planning Institute; John Osmond, Director, Institute of Welsh Affairs; David Prescott, Solicitor to the Authority, Pembrokeshire Coast National Park Authority; Peter Slater, Director of Economic Development, County Borough of Blaenau Gwent; Mark Tewdwr-Jones, University of Wales Cardiff.

SOCIAL SERVICES, 10 JUNE 1998
(IWA, CARDIFF)

Jane Davidson, Welsh Local Government Association; Graham Day, University of Wales Bangor; Mark Drakeford, University of Wales Cardiff; David Evans, Chief Inspector, The Welsh Office; Gerry Evans, Assistant Director, Social Care Research, Wales Office of Research and Development for Health and Social Care; Keith Fletcher; Steve Griffiths; Rhian Huws Williams, Head, CCETSW Cymru; Marie John, Senior Lecturer, University of

Glamorgan, Dept of Nursing & Midwifery; R Johnson, Nursing Division, The Welsh Office; Tony Newman, Policy Officer Research & Development, Barnardos; John Osmond, Director, Institute of Welsh Affairs; Julia Phillipson; Andy Pithouse, University of Wales Cardiff; Colin Preece, Director, Neath & Port Talbot Social Services Department; Angela Pulman, Director, Community Enterprise Wales; Mick Roberts, Divisional Manager, Include; David Smith, Anderley Associates.

FINDING OUR VOICES SEMINAR, 11 JUNE 1998
(IWA, CARDIFF)

Ceri Black, Institute of Welsh Affairs; Neil Caldwell, The Prince's Trust - BRO; Geraint Davies, Development Board for Rural Wales; John Davies, Porthcawl Town Council; Maggie Dawson, Amman Valley Enterprise; Graham Day, University of Wales Bangor; Mark Drakeford, University of Wales Cardiff; Keith Edwards, Director, TPAS; Val Feld, Equal Opportunities Commission Wales; Martin Fitton, National Park Officer, Brecon Beacons National Park; Mike Flynn, Royal Town Planning Institute; Jane Hutt, Director, Chwarae Teg; Nick Irvine, Institute of Public Policy Research; Alwyn Jones, University of Glamorgan; Richard Lewis, Groundwork Cymru; Colin P. Mann, Welsh Association of Community and Town Councils; Margaret McCabe, Management Planning & Review, Welsh Office; Margaret Minhinnick, Sustainable Wales; John Osmond, Director, Institute of Welsh Affairs; Nich Pearson, Welsh Consumer Council; Sian Phipps, Co-Ordinator, Environment Wales; Peter Polish, Red Kite; Angela Pulman, Director, Community Enterprise Wales; Simon Thomas, Co-ordinator of Jigso, Plaid Cymru; Alan Underwood, Ebbw Fach Development Trust; Suzanne Waldren, Local Agenda 21 Officer, Neath and Port Talbot County Council.

LEGISLATIVE PROCESS SEMINAR, 12 JUNE 1998
(IWA, CARDIFF)

J Barry Jones, University of Wales Cardiff; Jackie Jones, University of the West of England; David Lambert, Legal Group, Welsh Office; David Miers, Centre for Professional Legal Studies; John Osmond, Director, Institute of Welsh Affairs; Keith Patchett; Jackie Rees, Land Authority for Wales; Paul Silk, Public Bill Office, House of Commons; Gareth Thomas, MP for Clwyd West; Rhodri Walters, House of Lords; Dafydd Williams, Media and Communications Executive, Welsh Development Agency; Richard Wyn Jones, University of Wales Aberystwyth.

TOURISM SEMINAR, 9 JULY 1998
(BBC WALES, CARDIFF)

Tim Arthur, Chair, Wales Association of Self-Catering Operations; Ceri Black, Institute of Welsh Affairs; Sir Brooke Boothby, Chairman, Associated Quality Services; David Botterill, Head of School of Hospitality, Leisure & Tourism, UWIC; Dafydd Bowen Lewis; Peter Cole, Tourism South & West Wales; Jean M Davies; Lila Haines, Economic Policy Researcher, Plaid Cymru; Allan Wynne Jones; Gareth Jones, Institute of Welsh Affairs; Jonathan Jones, Director of Communications, Wales Tourist Board; Ffion Lloyd, Cardiff County Council; John Lloyd; Nigel Morgan, U.W.I.C, School of Leisure & Tourism; John Osmond, Director, Institute of Welsh Affairs; R Elwyn Owen; Annette Pritchard, U.W.I.C, School of Leisure & Tourism; Iain Skewis, The Development Consultancy; David Smith, Anderley Associates; Terry Stevens, Stevens and Associates; John Walsh Heron, Tourism Quality Services; Steve Webb, Director of Research, Wales Tourist Board; Nic Wheeler, National Park Officer, Pembrokeshire Coast National Park Authority; and Dafydd Wigley, MP for Caernarfon.

Additional comments on an early draft of the Chapter were received from Lowri Bevan, Stevens and Associates; John Walsh Heron, Tourism Quality Services; Vicki James, Stevens and Associates; Professor Gareth Wyn Jones, Institute of Welsh Affairs; Jim Moores, Chair, Brecon Beacons Tourism; Ashford Price, Dan yr Ogof Showcaves; and David Lea Wilson, Anglesey Sea Zoo.

SECOND MEDIA SEMINAR, 4 AUGUST 1998 (NATIONAL EISTEDDFOD, BRIDGEND)

Leighton Andrews, Political Context; Susan C Balsom, Francis Balsom Associates; Elan Closs Stephens, Chair, S4C; Neil Fowler, The Western Mail; Steve Hill, Cardiff Business School; Geoff Mungham, Centre for Journalism Studies, University of Wales Cardiff; John Osmond, Director, Institute of Welsh Affairs; Menna Richards, Managing Director, HTV Wales; Geraint Talfan Davies, Controller, BBC Wales; Brian Walters, South Wales Evening Post.

APPENDIX IV

IWA PUBLICATIONS

AGENDA

The Institute's regular journal appears three times a year. The Summer 98 issue is out now. £5 for a single issue, £15 yearly subscription.

THE GREGYNOG PAPERS

Polemical but informed policy papers by experts in the field:

The Place of North Wales by Huw Vaughan Thomas (July 1996) £5.

NHS Wales: Business or Public Service? by Professor David Cohen (February 1997) £5.

Lessons from the Sea Empress by Neil Caldwell and Clive Morgan (March 1997) £5.

The Welsh Image by John Smith MP (March 1998) £7.50.

State of the Arts by David Clarke (Oct 1998) £7.50.

IWA DISCUSSION PAPERS

No 1 *Why Snowdonia and North Wales Need a New Tourism Strategy* (bilingual), by John Osmond, Professor Gareth Wyn Jones and David Williams (July 1997) £5.

No 2 *The Welsh Baccalaureate: Matching International Standards* (bilingual) by John David and Colin Jenkins (October 1997) £5.

No 3 *An Effective National Assembly*, a report by the IWA Constitution Working Party (Jan 1998) £5.

No 4 *Rural Wales and the Agricultural Crisis* by a panel of Rural Studies experts (Jan 1998) £5.

No 5 *The Bonding of Wales - Housing the Assembly* - the IWA's contribution to the debate on finding a location for the Welsh Assembly (Jan 1998) £5.

No 6 *The Operation of the National Assembly* - the IWA's response to the National Assembly Advisory Group (May 1998) £5.

No 7 *The Information Gap* - the IWA's response to the Neill Committee enquiry into Standards in Public Life (May 1998) £5.

No 8 *The National Assembly and Broadcasting* - the IWA's Evidence to the Welsh Affairs Select Committee Inquiry (1999) £5.

CURRENT RESEARCH REPORTS

Quality of Service, Bilingualism & the Public Utility Services in Wales (Sept 1998 – available in Welsh or English versions) A joint report from the IWA and the Welsh Consumer Council. £10.

The Other Wales (July 1998) Examines Wales' entitlement to Objective 1 European funding. £10.

A Competitive Edge: Why Welsh Medium Schools Perform Better (June 1998) This bilingual study compares Welsh and English medium schools in the same pupil catchment area. £10.

Making the Assembly Work (Nov 1997) A bilingual report by the IWA Constitution Working Party containing 30 recommendations on how the Assembly can be improved within the framework of the White Paper. £10.

The Economic Impact of a Welsh Assembly (Sept 1997) By Professor Ross Mackay, Institute of Economic Research, University College of North Wales, Bangor; Brian Morgan, Cardiff Business School; and Gerald Holtham, Director IPPR. £10.

Bridging The Technology Skills Gap (Sept 1997) An examination of the ways of enhancing the image of careers for young people in Welsh manufacturing industry, commissioned from Coopers and Lybrand. £10.

Making the CAP Fit: An Integrated Development Strategy for Rural Wales (July 1997) Prepared by Dr Gillian Bristow, this report examines the impact of forthcoming changes to the EU's Common Agricultural Policy and calls for a single multi-functional Rural Development Agency for Wales. £10.

Wales in Europe: The Opportunity Presented by a Welsh Assembly (June 1997) The work of an IWA study group chaired by Sir John Gray, former Ambassador to Belgium and now Chairman of the Welsh Centre for International Affairs, with whom this bilingual study is jointly published. £10.

The Wales Information Society (June 1997) A wide-ranging bilingual study of the impact of the digital revolution on the Welsh economy, culture and society, written by IWA Director John Osmond. £10.

BSE - The Welsh Dimension In collaboration with the Welsh Institute of Rural Studies at Aberystwyth. £5.

Building our Future: The Housing Challenge for Wales (March 1997) Broad overview of all aspects of Welsh housing policy, calling for major new investment. £5.

The WelshBac: Educating Wales in the Next Century (March 1997) A bilingual study on all aspects of the IWA's new curriculum framework to replace A-levels. £7.50.

Wales 2010: Three Years On (Dec 1996) IWA Research Panel chairman Dr Gareth Jones reviews progress on his influential 1993 Wales 2010 report. £5.

PAST PUBLICATIONS

Towards an Educational Policy for Wales (1994) £5.

Cardiff Euro City (1994) £5.

Wales 2010: Creating our Future Main report £5, Summary Report £3.

EC Actions of Interest to Small and Medium-size Enterprises £5.

Cardiff Chancery/Commercial Bar Project £5.
South Wales Valleys: An Agenda for Action £5.

Rural Wales: Population Changes and Current Attitudes £5.

Channel Tunnel: Evidence to the Parliamentary Committee on Welsh Affairs £5.

Estimated Demand for Air Services between Cardiff and Paris and a West German Destination. £5.

North Wales: Prospects and Opportunities. £5.

A Study for New Facilities for the Visual Arts and Crafts in Wales £5.

West Wales: 1990 and Beyond £5.

Japanese Manufacturing Investment in Wales - published and available directly from the University of Wales Press, £25.

Wales: The Arts of the Possible £5. Summary Report £3.

ORDERING

To order a publication (there is a p&p charge of £1.50) contact:

IWA
Tŷ Oldfield
Llantrisant Road
Llandâf
Cardiff
CF5 2YQ

Tel: 01222 575511
Fax: 01222 575701
Email: wales@iwa.org.uk
Website: www.iwa.org.uk